There's been a lot of hype about the World Wide Web being an entirely new publishing medium. Although the Web is quite new in terms of organization, navigation, and quick access to information and media, the presentation isn't all that revolutionary. Despite all the technology, the Web is still essentially a medium for two-dimensional expression. A single unit of information on the Web is a "page," just as it is in a magazine or a book, and text and images are arranged left and right and top to bottom in a two-dimensional space.

So what if you want to do more, to create pages that aren't just flat text and images on a virtual page? 3D might be the solution you're looking for. The first step might be to simply add 3D effects to your pages—such as drop shadows in your images—or to create 3D-looking images by using modeling and rendering, or to experiment with 3D multimedia like animations and video.

Beyond simple graphics or multimedia effects, a more significant step might be to break free of the Web's page metaphor altogether and go to VRML (the Virtual Reality Modeling Language), where your site is a 3D representation of an actual place where you and your readers can roam around and interact with each other. Even if you don't want an entire site in VRML, adding VRML worlds to your site might be an good way to stay on the leading edge and get ahead of other Web developers.

If you've got the 3D bug, this book can help you. Nearly anything you might want to do with 3D and the Web is explored in this book, from simple graphics techniques all the way up to designing and creating complex 3D worlds and spaces using VRML. Through plenty of examples and ideas for real-life uses of these techniques, you'll be able to break your own Web site out of the flat world so many other Web sites belong to.

Good luck and enjoy!

Laura Lemay

lemay@lne.com
http://www.lne.com/lemay/

LAURA LEMAY'S
WEB WORKSHOP

3D GRAPHICS
&VRML 2.0

LAURA LEMAY'S
WEB WORKSHOP

3D GRAPHICS & VRML 2.0

Laura Lemay

Justin Couch

Kelly Murdock

201 West 103rd Street
Indianapolis, Indiana 46290

Copyright © 1996 by Sams.net Publishing

International Standard Book Number: 0-672-143-2

Library of Congress Catalog Card Number: 96-68591

99   98   97   4   3   2

Interpretation of the printing code: the rightmost double-digit number is the year of the book's printing; the rightmost single-digit, the number of the book's printing. For example, a printing code of 96-1 shows that the first printing of the book occurred in 1996.

Composed in Frutiger and MCPdigital by Macmillan Computer Publishing

Printed in the United States of America

President, Sams Publishing:	Richard K. Swadley
Publishing Manager:	Mark Taber
Managing Editor:	Cindy Morrow
Marketing Manager:	John Pierce
Assistant Marketing Managers:	Kristina Perry
	Rachel Wolfe

Acquisitions Editor
Beverly Eppink

Development Editor
Fran Hatton

Software Development Specialist
Bob Correll

Production Editor
Lisa M. Lord

Copy Editor
Howard A. Jones

Indexer
Cheryl Dietsch

Technical Reviewers
Sue Charlesworth
Alfonso Hermida

Editorial Coordinator
Bill Whitmer

Technical Edit Coordinator
Lorraine Schaffer

Resource Coordinator
Deborah Frisby

Formatter
Frank Sinclair

Editorial Assistants
Carol Ackerman, Andi Richter,
Rhonda Tinch-Mize

Cover Illustration
Eric Lindley

Cover Designer
Alyssa Yesh

Book Designer
Alyssa Yesh

Copy Writer
Peter Fuller

Production Team Supervisor
Brad Chinn

Production
Stephen Adams, Debra Bolhuis,
Mona Brown, Jason Hand, Daniel
Harris, Mike Henry, Ayanna Lacey,
Casey Price, Laura Robbins, Bobbi
Satterfield, Mark Walchle

Dedication

To my dear wife, Angela, for everything.

—Kelly Murdock

To Imagica, CYBERLady, Reflection, and Nemesis, friends from the heart of cyberspace.

—Justin Couch

Overview

Contents

Part V   Advanced VRML Techniques   289

Acknowledgments

Thanks to the many software companies who were so gracious in supporting this project. To my friends at Viewpoint, who remembered me after all these years. To all my friends at Sams who showed interest in this project, especially the Emerging Technologies team, and to Richard for letting me have a chance to write.

To my family, especially Mom and Mike. I don't know if I am the first to be published, but this book definitely has the prettiest cover. Dad, we're still waiting for your first book. To Eric and Thomas, the two cutest boys ever, be nice to one another.

—Kelly Murdock

Apart from the lack of sleep, I would like to thank the people from Sams.net for letting an Aussie write a book for them. Living on the right side of the globe makes life interesting when trying to communicate ideas and thoughts to Kelly (my co-author) and the editors. This has been a true adventure in using the Internet for global communications.

Many contributed to the content. First, to Cindy Reed—thanks for the cutest VRML pig around; keep hanging in there and you'll get the hang of scripting one day. Gavin Bell, Rikk Carey, and Chris Marrin, as well as the countless thousands on the VRML development list—thanks for putting up with incessant questions on a specification that wasn't finished. And thanks to my mate, Mark Webb, an Aussie feeling very lost in the United States; he spends his time reading the drafts and picking up those fine little corrections and clarifications.

The final acknowledgement must go to my friends from Terra Vista, a real virtual community built in the spirit of cyberspace. Regardless of ability or technical clout, they have pushed the electronic frontiers further in the past four months than any other community I have ever been involved in—real or virtual. Keep going and never give up the dream.

"Cyberspace. A consensual hallucination experienced daily by billions of legitimate operators, in every nation, by children being taught mathematical concepts.... A graphic representation of data abstracted from the banks of every computer in the human system. Unthinkable complexity. Lines of light ranged in the nonspace of the mind, clusters and constellations of data. Like city lights, receding."

(William Gibson, *Neuromancer*, p. 103)

—Justin Couch

About the Author

Kelly Murdock has led many different lives before this book, including as a missionary in Japan, a champion collegiate hurdler and decathlete, and a professional engineer, but none was as challenging as his current profession—being a husband and father. When not with his family (or in front of his computer), he can be found at Sams.net buried in his office, reading and developing computer books.

Kelly contributed to *Web Page Wizardry* and has written several articles on virtual reality. He graduated from Brigham Young University with a degree in mechanical engineering and has founded a multimedia production company named Tulip Multimedia with his wife. In his spare time, he likes to attend concerts and movies with his wife. He can be reached at kmurdock@sams.mcp.com.

Justin Couch (justin@vlc.com.au) works as a software engineer for ADI Ltd. When not working there, he also runs The Virtual Light Company, a small VRML and Java Web publishing company in Sydney, Australia. He is an active member of both the VRML standards and Java-VRML mailing lists. Currently, he's involved in research on using VRML to create seamless worlds on the Internet. When not pushing the limits, he relaxes by playing bassoon and clarinet and going gliding.

Justin can be found most days in the CyberGate community Point World under the name Mithrandir or can be reached through the Web at http://www.vlc.com.au/~justin.

Tell Us What You Think!

As a reader, you're the most important critic and commentator of our books. We value your opinion and want to know what we're doing right, what we could do better, what areas you'd like to see us publish in, and any other words of wisdom you're willing to pass our way. You can help us make strong books that meet your needs and give you the computer guidance you require.

Do you have access to CompuServe or the World Wide Web? Then check out our CompuServe forum by typing **GO SAMS** at any prompt. If you prefer the World Wide Web, check out our site at http://www.mcp.com.

NOTE: If you have a technical question about this book, call the technical support line at (800) 571-5840, ext. 3668.

As the team leader of the group that created this book, I welcome your comments. You can fax, e-mail, or write me directly to let me know what you did or didn't like about this book—as well as what we can do to make our books stronger. Here's the information:

FAX: 317/581-4669

E-mail: newtech_mgr@sams.mcp.com

Mail: Mark Taber
          Comments Department
          Sams Publishing
          201 W. 103rd Street
          Indianapolis, IN 46290

Introduction

As you can see from the title, this book really has a split personality—the first half is about 3D graphics and the second is about VRML. However, these two topics are very closely related. VRML scenes are 3D graphics, and 3D graphics are used in VRML scenes.

3D graphics on the Web are pervasive because they are graphics. VRML on the Web is a hot new technology that enables real-time 3D. By covering both, you get a broader look at how to enhance your site with many facets of 3D graphics, instead of just one.

In the past, we've all marveled at this technology from a distance. We've seen it in movies, in arcades, and in some of the latest research environments; now we're seeing it on our home PCs. The power of current processors coupled with 3D acceleration cards are making it possible to experience advanced 3D graphics everywhere, especially on the Web.

To begin, we will introduce this unique series, 3D graphics on the Web, and VRML 2.0. A lot is included, and there's a lot you can get out of it.

The Web Workshop Series

Back in 1994, Laura Lemay wrote a little book that changed a lot of people's lives— *Teach Yourself Web Publishing with HTML in a Week*. It taught everyday people how to present and publish their ideas on the Web. The results have been revolutionary.

Laura's book was popular with many people because of its simple, direct language and engaging, easy-to-understand examples. Laura followed up her best-selling book with several enhanced editions and another best-seller, *Teach Yourself Java in 21 Days*. It was clear to the publisher that Laura had developed a style people could relate to.

In the meantime, simple Web publishing with HTML has moved forward on many different fronts. You can publish on the Web by using one of many HTML editors, such as Microsoft's FrontPage and Netscape's Navigator Gold; you can enhance your site with audio, video, ActiveX controls, 3D VRML worlds, and specialized plug-ins, like Shockwave; you can program on the Web with powerful languages like Java or scripting languages, such as JavaScript and VBScript.

With all this happening, it became obvious that Laura would have her hands full trying to instruct her readers in all these new developments, so the Web Workshop series was born.

This series is directed toward readers who have mastered the basics of HTML and are now ready to move to the next level of Web development—to experiment with all the new technologies that are making the Web interactive, easier to use, and exciting.

This particular book focuses on 3D graphics and VRML 2.0. It doesn't assume you're familiar with either of these areas, but it guides you through the details of creating 3D content for your Web pages in that familiar, comfortable Laura Lemay style.

This book is a "do" book. The Workshop name means there are no fluff chapters on historical background, marketing hype, or conceptual discussions. Each chapter is full of hands-on examples that teach you, step-by-step, how to use these technologies.

In addition to the examples, several chapters have real-life examples. These workshops are found in the first two chapters of the book and at the end of each part.

3D Graphics on the Web

3D graphics on the Web typically show up in two forms—images and animations. As an HTML pro, you will have no trouble using either in your Web pages, but creating them is where the challenge lies.

The first half of this book teaches, by example, how to create these 3D images with 2D and 3D tools. It also covers creating animations using the latest mid-range 3D tools. The workshops show you how 3D graphics can enhance your site and keep people coming back.

In covering 3D graphics, many different tools are used to create 3D content. By focusing on several tools, the book isn't a guide to learning one package, but a broader look at the types of tools you're likely to use. It also lets you see some unique functions that aren't exclusive to each package. Here's a list of some of the packages used in these examples:

- ❏ Caligari's trueSpace 2
- ❏ Ray Dream Studio
- ❏ Martin Hash's 3D Animation
- ❏ Adobe Photoshop
- ❏ Strata Studio Pro Blitz
- ❏ Fractal Design Painter
- ❏ Adobe Premiere
- ❏ Strata MediaPaint
- ❏ Apple's QuickTime VR

Chapter 1, "Building a 3D Enhanced Web Site," is the fast track. It takes you through developing a site enhanced by 3D graphics and shows you the possibilities of what's covered in the rest of the chapters.

Chapter 3, "Adding Simple 3D Elements to Your Web Page," shows you how traditional 2D tools, such as image-editing programs and plug-in filters, can be used to create 3D effects.

Chapter 4, "Creating and Embedding 3D Rendered Images," gets into the basics of 3D image creation. It shows you how to build scenes by using models and how to apply textures and materials; it also gives you a basic overview of 3D graphics technology through simple examples.

Chapter 5, "Creating and Embedding Simple 3D Animations," introduces 3D animation and explains how to generate animations by moving the camera and moving the models.

Chapter 6, "Using Animation Plug-Ins in Your Web Page," covers animation plug-ins that help you display the 3D animations you've just created.

Chapter 7, "Real-Life Examples: Product Design on a Corporate Intranet: Advanced Telescope Design Corporation," is the real-life example for this part of the book. It illustrates using 3D enhanced graphics over an intranet to explain the latest product designs.

Chapter 8, "Creating Advanced 3D Rendered Images for Your Web Page," gets into advanced issues of creating 3D images for the Web, including complex modeling and rendering issues.

Chapter 9, "Creating Advanced 3D Animations for the Web," offers many advanced techniques of 3D animation creation, including character animation.

Chapter 10, "Using Apple's QuickTime VR," delves into a new technology for the Web developed by Apple—QuickTime VR. This chapter explains what it is and gives some examples of it.

Chapter 11, "Using Microsoft's ActiveVRML," previews Microsoft's ActiveVRML technology. Uniquely different from VRML, ActiveVRML offers some similarities to VRML and some not-so-similar options.

Chapter 12, "Real-Life Examples: Creating a MYST-like Adventure on the Web," is the real-life example for the third part of the book. You'll see how to create an adventure game with 3D graphics played over the Web.

VRML 2.0 on the Web

VRML is a new technology that's similar to HTML in many ways, but the end results are very different. VRML files are created by writing text files that define 3D worlds. These worlds can then be loaded into your favorite browser by using a VRML browser or a VRML plug-in. Within a VRML browser, you can move around these worlds in three dimensions, and the view updates in real-time. Imagine going inside the 3D images you create in the first part of the book and flying around the objects—that's what VRML can do.

VRML 2.0 offers more than just worlds you can roam about. With the 2.0 version, you can add behaviors to your objects that make them move and react to the world around them. This capability and many other improvements make VRML 2.0 a technology you really should learn to use in your Web sites. This book explains how it's done.

Although you'll be using a simple text editor to create most of the VRML worlds in the book, several VRML tools are presented, also:

- ❏ Caligari's Pioneer Pro
- ❏ Paragraph's Home Space Builder
- ❏ Netscape's Live3D
- ❏ Microsoft's ActiveVRML
- ❏ SGI's CosmoPlayer
- ❏ Sony's CyberPassage
- ❏ OnLive's Traveler
- ❏ BlackSun's CyberGate

NOTE:
At the time this book was going to press, Sony was in the process of changing the name CyberPassage to Community Place. Check the Sony site at `vs1.sony.co.jsp` for updates.

Chapter 2, "Up and Running: First VRML Creation," is a quick-start example using VRML; it extends Chapter 1 by adding a VRML showroom.

Chapter 13, "Exploring VRML Browsers and Development Tools," explores the VRML browsers you need to view VRML files. It also takes a look at several development tools that help you create VRML worlds easily.

Chapter 14, "Starting with Models," introduces how models are defined in the VRML world. Using basic shapes and models, you can start to lay out your VRML world.

Chapter 15, "Sprucing Up Models with Textures and Materials," teaches you how to enhance and manipulate your models by using textures and materials.

Chapter 16, "Adding a Dash of Reality," adds lights and viewpoints to your VRML world.

Chapter 17, "Real-Life Examples: The VRML Art Gallery: A VRML World by Hand," is a real-life example of a VRML world in action. The example creates an art gallery that's worth visiting.

Chapter 18, "Tricks to Optimize Your VRML Worlds for the Web," offers tricks to help you reduce the file sizes of your worlds and optimize them for the Web.

Chapter 19, "Using Built-in Animation Techniques," gives you your first look at animating objects within your world.

Chapter 20, "Interfacing VRML Worlds with Scripts," introduces you to scripting interaction with JavaScript.

Chapter 21, "Using Java to Add Behaviors to VRML," shows you how you can use Java to program specialized behaviors into your world's objects.

Chapter 22, "Adding Interactivity: The Future of VRML," explains where VRML is headed and covers some of the 3D chat environments that are beginning to appear.

Chapter 23, "Real-Life Examples: A 3D Gallery: An Advanced VRML World," concludes the book with a final VRML workshop. This real-life example extends the art gallery by using all these advanced techniques.

Get Ready...

The book is designed to present example after example of good ideas to enhance your Web pages, so it doesn't need to be read in order. If you're anxious to get into the VRML stuff, then jump straight to Chapter 13.

Every chapter ends with Workshop Wrap-up, Next Steps, and Q&A sections. The Next Steps section is designed to offer you information on where you might like to go to next.

Get Set...

A valuable resource that shouldn't be overlooked is the CD-ROM that comes with the book. We've put a lot of effort into finding many resources that will help you as you read the book. Many of the software packages covered in the book have a demo version available on the CD-ROM. These demo versions let you play around with the program to see whether it fits your needs before you buy it.

The CD-ROM also has a friendly HTML interface with all the book examples and an extensive resource guide with plenty of links.

Go!

We really hope you get a lot out of this book. 3D graphics can be a lot of fun; by using them, you can create some compelling Web sites. So without further hand-waving, read on! Good luck—and when you succeed, we'd love to hear about it.

—Kelly Murdock kmurdock@sams.mcp.com

—Justin Couch justin@vlc.com.au

I

Fast Track to 3D Graphics and VRML on the Web

ONE

Building a 3D Enhanced Web Site

—by Kelly Murdock

In this chapter, you

- ❏ Plan your Web site
- ❏ Add 3D elements
- ❏ Add rendered 3D images and image maps
- ❏ Add 3D animations

Tasks in this chapter:

- ❏ Adding 3D Text
- ❏ Including a 3D Background
- ❏ Embedding Navigation Buttons
- ❏ Adding 3D Images
- ❏ Spicing Up with 3D Animations

If you've thumbed through the book, you've seen the different examples of 3D elements that can enhance your Web site. If not, then go ahead and thumb through it now to look at some of the images. Every image you see in the book can be used in a Web page. Some of the techniques may look a little difficult, but they really aren't. Creating 3D graphics isn't difficult, although it can be tricky. The purpose of these first two chapters is to show you quickly that this book can unlock possibilities and to get you over any intimidation you might have about creating graphics. This is how this chapter will progress:

- ❏ Start with a plan—always a good idea that will save you time
- ❏ Add 3D elements, such as buttons, text, and backgrounds, to your site
- ❏ Next, add your rendered 3D images and image maps
- ❏ Finally, add 3D animations for extra pizzazz

Once you get this site up and looking good, Chapter 2, "Up and Running: First VRML Creation," extends it with a VRML world. At the end of these two quick-start chapters, you'll have a state-of-the-art 3D site.

I was in Bubsy's showroom the other day examining his new line of convertible dump trucks when talk turned to the Web. Bubsy was anxious to establish a Web presence for his business and asked if I could help. I accepted the challenge, and the results of Bubsy's Sport Car and Heavy Machinery Web site follow.

Planning the Site (with Bubsy's Blessing)

Bubsy is a fictional character and company and is meant in no way to demean or ridicule any actual people or corporations.

Bubsy has been in the business of selling vehicles for some time and has some definite ideas about what should go on the Web site. After considerable deliberation, we agree on the plan for the Web site and intend to include the following structure:

❏ Home page: with Bubsy's logo and company name and a personal welcome from Bubsy

❏ What's New page: presenting the latest vehicles, complete with images

❏ Vehicle Description pages: with break-downs and specifications of each machine in the lot

❏ Special Sale pages: showcasing Bubsy's sale of the week

❏ Bubsy's Favorite Links: providing links to replacement parts pages and other Web resources

Each page should have icons at the bottom of the page that link to the other pages to help you move around Bubsy's site. Now that you have a rough plan, move on to building the site by starting at the title page.

Starting with the Title Page

The title page is usually the first page the visitor sees. It's the first chance you have to show off your 3D wares. For this site, you want to include the company name in 3D text, present a 3D background, add navigation buttons, and include a rendered animation of Bubsy welcoming visitors to the site.

Adding 3D Text

Bubsy doesn't really have a logo. In fact, everywhere the name is mentioned, it looks different, so Bubsy thought it would be a good idea to present his company name as 3D text.

The size of the image needs to be rather large to get all the words in and to make it readable, but you don't want to blank out the background, so use a transparent GIF image:

1. The text was rendered with trueSpace and saved as a Targa image.
2. This image was then loaded into Paint Shop Pro, converted to a 256-color image, and saved as a transparent GIF image, shown in Figure 1.1.

CAUTION: You should usually embed your 3D images as JPEG files. JPEG is better at subtle color changes, which are common for 3D images. Notice how the colors in the Bubsy title look kind of splotchy and how the edges are ragged. But if you want transparency, GIF is the only option for now.

3. The image was then centered and placed by using standard HTML tags.

Figure 1.1.

Title page for Bubsy's Sports Cars and Heavy Machinery Web site.

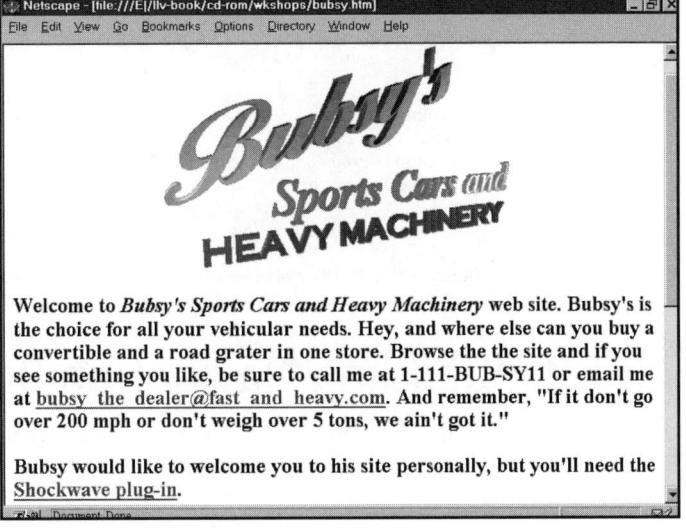

 ## Including a 3D Background

Backgrounds are a two-edged sword. They can effectively hide some ragged edges caused by making 3D images transparent, but when they have too much detail, they can make the text on the page illegible. For the background on the title page, I did the following:

1. I started with a low-resolution texture image and enhanced it by using Photoshop's Extrude filter.

2. Then in Photoshop, I increased the brightness of the image by 35 percent. This washed the image out enough that the text is legible, but it still covers the ragged edges somewhat.

3. I used a standard background image tag to embed the background in my title page. (See Figure 1.2.)

Figure 1.2.
Title page again, this time with a brightened background.

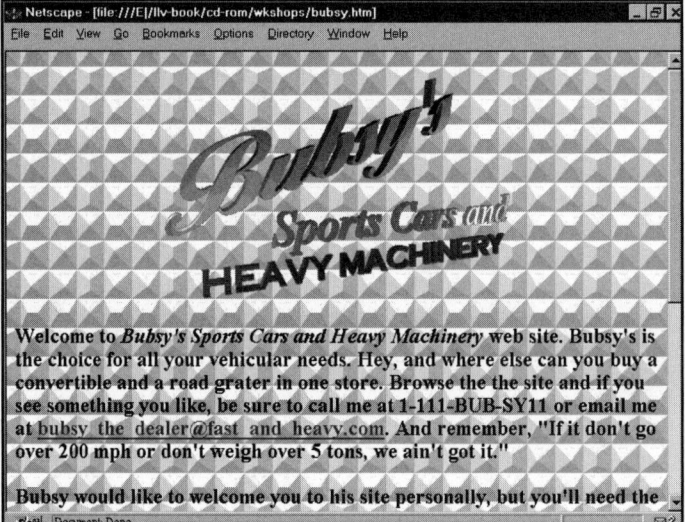

 ## Embedding Navigation Buttons

Now that the title page is shaping up, you need some links to guide visitors into the site. According to the plan, there should be five buttons that appear on every page in the site.

1. Starting with a plain red oval in Photoshop, I used the text tool to center the text.

NOTE: I've used Photoshop throughout this example, but I could just as easily have used Paint Shop Pro or any other image-editing software.

2. I then selected the oval and used the Glass Lens filter from the Kai's Power Tools plug-in to add the 3D look.

3. I saved the buttons as GIF files. I didn't have to worry about ragged edges since I started with a simple shape. The GIF images were easily embedded into the HTML file, as Figure 1.3 shows.

Figure 1.3.
Bubsy's Web site after adding 3D navigation buttons.

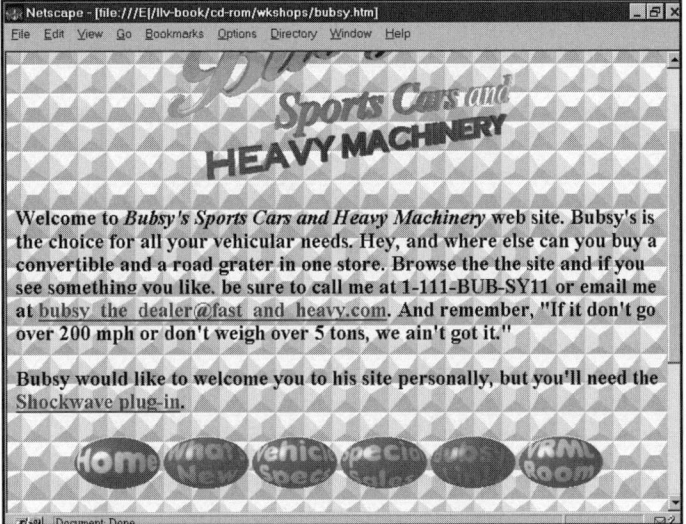

Embedding an Introduction Animation

One thing about Bubsy is that he has a large ego. He insisted that he be placed on the home page to personally welcome visitors to his site. However, he won't let anyone take a video of him, so I created a 3D character to do the introduction animation. It's a good thing Bubsy has a cartoon-like face.

Lucky for me, Bubsy happened to be a dead ringer for FlimFlam, a demo character that ships on Martin Hash's 3D Animation CD-ROM—except Bubsy has a large nose and bigger ears.

1. Using Martin Hash's 3D Animation, I animated the cartoonish Bubsy and output the animation as a series of Targa images.

2. I then recorded Bubsy's welcome and loaded the Targa images and the sound file into Director, where I synchronized the two.

3. After saving the Director file, I compressed it for the Web with the After-burner utility.

4. Finally, I embedded the animation as a Shockwave movie using the standard `<EMBED>` tag.

5. The note just before the animation lets visitors know where to get the Shockwave plug-in for viewing the animation.

Figure 1.4.

The final element on the title page is a personalized welcome from Bubsy himself in a Shockwave movie.

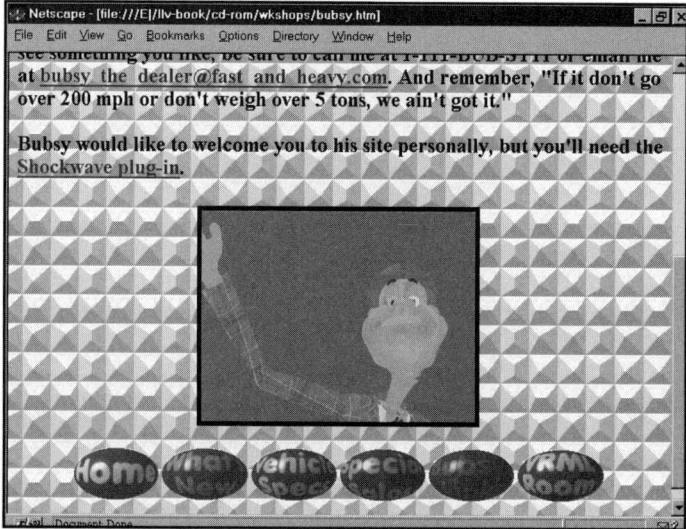

TASK   Adding 3D Images

The core of the Web site is where you present your products. Bubsy wanted these split between three different pages: the What's New page, where the latest and greatest can be found, the Vehicle Specification pages, where the bulk of the items will go; and the Special Sales page, where discounted vehicles are highlighted.

Each of these sections has the Bubsy logo and the navigation buttons, but the new element will be the 3D images of the vehicles. Bubsy also earns some revenue by offering his customers custom-paint jobs, so you naturally want to show this to the site visitors.

1. Start by loading your pre-built models into a 3D package. I used both trueSpace and Ray Dream Studio.

2. The materials on the vehicle model can be easily changed using the material selector functions. Each image needs to be rendered separately.

3. Thumbnails can be created by rendering the image again at a smaller resolution or by resizing the final image.

4. You know how to embed images; keep in mind that they usually look best when surrounded by a border of some kind.

The Viper and Forklift models were both taken from the DreamModels set that ships with Ray Dream Studio.

Using thumbnails, you can present many examples without taking up too much bandwidth, as shown in Figure 1.5. The thumbnails all link to larger images.

Figure 1.5.
3D images added to Bubsy's products page; the thumbnail images link to larger images.

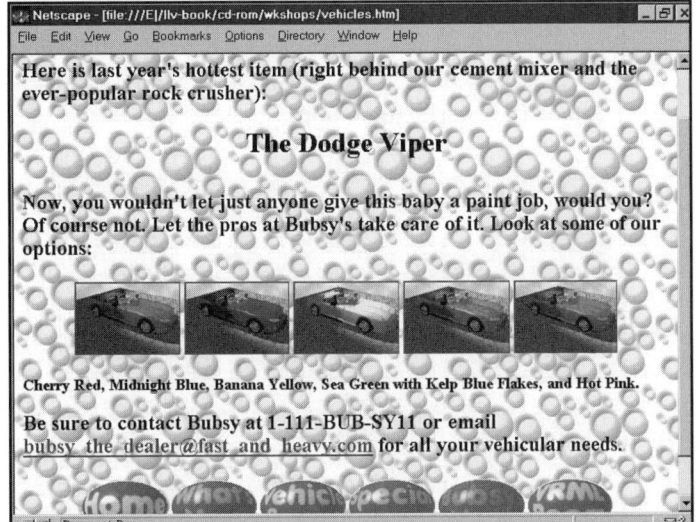

TASK Spicing Up with 3D Animations

When you go into a showroom to look at cars, you usually wander around the car to view it from all sides. With animations on your site, you can simulate this experience. Rotating a 3D object to create an animation is fairly painless, but embedding it is another story.

There are many ways to embed animations in your Web site; several will be covered here. If you don't like any of these methods, then just wait—new methods are showing up all the time. For the vehicle demonstrations on Bubsy's site, I decided to use Shockwave movies. They work about the same way as Bubsy's introduction animation.

The GIF Construction Kit can be downloaded from Alchemy Mindworks Web site at `http://www.mindworkshop.com`. It's a shareware product.

Another way to add small animations is using GIF animations, which were used on Bubsy's Special Sales page:

1. Create your 3D animation in the usual manner, but make sure the size is fairly small. Output the animation as a series of images.

2. Load the individual images into a GIF animation tool, such as the GIF Construction Kit, and save the file as a GIF file.

3. The GIF animation can be embedded just like any other GIF image.

When using GIF animations, it's important to remember not to place too many on one page, not to use large images, and not to use too many frames. Small files like the ones in Figure 1.6 are just about right.

Figure 1.6.
Bubsy's Special Sales page makes use of GIF animations to draw attention to deals you can't pass up.

Don't write off GIF animations because of the warning on file size. You can do quite a bit with these little files.

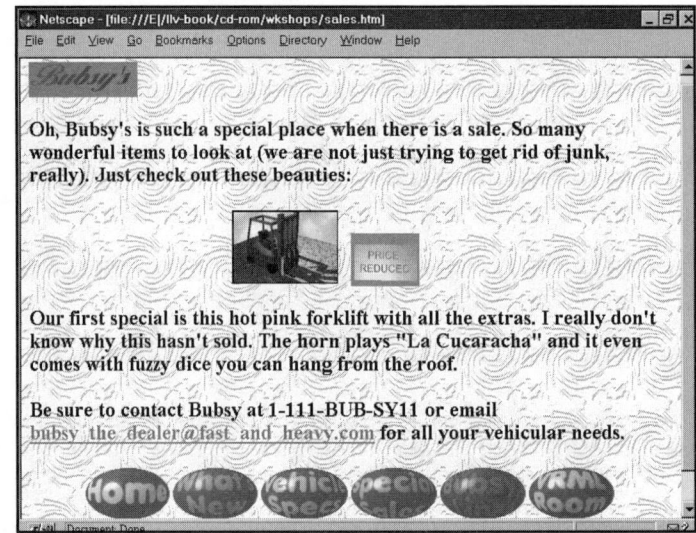

Workshop Wrap-up

The completed Bubsy site can be viewed on this book's CD-ROM. It's a rather small site but has enough to show you a sampling of what this book will enable you to do. Bubsy's not done with you yet, though. In the next chapter, you'll add a VRML showroom to Bubsy's site.

Next Steps

Boy, Bubsy is demanding. Not only did he get me to work on his site, but he managed to get my co-author to add a VRML showroom as well.

- ❏ The next chapter, "Up and Running: First VRML Creation,"extends Bubsy's site by adding a VRML showroom where you can move around the vehicles in real time.
- ❏ Just beyond Bubsy's world is where the tricks lie; Chapter 3, "Adding Simple 3D Elements to Your Web Page," starts it all off.
- ❏ The first workshop that shows real-world examples like Bubsy's can be found in Chapter 7, "Real-Life Examples: Product Design on a Corporate Intranet: Advanced Telescope Design Corporation."
- ❏ If you're eager to jump into VRML building, see Chapter 13, "Exploring VRML Browsers and Development Tools."

Q&A

Q: What kind of tools did you use to create these 3D images? Are they affordable?

A: I must admit, I did use some expensive tools in the process of creating this example, but not as expensive as I could have. In the 3D world, tools such as Ray Dream Studio and trueSpace are real bargains at around $500.

The CD-ROM that goes with this book has a number of good demos that will let you play with these tools to help you decide whether they're right for you before you lay your money down. Appendix A, "3D Software Resource Guide," is another reference that can help you see what kinds of tools are available.

If you're still not satisfied, try checking out the shareware scene. There are several shareware and freeware programs that will help you get started. The book's CD-ROM is full of these kinds of programs.

Q: I've been working in 3D for a long time, and it seems that it would be a lot of work to put my existing images and animations on the Web. Is there an easier way?

A: If you don't like the way something is done on the Web, then check back in about three months. The Web is continually changing and improving. Currently, it's somewhat difficult to get 3D content on the Web; that's why this book is being published.

Easier methods for publishing 3D are in the works by several different companies. One to watch is Shockwave for Extreme 3D, which will make it possible to embed your existing 3D work easily into your Web pages. Tools like that will make this book and a lot of headaches disappear, but I'm not worried—there will still be plenty to write about!

TWO

Up and Running: First VRML Creation

—by Justin Couch

Subject: VRML Showroom for Bubsy's Site Wanted!
Date: Monday, July 15 1996 16:44:04 -0500
From: kmurdock@mail.mcp.com (Kelly Murdock)
To: justin@localnet.com.au

Attention: Mr. Justin Couch

My name is Kelly Murdock and I've been fortunate to have the opportunity to oversee the development of a Web site for Bubsy's Sports Cars and Heavy Machinery. Bubsy is a great person who is always looking for the latest way to promote his successful business (like the time he tried to spell out Bubsy with fireworks).

Bubsy read this article about VRML and thought we could create a VRML showroom to show off some of Bubsy's latest models. To create a great showroom, Bubsy thought it would be best to pull in a ringer, and that's you. Please consider creating a compelling VRML showroom for this site. Bubsy will reward you plenty for your help and even give you discounts on his new line of bulldozers.

Thanks for helping out.

Kelly Murdock
Chief Web Developer for Bubsy

In this chapter, you

- ❏ Learn what VRML is, what you need to view it, and how to create it
- ❏ Create a floor plan for Bubsy's showroom
- ❏ Perform the basics of setting a world up
- ❏ Create links to HTML pages
- ❏ Set up a Web site for the showroom

Tasks in this chapter:

- ❏ Creating the Showroom
- ❏ Adding the Logo and Vehicles
- ❏ Adding a Roof
- ❏ Sprucing Up the World with Scenery
- ❏ Putting the World on the Web

Hmmm. This looks like something interesting—a new virtual showroom. (Besides, I need a new family bulldozer, so this will be worth it.) Lucky for me he attached a whole heap of files he used for creating the Web pages to guide me in the style of the VRML model.

Creating a Web page is a fairly well-understood process these days, but creating a 3D scene you can wander around in on the Web is not so well understood. Before you delve into the wonders of VRML, you'll get a quick introduction to what it is and how to use it. In this chapter, you'll cover the following tasks:

- ❏ First, you need to know what VRML is, what you need to view it, and how to create it.

- ❏ After you've worked out how to create it, you need another plan—this time, a floor plan of what the shop will look like, where things will be placed, and so forth.

- ❏ Next, you'll get on with creating the showroom. You'll run through the basics of getting a world set up, add a few links here and there back to the HTML pages, and get ready to set up the Web site.

What Is VRML?

The Virtual Reality Modeling Language (VRML) is the de facto standard for delivering platform-independent virtual reality over the Internet. VRML is to 3D graphics what HTML is to document formatting. With a simple text file, you can describe how a virtual world looks and behaves and navigate around it without restrictions.

VRML is a relatively new technology. Version 1 was completed in August 1995, and the next major version will be finished by the time you read this. A VRML file works a bit like HTML because it's all done in text. However, instead of working with 2D text documents, you're placing objects in 3D space, then wandering around in it.

However, the question you really want answered is, "What can I use it for?" Well, what would you like it to do? VRML can be used in a wide variety of situations. VRML 1.0 described purely static scenes, which meant it was good for producing virtual art galleries and designing mock-ups of buildings, but it lacked any real interactive element. For example, there was no way to watch a real-time virtual Wall Street. With the arrival of the second version, though, you'll be able to create worlds that respond to input of almost any form. You could create a complete VRML airline reservation system, design a virtual factory that controls a real one from a distance, or just have a great homeworld to impress your virtual neighbors.

Experiencing VRML: Browsers

To enjoy the wonders of virtual reality, you need a browser with VRML capabilities. With the current popularity of Netscape and its plug-in capabilities, many different browsers are available. Companies like BlackSun, IDS-software, and Silicon Graphics all offer VRML plug-ins for Netscape. The latest versions of Netscape now include their own VRML browser called Live3D. For most people, this is all they need to get VRML capabilities.

A typical session using Live3D is shown in Figure 2.1. The creators of Live3D were careful when they chose their navigation interface; they based it directly on DOOM. Now, if you haven't heard about DOOM or played it, then where have you been hiding for the past few years? To make your way around the scene, just use the arrow keys to move forward or backward and to turn. Other navigation options, including ones for the mouse, are covered in Chapter 13, "Exploring VRML Browsers and Development Tools."

Figure 2.1.

A typical screenshot of a VRML world when using Live3D. The Talosian world of Len Bullard from Terra Vista.

VRML Made Easy: VRML Tools

Even though VRML is just over two years old, a wealth of content creation tools are already available. They vary in both cost and suitability. The first tools were just conversion programs from other file formats to VRML; they were followed by options to export VRML from existing programs. Finally, dedicated VRML editors are now available.

Since my partner developed all his logos with trueSpace, I'll use its sister product, Pioneer, to develop the VRML version of Bubsy's showroom. This makes my task easy because I can just import the original trueSpace file and export it as VRML. The Pioneer look and feel is almost identical to trueSpace, which means all the time you invested learning how to use trueSpace won't go to waste.

Planning Bubsy's VRML Site

Despite his interesting choice in clothes, Bubsy is a pretty traditional sort of guy when it comes to his showroom. He wants his showroom to be a typically earthbound style—one large room for the cars and, of course, the heavy machinery stays outside. Like all business owners, he wants it done yesterday, so the showroom will have to be fairly simple.

What have I got to use? Well, Kelly gave me a copy of Bubsy's logo, so I can use that as a sign. There's a couple of models for the vehicles, and Bubsy wants a room to put the cars in. Sounds fairly simple to do. He also wants to link back to his HTML pages, so I have to accommodate that, too. It looks like the best way to tackle this job is to start with a basic showroom, then add other parts later.

Starting with the Showroom

The showroom can be simply constructed from a box for the main part and a couple of polygons for the roof. On the outside, put the sign in the traditional place above the door.

Creating the Showroom

The basic showroom is constructed by creating one box, then using Pioneer's boolean functions to subtract other objects from it. The outside of the showroom is created first, then the inside box is subtracted from it to get the interior room. A large window and door are created in the same fashion. Subtracting from the box means there's no floor, so a plane is used for that.

TIP: Later on, when you add some grass outside the building, it will also cover the floor because it has the same height as the outside ground. To make sure the floor is visible, offset it by a very small amount, like 0.01.

Now, Bubsy is fairly fussy because he wants the virtual showroom to look just like his real one, so follow these steps to accomplish that:

1. The real showroom is a standard brick building. First, create the basic room by placing two boxes in the scene—one slightly smaller and inside the other. Use the boolean functions to subtract the inside box from the outside one to make a room.

2. Use Pioneer's brick texture to make the outer box look like a brick building. You might want to switch to the Rendered mode rather than Wireframe so you can see the effects of the textures. To add a texture, in the Object Paint menu choose the Top option, which paints the entire object. The default selection is to paint only a single surface at a time.

3. To make it look right, you need to scale the texture to the right proportions. For Bubsy's showroom, I used 100 bricks by 20. This can be done by using the Scale dialog box and adjusting the values while watching the effects.

4. Immaculate as ever, Bubsy has a white floor to display the Viper on. Just add a normal plane and size it so that it's bigger than the inside of the room but smaller than the outside of the building. This will give you a nice smooth connection between wall and floor.

5. Using the material properties, turn off the texture map and adjust the color to what you want—a nice bright white with plenty of reflection, in this case.

The real showroom has writing on the windows advertising the specials for that week.

1. You can easily do this for the virtual showroom by putting in another object and again using the boolean functions to subtract areas for the windows and the doors.

2. To create a window with sign writing on it, place a plane where the window is and apply to its face a GIF image that has a transparent background. Lucky for me, the 3D title image Kelly created in the previous chapter is just like the writing on the windows.

Pioneer doesn't display GIF textures, so I told Pioneer to use the texture and generated the correct file anyway. You could use a JPEG image if it supported transparent background images. In this case, though, it was just easier to use what was already defined.

3. Some browsers may not support GIF images, so to keep up the realism the window has the Material property set the transparency to almost 1.

At this stage, the roof has been left off so you can still see inside when the car is placed. However, the floor has been added to use as a reference later.

Figure 2.2.
The basic room structure in wireframe. Notice that the walls and doors have been removed.

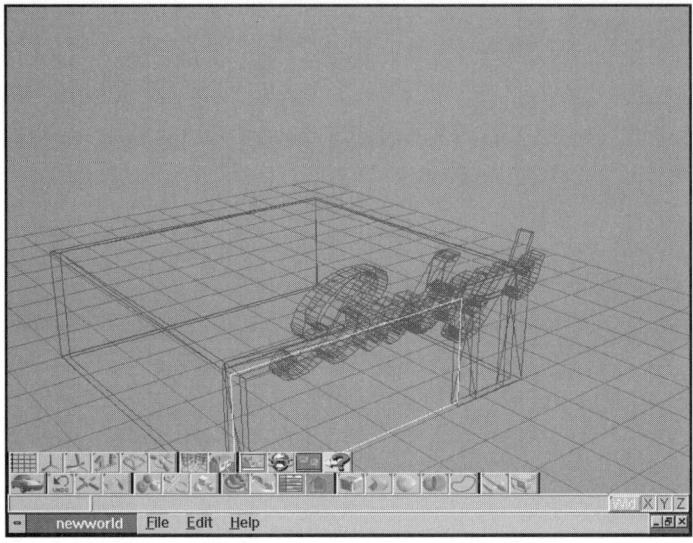

TASK Adding the Logo and Vehicles

The loading of the logo is a very simple thing.

1. Choose Select I Object from the menu, pick the logo file created by Kelly with trueSpace, and insert it directly into the scene. I used the standard trueSpace file Kelly sent me and adjusted it to fit the scene.

2. The usual scaling and translation were done to make the logo look right in the scene because the original file produced a logo bigger than the rest of the building.

3. I placed the logo just above the building over the entrance. In a concession to virtual reality, the logo floats in space. It looks much better than creating lots of visually unappealing supports. Besides, it's easier to do it that way!

4. The two vehicles are added in the same way. Place the Viper inside the showroom and leave the forklift outside in front of the building. The models came from the Viewpoint collection included on this book's CD-ROM. The Viper model is so large it created problems in Pioneer, so I had Kelly remove a lot of details from the original file before he sent it on to me. Originally, it was so big that Pioneer would create error messages and just not display it at all. Once it was trimmed down substantially, I could add it to the scene directly.

5. Sometimes you will find it necessary to hand-edit the file to include it in the right position. The forklift, being much simpler, was easy to do automatically.

Pioneer doesn't display the .scn files from trueSpace in the list of supported file formats. When the dialog box opens, then type `*.scn` in the Filename box and select the appropriate file.

TIP: The models are very high detail, so when you save them, make sure you turn the precision down. A precision value of 2 should be enough to get reasonably accurate models.

Adding a Roof

Now that you've placed some vehicles in the scene, you need to add a roof. The simplest method of doing this is to create a box and deform it to a pyramid shape by using the Deformation tool.

1. First, create a box and place it in the right position so its base lines up with the top of the walls.

2. Select the scale in the Z axis. Select the top of the cube and move it so that the corners meet in the middle.

3. You need to expand the bottom out so that it spans the sides of the building.

The end result is a roof pitched on all four sides just like a real one. To finish it off, use a gray tile for a realistic look in the same method as the brick texture was added to the walls.

Sprucing Up the World with Scenery

If you look at this file with a VRML browser, then you'll notice that the forklift is floating in mid-air. To remedy that, you'll add a bit of surrounding scenery.

First, the forklift needs to have some ground to sit on. I made it from a normal polygon that I added a grass texture to. The default setting for the grass texture looks fairly ordinary, so you can increase the amount of wrapping as I did with the brick walls and roof, which produces a much better grass effect.

Trees were constructed by placing a cylinder and then stacking a few cones on top. Once you're satisfied with the first one, then add a couple more by collecting the primitives in the first one as siblings and then choosing the Edit I Copy function from the menu. This function places the copy on top of the original, so you'll need to move the copy to the location you want. For my scene, I made four trees and placed them in a clump on the right-hand side. (See Figure 2.3.)

Figure 2.3.
The completed showroom ready to be put on the Web.

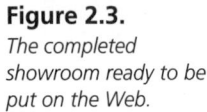 ## Putting the World on the Web

After creating your VRML world, you need to display it somewhere. The file extension for VRML files is .wrl, so from an HTML page all you need to do is make the anchor tag point to the VRML file.

1. Add a link to the VRML world from the HTML page. You can use a statement like this to add a link to the VRML world:

   ```
   Come and see my <A HREF="showroom.wrl">virtual showroom</A>
   ```

2. Click on this link. Two things might happen. If you're loading the file from the hard drive, then it will probably appear the way it should. If you're loading it from the Web, you might be lucky enough to have the same result. If so, then there's nothing more to do—just upload the files you need.

3. However, if all you get is a text document showing you the file's source, then some more work is in order. This result, by the way, means your Web server isn't configured to handle VRML files. You need to hassle your service provider or system administrator to add the correct configuration, which involves adding a new MIME type for the VRML files, like this:

   ```
   x-world/x-vrml    .wrl
   ```

The actual configuration varies depending on the brand of the Web server. Giving them this information should be enough to get you up and running. Once that's done, you should be able to load the file properly.

Workshop Wrap-up

There's your first world, ready to be published on the Web. As you have seen, it's possible to create a great-looking world without even knowing what VRML is. Graphics editors make creating cool worlds easy. However, these worlds were all static. You haven't even seen the latest version of VRML, the real subject of this book. In this chapter, you used just version 1.0—still an effective tool for 3D content, but the real fun hasn't started yet!

Next Steps

Now that you've had your first taste of both 3D graphics effects and 3D worlds, you need to go and learn some more. You can learn how to create all sorts of wonderful 3D graphics effects in the next two parts of the book. My co-author, Kelly, will look at everything from simple 3D buttons to animated logos.

❑ If you want to know more about VRML, then head straight to Chapter 13, "Exploring VRML Browsers and Development Tools," which introduces the basics of browsing and building VRML worlds.

❑ After you've learned the basics, then Chapters 14, "Starting with Models," 15, "Sprucing Up Models with Textures and Materials," and 16, "Adding a Dash of Reality," lead you through a series of exercises to produce a range of common objects that will become part of your everyday library of components.

❑ In Chapter 17, "Real-Life Examples: The VRML Art Gallery: A VRML World by Hand," you'll create a new VRML 2.0 world by hand, putting together all you've learned in the preceding chapters.

❑ Part V, "Advanced VRML Techniques," takes you into the realm of creating interactive VRML worlds. Here you'll find everything from simple animations to complex behaviors.

❑ The final VRML chapter, Chapter 23, "Real-Life Examples: A 3D Gallery: An Advanced VRML World," completes the art gallery begun in Chapter 17 by creating a world with flying pigs and sound.

Q&A

Q: What sort of tools did you use to create the VRML world?

A: Apart from Caligari's Pioneer, no other tools were used to create the world. Some parts were given to me by my co-author as files created in non-VRML tools like trueSpace. They could just as easily have been created in

Pioneer, but a lot of VRML site design ends up being done this way. Often your client has a collection of 3D models and 2D images that he or she would like to use.

I have to admit I did cheat for one little section—including the Viper model. It came from a very complex original model that was just too big for Pioneer to handle when loaded in with other scenery. So I added it by hand-editing the text source file in Notepad. You'll probably find that this is the way much day-to-day work is done—the basic model is created with a modeling tool, then finished in a text editor.

Q: Besides Pioneer/trueSpace, is there any other combination of tools available?

A: A difficult one to answer, because new products are coming out all the time. What's true today may not be true tomorrow. However, an increasingly popular choice is releasing a browser and builder together. A number of companies, such as IDS Software, Sony, and Silicon Graphics, do this, and many of them can import external formats like DXF.

Chapter 13 looks at the different methods of generating VRML files. The good thing is that most of your standard 3D modeling tools now either directly or indirectly support VRML output.

PART

II

Creating and Using 3D Elements in Your Web Page

THREE

Adding Simple 3D Elements to Your Web Page

—by Kelly Murdock

Welcome to Chapter 3. Hopefully, you're here because you liked the Web pages you saw in the first two chapters and want to do the same to your own pages. Well, just as every voyage begins with one step, learning to make a 3D Web site begins with one chapter—and this is it.

If you're convinced that adding 3D elements to your Web page will give it the look you want, you may be ready to run out and buy an advanced package to do 3D graphics. Before you do, you might want to consider using the tools you already have in your arsenal. Several fancy 3D graphics effects can be produced with simple paint programs, such as Paint Shop Pro (which is on this book's CD-ROM):

- ❏ Learn to quickly add a 3D look to text and objects by using drop shadows.
- ❏ Use the Emboss filter to make elements appear raised from the surface.
- ❏ Discover how to add perspective to your images.
- ❏ Adjust the brightness of your background images to make the foreground text more legible.
- ❏ Create tiled backgrounds that are seamless.

In this chapter, you

- ❏ Use drop shadows and the Emboss filter to add a 3D look to text and objects
- ❏ Add perspective to your images
- ❏ Create seamless tiled backgrounds
- ❏ Use Photoshop to add specialized 3D effects

Tasks in this chapter:

- ❏ Adding a 3D Look by Using Drop Shadows
- ❏ Using the Emboss Filter
- ❏ Using Perspective Deformations
- ❏ Manually Creating Tiled Backgrounds with Paint Shop Pro
- ❏ Using Photoshop's Emboss Filter
- ❏ Using Photoshop's Lighting Effects
- ❏ Adding Stylized Depth Effects by Extruding with Photoshop
- ❏ Creating Quick and Easy Tiled Backgrounds with Fractal Design Painter
- ❏ Creating Extruded Outlines with CorelDRAW!

If you're lucky enough to have more sophisticated 2D packages, such as Photoshop or CorelDRAW!, then countless effects are possible; this chapter will also teach you how to use them in your Web pages.

❏ Use Photoshop's lighting effects to add realism to your images.

❏ Create stylized depth effects with Photoshop's extrude filter.

❏ Learn how Fractal Design Painter can be used to quickly create seamless tiled background patterns.

❏ Take a look at CorelDRAW!'s powerful extrude features.

❏ Discover how Photoshop plug-ins can add specialized 3D effects.

That's a lot to cover in one short chapter, but then 2D packages shouldn't be sold short. They have been around much longer than their 3D counterparts and have learned a thing or two about "faking" 3D.

Adding a 3D Look by Using Drop Shadows

Perhaps the simplest effect is to add a shadow to 2D objects. This is done by copying the object and changing its color (most often black is used), then positioning the original object diagonally offset from the shadow. Many paint packages have commands that automate this process. Paint Shop Pro, for example, offers a couple of ways to do this.

Drop Shadows on Text

The Text dialog box in Paint Shop Pro has a Shadow option; to use it, follow these steps:

1. Select the text tool by clicking on the icon with a capital *T* in the Paint toolbar.

2. With the tool selected, click anywhere in the image to open a dialog box, where you can specify the font, size, and style of the text. There is also a checkbox for enabling a shadow. Type in your text and select this checkbox, and your text will be displayed with a shadow when you hit the OK button.

3. Position the text where you want it and click the button to set it. The color of the text and the shadow will be determined by the foreground and background colors selected in the Paint toolbar.

The resulting text from the drop shadow option set in the Text dialog box can be seen in the top of Figure 3.1. The drawback to using this method is that it's limited to text and the 1-pixel shadow offset cannot be changed. So take a look at how this same effect can be done by hand:

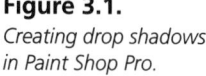

Figure 3.1.

Creating drop shadows in Paint Shop Pro.

1. Open a new image and select black as the foreground color and green as the background color.

2. Next, select the text tool and click anywhere in the image workspace to open the Text dialog box. Type your text in the text field, make sure the shadow checkbox is cleared, and click the OK button. The text appears as a floating object that moves around with the cursor. Position the text and click the mouse; the text appears in black.

Using the Soften filter, which can be found by choosing Image I Normal Filters I Soften, on the shadow before overlaying the original text gives the edges a realistic, blurred look.

TIP: Floating objects are objects that aren't yet part of the image. Their position is controlled by the mouse movements. By holding the mouse still, the object looks the way it will when set in the image. Click the mouse button, and the object is permanently set in the image. This technique lets you see what the final image will look like before it's set.

3. Now, double-click the small *R* icon next to the foreground and background colors to reverse the colors.

4. Then, with the text tool still active, click in the image workspace again and click OK in the Text dialog box. The same text will become a floating object. Position the text above and slightly to the left of the black text and click the left mouse button. The resulting green text will have a black shadow offset.

Applying Drop Shadows to Nontext Objects

Besides text, this method can be used for any type of 2D object as well. The embellishments in Figure 3.1 used the same technique except that the Magic Wand tool and the Cut, Copy, and Paste functions were used to select and position the object. Be sure to place the shadow down first so that the actual object isn't obscured. The bottom half of Figure 3.1 shows the possibilities of using this second method.

Remember to use transparent GIF images. The subtleties of shadows and highlights look better when 3D elements can rise above the background surface.

CAUTION:
Notice in Figure 3.1 that the holes in the embellishment don't have a shadow. In Paint Shop Pro, you can't select interior areas that are a different color with the Magic Wand tool. A workaround solution is to connect the interior sections to the background with a thin line that you can erase once the effect is complete.

Creating Skewed Drop Shadows

For a more realistic effect, the shadow can be skewed to give the perception that the light source is located in a different position. Try using the Image l Deformations l Skew command on the shadow copy. Then position the original on top of it, matching up the bottom lines. This can be used to create the effect of different times of the day, as shown in Figure 3.2.

Figure 3.2.
Using skewed shadows to give the appearance of a light source at different positions.

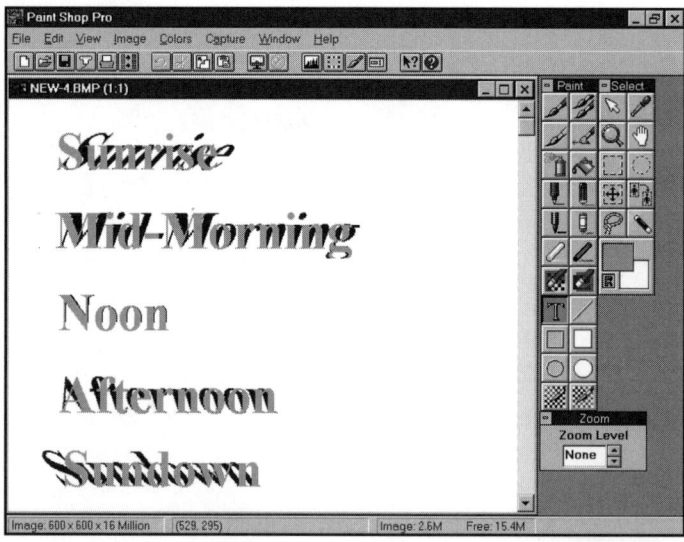

Don't be limited to only the Skew deformation; try using the Perspective deformation and aligning the unchanged edge.

The Emboss filter can be tricky because it changes the colors of the image.

Using the Emboss Filter

Filters are mathematical algorithms that change the image in preprogrammed ways. They can be used to alter an image in one bold process, thereby replacing a lot of tedious handwork. Several of these processes can be used to create 3D effects.

The drop shadow effect adds only a shadow to the object, but the Emboss filter adds a highlight and a shadow. This gives the embossed object a *relief* look, as if the embossed object sticks up from the surface. The filter does this by changing the original object to gray, using the object color for the highlight on one side of the object, and using a complementary color for the shadow on the opposite side.

The Emboss filter is fairly common and can be found in most paint programs, including Paint Shop Pro. As an example of applying the Emboss filter, the results of the Web Tournament of Champions are assembled in Figure 3.3.

CAUTION: Filters can be applied only to high-resolution images. In the lower-left corner of the status bar, you can see the size and color depth of the current image. If your image is not in 16 million color format, select Colors | Increase Color Depth | 16 Million Colors (24 Bit).

Since you want to apply the Emboss filter to the entire image, there is only one step. Select Image | Special Filters | Emboss. The results can be seen in Figure 3.3. Notice that the angle of the emboss effect is parallel to some of the lines, so they seem to disappear.

Figure 3.3.
Results of your Web Tournament of Champions with the Emboss filter applied.

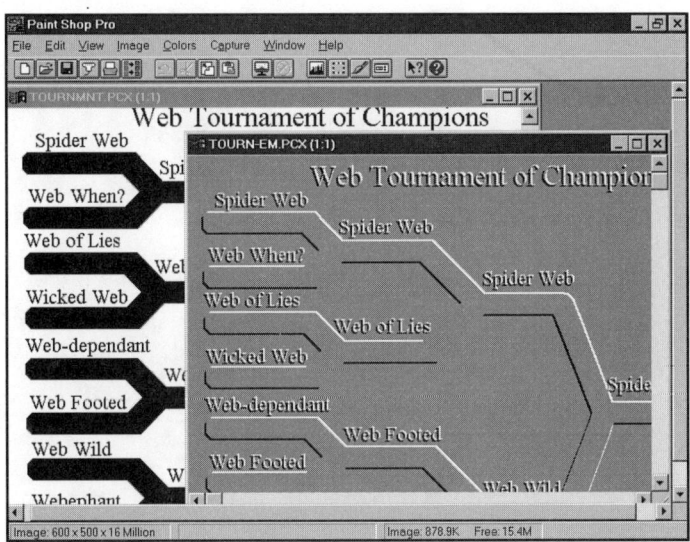

The Emboss filter can also be used to quickly make buttons. Try applying it to outlined shapes with a thick border.

Horizontal perspective works great for rows of similar objects, like parked cars, trees, and telephone poles.

Using Perspective Deformations

One of the deformation filters that can be used to create a 3D look is the Perspective filter. If you're looking down a country road lined with trees, you will notice that the farther away the tree is, the smaller it looks. That's how perspective works.

In Paint Shop Pro, there are two such filters: one for horizontal perspective and the other for vertical perspective. Each gives you a dialog box with a preview window and a control to change the percent of the effect.

Try using the Horizontal and Vertical Perspective deformation filters to create a wood box for your Web page:

1. Open a new image and duplicate it by using the Window I Duplicate command.

2. Next, resize the image to 100 × 200 with the Image I Resize command and apply the Perspective filter with the command Image I Deformations I Horizontal Perspective. Enter the value of **90%** into the dialog box and click OK. The right edge of the image will shrink.

3. Make a copy with the Windows I Duplicate command and create the opposite face with the Image I Mirror command; this creates a mirror image.

4. Select the original image, resize it to 200 × 100, and apply the Vertical Perspective deformation at 90 percent.

5. Duplicate the image and select Image I Flip to create the final face.

6. Now copy all the images into a new 250 × 250 image file and position them as shown in Figure 3.4. Finally, add the borders in with the fill tool.

Figure 3.4.
Using the Perspective filter in Paint Shop Pro to create a four-sided perspective image.

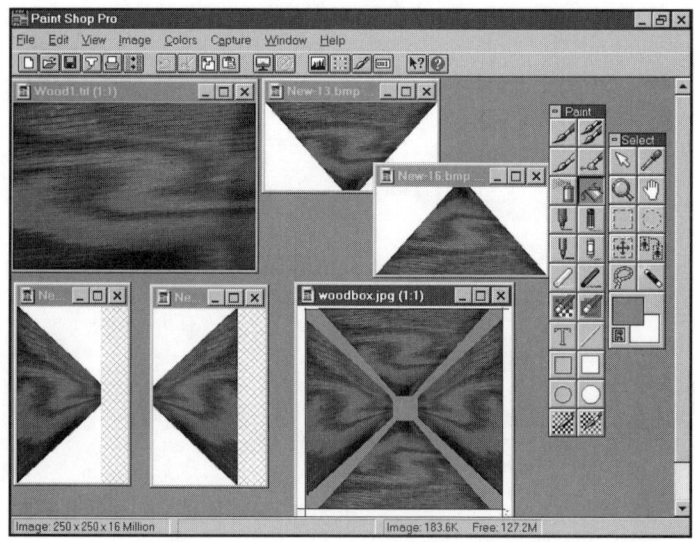

To save your image as a transparent GIF file, select File I Save As to open the Save dialog box. Choose the GIF file type from the List Files of Type drop-down menu and click the Options button to open the Options dialog box. Select the option to Set the Transparency Value to the Background Color.

Once you're finished with your image, you can decrease the color depth again by using Colors I Decrease Color Depth I 256 Colors to significantly reduce the file size. The image can then be saved as a GIF file. You can also save the image as a JPG file without reducing the color depth. JPG save options allow you to specify the amount of compression to be applied to the image. The greater the compression setting, the smaller the image file size, but the worse the quality. Most images can be set to a 50 percent compression setting without noticeably affecting the image quality.

Using 3D Backgrounds in Your Web Page

Backgrounds can really give your Web site that 3D feel, but they need to be used with care. Placing a detailed 3D image as your background looks great, but it also makes it difficult for visitors to read the text on your Web page, no matter what text color you use.

Another difficulty is dealing with the file size of backgrounds. Nobody likes a slow-loading Web site. The two best ways to reduce file sizes are to reduce the color depth and to reduce the overall size of your image. It's not often recommended that you use fewer than 256 colors for your 3D images, so one of the best ways to use smaller images is to tile them across the page. HTML does this automatically for background images.

Increasing Brightness of Backgrounds to Emphasize Text

If you are intent on using one of your 3D images as a background, there is a simple way to ensure that the text is legible. Increasing the brightness of the image fades the details and still lets users see the image. A background image brightened by 50 percent lets you use a dark text color that will be legible.

If you use a brightened image as a background, be sure to include the unbrightened image somewhere in your pages so Web visitors can see the original image in all its glory.

In Paint Shop Pro, use the Colors I Adjust I Brightness/Contrast command and set the value between 50 and 80 percent. A setting of 100 percent will wash out the image entirely, leaving a pure white image—and there are easier ways to do that.

Figure 3.5 shows a good example of using a background in this manner. For this example, I used a brightness setting of 40 percent.

However, notice the strong seams at each edge of the image. It's easy to tell that the background is tiled from one image. If you can match the opposite edges, you can make your backgrounds look like one consistent image.

Figure 3.5.

Adjusting the brightness of the background image to ensure that the text is legible.

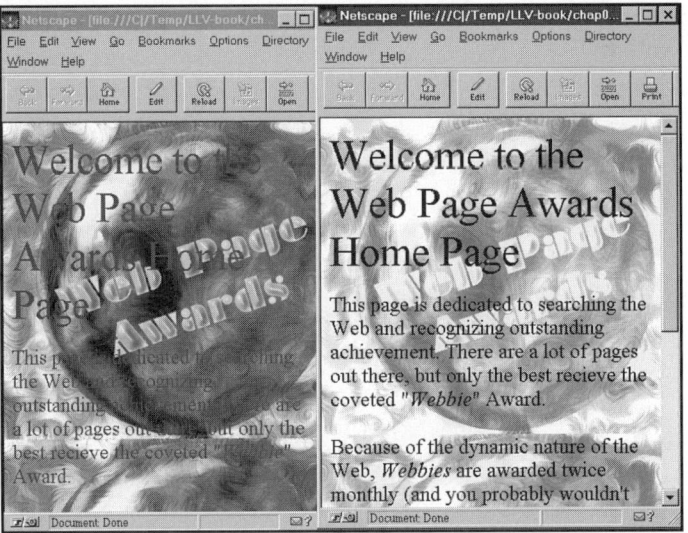

Manually Creating Tiled Backgrounds with Paint Shop Pro

Tiled backgrounds are one of the best ways to get a lot of benefit out of small image files. A small image can be repeated to cover entire Web pages no matter what the size is. The trick to making the images look good is to eliminate the seams by matching each edge to the opposite edge.

Simple image-editing packages like Paint Shop Pro can be used to create seamless tiled backgrounds with a special trick. The trick is to divide your image so that the seams on opposite sides match up. You can do this by splitting the image into four quadrants and copying each quadrant diagonally to the opposite quadrant, then removing the newly created seams.

Because each quadrant of the original image is repositioned, this isn't a good technique to use for objects that need to remain consistent, such as a picture of an eye or a car. However, it works well for abstract backgrounds. To do this with Paint Shop Pro, try the following:

1. Create a new image that is 96 × 96 pixels.

2. Next, use the rectangular selector tool to select the upper-left quadrant of the image from 0,0 to 47,47 and copy it onto the Clipboard. The coordinates are shown on the status bar at the bottom of the window.

3. Create another new image that is 96 × 96 pixels, and paste the image quarter with the Edit I Paste I As New Selection command into the new image. Then position it in the lower-right corner and click the button.

4. Repeat this copy-and-paste process for the other three quadrants, copying each quadrant to its opposite corner.

5. When you're finished, two seams remain, running horizontally and vertically through the image. Use the drawing tools to hide these seams, then save the image.

6. As a final step, apply the Emboss filter and save the image as a JPG file to be used as a background.

You should wait to apply the 3D effect until after the quadrants have been repositioned because it's easier to fix the seams before the effect is applied.

Figure 3.6 shows this process in four windows. The upper-left window shows the original image, and the upper-right shows the new image created from the pasted corners. The lower-left window shows the image after the seams have been touched up, and the lower-right window shows the image after you've applied the Emboss filter. The larger image to the right is an example of the tiled image.

Figure 3.6.

Creating a seamless background with Paint Shop Pro by moving each quadrant to the opposite corner.

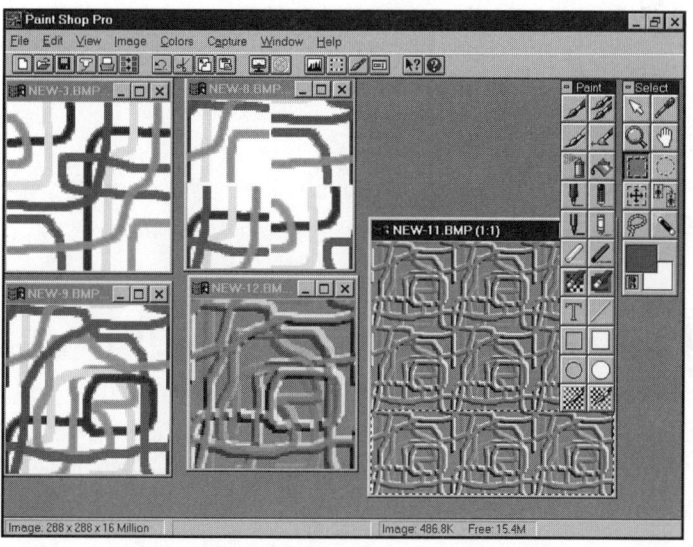

Using High-End 2D Tools

Low-end tools like Paint Shop Pro are a good place to start, but they often require a lot more work to accomplish simple effects. There are many advantages to working with high-end image-editing packages, such as Adobe Photoshop, Corel PHOTO-PAINT, and Fractal Design Painter.

Of course, there are many more image-editing packages than the ones I've listed here; these are just popular representations. Sorry if I left your favorite off the list!

These packages make a lot of effects easy to accomplish, but they're very sophisticated and often require some time to learn. Many artists and designers spend years learning these tools. Without getting too deep, take a look at some 3D tricks that these products make easy.

 ## Using Photoshop's Emboss Filter

Adobe Photoshop can also create the drop shadow and emboss effects you just learned with Paint Shop Pro. The advantage to Photoshop is the ease and control you have. For example, Paint Shop Pro won't let you select separate areas not connected by similar colors, so it becomes cumbersome to apply filters on text.

Take a look at how Photoshop does embossing:

❏ First, select the line or object you want to emboss by using the Magic Wand tool. You can easily select other areas regardless of color by holding down the Shift key and selecting elsewhere.

❏ Once you're satisfied with your selection, then choose Filter | Stylize | Emboss. This activates a dialog box that lets you specify the direction and height of the emboss and the percentage amount of the original image that the Emboss filter uses. These added controls are one of the chief advantages of high-end tools.

TIP: The most recently used filter jumps to the top of the Filter menu and can be selected quickly without navigating the menu choices.

 ## Using Photoshop's Lighting Effects

In addition to the effects already covered, Photoshop is capable of several unique 3D effects that aren't possible with low-end tools. One of these is lighting effects. Photoshop can control the direction, amount, and angles at which the light falls on an object.

1. Open the image you want to apply lighting effects to in Photoshop. I'm using the rubber duckie image from the Photoshop Deluxe CD-ROM for this example.

2. Select the Filters | Render | Lighting Effects filter to open a dialog box for selecting the light type, properties, and textures.

3. From the pull-down menu at the top of the dialog box, select the Xdown light style.

You can also choose to place multiple lights in an image and change their colors.

4. In the preview window, drag the handles to change the direction of the light and click OK when you're satisfied.

Figure 3.7 shows a before-and-after example that uses the Lighting Effects filter.

Figure 3.7.
Using lighting effects in Photoshop can add an element of realism to the image.

Adding Stylized Depth Effects by Extruding with Photoshop

The Photoshop method of extruding is somewhat different from the way you generally think of extruding. It's capable of some impressive special effects, but the CorelDRAW! method shown later in the chapter is more traditional.

Do you remember in grade school when you learned to make a cube out of a simple square by drawing parallel diagonal lines? Well, the same method can be used to create 3D elements for your Web page. *Extruding* is just that—adding depth to an object by extending parallel lines from each corner.

In Photoshop, the filter breaks the selected area up into squares and separates them with an extrusion depth. The size of the squares and the extrusion depth are controlled by using dialog box, opened with the Filters I Stylize I Extrude command. This dialog box, along with an example, is shown in Figure 3.8.

Figure 3.8.
Using Photoshop's Extrude filter to create a special 3D look.

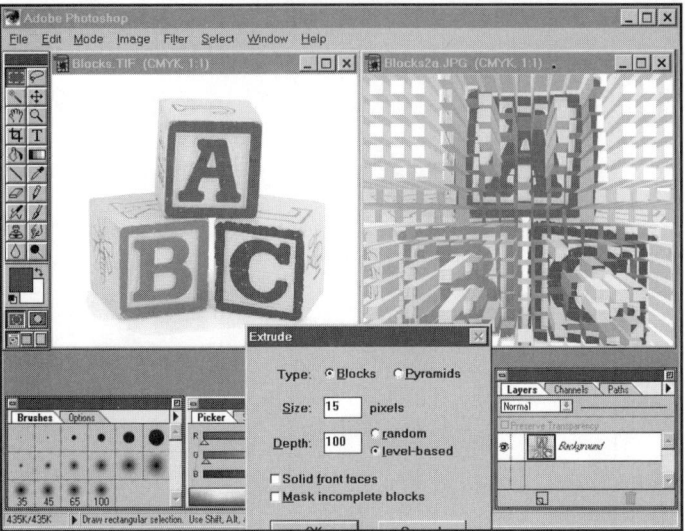

Creating Quick and Easy Tiled Backgrounds with Fractal Design Painter

Remember the trouble you had to go through to create a seamless tiled background in Paint Shop Pro? Perhaps the slickest way I've found to create these backgrounds is by using Fractal Design Painter. Painter has a feature that lets you paint an image and match the opposite edges automatically.

Creating tiled backgrounds in Painter is as easy as this:

1. Start with a new file of any size. Under the Pattern menu in the Art Materials dialog box, choose Define Pattern.

2. Now, as you begin painting in the new workspace, the colors wrap around to the far edge as you cross over them.

3. Try painting with the Image Hose, found in the Brushes drawer. This tool overlays several different images as you drag the pointer over the image. As you paint near an edge, notice how half the image shows up on the opposite edge.

4. When you are done painting, you can check the background by saving the pattern to the library with the command Pattern I Add Image to Library. Give the pattern a name, then open a new image larger than the pattern and fill it by using the fill tool.

5. Save the file and use it as your background image.

A good sampling of tiled 3D backgrounds can be seen in Figure 3.9. These backgrounds took about five minutes to create using the Image Hose tool and several of the nozzles found on the Painter 4 CD-ROM. The Painter Help file has a warning that creating patterns can be addictive, and I can testify that this is true. Once you start creating patterns in this way, you won't want to go back to any other tool.

Figure 3.9.
Using Fractal Design Painter, you can easily and quickly create tiled backgrounds.

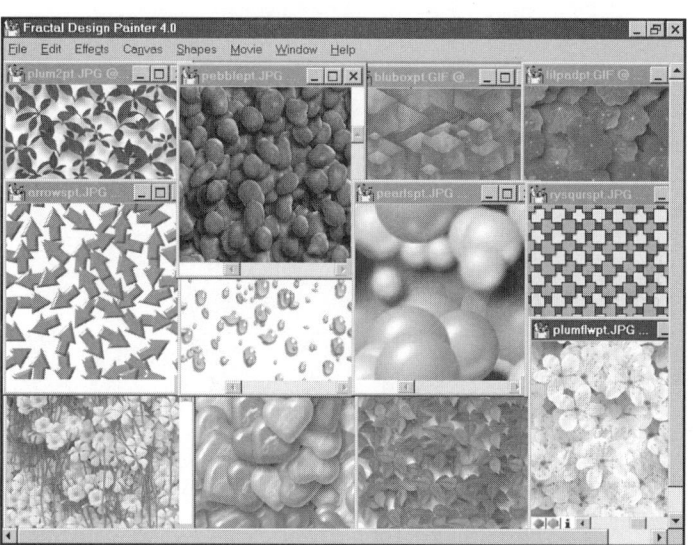

Fractal Design Painter is a special type of image-editing package. It was built specifically for artists and has some truly unique features. You'll visit this package again when you start to create your own model materials.

Because Painter is a tool that simulates working with natural media, it allows you to use all types of textures, like canvas, wood, and different grades of paper. These textures, when applied to images, give them a look of depth. For subtle textures with a 3D look to them, you should look into using Painter.

 # Creating Extruded Outlines with CorelDRAW!

Although image-editing software, such as Photoshop, has capabilities for tasks like extruding and adding perspective, the real pros at these effects are vector-based drawing packages, like Adobe's Illustrator, Macromedia's FreeHand, and CorelDRAW!.

Take a look at how you would use the extrude feature of CorelDRAW! 6:

1. Open a new image and place a 2D outline within the image. For this example, I selected a symbol from the symbol library by using the Tools I Symbols command.

2. From the Stars1 font, set the size to 7 and drag the symbol over to the page. The star outline shows up on the page.

3. Access the Extrude roll-up menu by choosing Effects | Extrude. The Extrude roll-up menu has five tabs. The first lets you select preset options, the second controls the type and level of depth, the third controls the rotation, the fourth the lighting options, and the final tab controls the colors.

CorelDRAW!'s extrude feature offers both extruding and lighting effects together. The lighting effects help emphasize the 3D nature of the extruded objects.

Once you've set the options you like, click the Apply button and the outline will appear on the page.

You can see from this example in Figure 3.10 the types of features that drawing packages offer. Because these packages deal with vector lines, they have precise control over how the outlines are manipulated.

Figure 3.10.

A simple extrusion of a star outline done with CorelDRAW! 6.

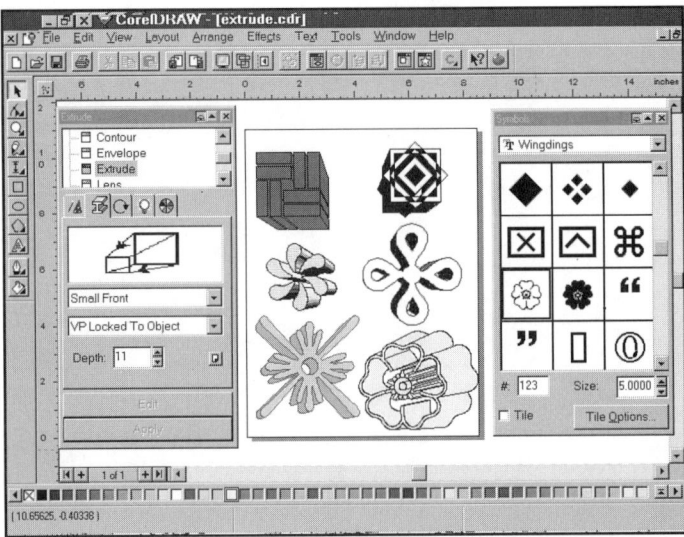

Keep in mind when working with drawing packages that you can't save them as GIF or JPG files. To use images created with vector-based drawing packages, you have to export the file to a raster format, like BMP, GIF, or JPG. If GIF or JPG isn't an export option (as in CorelDRAW!), then export the image to BMP and convert the file in Paint Shop Pro by opening the file and using the File | Save As command to specify the format you want.

3D Effects Made Easy with Plug-In Filters

The easiest 3D effects to use are the ones built in to Photoshop, like the Emboss or Extrude filters. However, because of the open nature of the software, Photoshop isn't limited to these built-in functions. Many third-party companies build plug-in modules that add functions to the existing package.

These plug-in packages work like the plug-ins for Netscape Navigator do. From within Photoshop, they show up as additional menu items launching helper applications that work within Photoshop. There are several of these applications that can add amazing 3D effects very easily.

Plug-ins have become a popular way to add additional functions to your product. You'll see plug-ins not only in the browser and image-editing world, but also in the 3D tools market as well.

In addition, many other image-editing packages support this same technology, so these plug-in filters aren't limited to working only with Photoshop. Fractal Design Painter, Corel PHOTO-PAINT, and even Paint Shop Pro can use these filters also.

Using Alien Skin Software's The Black Box

Alien Skin Software has a set of plug-in filters called The Black Box; although not the most popular of the third-party plug-in filters, it's probably one of the best for adding 3D effects. The Black Box 2.0 contains 10 plug-in filters, including several that apply 3D effects:

- ❏ **Drop Shadow**—allows precise control over the X and Y offset and the blur and opacity of the shadow.
- ❏ **Cutout**—inverted shadow effect creates a hole in the image out of the selected area.
- ❏ **Inner Bevel**—makes the selected area appear raised from the image surface by adding highlights to the inner edge of the selection; works great for creating buttons.
- ❏ **Outer Bevel**—another type of bevel that highlights the edges outside the selection.
- ❏ **Carve**—is the opposite of the Inner Bevel filter and makes the selection look indented into the image surface.

The Black Box has other filters that can add interesting effects to whatever image you're creating. A sampling of the types of effects possible with The Black Box are shown in Figure 3.11.

Take a quick look at how the Cutout filter works in Photoshop. This filter is included on the book's CD-ROM as a sample, courtesy of Alien Skin Software.

TIP: Most plug-in filters work only when the computer is set to display 24-bit color (16 million colors). They can be used at other color depths, but the interfaces are difficult to see.

Figure 3.11.

Using The Black Box filters by Alien Skin Software to create 3D snowflakes.

CAUTION: The Black Box filters will not work in Paint Shop Pro. The filters load okay and run okay, but seem to cause the program to shut down when applied. So, if you try using the filters in Paint Shop Pro, save your images before testing them.

1. Run the setup disk to install the filters, which are typically saved and accessed from the plug-ins subdirectory of your image-editing package.

2. Now run Photoshop and open an image. If you choose Filters | Alien Skin, the Cutout filter becomes available.

3. Use the Magic Wand tool to make a selection in the image and access the Cutout filter. A dialog box opens with controls that allow you to change the X and Y offset, blur, and opacity of the shadow. You can also select the color of the shadow and the fill with the foreground and background options.

4. Unique settings can be saved and added to the selection drop-down menu above the preview window. Choose the Subtle option and click the OK button.

5. After applying the filter, the image looks like a hole has been cut out of it.

Creating 3D Effects with Metatool's Kai's Power Tools

One of the best-selling plug-in filter sets is Kai's Power Tools (KPT) by Metatools. Among the vast array of tools included in this package are several that are excellent at creating 3D effects, including filters for glass lens, page curl, and the new spheroid designer.

KPT's Glass Lens Filter

Kai's Power Tools have a wide assortment of filters with an endless number of options. If you get only one plug-in filter package, this would be the one to consider.

Remember the old magnifying glass you used to burn ants? Well, Kai's Power Tools has a filter that distorts your selection in a similar manner. It's called the Glass Lens filter and is fairly easy to use (and not nearly as dangerous for small bugs):

1. Select the area of the image you want to distort.

2. Use the Filter I KPT 3.0 I KPT Glass Lens 3.0 command to open a dialog box for setting how the effect interacts with the image.

3. Apply the filter by clicking the small green button in the lower-right corner of the dialog box.

This effect, along with some others done with KPT, can be seen in Figure 3.12.

Figure 3.12.

Three examples using Kai's Power Tools: Glass Lens effect, the Page Curl effect, and an effect using the Spheroid Designer.

Both Paint Shop Pro (Image I Deformation I Circle) and Photoshop (Filter I Distort I Spherize) have similar filters, but neither offers the many controls that Kai's Power Tools do.

KPT's Page Curl Effect

The Page Curl effect is just that—an effect that makes the page look like its edge is curled. This filter is applied much the same way as the Glass Lens filter explained previously. It lets you control the corner and direction of the page curl as well as the opacity of the curled edge. You can see an example of this effect in Figure 3.12.

KPT's Spheroid Designer

This filter is much more versatile than the other KPT filters covered so far. It's actually a helper application that gives you precise control over the spheroids you place in your image. The example in Figure 3.12 uses the Spheroid Designer for a simple effect, but much more complex and distorting options are available.

Some of the controls in the Spheroid Designer include the illumination of spheres, the number of spheres, the curvature and transparency of spheres, and the randomness of all the spheres. Boy, there are spheres showing up everywhere! You can also use bump maps, which are images that help define how the surface is textured.

Workshop Wrap-up

By now your 2D tools are probably exhausted, so why don't you give them a chance to catch their breath? Not too long, though, because you'll use them again. They will be instrumental in creating textures and materials used to dress up your 3D models.

If you take the 3D effects gleaned from this chapter and place them in your Web page, you will earn a few hurrahs—and you've just started. It's time to move on; the third dimension awaits. Now, where did I put that other dimension?

Next Steps

Don't feel like you have to take this book chapter by chapter. The end of each chapter includes a "jump list" like this one to guide you in your journey:

- ❑ To jump into the 3D world and learn how to produce and use true 3D images, move on to Chapter 4, "Creating and Embedding 3D Rendered Images."
- ❑ If you've had enough images and are ready for animation, skip to Chapter 6, "Using Animation Plug-Ins in Your Web Page."
- ❑ To see an example of how these 3D elements are used in a real-world example, jump to Chapter 12, "Real-Life Examples: Creating a MYST-like Adventure on the Web."
- ❑ If you're anxious to get into VRML, then hop over to Chapter 11, "Using Microsoft's ActiveVRML."

Q&A

Q: **What are the differences between image-editing packages like Photoshop and drawing packages like CorelDRAW!?**

A: Image-editing packages, also called paint packages, are *raster-based*, which means they deal with pixels—rows and columns of dots that make up the screen. Each pixel can hold essentially one color. If you zoom in on an image, you will eventually see the individual pixels.

Drawing packages are vector-based. *Vectors* are line elements defined mathematically. Every time the screen is redrawn, the vectors are recalculated; therefore, when you zoom in on a vector, it still looks like a line. Some fonts use vectors so that they stay smooth at any size.

Q: **Which are better at producing 3D effects, image-editing packages or drawing packages?**

A: It really depends on the type of effect you're looking for. You have more control with effects involving lines, such as extruding, if you use a drawing package. Softer effects, such as a blurry look to drop shadows, look better done with a paint package because you can more easily spread the pixels around.

Q: **Can I use the images created in this chapter in my 3D software and vice versa?**

A: I'm afraid the answer is like a one-way street. Still images created in a 3D environment can be saved as a picture and edited in an image editing-package, but when they're saved, all 3D information is lost. A 2D package doesn't know what to do with the 3D information, so it simply discards it. Conversely, when 2D images are imported into 3D packages, they show up as flat images. They can be viewed or even wrapped around 3D objects, but they are still flat.

FOUR

Creating and Embedding 3D Rendered Images

—by Kelly Murdock

If you've added some 3D elements to your Web page and pushed your 2D tools to their limits, but you still think your Web pages are lacking, then you might need some real 3D images. It's tricky to say "real 3D" images because all images seen on the computer screen are still two-dimensional, so it's clearer to say that this chapter deals with images created by using 3D RMA (Rendering, Modeling, and Animation) packages. You will use these packages in this chapter to create what are known as *stills*, or *still images*. Still images are simply images that don't move. If you're anxious to get into animation, hold your horses—you'll get into animation in the next chapter.

In this chapter, you learn to set up 3D scenes by placing 3D objects called *models*, dressing up those models with materials, and positioning lights and cameras, just as a real photographer does. With the 3D scene setup, you can quickly reshoot images from different viewpoints without redrawing the entire scene. More specifically, this chapter covers the following tasks:

- ❏ Set up different views within your 3D scene.
- ❏ Learn where to find and borrow 3D models.
- ❏ Personalize your models by modifying them.
- ❏ Learn how to create new models.

In this chapter, you

- ❏ Set up different views in your 3D scene
- ❏ Find, borrow, and modify 3D models
- ❏ Create new models and add materials to them
- ❏ Position and control lights
- ❏ Place cameras in your 3D scene
- ❏ Use 3D still images in your Web page

Tasks in this chapter:

- ❏ Creating New Models by Modifying Existing Ones
- ❏ Creating Original Models with Ray Dream Studio
- ❏ Using trueSpace to Create New Materials
- ❏ Creating Texture Maps
- ❏ Positioning and Controlling Lights
- ❏ Placing Cameras and Capturing an Image
- ❏ Outputting and Using 3D Images in Your Web Pages
- ❏ Creating Reference Thumbnails

❑ Add materials to your models.

❑ Create and use new materials, both within 3D packages and by importing texture maps.

❑ Position and control lights and lighting effects.

❑ Learn to place cameras and control viewpoint.

❑ Use captured 3D still images in your Web pages.

From the looks of this list, you have a ways to go, so begin with an overview of 3D RMA packages.

3D RMA (Rendering, Modeling, and Animation) Packages

Many 3D packages are available, and they span a wide range in cost and performance. It's beyond the scope of this book to cover all of them, but a good starting list can be found in Appendix A, "3D Software Resource Guide."

These 3D packages allow you to *model* objects—that is, to build three-dimensional representations of objects; to *render* images, which means to calculate the effects of models' lights, shadows, and positions; and to *animate* images, meaning to move the objects over time.

Just like other types of software, 3D packages are very different from one another in the way they work. There are some wonderful packages that do everything you could possibly want, but they are very expensive. However, among the low-end packages, different features are available. I'll try to show you a variety of packages—not to confuse you, but rather to cover the basic concepts by presenting the best features of different packages.

For the examples in this chapter, you will focus on two packages: Caligari's trueSpace, currently in the 2.0 version, and Ray Dream Studio. Both these packages fit into the midrange price level at around $500, yet have surprisingly powerful features. Before you put your money down, play with the demo versions on the CD-ROM to decide whether these packages are right for you.

How Is the View?

One of the first lessons in the 3D world is coming to grips with the multitude of views. If you go to a museum and look at a picture of a fire hydrant hanging on the wall, you see it from only one viewpoint. You can walk to the other side of the room, walk up close, or even stand on your head, but the image is still the same.

If you walk outside the museum and look at a fire hydrant on the street, the image you see changes as you move about it. From behind it you see a shadow, on top of it you see a circular dome, and to the side you see where the firehose connects. This is the key advantage of working in the 3D world. Once a scene is created, an infinite number of images can be created just by changing the viewpoint.

In the 3D world, you deal with a third axis, the notorious *Z-axis*. Using this Z-axis allows your objects to go forward and back and can also make it tricky to line up various objects. An object can look like it's right next to another in one view but actually be in the far distance, as it is in Figure 4.1. In the upper-left image, the words *front* and *back* seem to be side-by-side, but in the next three windows, you can see as you rotate around that there's some distance between the two.

Figure 4.1.
Even though objects seem to be side-by-side in one view, that doesn't mean they're actually next to one another.

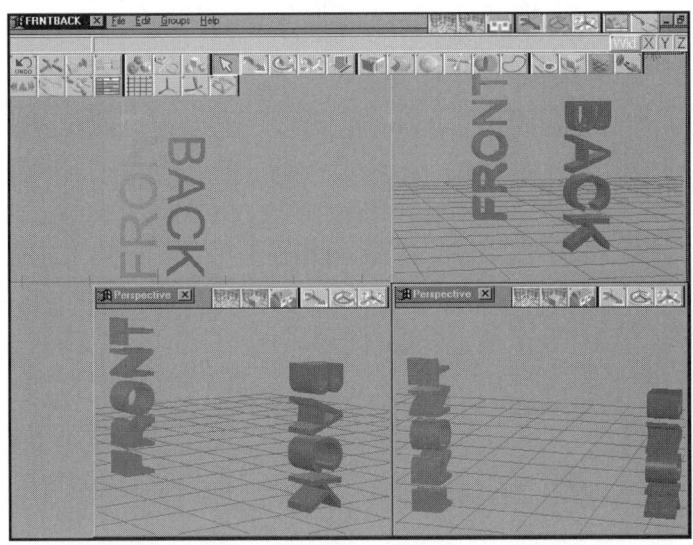

To handle the relative positions of objects, many 3D packages deal with four viewpoints at the same time: top view, right view, front view, and perspective view. This allows the user to quickly look at the objects in relation to one another.

The 3D package trueSpace starts with only one window set to the Perspective view, but new views can be selected by clicking and dragging the View button in the View Group. There are several preset views, including Top, Left, Front, Perspective, and View from Object.

In trueSpace, the toolbar and menus start out located at the bottom of the screen, but they can be moved to the top of the screen to look like other Windows programs, by toggling the Top View option in the panel opened by the File | Preference command.

The View Group also includes the Eye tools, which let you move, rotate, and zoom the viewpoint. If you click one of these buttons, they toggle on. You are then in that mode until you select another tool. Click on the Eye Move button and drag the cursor in the main window. Notice how the grid moves up and down and forward and back with the mouse. The up and down directions are controlled by dragging with the right mouse button.

The View Group is a toolbar that's part of the title bar; it's separate from the other toolbars. All other groups can be turned on and off with the Groups menu option.

NOTE: In trueSpace, a default grid is placed in the scene to help you orient your models. It doesn't show up in the rendered image.

Another tool in the View Group allows you to open new windows, which have their own View Group buttons for navigating around the view.

TIP:

When you start changing your view in trueSpace, you can easily get lost, but two other View Group tools can help you when you start. The Reset View button restores your view to your original starting point, and the Look At Object button automatically positions your view so that the selected object is in the center of the screen.

It's great that you can control the views of your scene, but what are you supposed to see? Why, models of course, so now you'll see how to find some.

Where and How to Find and Borrow 3D Models

Now, if you have a 3D rendering piece of software and you're ready to go, the first thing you need is a model. Models are to 3D packages what paint is to a painting.

The simplest models are called *primitives*, which include objects like cubes, spheres, and cones. These primitives are usually built into the software and can be dropped into a scene with a single command.

The primitives in trueSpace include a plane, cube, cylinder, cone, sphere, and torus (a doughnut). The Primitive Panel is also used to add cameras, horizontal and vertical text, and deformation planes to the scene. Deformation planes allow you to alter the surface of an object. They will be covered in Chapter 8, "Creating Advanced 3D Rendered Images for Your Web Page."

In trueSpace, primitives are placed in a scene by using the Primitives Panel. Click the tool button, then click on the primitive you want to place. The object shows up in the center of the window.

Complex models can be created from these primitives by combining them in different ways or by distorting their shapes. Different packages have different methods of modeling objects, but before you delve into modeling, take a look at where you can borrow ready-made 3D objects.

The first place to look is on this book's CD-ROM. Several companies make 3D models, so a sample of their products is included on the CD-ROM.

NOTE:

Just as there are different image formats, such as BMP and JPG, there are also several different 3D file formats. The native AutoCAD format (DXF) is probably the most widely supported one for PCs.

Almost every 3D package has its own proprietary file format. Other useful formats include Wavefront (OBJ), 3D Studio Binary (3DS), Lightwave (LWO), trueSpace (COB), and Ray Dream Designer (RD4).

Once you've explored the models on the CD-ROM, then move on to the Web, which offers a plethora of models. The first place to visit is Avalon, a huge repository of 3D models, textures, and utilities available in the public domain. Avalon used to be located at the China Lake Naval Base until it was taken over by Viewpoint. It can now be found at the following site:

`http://www.viewpoint.com/avalon/`

Figure 4.2.

Viewpoint maintains the Avalon site, an immense collection of public domain models, textures, and utilities.

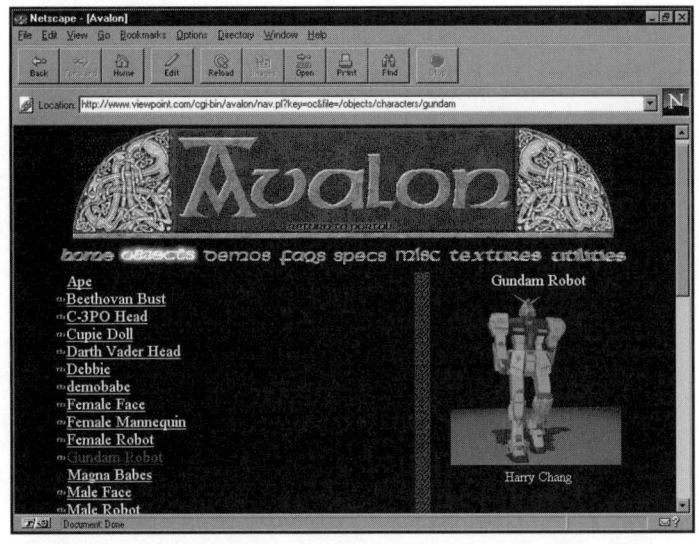

There are several mirror sites for Avalon throughout the Web, so don't be surprised to see the same models in several places.

Viewpoint regularly archives the entire collection and makes it available on CD-ROM for a nominal cost.

Besides maintaining the Avalon site, Viewpoint is a premier model-generating company; many of the sample models on the CD-ROM were graciously donated by them.

Another great site is the 3D Café, found at this location:

`http://156.46.199.2/3dcafe/`

Note that some of the objects at the 3D Café are for sale. It's common for sites that offer free models to also sell some of their higher-end models.

There's some overlap with the Avalon site, which is to be expected, but there are also some new models.

Once downloaded, these objects can be loaded into your 3D package. In trueSpace, use the File I Load command to bring up a dialog box for selecting the downloaded model's location. Depending on the object's format, you might need to specify some import options.

Figure 4.3.

You can find a good collection of free 3D models at the 3D Café Web site; shown here are the thumbnails for the Toys collection.

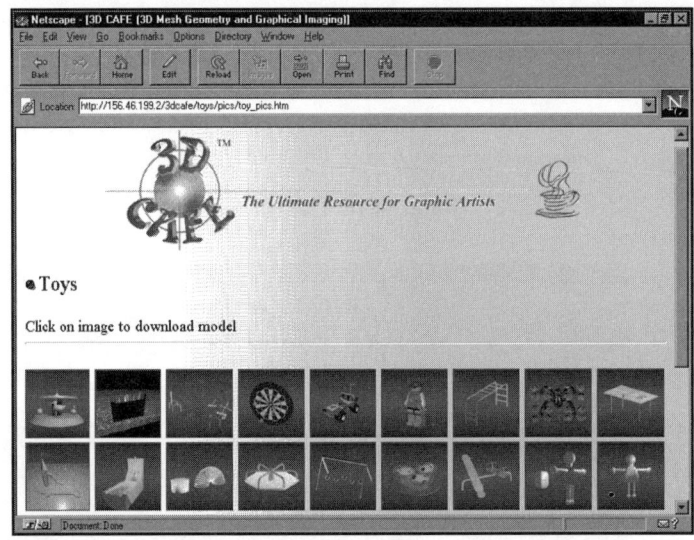

> **TIP:** Don't think you have to use only free models. Companies like Viewpoint offer a wide variety of models they sell as collections, or you can even commission them to custom-build a model for you. If you're working for a client and have the funds, models made by the real pros are worth the money, saving you the time needed to build the model yourself.

Before you move on, one more good model site is supported by Richard Tilman. Mesh Mart can be found at this site:

```
http://cedar.cic.net/~rtilmann/mm/index.htm
```

It offers a good assortment of models and textures and is another mirror to the Avalon site.

Manipulating Your Model

All the icons in the toolbar can be toggled on and off by using the Groups menu option. The groups in trueSpace include the Edit, Libs, Nav, Model, Render, Animate, and Util Groups. The View Group is always present and cannot be turned off.

Once imported, objects can be moved, rotated, and scaled in a scene. In trueSpace, these three navigation tools are located in the Nav Group to the right of the Object tool.

Just as you can move the viewpoint around, you can use similar tools to control the individual objects within the scene. In trueSpace, use the mouse's left button to control two axes and the right button to control the third axis. It's a good thing you don't work in four or more dimensions because you'd run out of buttons!

For example, select your model by clicking the Object tool, then clicking on the object within your scene. The object turns white to indicate that it's the currently selected object. Next, select the Object Move tool. Dragging with the left mouse button while you're in the Perspective view moves the model left and right or forward and back. Clicking and dragging with the right mouse button moves the object up and down, depending on the coordinate system you've selected.

You can also constrain the object to move only along certain axes by clicking and holding the right mouse button on the tool. This brings up the Coordspanel where you can toggle the axes on and off.

Many of the tools in trueSpace have additional panels that can be accessed by clicking them with the right mouse button. All tools with such panels have a small red mark in their upper-right corners. The small green mark in the upper-left corner indicates that more tools are available by dragging down with the left mouse button.

CAUTION: As you saw in Figure 4.1, it can be tricky to line up objects in three dimensions. When you place objects, be sure to check the alignment from more than one view.

The Coords panel also includes buttons for selecting the coordinate system; in trueSpace, you can select between Object, World, and Screen coordinate systems. The coordinate system alters which movements are controlled by the left mouse button and which are controlled by the right. It can be difficult to mix and match coordinate systems, so it's best to discover which one is easiest for you to use and stick with it.

Coordinate systems can also be changed for the Eye Move, Eye Rotate, and Zoom controls by right-clicking their respective toolbar buttons.

The Navigation tools move, rotate, and scale objects around the object's origin point, which is the center of the object for new primitives. For example, if you rotate a sphere, then it spins around the object's center point, but if you move the origin point, then the object rotates around the origin's new position. This origin point can be moved, rotated, and scaled just like any other object. To see the origin point, click the Axis button in the Util Group.

Also in the Util Group are tools that help you restore your object if you get lost. The Normalize buttons align your object according to the World coordinate system, and the Move Axis to Center of Object button does just what it says—it can be invaluable if you get confused about where your origin point is.

TASK

Creating New Models by Modifying Existing Ones

If you've searched high and low through the available models but just can't find the right one for your creation, then the next best bet is to find something that's close and modify it as needed.

Most 3D packages have a number of features to help you with your task. The first is the scaling command, mainly used to control the size of your models. This alone doesn't do much for you, because size in the virtual world is all relative. A model of an airplane is perceived as such when positioned next to an airport, but placed next to a teddy bear, you see it as just a child's toy.

TIP:

To scale an object along all axes simultaneously, hold down both buttons while dragging the mouse. This increases or decreases the object's overall size equally in all directions.

Non-uniform Scaling

Scaling becomes interesting when done on only one part of an object or along only one axis—this is called *non-uniform scaling*. Using this technique, not only can square boxes become rectangles, but a model of a man can become a clown by enlarging the size of his feet disproportionately, or a car can turn into a limosine by stretching its midsection.

So how can scaling help you modify a model? If you right-click the Scale tool and toggle off two of the axes, then by dragging the mouse, the object is scaled only in the one remaining axis. Try an example by following these steps:

The park bench model was downloaded from the collection at the 3D Café site.

1. The first step is to import the 3D model with the File I Load Object command. For this example, I've selected a park bench minus the pigeons.

2. The imported object shows up selected in the center of the scene. If you can't see the object, try using the Zoom tool to zoom out of the scene or use the Look At Current Object tool.

3. Once you can see the object, it should be white to indicate that it's the current object. If it's not, then make it the current object by clicking the Object tool, then clicking on the park bench.

4. With the object selected, click on the Object Scale tool. Notice that the object stretches in two different directions as you drag the mouse. The right mouse button lets you stretch the object along the third axis. Click the Undo button to restore the object to its original size.

5. Click with the right mouse button on the Object Scale button to open a pop-up window of six toggle buttons. Use the top buttons to change the coordinate system and the bottom buttons to constrain certain axes. Toggle the Y and Z axes off, then drag the mouse to lengthen the object along the X axis.

Using this method, I lengthened the park bench model to accommodate a couple of families, rather than one or two people. Pretty nice of me, wasn't it? The original bench is seen back to the left, and the new bench is in the foreground of Figure 4.4.

Figure 4.4.
Using non-uniform scaling, the park bench was lengthened to hold more people.

Sculpting Your Models by Surface Deformation

Another common technique for modifying your models is *surface deformation*. Other 3D packages call this method *sculpting* or *planar distortion*, but it's all the same basic idea. Surface deformation alters an object's surface by moving, rotating, or scaling a point, line, or polygon face on the object.

NOTE: Most 3D packages are polygon-based, which means that their models are composed of a series of polygons. I say "most" because some 3D packages use splines or patches, as Animation Master does, but I'll save that for Chapter 8.

You can control the number of lines that make up the primitives by right-clicking the primitives buttons to access another small panel, where you can designate parameters such as the number of latitude and longitude lines that make up the object.

Surface deformation can be an extremely useful feature for creating new models from existing models or primitives. Take a look at how this is done in trueSpace:

1. Start by creating a sphere. Open the Primitives panel by clicking the Primitives Panel button. Click the Add Sphere button, and the sphere pops up in the center of the scene.

2. Before you deform the sphere's surface, increase its resolution by subdividing all the polygons. Use the Quad Divide tool in the Util Group. This results in a sphere with four times the number of polygons and enough resolution for the deformations to show up smoothly.

3. Click the Deform Object tool in the Model Group, then select a point on the surface of the sphere. With a point selected, you can move, twist, or stretch it by using the pop-up panel. For the bunny rabbit in Figure 4.5, I selected three distinct points on the sphere and pulled them away from the surface to form a nose and two ears.

Figure 4.5.

The bunny shape was made from a simple sphere, using the Deform Object tool to pull points away from the surface.

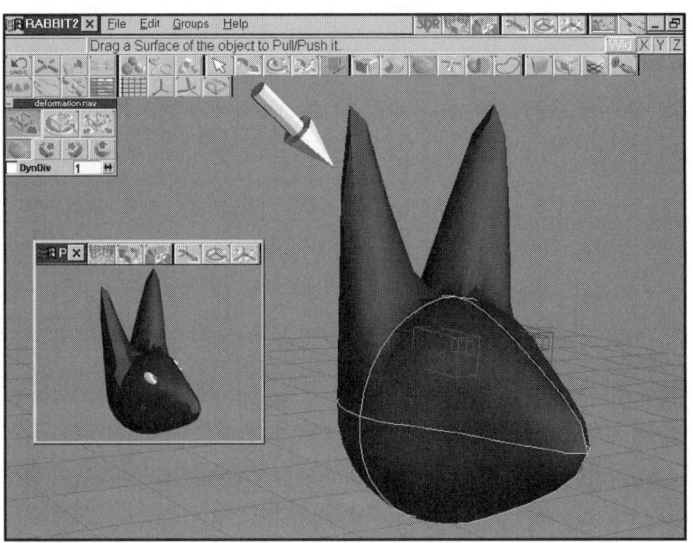

Another option in the Util Group is the Smooth Quad Divide button. Use it to smooth out the transitions between adjacent polygons to make the object look rounder.

CAUTION: The Quad Divide and Smooth Quad Divide tools increase the number of polygons by four times each time they are used. This also increases the overall file size of your model, so use it cautiously.

Boolean Operations

Recall for a moment how you make sugar cookies. You roll out the dough, then press in a cookie cutter that cuts the shape out of the dough. Similar types of operations are possible in the 3D world—they're called *boolean operations*.

Three common boolean operations—Union, Subtraction, and Intersection—apply to any overlapping areas of two objects. The Union operator joins overlapping areas, the Subtraction operator removes overlapping areas, and the Intersection operators remove everything except the overlapping areas.

Suppose you want to model an apple with a bite taken out of it. If you position a sphere primitive so that it overlaps the surface of the apple model and use the Subtraction boolean operation, then the area that overlaps is removed. You're left with a big bite taken out of the apple, and you don't even have to worry about digestion!

These operations are key to building complex models. The trueSpace modelers typically use primitive shapes and these boolean operations to get the model close to where it needs to be, then finish the details by sculpting the surface. Combined with the other techniques, you can model just about anything. Look at an example that uses boolean operations:

Since boolean opera-
tions apply only to
overlapping areas that
are common to both
objects, applying it to
objects that don't
overlap is futile. Also
keep in mind that when
subtracting objects, the
object selected second is
removed from the
object selected first.

1. These operations work only when applied to two unique models, so load two models or use two primitive shapes and make sure they overlap.

2. Then select one of the overlapped models and click one of the boolean operation buttons found in the Model Group. The cursor changes to a glue bottle. Click the other model to perform the operation.

3. As a final step, check the model by clicking the Render Object button in the View Group. This lets you see whether the operation was successful. Figure 4.6 shows examples of each of the boolean operations.

Figure 4.6.
*Examples of the Union,
Intersection, and
Subtraction boolean
operations.*

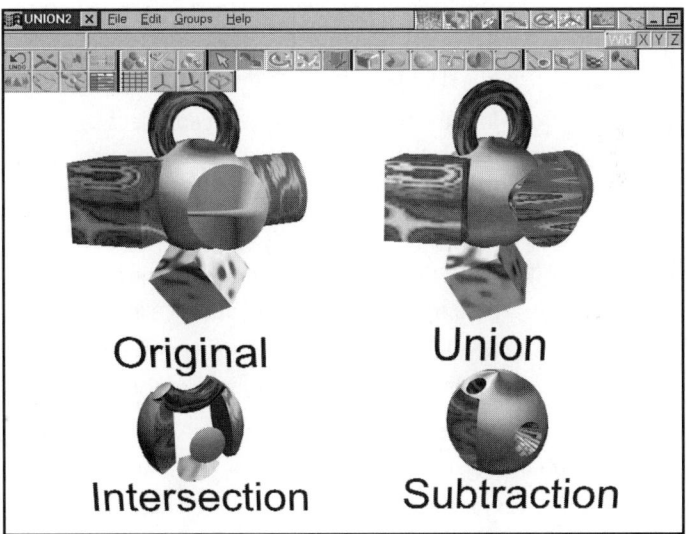

The techniques in this section form some of the basic modeling features found in trueSpace. There are several more advanced features for modeling, and you'll delve into some of them in Chapter 8. However, trueSpace's method of modeling isn't the only game in town, and there's more than one way to skin a cat, so without anymore clichés, let's get down to brass tacks and take a brief look at Ray Dream's approach to modeling.

Creating Original Models with Ray Dream Studio

The modeling module of Ray Dream Studio has been around for some time and is still sold separately as Ray Dream Designer.

Now that you've seen the basis of modeling in trueSpace, take a look at how Ray Dream Studio tackles the problem. Ray Dream Studio builds models from 2D lines in a modeling module called the Free Form Modeling Window. This technique gives you precise control over the model's surface but can be confusing. To simplify using it, the package has a Modeling Wizard that automates the building of some basic models.

The Modeling Wizard steps you through the process of building simple models by offering you choices in various windows. You will use the Modeling Wizard to generate a spring, which is a difficult modeling task by hand.

Not only does Ray Dream have a Modeling Wizard, but it also has a Scene Wizard for creating scenes quickly and easily. Be cautioned that the wizards are fairly limited, but they give you a good place to start and can be modified later.

The choices in the Modeling Wizard are various types of models that can be created by using the Free Form Modeling Window. Launch this window by dragging the Free Form icon, located on the left toolbar, into the scene.

1. When Ray Dream starts, a dialog box opens that asks whether you want to use the Scene Wizard, open a new scene, or open an existing file. Click the Create Empty Scene button to start with a blank scene window.

2. Select the Modeling Wizard icon, which is in the toolbar to the left of the screen directly under the Sphere tool, and drag it into the scene. This launches the Modeling Wizard.

3. The Modeling Wizard starts by offering you six choices: Lathe Object, Extrusion, Pipeline, Skin Object, Spiral Object, and Twisted Object. Select Spiral Object and click the Next button to move on.

4. In the next dialog box, you can select several premade spiral objects, such as a corkscrew, a shell, and a telephone cord, but try the first option, which is Create Your Own Object.

5. Next, choose the cross section of the object. Select the Circle cross section.

6. Enter the number of turns the spring will have; for this example, 10 seems to be a good number. Leave the scaling parameters at 100%.

7. Finally, specify the dimensions of the spring: Enter the values 4 for the height, 32 for the width, and 12 for the depth, then click the Finish button. This produces a nice spring, like the one in Figure 4.7.

Any model created with the wizard can be edited by double-clicking on the model. This loads the model into the Free Form Modeling Window where you have complete control over the model's geometry and control paths.

Figure 4.7.

A spring created with Ray Dream's Modeling Wizard.

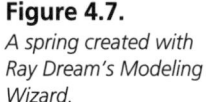

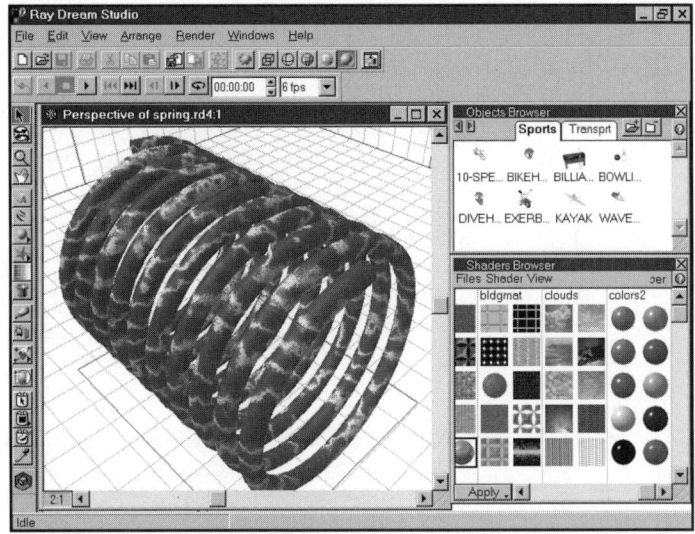

Navigating the Model's Hierarchy

You've now learned how to find, edit, and build models. Along the way, you might have noticed that some models are made up of several different parts. These different parts are not only key to building complex yet organized models, they also allow you to animate parts independently once you get to the animation section.

Models with several different parts combined are organized into a *hierarchy*, which is just a way of organizing various parts that make up the whole. Think of that classic gospel song, "the foot bone's connected to the leg bone…." You naturally want all the fingers grouped together in the hand group.

The Viper model is one of the models in the Dream Models collection that ships with Ray Dream Studio.

Look at the Object tab in the Time Line Window of Ray Dream for the model of a Viper (the car, not the snake) in Figure 4.8. What you see is the hierarchy for this model. This tells you at a glance how this model is put together. Notice also that the hierarchy includes elements of the scene, such as scene lights and cameras, and that the similar object parts are grouped together—the lights group is broken down into headlights and fog lights. This helps when you start applying materials and colors to certain parts of the model. With a hierarchy, it's easy to specify that, for example, all body parts get painted red and all windows and lights are made out of glass.

NOTE: In trueSpace, the Navigation tool (which shows up as an arrow pointing down) lets you move around the hierarchy. The selected object shows up in white, and all other objects are brown. With the left- and right-arrow keys, you select objects in that same level; the down-arrow key moves you further down into the current object.

To set up hierarchies in trueSpace, use the Glue tool. Glue as Sibling makes objects equal rank in the hierarchy, and Glue As Child makes the object you point to a child node under the currently selected object. The Unglue command, of course, breaks the object from the hierarchy.

Figure 4.8.
The hierarchy of the Viper model is shown in the Model window.

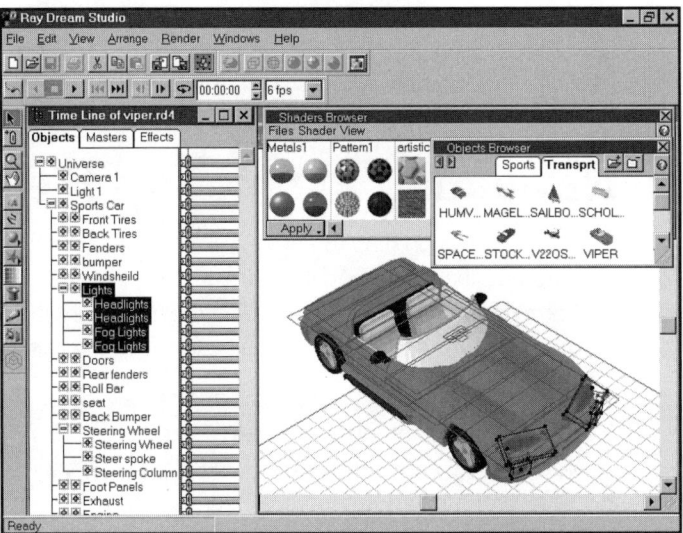

Adding Materials to Models

Once your model is built and you're happy with it, you can render the object. Switch back to trueSpace and look for the Render Object button in the View Group. If you render the objects you've built so far in this chapter, it will probably look pretty plain—that's where materials come in. Applying materials to models helps enliven your models, much like a new coat of paint on the old red wagon.

In trueSpace, you'll find materials stored in libraries, which can be accessed by clicking the Materials Library button in the Lib Group. After selecting a material in the library, it can be applied to the entire model, to an object in the model by navigating the hierarchy, or to a single polygon. Try practicing by dressing up a model.

For this example, I've selected a stormtrooper's helmet taken from the collection of *Star Wars* models done by Harry Chang (`http://www.loop.com/~hhc/starwars.html`). Harry has some beautiful models, and he hosts a collection of *Star Wars*–specific models that's worth checking out.

1. After loading the model, navigate the hierarchy until you have isolated the part you want to alter. Now find a material to apply.

2. Click the Material Library button to open the library. Material sets are saved as MLB files. Click on the library name at the bottom of the library toolbar to access a File menu that will let you load, save, and create new libraries. Select the material by clicking the colored spheres. The materials name shows up in the lower-right field.

3. Once you've selected a material, click the Apply Material button to apply it to the model part. The part immediately begins rendering in that material. Repeat this process for all parts you want to apply materials to.

4. When you've applied all the materials, navigate to the top of the hierarchy by clicking on the Hierarchy navigation arrow in the Nav Group. The arrow will now be an up-arrow since you have descended the hierarchy. Click the Render Object button to render the entire object or the Render Scene button for the entire scene.

The finished stormtrooper helmet with applied materials is shown in Figure 4.9 next to the original model.

Figure 4.9.

What is a Stormtrooper to wear to a party? Well, luckily you can apply materials to the helmet to make it more jazzy.

Other tools in the Render Group let you paint individual polygon faces or vertices or paint over existing materials. The Inspect tool can be used to access and load the selected material into the Material Attributes panels, where they can be edited to create new and interesting materials.

TASK

Using trueSpace to Create New Materials

You should notice that I called these "materials" and not just "colors" because materials have many more properties than just color. The following list describes some of the common properties materials can use:

- ❏ **Color** Of course, you can change the color and brightness by using the tools in the Material Color panel.

- ❏ **Ambient Glow** Sets how much light radiates from the object without any lights around.

- ❏ **Shininess** Used to control how the light reflects off the object, like a Christmas tree ornament compared to a dirt clod.

- ❏ **Roughness** The opposite of shininess, this property helps determine how the light scatters when it hits the object.

- ❏ **Transparency** This property has settings from opaque, where no light passes through, to transparent, where all light passes through the object as though it were glass.

- ❏ **Index of Refraction** Determines the extent to which light bends through the object. Thick glass, for example, has a high index of refraction.

  In addition to material attributes, there are several special operations that the render engine picks up when determining how to draw the object. They are controlled by the Shaders/Maps panel.

- ❏ **Faceted, Auto Facet, Smooth** This setting tells the render engine how to deal with the edges between polygons. Faceted doesn't smooth any of the edges, and Smooth smoothes all of them. Auto Facet is somewhere in between and should be used when you have both smooth and hard edges.

- ❏ **Flat, Phong, Metal Shading** This setting determines how the lights in the scene highlight the surface. Flat shading is very quick, but makes the entire polygon surface the same color. Phong is slower but creates a smoothly shaded surface from bright, where the highlights are, to darker the further you move away. Metal features sharp highlights for shiny surfaces, such as metal and glass.

Other render engines frequently use a shading method known as *Gourand shading*. It was around before Phong shading and is slightly faster but has poorer quality.

Yet another shading method known as *radiosity* computes the effect of light bouncing off surfaces. It's used to create very realistic interiors in which lights down the hall can still light up an adjacent room.

❏ **Texture Maps**   This setting lets you wrap 2D images around your objects. You'll take a closer look at this one in the following section.

❏ **Bump Maps**   These maps can be wrapped around objects much the way texture maps can, but they use the image's brightness to represent bumps on the surface. They can be used to control the bumps, ridges, and texture of the object.

❏ **Environment Maps**   Wrap a reflected view of the environment onto the object.

❏ **Procedural Maps**   There are three types in trueSpace: Granite, Marble, and Wood. Their attributes let you change the color and other properties.

In trueSpace, you also have property panels for controlling the values of all these properties. They are used to create new materials that can be saved and applied to models. Try enhancing your current model with some wild colors you'll create yourself:

1. Load the piano model and duplicate it with the Copy button in the Edit Group. I duplicated it six times to show some variety.

2. Select the Inspect tool in the Render Group and click on any part of the piano. The current material applied to that part shows up in the Material sphere.

3. Activate the Material Library by clicking its button. Samples from the current library are displayed, and the name of the library is at the bottom of the panel. By clicking on this name, you open a pop-up menu for loading new libraries.

4. To make the glass piano, move the transparency slider (the fourth column) in the Shader Attributes panel near the top. Make sure that all texture maps are turned off in the Shaders/Maps panel.

5. When you're comfortable with the color, shininess, and other attributes, click the Paint Object button to render the object in the newly created material.

To round out your collection of pianos that would make Liberace jealous, in Figure 4.10 you have the original piano with original materials, a texture map piano, a wood grain procedural map piano, a blue glass piano, a bump map piano, and finally a red marble piano.

Figure 4.10.

Your fine collection of pianos with various materials applied, sure to make Liberace jealous.

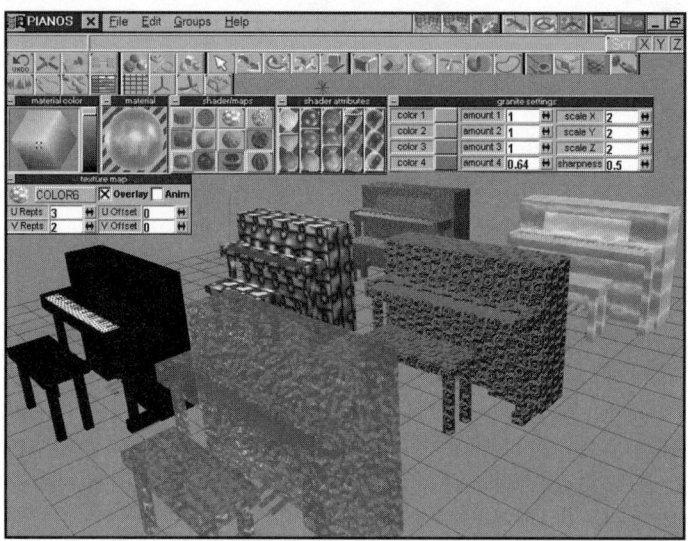

TASK Creating Texture Maps

The material-editing capabilities native to trueSpace are great, but one of the greatest benefits of materials is the ability to use additional texture maps created externally and imported.

Using Paint Shop Pro, Photoshop, or Fractal Design Painter to create texture maps lets you add a specific look to your model. Take a look at how this is done using the tiled ivy background you created with Fractal Design Painter in Chapter 3, "Adding Simple 3D Elements to Your Web Page." You'll apply this pattern to get a floral look for the loveseat:

1. With the Material Attributes panel open, right-click the Texture Map button to reveal a separate Attributes panel specific to texture maps. This panel can be used to control the offset of the texture map and the number of times the texture repeats in both the horizontal and vertical directions.

2. Click on the texture name to open a dialog box for selecting a new texture. Pick the ivy background and click OK.

3. The texture is loaded into the Material Attributes panel. You might have to adjust the U and V repetition factors to make the texture look good.

TIP:
Using tiled patterns for texture maps makes the final image look much cleaner because there are no seams in the pattern covering the surface.

Both the piano model in the last example and the loveseat in this example can be found on the trueClips CD-ROM that ships with trueSpace 2.

4. Another aspect of using texture maps is how the texture is projected onto the object. With trueSpace you have three options for using the UV Projection tool. They tell the program to project the texture map as though the object were a cube, a cylinder, or a sphere. Descend the hierarchy and use the spherical projection for the arms and back of the loveseat and the planar projection for the seat.

CAUTION:

Using the wrong type of projection causes the texture map to smear or run across the surface. For example, applying the ivy texture to a cube will look fine on the front and back faces, but will smear the edges of the texture across the side faces.

5. Finally, to apply the material to each part, click the Paint Object button to render the object as shown in Figure 4.11.

Figure 4.11.

The ivy-endowed loveseat features the ultimate in floral patterns, compliments of Painter's patterns and trueSpace's rendering.

TASK   Positioning and Controlling Lights

Suppose your model is complete, materials have been added, and you render your model. What do you get? Nothing but a black screen. Well, not exactly. To prevent this tragic occurrence, trueSpace automatically adds a default light to a scene when you start. However, if there were no light, you wouldn't see anything.

The point is that lights are a necessity, but they can be so much more than that. For starters, there are several different types of lights; trueSpace has three types:

❑ **Infinite lights** This light illuminates object surfaces with many parallel rays coming from a distance, much like sunshine. You can control in what direction this type of light shines.

❑ **Local lights** These lights spread light equally in all directions, as a candle or light bulb would.

❑ **Spot lights** Just like the ones on a stage, you can control the diameter of the beam.

Lights essentially have two properties: brightness and color. They can also be positioned anywhere in the 3D scene, even within objects. For instance, placing a light inside a semitransparent model makes the model seem to glow. Follow these numbered steps to try using lights in trueSpace:

1. Start by positioning your models in the scene. Figure 4.12 shows a model of a car positioned at a stoplight under a street lamp.

2. Next, remove the default lights that appear as a group of radiating lines. If you zoom out from the top view, you can easily pick them out and remove them with the Delete key.

3. Add new lights to the scene by opening the Primitives panel. Click on the light button of the type you want to use in your scene. The light will appear selected in the scene.

4. Lights can be moved, rotated, and scaled just as any other object can. Position the lights in the scene. For the scene in Figure 4.12, I placed a spot light in the street lamp, three local lights in the stoplight object, and a local light in the car taillights.

5. With the light selected, an attributes panel pops up that lets you change the color and brightness of the light and whether it casts shadows.

The final scene is shown in Figure 4.12. Notice how some light spreads throughout the scene, such as the green highlights on the inside of the car. This is the tricky nature of working with lights.

Lights in Wireframe mode show up as arrows for infinite lights, radial lines for local lights, and cones for spot lights. Although you can see these lights in Wireframe mode, they become invisible when the scene is rendered, except for their light.

The car, stoplight, and street lamp are all models from the trueClips CD-ROM that ships with trueSpace 2.

Moving, rotating, and scaling certain types of lights have no effect on them. For instance, rotating a local light or scaling an infinite light has no effect on the light.

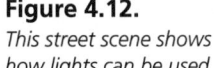

Figure 4.12.
This street scene shows how lights can be used within a scene.

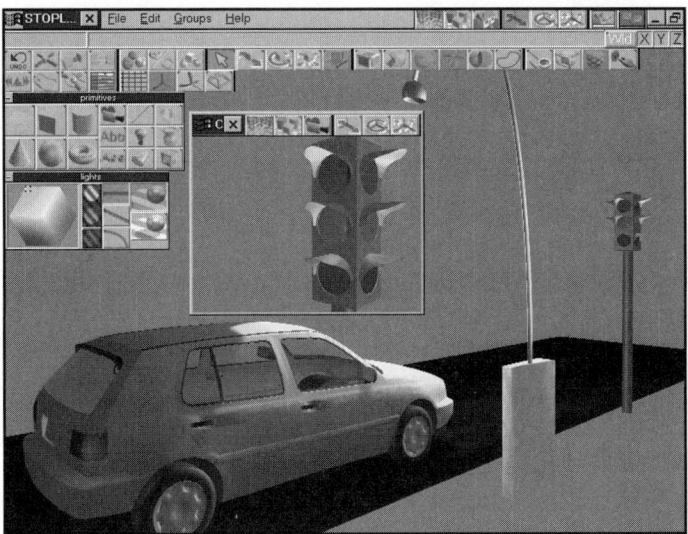

TASK Placing Cameras and Capturing an Image

Navigation around any 3D world is tricky. If you find a shot that looks just right, a good way to remember the spot is to place a camera. *Cameras* give you another window through which you can look at your scene.

Cameras have the unique ability of being invisible in the final rendered scene, so they can be positioned anywhere without affecting the output image. Both lights and cameras can be moved during an animation sequence, but details on that are covered in Chapter 5, "Creating and Embedding Simple 3D Animations."

Notice in Figure 4.12 that a camera was used to get a close-up picture of the stoplight. To place a camera in the scene, follow these steps:

1. Cameras are selected from the Primitives library. Click the Camera button to place a camera in the scene.
2. Cameras can be moved, rotated, and scaled, just like other objects can. Position the camera where you want to look.
3. Cameras can also be frozen to a particular object. With the camera selected, click the Look At button in the Util Group. The cursor changes to a glue icon and the next object you click on in the scene will be where the camera points. The camera continues to point toward the object you indicated as you move and rotate it about the scene.

4. To see the Camera view in a new window, click the New Perspective View button in the View Group. A new window appears with its own View Group toolbar. Select the camera object, then click the View from Object button in the View Group. The view from the camera's viewpoint shows up in the new window.

Cameras are also very useful in capturing a final image. Before you actually capture an image, though, look first at the different shading methods.

Shading Techniques for Final Output

There are several different ways to output your final image and the trade-off is quality versus speed of rendering. Wireframe mode can be seen instantaneously but is not very realistic; on the other hand, Ray Tracing takes considerable time to complete but is photo-realistic.

The render option you use really depends on the speed of your machine. For Pentium machines, you can comfortably run in Solid Render mode, although there are advantages to Wireframe mode. The Render Mode buttons can be found in the View Group, and you can get to the Render Options panel by right-clicking the Render Object button. Here's a list of shading modes and options:

- ❏ **Wireframe**   This is the simplest method; it represents the model as a series of lines that make up the individual polygons. This isn't really a shading method, but the lack of one.

- ❏ **Solid Render Display**   This option allows the objects to be shaded and displayed in real-time. It helps to have this option on to give you immediate visual feedback.

- ❏ **Draft**   This mode renders the scene quickly at low quality.

- ❏ **Normal**   Somewhere between draft and ray tracing is the Normal render mode. It is the default, with no special features thrown in.

- ❏ **Ray Tracing**   This render method is photo-realistic and requires a great deal of computation. It produces superb results but takes some time to generate. Ray Tracing traces the path of each light beam in the entire scene, whether it bounces off reflective surfaces or refracts through glass.

TIP: An alternative to using Ray Tracing is using Environment Maps, which compute the scene's reflection and apply it as a map onto the object. The tricky part is that every object that reflects needs to have an environment map.

Once again, the models for this scene were borrowed from the trueClips CD-ROM. Having at least one good collection (like the models that come with this book) of models can take you a long way.

An example of four render modes is shown in Figure 4.13.

CAUTION: Although Ray Tracing can produce some incredible images, it's time-consuming and requires a lot of memory for high-resolution objects. Use it with caution.

Figure 4.13.

Four rendering options in trueSpace. The upper-left image is Wireframe, the upper-right image is rendered in Draft mode, the lower-left image is Normal mode, and the lower-right is done in Ray Tracing.

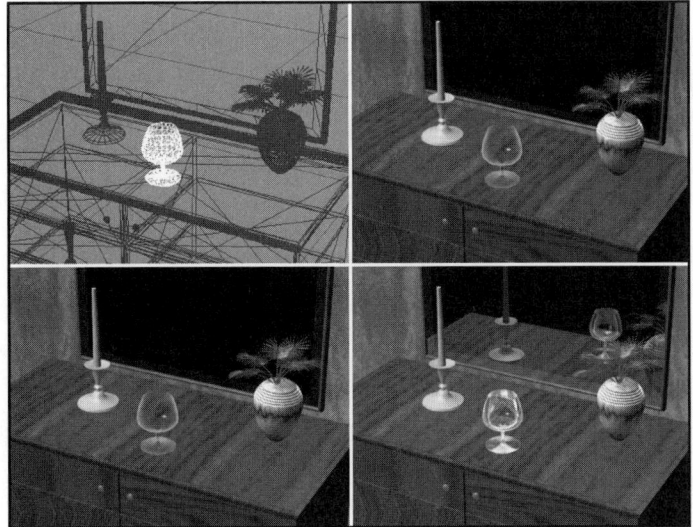

You've reviewed the 3D capabilities of these packages enough, so now try producing something you can use in your Web page—a 3D rendered image, or *still*, as they are called.

Outputting and Using 3D Images in Your Web Pages

Creating the final image is relatively easy. In the View Group is an option to Render Scene to File; use this button to capture your 3D image.

1. When you're pleased with the image and are ready to capture it, click the Render Scene to File button.
2. A dialog box opens and asks where you want to save the file. You can also indicate the file type (JPEG is an option, and one that's recommended), the image size, some special effects, and some animation options. Ignore the

animation and effects options for now—you'll get there soon enough. Give the file a name, select the JPG file type, and click Other for the resolution. This produces an image the same size as the current window.

3. Place the file into the same directory as your HTML file and include it by using the standard <IMG SRC> tag.

There is nothing that makes the 3D image you just created different from the other images used on your Web site. However, some tips will make the image look better on your Web site.

 ## Creating Reference Thumbnails

To see your 3D images in all their glory, you normally have to make them larger than your other images, but this can be deadly to some visitors who stumble across these serious images and aren't willing to wait to see your masterpiece. They will more than likely run away and never come back.

A good solution to this problem is creating a small thumbnail of the image that links to another page where the 3D image can be viewed in a larger format. These thumbnails take very little space and give visitors an idea of whether they want to look at the image.

Creating these thumbnails is simple. Return to the scene where the original image was created and simply reduce the size of the output image. A good rule of thumb (no pun intended) is to make your thumbnails about 1/8 the size of the original.

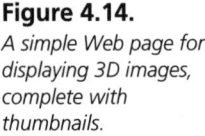

Figure 4.14.
A simple Web page for displaying 3D images, complete with thumbnails.

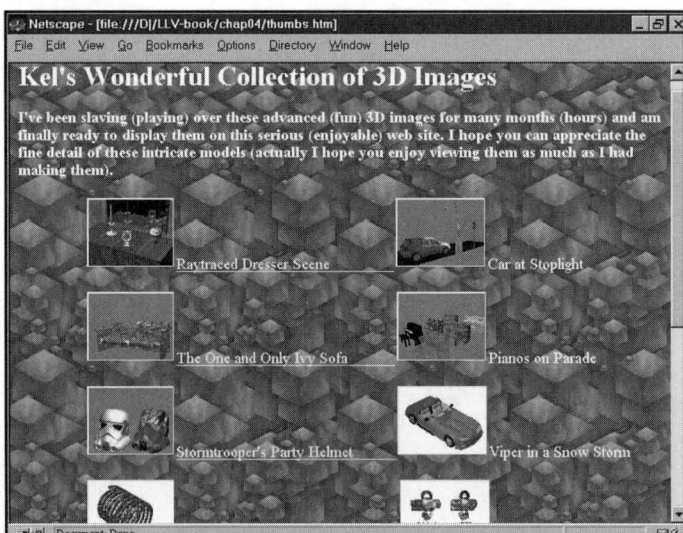

Optimizing Images: JPEG Versus GIF

Just because your 3D package doesn't output to either of these formats—JPEG or GIF—doesn't mean you can't use them. Paint Shop Pro can convert almost any graphic format with ease. It even can do batch conversions (see the File | Batch Convert command).

GIF format works well at reducing the file size because it's limited to 256 colors. Without all the colors to remember, it doesn't take up as much space. However, be warned—3D images are usually rendered by casting light across objects, so they typically have subtle gradations that rely on gradual changes in color. Use GIF if you must, but it shouldn't be the preferred format for 3D images.

JPEG, on the other hand, is good for working with images that have subtle color changes. It works in 24-bit with 16.7 million colors. Because it has so many colors to remember, it uses a *lossy* compression technique to reduce file size, meaning some of the image quality is lost as a result of the compression. On the plus side, the algorithm is designed to first eliminate the image information that affects the image quality the least. In most cases, you can't detect a degradation in image quality until it reaches the 60 percent compression level.

Another alternative that's becoming popular since the GIF format legal troubles is the PNG format. It offers 24-bit capability and includes the ability to save alpha channel transparency, which allows greater flexibility than GIF transparency.

Workshop Wrap-up

This has been a busy chapter, but I hope you feel comfortable working with 3D packages by now. You've really just cracked open the door of possibilities. You can learn much more by experimentation, so jump in and see what's possible. When you're ready to continue, come back to explore animation.

Next Steps

❏ Now that you have the static images looking good, the next step is to animate them. Check out Chapter 5, "Creating and Embedding Simple 3D Animations."

❏ If you want a glimpse at the higher end of creating 3D images, move on up to Chapter 8, "Creating Advanced 3D Rendered Images for Your Web Page."

❏ The VRML material is still a part and a half away, but you can always "hyper-jump" to it by checking out Chapter 13, "Exploring VRML Browsers and Development Tools."

❏ You can also learn how modeling is done for the VRML environment by reading Chapter 14, "Starting with Models."

Q&A

Q: After reading this chapter, I feel comfortable in the trueSpace environment, but how different is this environment from other 3D packages?

A: When learning 3D, certain conceptual principles, such as modeling, materials, and lighting, are common regardless of the package you're using. The main differences you find will be in the special features offered by various packages. These features are usually high-end options, but the basics should be similiar.

The basic commands may be called something different in another package, but they work the same way.

Q: If I download a model from the Web, do I have to pay the creator when I use it?

A: Every site that offers free models for downloading has specific instructions on using its models. Be sure to read the posted messages because models can be copyrighted and can lead to legal difficulties if used improperly. Beyond legal ramifications, it's ethically smart to always give the creator credit where credit is due.

Q: I've shopped around and there are a lot of 3D packages available. Which one is the best package to use for Web page design?

A: First of all, you probably won't be able to afford the best overall 3D packages, but if you're looking for a package to use in Web page design, the choice becomes easier. Many of the available packages are overkill for simple 3D Web page design. It really depends on what you can afford. A good comparative list can be found in Appendix A, "3D Software Resource Guide."

Several companies have heard this request and responded. Lately, a number of 3D Web page design packages have appeared, including Asymetrix's 3D Web and Specular's 3D Web Workshop (they get an A+ for the name). You might want to check out these new products and see whether they fit the bill.

FIVE

Creating and Embedding Simple 3D Animations

—by Kelly Murdock

This is the chapter where you make the bold move from photographer to movie director. Animation is more than just moving objects; it's a visual language and one that we all identify with because it mimics real life.

In the last chapter, you learned to set up scenes and create 3D images. Now suppose in that same scene, you move the camera a little bit and capture another image. If you keep doing this and link all the images together, you end up with an animation. Even easier than that, 3D packages have ways to automate the movements within a scene. In this chapter, you'll cover various ways of creating animations with 3D packages and how to embed them in your Web page. Here's what you'll accomplish in this chapter:

❏ Create animations by simply moving the camera, also known as a camera fly-by.

❏ Animate models by using keyframes. *Keyframes* are the beginning, intermediate, and ending model positions. Once the computer knows these, it will happily generate all the in-between positions.

In this chapter, you

❏ Create animations with a camera fly-by

❏ Animate models by using keyframes

❏ Learn to work with paths

❏ Create special effects with animated materials

❏ Embed your 3D animations as GIF animations

❏ Learn about client-pull and server-push animation methods

Tasks in this chapter:

❏ Animation by Moving the Camera

❏ Animation by Moving the Models

❏ Working with Paths

❏ Animating Materials

❏ Creating GIF Animations with the GIF Construction Set

❏ Client-Pull Animations Using the <Meta> Tag

❏ Learn to work with paths.

❏ Create special effects with animated materials.

❏ Learn to embed your 3D animations as GIF animations with the GIF Construction Set.

❏ Learn to use the client-pull and server-push methods for adding 3D animations to the Web.

You'll be surprised how easy it is to create animations; the difficult part is already behind you. So round out your skills in using these 3D packages and learn how you can display them to the world over the Web. Maybe this is the start to your earning an Oscar.

For this chapter, you'll use trueSpace again. You should be feeling comfortable with this product by now; trueSpace does a good job with the animation basics, and it's easy to learn to use. There are several advanced animation techniques that other packages have, but you'll explore them in Chapter 9, "Creating Advanced 3D Animations for the Web."

Animation by Moving the Camera

Animations can be created very simply from a scene that's already set up by moving the camera around the scene. This is usually called a *camera fly-by*. In the previous chapter, you learned how to navigate objects. To perform a camera fly-by, you simply move and rotate the camera, but it's really even easier than that.

Using the Object Scale tool on cameras causes the camera to zoom in and out. Pressing both mouse buttons simultaneously makes the camera larger or smaller in the scene, but it has no impact on the image.

Clicking on any of the controls in the Animation panel brings up the Keyframe Monitor panel. This panel shows the keyframes associated with each frame and also lets you copy, shift, and stretch keyframes between frames.

Because the computer knows the location of all objects in the scene and their relationships to each other, all that's necessary to animate a scene is to position the camera at the locations where the animation should start and end. These positions are known as *keyframes*.

If you want to move the camera through an intermediate position, then you can do that, too. Just tell the computer where the camera looks at which frame. The computer can then generate all the intermediate frames automatically. Take a look at this example:

1. Set up your scene by loading your model and background. For this example, a model of the Chrysler building and a sky background are used. Place a camera in the scene, open a new View window, and set it to the camera view. Position this camera to the first frame of the animation.

2. Click the Animation tool in the Animate Group. This opens the Animation panel that lets you control the animation frames. Notice that the current frame is set to 0.

3. Make sure the camera is selected, then enter 30 in the Current Frame Number field and hit the Enter key.

4. Reposition the camera to show the final frame of the animation in the camera window. Frames 1–29 are computed automatically at points between the first and last frames.

5. To see the animation, click the Play button in the Animation panel. The animation will be shown in the active window in either Wireframe or Solid Render mode, depending on which setting is active in the View Group.

The Solid Render mode cycles through the animation at a slower rate than Wireframe mode does. You might want to switch to Wireframe mode to view your animation.

6. If you're happy with what you see, then click the Render Scene to File button in the View Group to open the Directory dialog box. Give the file a name and select the type of file you want to save. Select the animation resolution and make sure the All Frames option is set and the Frame Rate is set to 30, then click OK.

Selecting a frame rate of 15 renders every other frame in your animation. To render all the frames, make sure you specify 30 for the frame rate.

TIP: The type of file you save your animation as really depends on the way you intend to use it on your Web page. In trueSpace, you can save animations as a series of images (BMP, TGA, or JPG) or as a video file (AVI, FLI).

If you intend to embed your animations as animated GIF or client-pull animations, then save your file as a series of images. trueSpace automatically attaches a number at the end of each image. Therefore, the first frame is file0000.jpg, the second file0001.jpg, and so on.

In Figure 5.1, you can see Frame 17 of a camera fly-by of the Chrysler Building. Figure 5.2 shows how the animation progresses. In the background window, you can see the camera and lights.

TIP: If your animation is one that loops continuously, make sure the beginning and ending views of the animation match. This makes the animation run smoothly as it loops.

Figure 5.1.

Creating a camera fly-by past the Chrysler Building by specifying the first and last keyframes.

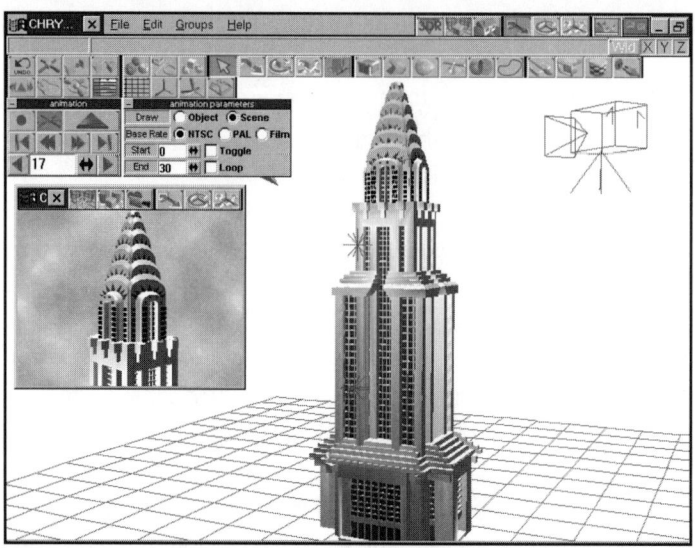

Figure 5.2.

Frames from the Chrysler Building fly-by animation.

That's all there is to it. However, being able to move only the camera for fly-bys is rather limited and can grow old quickly. Luckily, trueSpace offers many other means of animating not only models, but even materials, so move on to find out more.

TASK # Animation by Moving the Models

Another way to produce animations is to keep the camera stationary and move the models. Although this method is slightly more complex, the animations are made the same way, by using keyframes. Take a look at how this is done in the following example.

TIP: Of course, you can still move the camera around as objects move in the scene. A powerful technique is linking the object to a moving object with the Look At tool in the Util Group, then moving the camera independently.

After loading your models, you need to determine what needs to be animated. For the helicopter in this example, it wouldn't look right if the main and tail rotors didn't spin, so start there:

1. Move through the hierarchy until you've located the main rotor and switch to the Top view. First, you need to make sure the rotor will rotate around the center of the blades. Click the Axis button in the Util Group. The rotor will be dimmed, and the axes associated with the rotor will be white. Move the axis to the center of the rotor, then click the Axis button again to return to the rotor object.

2. With the axes centered, click the Animation tool button and enter 6 for the Current Frame Number. Click the Object Rotate button and spin the rotor about 160 degrees, using the right mouse button.

CAUTION: You may be tempted to rotate the rotor beyond 180 degrees, but if you do, the rotor will spin backward to that position. The computer always takes the shortest path between two keyframes.

3. Next, enter 12 as the Current Frame Number in the Animation panel and rotate the rotor another 160 degrees. If the rotor starts to stray, then the rotor's axis is still misaligned. In that case, go back to Step 1 and line up the axes. Repeat this step, incrementing by six frames each time until you reach Frame 30.

4. Now that you've completed the keyframes for the rotor blades, you should have noticed that the rotor center is separate from the blades. Repeat the previous actions for the rotor center, and use the blades to line up the rotor center.

You can click with the right mouse button on the Animation tool to access the Animation Parameters panel. You can use this panel to animate the whole scene, or just the object, and to set looping for the animation.

5. Once you've got the rotor set, switch to the Perspective view and click the Play button to see how the spinning rotor looks.

6. Now switch to the Left view and zoom in on the tail rotor. Repeat the previous steps for the tail rotor and blades, but set your keyframes every three frames because you want the tail rotor to spin faster.

7. Select the entire helicopter and enter 30 for the Current Frame Number. From the Top view, move the helicopter a good distance toward the top of the screen. Click the Rotate Object button and rotate the helicopter slightly.

8. For a realistic touch, set a keyframe at 10 and rotate the helicopter about 20 degrees so that the nose is down; this adds a slight tilt to the helicopter in the Left view.

9. Finally, load the sky background image in the Render Options panel. Next, make a cube to represent some land below the helicopter and move it left in the Top view to simulate the moving ground. Frame 1 of the animation should look like Figure 5.3.

Figure 5.3.

A helicopter that flies into the distance. This example shows how moving parts can be animated.

There are quite a few techniques in this example, such as moving axes, setting multiple keyframes, and animating object parts. It can be some work, but look at the flexibility you've gained. Using these simple techniques, you can animate any 3D model. Take a look at the finished animation in Figure 5.4.

Figure 5.4.

A frame-by-frame look at the helicopter animation.

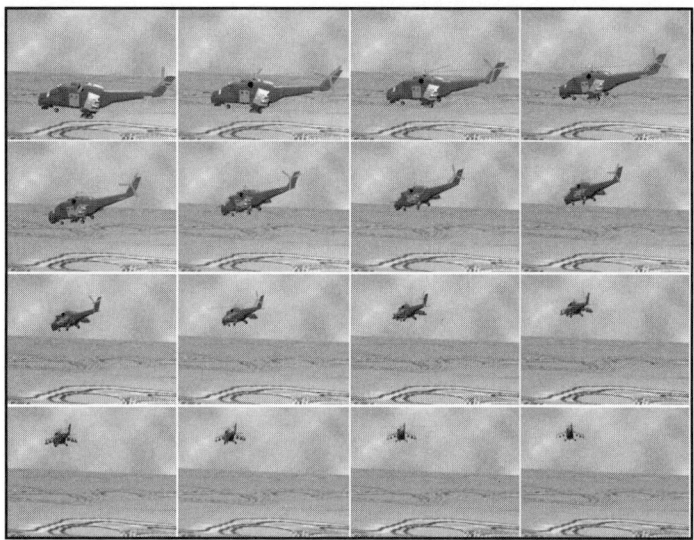

TASK Working with Paths

Any moving object has an associated path. These paths are standard splines and can be saved and loaded from the Path Library. Occasionally, you can edit these paths without having to reset keyframes.

Splines are beneficial because of the power and control you have in manipulating them. Each spline has several control points that define its curvature. By selecting these control points, you can alter the way the curve looks. Each point also has handles, which change the way the curves approach and leave the control point. Handles can be set to make the control point a sharp point or a smooth curve.

Perhaps the best use of paths in trueSpace is attaching them to cameras. This allows you to save your favorite camera movements to be applied wherever you want.

Now to the example. In this example, you'll use a path to create an abstract tube, then match the tube with a camera on a similar path that will fly through the tube:

1. Start by placing a camera, then attach a path to it by clicking the Path button in the Animate Group. trueSpace will go into Spline Drawing mode. Click around in the view to set control points. The spline will automatically be drawn between the points you select. Click the right mouse button to make the curve a complete loop.

Within the Draw Path panel are controls that let you add, delete, or move control points.

2. When you've finished your path, click the Play button in the Animation panel. The camera will move along the path. This looks nice, but it would be helpful if you could see where you're going. Click the Look Ahead button in the Animate Group, then click the Play button again. The Look Ahead button realigns the camera so that the lens is always facing forward.

3. Open the Path Library, which is a button in the Lib Group, and click the Add Path to Library button. This adds the path you just drew to the Path Library under the name *Anim*.

4. Next, you need something to move through. Click the Regular Polygon button in the Model Group to open the Poly Modes panel. Enter 16 in the Set Number of Edges field at the bottom of the panel, which gives you enough edges to represent a small-diameter circle. Next, click in the Perspective view and drag the mouse until you have a small 2D circle about the size of the camera.

5. Rotate the circle 90 degrees so that it's perpendicular to the reference grid.

6. Click the Sweep/Macro button in the Model Group and make sure the new Anim path you created is selected in the Path Library panel. The path will be attached to the circle you created. Change to the Left view and rotate the path so that it lines up with the grid.

7. Once the path is lined up, click the Sweep/Macro button again to create a tube that looks like the path, with the circle for a cross section.

8. Shift back to the Top view and select the camera object, then click the Path button in the Animate Group to show the linked path. Rotate and move the camera and its path until it lines up on the tube you created, as Figure 5.5 shows.

9. Now you're ready to create the animation. Apply a material to the tube, choose a background color, and switch to Camera view. My example has a slightly transparent red tube with a texture map and a blue background, so the tube looks purple.

The number of frames in this animation depend on the number of points in your spline. Figure 5.6 gives you a small sampling of this animation, but to see the whole thing you'll need to go to the CD-ROM. The one I created had 140 frames, so you might want to create this as an AVI file. In the next chapter, you'll learn how to deal with AVI files by using plug-ins.

Figure 5.5.

Lining up the camera with its linked path to the tube created from the same path.

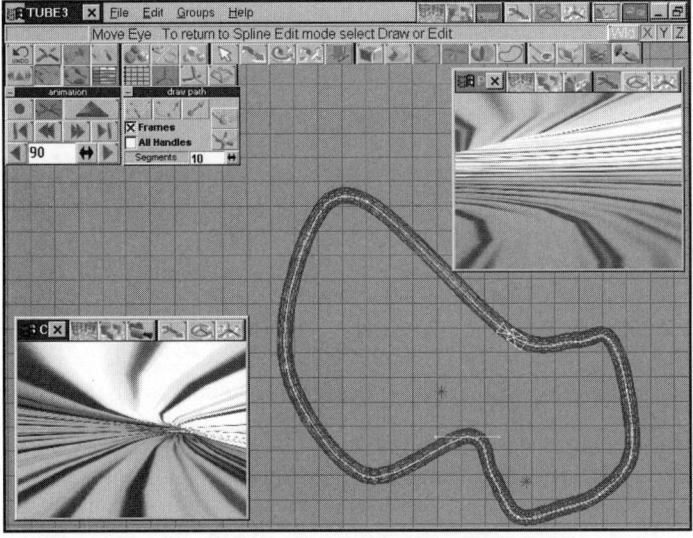

Figure 5.6.

How about a waterslide in space? Using the same path to create a tube and link it to the camera, it's easy.

Notice how you go outside the tube at a few places along your trip. This is because the tube was constructed from a 2D circle.

 # Animating Materials

Not only can you animate cameras, lights, and models, but with trueSpace you can animate materials on the surface of your objects. This is done by applying a material to an object, then applying a different material at a later keyframe. As the animation progresses, the surface material changes from one material to the other.

You can also apply materials to designated rectangles that are projected on top of the model. The materials for these rectangles can be different from the model's base material. These material rectangles can be animated as well. Think of how a model of a television set could use an animated material rectangle:

1. Load the model of a television set (the television set was taken from the TrueClips CD-ROM that ships with trueSpace) and move through the hierarchy until the television's front screen is selected.

2. Click the Material Rectangle button in the Render Group. The Material Rectangle panel with several controls appears.

3. Click the New button and a small rectangle will be selected in the center of the television screen. This rectangle can be moved and scaled by using the Move and Scale buttons at the top of the Material Rectangle panel.

4. Move the material rectangle so that its upper-left corner matches the upper-left corner of the television screen. Next, scale the rectangle so that the upper-right corners match and the rectangle's lower edge falls about two-thirds of the way down the height of the television screen.

5. Bring up the Animation panel and enter 30 as the Current Frame Number. In the Material Rectangle panel, move the rectangle up so that the bottom edge of the rectangle and the television set match.

6. Finally, select a material for the material rectangle, and you're done.

When the material rectangle is active, trueSpace is in a special mode. To apply materials to the rectangle, you need to click on the Paint Material Rectangle button in the Material Rectangle panel, rather than using the Paint Object button in the Render Group.

The final animation is difficult to show as a figure because the animated material is just a series of blue lines that scroll up the screen (I guess this television set is broken). Figure 5.7 shows the scene as it's being created with the material rectangle in the middle of the television screen.

Figure 5.7.
Using material rectangles to animate materials on objects. Here you can see static on the television set.

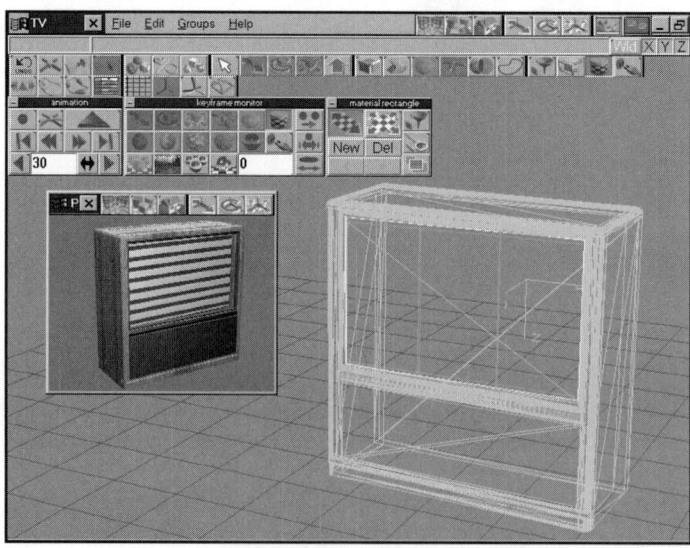

Creating GIF Animations with the GIF Construction Set

There are several ways to embed animations in your Web page. With 3D packages, you can create your animation as either a video format, like AVI or QuickTime, or as a series of images, like JPG, BMP, or TGA. In this section, you'll see how to use each of these formats, starting with using animations saved as a series of images.

GIF animations are easy to use because they don't require using plug-ins or special HTML tags. The browser interprets GIF animations the same way it does regular GIF images, so to embed GIF animations you can use the standard <IMG SRC> tag. When the image loads, the images are loaded in successively to create the animation effect. The trick is to create the image in such a way that the frames of the animation line up.

Luckily, there's a simple package that makes it easy to line up the animation frames. The GIF Construction Set is an easy-to-use shareware program, created by the people at Alchemy Mindworks, that automates this process. Try using this program to create a GIF animation of your tube animation from the earlier section:

1. The successive images for the animation were created as a series of TGA images, which will work well with the GIF Construction Set. Start the program, and you'll see a dialog box interface with buttons along the top and menu items.

2. Create a new file by choosing the File I New command. The program will place a header at the top of the list. The dimensions listed in the header determine the size of the image. You can change the dimensions by double-clicking on the header and entering the new dimensions.

3. Click the Insert button and select Image from the pop-up menu. This brings up a Directory dialog box.

4. Find and select all the images associated with the animation. You can hold down the Shift key to insert multiple images at once.

5. A dialog box opens, letting you specify how you want to control the palette conversion. For each image, select the Use a Local Palette for This Image option. You also want to select the Use This Setting For All Remaining Images option to load all the images at once.

6. When all the images are loaded, click the View button to see the animation, then save the file.

There are several options in the Insert pop-up menu. You can add comments, loops, controls like Pause and Transparency, and text.

Figure 5.8 shows the GIF animation for the tube you created earlier.

Figure 5.8.

The GIF Construction Set is used to create GIF animations from a series of images created by trueSpace.

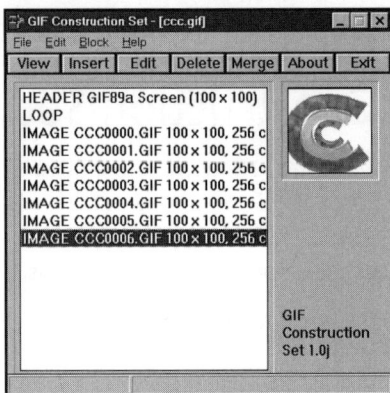

Embedding the GIF animation is no different than embedding a regular GIF image. The browser will load the different frames automatically. Figure 5.9 shows a sample Web page that uses a GIF animation.

Figure 5.9.

A simple GIF animation is used to animate the logo for the Cookie Construction Company.

Notice how the animation background and the Web page background match.

 **TASK**

Client-Pull Animations Using the <Meta> Tag

The idea behind client-pull animations is to load an HTML page, then load another page right over the top of the first, and continue in this manner until the animation is finished. Some people are opposed to client-pull animations because of the strain they can put on the client.

As you can guess, it's probably not a good idea to use a lot of frames for an animation of this type. It works well for small files like logos and such. The steps below show you how to create a client-pull animation.

1. Create a simple animation and save the images as a series of JPG images.

2. Build an HTML page with the image displayed somewhere on the page using the `<IMG SRC="logo1.jpg">` tag. Save the file as `logo1.htm`. Within the `<HEAD>` tag, include a `<META>` tag that looks like this:

   `<META HTTP-EQUIV="refresh" CONTENT="1; URL=logo2.htm">`

3. With the HTML file still open, change the `<IMG>` tag so that it displays the second frame of your animation, and change the `<META>` tag to open `logo3.htm` and save the file as `logo2.htm`.

4. Repeat this process for all frames of the animation.

When the browser encounters the `<META>` tag, it gets a message to fetch the second HTML file in the series. This continues until the last frame of the animation, where no `<META>` tag is needed.

Server-Push Animations

Server-push animations are accomplished in the same way as client-pull animations, except the server is in control of sending the series of HTML pages down. The other difference is that a program residing on the server is needed to control the action. These programs are usually written as CGI scripts that reside on the server.

With the ever-changing nature of the Web, these two techniques are slowly being discarded as cheap, dirty, old methods. They are "cheap" because they don't require much work; "dirty" because they task the machines, are inefficient for creating animation, and seldom produce smooth results; and "old" because they've been around for a while. Newer methods are quickly replacing these old dogs, and Chapter 6, "Using Animation Plug-Ins in Your Web Page," covers a number of them. I suppose these methods could be modified, but you can't teach an old dog new tricks (sorry, I couldn't resist).

Workshop Wrap-up

With this chapter, you've earned the final letter in RMA packages—animation. You've learned about several key concepts of animation that should apply to all 3D packages, and you now have the means to create Web pages with dynamic animations.

Next Steps

I hope you're still anxious to move on because there's still more to learn.

❑ To learn what to do with the AVI and QuickTime movies you've had your 3D packages spit out, check out the next chapter, Chapter 6, "Using Animation Plug-Ins in Your Web Page."

❑ You haven't exhausted the animation realm, either. Advanced animations are covered in Chapter 9, "Creating Advanced 3D Animations for the Web."

❑ If you're ready for VRML, you don't really need to read the stuff in between. The VRML sections start from the basics in Chapter 13, "Exploring VRML Browsers and Development Tools."

Q&A

Q: Do I have to use a 3D software package to create animations?

A: No. Traditional animation uses 2D images that are changed slightly from frame to frame. These techniques work fine, but tend to be more time-consuming than the animations produced by 3D software packages.

The chief benefit of 3D packages is that the computer can calculate in-between images without requiring the artist to redraw every image by hand because it knows the relationship of all objects to each other.

If you decide to use a 2D animation package, look for one that has *onion skin* features. This lets the adjoining images show through onto the current image, which will help you line up the images.

Q: Are there any 3D packages that can create animations as GIF animations, without requiring you to use another package like the GIF Construction Set?

A: We all know that the Web has sneaked up on us. Many software vendors are working to incorporate export capabilities for their products; in time, you'll likely see such features.

Two products have recently appeared that are focused on producing 3D graphics for the Web. If you're a PC user, check out Asymetrix's 3D Web product; you can use it to create animations as GIF animations. For Mac users, there's Specular's 3D Web Workshop product.

Q: What's the difference between 3D animations and video? It seems like it would be easier to record something with a camera than to generate and animate a scene. Which is best for the Web?

A: These are really two very different technologies. Video is real-time and photo-realistic; as such, it requires very large file sizes for low-quality videos. However, there are many places on the Web where video would be the better choice, such as an interview. It would take far more time to animate a person talking than it would to simply push the record button. On the other hand, it's a little difficult to take a video of aliens on the planet Mars.

3D animation does take some time to set up the initial scene, but many images can be created with computer graphics that would otherwise be impossible (or very dangerous) with video techniques.

What's best for the Web depends on what you really want to do. If you plan on having a person talk about a new product, use video, but if you want a space animation with special effects, use 3D animation—and don't rent the space shuttle!

SIX

Using Animation Plug-Ins in Your Web Page

—by Kelly Murdock

Client-push, server-pull, and GIF animations work okay for Web pages, but they can task the hardware or just be difficult to use. Often your 3D package conveniently outputs an animation as an AVI, an MPEG, or a QuickTime file. It would be nice to have a browser that could handle these video files without having to load a helper application. Well, someone is listening because this is becoming possible through browser plug-ins.

There are many video and animation plug-ins out there, and they are all very new. As a result, they probably won't produce the results you want right away, especially on machines with slower Internet connections. However, many groups are working on solutions—so surely one of them will get it right.

In this chapter, you

- ❏ See how to create Shockwave movies
- ❏ Learn how 3D animations are converted and embedded in Web pages with the Sizzler editor and plug-in
- ❏ Find out about Netscape plug-ins for embedding video files
- ❏ Learn about the Active Movie family of technologies

Tasks in this chapter:

- ❏ Creating 3D Shockwave Movies
- ❏ Converting AVI Movies to Sizzler Animations
- ❏ Embedding and Playing AVI Files with CoolFusion
- ❏ Animation Using Microsoft's Internet Explorer
- ❏ Using the ActiveMovie Control and ActiveMovie Stream

A majority of the available plug-ins work with Netscape's Navigator browser, but Microsoft is working on their own solutions for Internet Explorer. In this chapter, you'll start by looking at a few of the Netscape plug-ins that will enable you to play your 3D animations on the Web:

❏ Perhaps the most popular Netscape plug-in for doing animation is Macromedia's Shockwave; you'll see how to create Shockwave movies.

❏ 3D animations can be converted and embedded into Web pages using the Sizzler editor and plug-in.

❏ Several different plug-ins enable you to embed video files, including plug-ins for AVI, MPEG, and QuickTime video formats.

Once you've looked into the Netscape corner, you'll be moving over to Microsoft's corner and seeing what they have up their sleeves. The biggest Web thing you'll hear out of Microsoft is ActiveX.

❏ The X in the first case stands for "Movie." ActiveMovie is a streaming animation player built into the browser.

❏ Another X is for VRML. This chapter introduces ActiveVRML, but the really interesting material is covered in Chapter 11, "Using Microsoft's ActiveVRML."

Some great tools are coming onto the market that will make it possible to place your amazing 3D animations easily on your Web page, so take a look at them.

Animation Plug-Ins for Netscape's Navigator

There are many plug-ins available for Netscape Navigator. You won't get a chance to look at all of them in this chapter, but if you check out Netscape's Web site, they keep an up-to-date list of available plug-ins:

```
http://home.netscape.com/comprod/products/navigator/version_2.0/plugins/
➥index.html
```

Another good source for plug-ins is the Soup's Up E-zine, which can be found at this site:

```
http://athos.phoenixat.com/scott/plugins.html
```

All these plug-ins are fairly new, so they haven't been widely used. This chapter will cover a few of the plug-ins that will most likely be valuable to you as you deal with 3D animations on your Web pages.

Creating 3D Shockwave Movies

First, Macromedia's Shockwave is by far the most popular animation plug-in for Netscape. That's because Shockwave movies are created with Director, which is the tool of choice for a majority of multimedia developers.

Extreme 3D is Macromedia's modeling, rendering, and animation package.

Macromedia is really pushing the envelope with Shockwave. Not only is there Shockwave for Director, but Shockwave for Authorware and Shockwave for Freehand are also available. In the future, you can probably expect a Shockwave for Extreme 3D to show up, which will enable users to easily publish their 3D content on the Web.

The Shockwave plug-ins are available from Macromedia at this site:

```
http://www-1.macromedia.com/Tools/Shockwave/Plugin/plugin.cgi
```

Director is a multimedia authoring package that enables users to create interactive multimedia content.

After installing the plug-in, you can view Shockwave movies as you navigate the Web, but to create Shockwave movies, you need Macromedia's Director.

NOTE:
Shockwave is also available as an ActiveX control. This enables Shockwave to be viewed with Microsoft's Internet Explorer. It can be downloaded from Macromedia's Web site.

To turn your 3D animations into Shockwave movies with Director, you need to import your animation into Director and have it saved as a Shockwave movie. To do that, follow these steps:

1. In Director 5, you can import video clips by using the File | Import command. Once the Open dialog box comes up, select Video clips from the file type box and click the OK button. This loads the clip into the Cast window.

2. Select the video clip in the Cast window and drag it onto the Stage. The Stage is the rectangle in the background; it represents the edges of the actual Director movie. (See Figure 6.1.) The Stage size and position can be changed with the Modify | Movie | Properties command.

Figure 6.1.

The Director environment, showing the Stage window in the background, the Score window in the upper-left, the Control Panel upper-right, and the Cast window at the bottom.

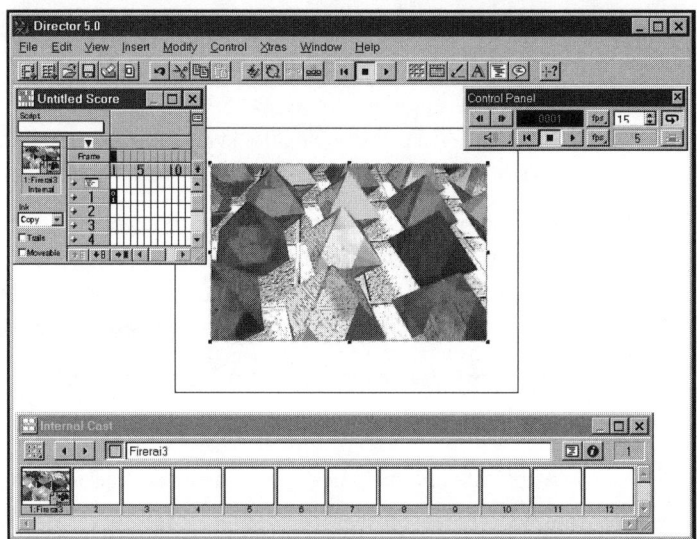

3. To see what the movie looks like, press the Play button on the Control Panel, which can be opened by using the Windows I Control Panel command. Once the movie has played, click the Rewind button to return it to the first frame.

4. Save the file as a Director movie (DIR) with the File I Save As command.

5. Use the Afterburner utility, available at Macromedia's Web site for no charge:

    `http://www.macromedia.com/Tools/Shockwave/Director/aftrbrnr.html`

    This utility compresses Director movies so they can run quickly over the Web. The format for Afterburned files is DCR.

6. Within your HTML file, place the following tag line:

    ```
    <EMBED SRC="filename.dcr" WIDTH=xx HEIGHT=yy>
    <NOEMBED> <IMG SRC="filename.gif"> </NOEMBED>
    ```

    `filename.dcr` is the saved Shockwave movie, and xx and yy are the width and height values. The `<NOEMBED>` tag isn't needed, but it replaces the selection with the filename.gif image if the Shockwave plug-in isn't available. An example is shown in Figure 6.2.

Figure 6.2.

A Web page with an embedded Shockwave movie.

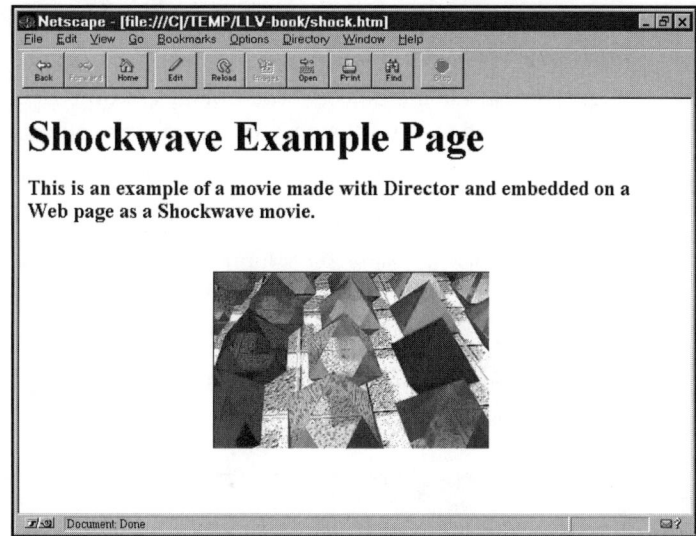

You will find throughout this chapter that I'm using the words *video*, *animation*, and *movie* synonymously. They are all different formats of the same thing. They all present several images in succession called *frames*. The difference is that you watch movies at the theatre, videos at home, and animations on Saturday mornings.

With Director, it's fairly easy to include 3D Shockwave movies in your Web pages and build interactivity into your movies. This added feature makes Shockwave a lot of fun to play with.

Converting AVI Movies to Sizzler Animations

In the computer world, videos are usually imported from a video camera, but an animation is usually produced using a piece of software. However, animations are usually saved in a video format like AVI or QuickTime. So, an animation can be a video, but a video isn't necessarily an animation. That's why your output is called a 3D animation, even though it's a video format. Get all that?

Another plug-in for Netscape Navigator is called Sizzler by Totally Hip Software. This plug-in enables what is known as *streaming animation*. The benefit of streaming animation is that it begins playing as soon as the animation file begins to download. The file starts in a very low resolution, and the details fill in as the file continues to download.

The Sizzler plug-in can be found at this site:

`http://www.totallyhip.com/sizzler/6b_sizz.html`

The Sizzler Editor is also available at the Totally Hip Software site. This editor is simple to use and allows you to convert an AVI file or a series of images in DIB format into the SPRITE format that Sizzler reads. Converting an existing 3D animation AVI file is as easy as this:

1. Download and set up the Sizzler Editor program from the address given above.

The ability to stream animations is one of the advantages that Sizzler has over Shockwave. Shockwave files have to load completely before you can view them.

2. Use the Objects I Insert Images I AVI File command to load the individual AVI frames into the Editor.

3. You can use the Objects I Insert Modifier I Goto URL on Mouse Click command to make the animation a link to another Web page.

4. Save the file as *filename*.SPR in the same directory as your HTML file.

5. Add the following lines to your HTML file:

```
<EMBED SRC="filename.spr" WIDTH=xx HEIGHT=yy>
<NOEMBED> <IMG SRC="filename.gif"> </NOEMBED>
```

Do these HTML tags look familiar? The animation will play for any Netscape browser with the Sizzler plug-in installed. A sample Web page using Sizzler animation is shown in Figure 6.3.

Figure 6.3.
A Web page with an embedded animation using the Sizzler plug-in.

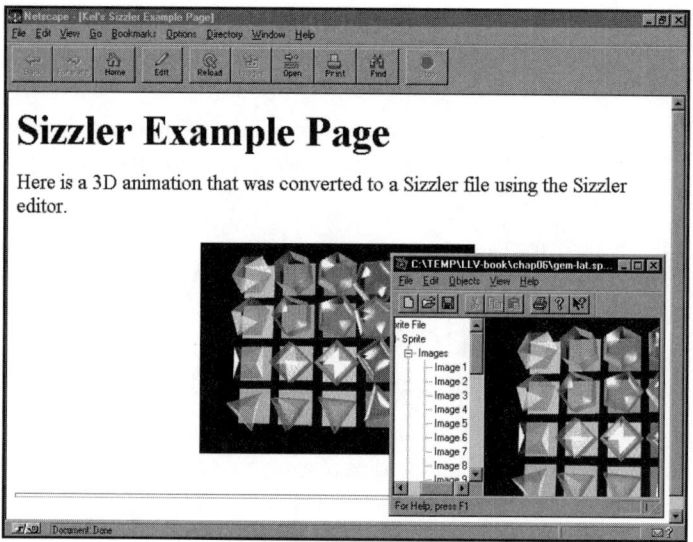

Totally Hip Software is working on a cel animation/painting program called WebPainter that will let users create their own animations and a larger multimedia creation product called Object Scenario.

Other video formats exist, but these three— MPEG, AVI, and QuickTime—are the main ones. UNIX stations use PPM, YUV, or Silicon Graphics MV video formats.

Using Existing Video Animations with the Netscape Plug-Ins

Several plug-ins let you embed video files into your Web page; they can be used to play existing 3D animations saved as video clips. Different video formats are now available, including MPEG, AVI, and QuickTime (MOV). Each has its unique strengths, but luckily, there are plug-ins available for each format. Currently, plug-in makers are working on a single plug-in that will support all the different formats, but until one arrives, you must use several different plug-ins to cover all the different formats.

Embedding and Playing AVI Files with CoolFusion

Iterated Systems has created a plug-in for embedding AVI files into your Web page and streaming them as they play. The advantage of streaming video is that the user can stop the video without having to wait for the entire file to download. The CoolFusion plug-in can be found at this site:

```
http://www.iterated.com/coolfusn/download/cf-loadp.htm
```

The <EMBED> tag is a Netscape extension to HTML. It can be used to embed all sorts of objects, including audio files.

To embed a video in your Web page, use the <EMBED> tag once again, like so:

```
<EMBED SRC="filename.avi" WIDTH=xx HEIGHT=yy>
<NOEMBED> <IMG SRC="filename.gif"> </NOEMBED>
```

The video will show up in the Web page as soon as it begins loading. This is a great way to display your existing animations without having to convert them, as shown in Figure 6.4.

Figure 6.4.
A Web page with an embedded AVI file, created using the CoolFusion plug-in.

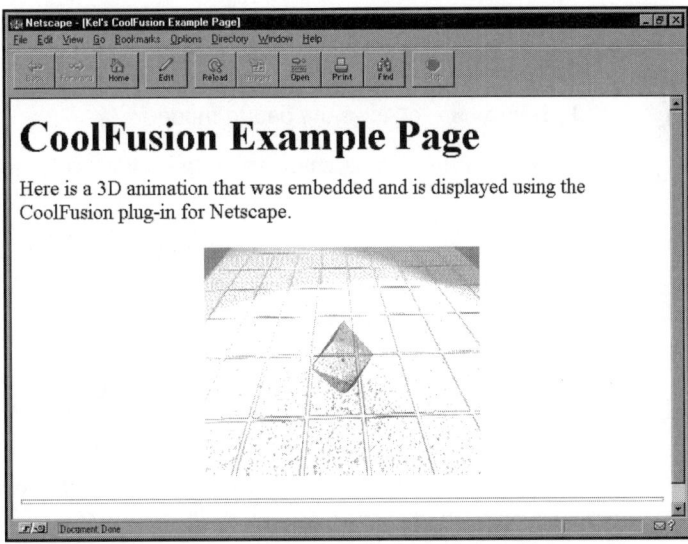

Embedding and Playing MPEG Videos with the Action Plug-In

The Action plug-in made by Open2u enables Web pages to be embedded with MPEG videos and WAV files. You can get it from the following site:

```
http://www.open2u.com/action/action.html
```

To include the file in an HTML file, the standard `<EMBED>` tag is used. The syntax looks like this:

```
<EMBED src="filename.mpg" width=xx height=yy [options]>
```

Many plug-ins use these types of parameter statements to add more functions to their plug-ins. Check the Web site where you get the plug-in for functions like those listed here.

Once included in your HTML file, the file is activated with a pop-up menu that appears when the left mouse button is clicked on the movie. The Action plug-in includes some additional options for playing back the video:

❑ **palette=`foreground or background`**—controls whether the video should impose its palette (foreground) or submit to the current palette (background). The default is `background`.

❑ **autostart=`true`**—tells the movie to start as soon as the page is loaded.

❑ **loop=`true`**—causes the movie to play continuously.

❑ **sync=`true`**—enables synchronizing audio and video.

❑ **size=`double`**—causes the video to be displayed twice its actual size.

❑ **color=`mono`**—plays the movie in gray scale.

❑ **debug=`on`**—enables the debug mode.

All these attributes can be changed by the home page visitor by using the pop-up menu.

Open2u is also developing an Encoder package so that users can combine audio and video into the same file and a Converter package so they can convert other video formats to MPEG.

Using QuickTime Plug-Ins for PCs and Macs

Apple created QuickTime video as the video format for the Macintosh. It has become so popular and robust that it has been ported to Windows machines and now is available on both platforms, as well as UNIX workstations. Several companies offer QuickTime plug-ins for Netscape Navigator, but the one to watch for won't be a plug-in at all.

QuickTime is more than just movies. Apple has added QuickTime tools for audio and MIDI as well as advanced technologies like QuickTime VR, which are panoramic scenes with a controlled viewpoint.

Apple has announced that it's working with Netscape to embed QuickTime technology into the Netscape Navigator 3. This will allow users to view QuickTime movies without a plug-in and navigate QuickTime VR worlds with a small plug-in. More details about QuickTime VR are in Chapter 10, "Using Apple's QuickTime VR." Nobody knows QuickTime video better than Apple, so when the plug-in finally shows up, you can expect it to be a strong tool.

Check this site for news about the QuickTime plug-in:

`http://quicktime.apple.com/`

Although the QuickTime in Netscape Navigator 3 isn't a streaming format, it has a feature called "Fast Start" that loads the first frame of the movie almost immediately, before the rest of the movie downloads. This preview gives you a good idea of what the video shows and lets you decide whether you want to wait for it to download.

To create a QuickTime movie with the Fast Start feature, you need to convert the file by using the Internet Movie Tool available at the QuickTime Web site. Once the movie is converted, embed it in your Web page with the standard <EMBED> tag. Figure 6.5 shows a sample Web page with a QuickTime movie embedded. Several other parameters control the playback options. A complete list of them is at this site:

`http://quicktime.apple.com/qt/dev/devWeb.html`

Figure 6.5.

A Web page with a QuickTime movie embedded.

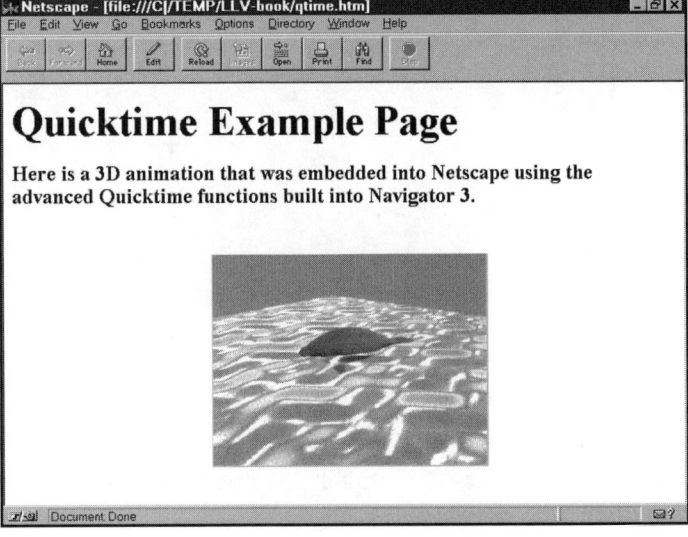

Animation Using Microsoft's Internet Explorer

Of course, Netscape isn't the only browser available; Microsoft is hard at work to add new features to Internet Explorer. Some of these new features will make it easy to embed your 3D animations.

The first solution doesn't use a plug-in at all. Microsoft is incorporating an extension to HTML that will enable users to embed AVI files by using the <IMG> tag. This new attribute called DYNSRC, which stands for Dynamic Source, looks like this:

```
<IMG DYNSRC="filename.avi" SRC="filename.gif"
      WIDTH=46 HEIGHT=46 LOOP=INFINITE ALIGN=CENTER>
```

Browsers that don't support this extension will still see the GIF file, but Internet Explorer will display the animation, as shown in Figure 6.6.

Figure 6.6.
AVI videos embedded in Internet Explorer with the <IMG DYNSRC= "filename.avi"> *tag.*

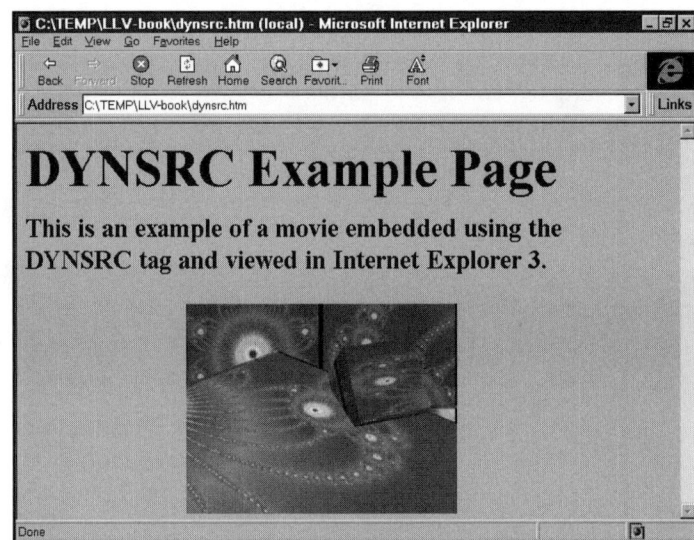

Both Netscape and Microsoft have proposed extensions to HTML that have been built into their respective browsers. The World Wide Web Consortium (W3C), the organization that controls the HTML spec, has reviewed these proposals and included many of them in the HTML 3.2 specification, which recently became available. Check out http://www.w3.org/ pub/WWW/ for more information.

Besides the common width, height, and align attributes, some special attributes are useful for controlling the animation:

❏ **CONTROLS**—This attribute displays start, stop, and pause controls underneath the video clip.

❏ **LOOP=x, LOOP=INFINITE**—This causes the video to loop x number of times, or infinitely.

❑ **START=FILEOPEN, START=MOUSEOVER**—FILEOPEN causes the video to begin playing as soon as the file is opened. MOUSEOVER starts the animation when the user moves the mouse over the video. Using them together, START=FILEOPEN, MOUSEOVER causes the video to play once, stop, and play again when the user moves the mouse over the video.

 **TASK**

Using the ActiveMovie Control and ActiveMovie Stream

ActiveMovie is a whole family of technologies specifically designed to stream media over the Internet; they include the following:

❑ The ActiveMovie streaming format (ASF) is a new streaming video format specifically designed for low-bandwidth Internet connections.

❑ The ActiveMovie player is a helper application that lets you play ASF files over the Web. The player is also designed to play back other media formats, such as AVI, MPEG, and QuickTime.

❑ The ActiveMovie Stream Editor lets you create ASF files optimized for various bit rates.

Currently, the ActiveMovie Add-On for Internet Explorer 3 is available, but the Stream Editor is being updated. The ActiveMovie site at Microsoft provides the latest information on these products. Check it out at this address:

```
http://www.microsoft.com/advtech/activemovie/amstream.htm
```

When the ActiveMovie Stream Editor is ready, you can download it from that address.

ActiveMovie is an ActiveX control, so embedding it in your Web page follows the same procedure as other ActiveX controls:

1. The main tag is the `<OBJECT>` tag. Within that tag is the `classid`, which is unique for ActiveMovie. You can also specify several other properties, such as height and width.

```
<OBJECT
    classid="clsid:{05589FA1-C356-11CE-BF01-00AA0055595A}"
    id=VideoWindow
    width=400
    height=250>
```

2. Below the `<OBJECT>` tag can be several `<PARAM>` tags that define the control of the movie:

```
<PARAM name="FileName" value="filename.asf">
<PARAM name="ShowControls" value="true">
<PARAM name="AutoStart" value="true">
</OBJECT>
```

NOTE: The value of the filename property can contain either ASF or AVI file formats.

3. The ActiveMovie control also has methods, like Run, Stop, and Pause, and events, like Error and Timer, associated with it. They can be called by using VBScripts in the HTML file. For example, you can build a button and attach the Run method to it to build your own interface.

The chief benefit of ActiveMovie will be its ability to play any video format. With this capability, you can use one control to embed and play any video files, regardless of the type. Microsoft isn't stopping with that, either. They have many other ActiveX controls, including one to create VRML worlds.

Introducing ActiveVRML

Another powerful ActiveX control that Microsoft has been working on is the ActiveVRML control, Microsoft's proposal to the VRML community for the 2.0 specification. The VRML community selected a different proposal, Moving Worlds, as the official 2.0 specification, but this didn't stop Microsoft from developing their product—and it's a good thing.

ActiveVRML has a lot of great features that not only enable 3D VRML worlds to be embedded within the Internet Explorer browser, but also enable controls of 2D animations within Web pages as well.

Even though ActiveVRML wasn't accepted by the VRML community as the 2.0 specification, it's still supported by several companies because of its easy-to-use features. For this reason, it's covered in Chapter 11, "Using Microsoft's ActiveVRML."

Plug-In Recommendations

With so many different plug-ins to choose from, you might be asking yourself which one is the best to use. Here are some recommendations:

❑ If you want to use full-size animations with interactive elements built in, then look into Shockwave. Shockwave also has the benefit (or curse) of downloading the entire file before playing it. This results in the animation being played as close to your original as possible.

❑ If you're dealing with smaller animations that will loop continuously, check out the Sizzler plug-in, but you should also consider GIF animations because they don't require a plug-in. Sizzler does stream the animation, however.

❏ If you plan to use existing animations on a Netscape browser, consider converting them to QuickTime format and playing them natively.

❏ For the Internet Explorer browser, use the DYNSRC tag to embed AVI files directly or the ActiveMovie control if you want streaming files.

My last bit of advice for plug-ins is that if you're using them, use them extensively or not at all. If visitors to your site have to go through the trouble of downloading and installing a plug-in, then make it worth their trouble by offering several animations throughout your site that use that plug-in.

Workshop Wrap-up

Once you've created 3D animations, there are several ways to get them on your site. If you use Netscape plug-ins or the functionality built into Internet Explorer, the process becomes rather simple.

Next Steps

Now that you've learned about several tools that will enable you to show off your dazzling 3D animation skills, you're probably going to cast this book aside to try them out. That's fine, but when you come back, here's a list of where to go next:

❏ To see a real-life example of how this is done, move on to the next chapter, Chapter 12, "Real-Life Examples: Creating a MYST-like Adventure on the Web."

❏ If you're fascinated with 3D animations and are anxious to learn more advanced techniques, skip to Chapter 9, "Creating Advanced 3D Animations for the Web."

❏ If you're intrigued by ActiveVRML, then Chapter 11, "Using Microsoft's ActiveVRML," is the place for you.

❏ If all this 3D stuff is fine, but you really want to get into VRML, jump to Chapter 13, "Exploring VRML Browsers and Development Tools."

Q&A

Q: What if I have a plug-in to play one type of video, but my animations are created in a different format?

A: Well, you could either find and use a different plug-in, or you could convert the video format by using a conversion utility.

Video-editing packages like Adobe Premiere let you convert video or animations to different formats. There are also some shareware applications that will work.

Q: I've seen the plug-in list for Netscape Navigator, and it's pretty extensive. Which is the best Netscape plug-in for 3D animations?

A: No plug-in is singled out as the best. However, in my opinion, Shockwave is leagues above the others in acceptance and robustness, but it has some serious drawbacks as well. It really depends on the operating system, the speed of your connection, and where you like to browse. Certain Web sites require certain plug-ins to view their content.

Q: I've tried to use the more popular plug-ins so that most of the visitors to my site can see my animations, but what if the visitors to my site don't have the plug-in I'm using?

A: Web pages that use a certain plug-in should let the readers know which plug-in the page content works best in. Plug-in companies usually have some kind of icon you can put on your site that will link back to the plug-in's site so users can download it, much like the Netscape Navigator icons you see everywhere.

Also, there are countermeasures to guard unprepared visitors against seeing a blank screen or a trouble icon, such as the <NOEMBED> tag. The HTML code in the <NOEMBED> tag is executed if the needed plug-in isn't available. This is a good place to explain to the reader what's needed to view the site. Be sure to use these in your pages.

SEVEN

Product Design on a Corporate Intranet: Advanced Telescope Design Corporation

—by Kelly Murdock

Now that you've got some ideas on how to enhance your Web site with 3D graphics, take a real-life look at where 3D graphics can really be valuable to the company.

At this fictional company, Advanced Telescope Design Corporate (ATDC), several design engineers work daily in 3D graphics. Their problem is explaining the construction of their latest design to the advertising group, the manufacturing team, and especially their managers.

Lucky for the engineering team, a bright Web designer has set up a corporate intranet, and now the engineering team can create a Web site to get the message out. This chapter examines the process involved in creating such a Web site; along the way the following topics will be covered:

❏ Starting with a plan for implementation, which you should discuss with both those creating the designs and those receiving the information, outline your site and goals.

❏ Creating your content by using the techniques learned in the last four chapters and following the plan to generate the images and animations needed.

❏ Writing out the HTML file after practicing with the embed tips learned in the preceding chapters.

This really shouldn't be too long of a chapter because you're already a pro at HTML and you've just learned all the techniques. However, it will give you a close look at how HTML is used to deal with 3D elements.

Step 1: Plan Your Web Site

Just because this material is easy doesn't mean you shouldn't have a plan. Designing your Web site before you create any of the content saves a lot of extra work later on. Also keep in mind that this site may grow, and plan accordingly.

Start by asking questions. Who will create the information? Who will access the information? Who will update the site? How many cookies did I bring for lunch? Once you have all the questions, go find the answers.

Talk with all people who will be involved. Find out what kind of 3D content your design engineers can supply, then talk with each of the groups who will browse the site internally. What kind of information do they want to see?

Many site-management tools offer the ability to visually map out how the site structure is organized. These tools can be especially helpful as you plan your site.

A Web site plan doesn't have to be complex. A simple flowchart sketched on a piece of paper will do. Circulate the plan to the various groups and ask for feedback. Be open to their ideas.

NOTE: In such a situation, you will probably start the Web site, but you really should get the different teams involved in creating the content and updating the site. The entire idea behind the Web is that it makes it easy for anyone to publish.

Step 2: Creating the 3D Content

For this scenario, creating 3D content will be a breeze because all the design engineers use advanced CAD systems. CAD systems typically work in 3D and usually have some sort of shading method available.

For the two most recent telescope designs, the design team has been asked to create a shaded image of the design and another image with all the parts separated, as shown in Figure 7.1.

Figure 7.1.
3D images of the latest telescope designs for your Web site.

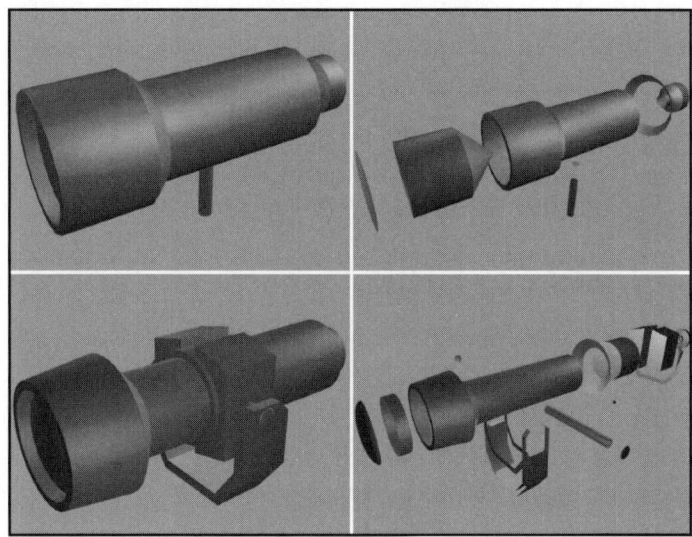

Although CAD systems are typically not listed along with 3D RMA packages because of the specialized function they perform, they are actually quite capable of producing rendered images and animation sequences. For a good example of this type of software, check out bCAD 2.0 on the CD-ROM.

The telescope models were taken from the Avalon site maintained by Viewpoint Datalabs. The more complex model can be found on the CD-ROM in the Viewpoint collection.

Another handy piece of content you want to use is a simple animation that shows the telescopes separating into their different parts. When it comes to embedding these animations, you should try to present the animations in a couple of formats to handle a wider array of browsers. A key advantage to an intranet is that the browser environments will be fairly consistent throughout the company. Companies typically have MIS departments that supply the software for the entire company.

If you don't want to have to worry about loading any plug-ins, use AVI video files for Internet Explorer and GIF animations for Netscape browsers. One of the animations is broken down in Figure 7.2.

Figure 7.2.

A frame-by-frame look at the parts that make up the latest telescope.

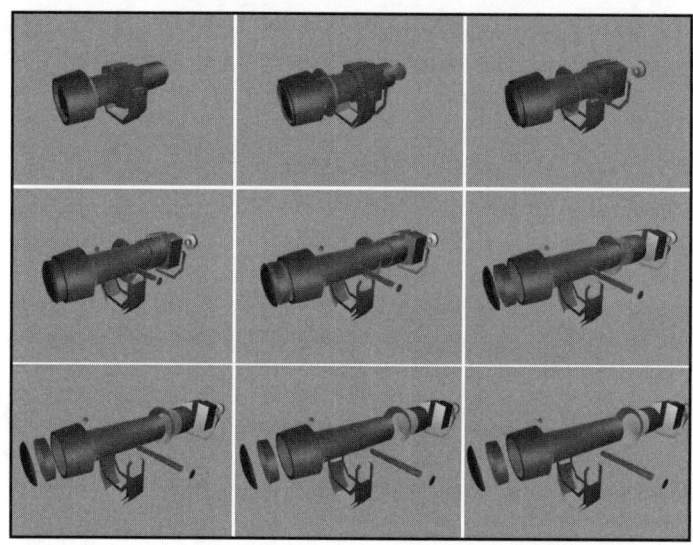

So which is better, GIF animation or AVI files? GIF animation files require you to create the files using a separate program like GIF Construction Set, but they seem to be widely supported. AVI files can use video compression to greatly reduce the file size, but video files aren't yet widely supported without plug-ins. As Internet Explorer becomes available, this will change. In the future, it looks like Netscape will have the ability to embed QuickTime movies, and Microsoft's Internet Explorer will have the ability to embed AVI files.

Step 3: Building Your Web Site

Once you have the 3D images, you can build your Web site. Following the plan, include all the standard elements that define a good Web site, including a home page and a what's new page.

When using graphics and animation content, it's important to remember to include thumbnails and warnings for low bandwidth viewers, as shown in Figure 7.3.

Figure 7.3.

Thumbnail images give viewers an idea of what the image looks like before spending time downloading it.

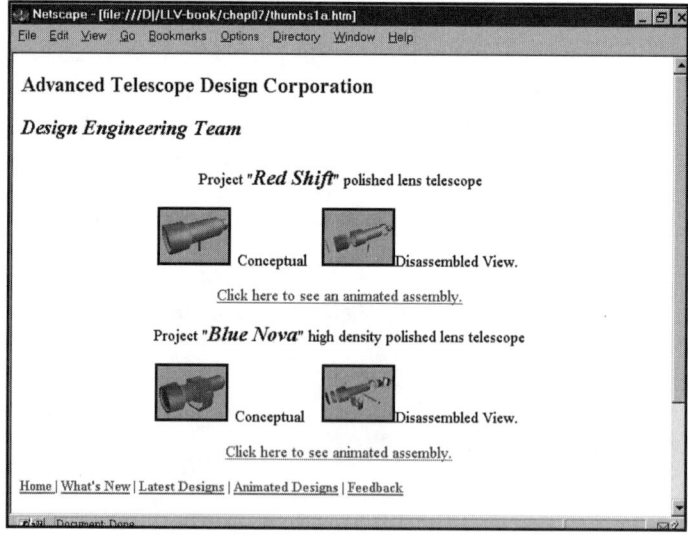

The company name and department are positioned at the top of all the Web pages on the site, and navigation links are placed at the bottom of the page.

Enhancing the Web Pages with 3D Elements

Now that you have images, animations, and text in the site, most people would call it a day and throw it to the Web, but not you—you've learned plenty of tricks to enhance the site and make it a place worth visiting.

Start with 3D navigation buttons. Using 2D tools, you can quickly create some raised buttons to be placed at the bottom of each page.

Since this is an intranet, you really should have the company logo displayed. But who says you can't give it a special look? You can enhance the logo, which is normally just black 2D letters, by extruding the letters and adding some colors and lighting effects.

Finally, try using a 3D background. These elements, shown in Figure 7.4, give the site a 3D look and are pleasing to the eye (maybe advertising won't think the engineers are so square, after all).

Figure 7.4.
Your thumbnail Web page enhanced with 3D elements.

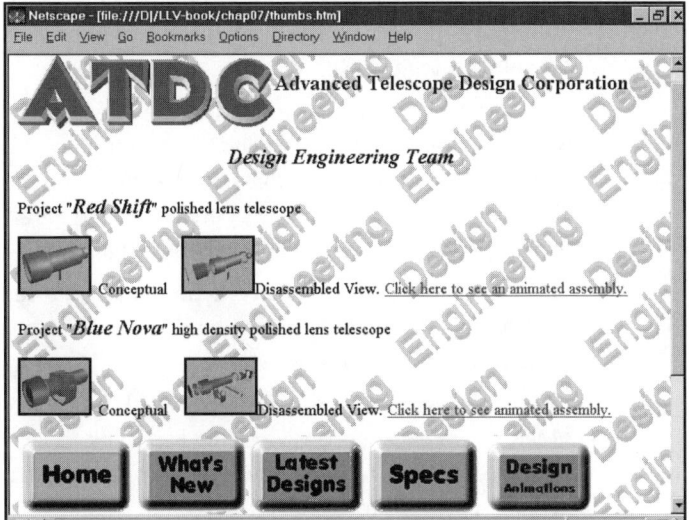

Workshop Wrap-up

If you're curious to see how the site turned out, you won't find it on the Web. This was developed for the corporate intranet (you didn't think we'd throw our latest telescope designs out to the world, did you?). Well, don't despair; the complete site is included on the CD-ROM for you to examine. I think the site turned out OK, but you should see it after the marketing staff got involved.

Next Steps

Before you say sayonara to this chapter, look at what's up ahead:

❑ The next chapter moves into the advanced arena. Chapter 8 covers "Creating Advanced 3D Rendered Images for Your Web Page."

❑ Another real-world example can be found in Chapter 12, "Real-Life Examples: Creating a MYST-like Adventure on the Web."

❑ VRML still awaits. It begins in Chapter 13, "Exploring VRML Browsers and Development Tools."

Q&A

Q: How is a corporate intranet different from the Internet?

A: Corporate intranets use the same tools as the Internet, but they are limited to employees within the company. You know the Internet as a wonderful place to share information, but there's a dark side of the Internet that looms with viruses, crackers, and other evils.

Corporations across the world have the same goal of sharing information, but the Internet holds too many threats for many of them. Many companies who worried about these threats have started up their own Web domains that run across the company's network. These intranets are confined to the company and separated from the Internet's threats.

Q: I've traditionally built Web pages using a text editor, but now many new HTML editors are beginning to appear. Are these tools any good, and which one is best?

A: Soon after the appearance of HTML, HTML editors began to appear. Many shareware versions were the first to hit the market, and although some of them were quite powerful, they had shortcomings and really couldn't be used to manage a Web site.

As the Web has grown, many large software companies have stepped into the realm of creating Web tools, such as HTML editors and site-management suites. Which tool is best really depends on your individual preferences. These tools are all top-notch and will help you build sites quickly. Here are several to consider:

❏ Netscape's Navigator Gold

❏ Adobe's PageMill and SiteMill

❏ Macromedia's Backstage

❏ Microsoft's FrontPage

PART

III

Advanced 3D
Graphics on the Web

EIGHT

Creating Advanced 3D Rendered Images for Your Web Page

—by Kelly Murdock

As you work in 3D graphics, you will begin to notice an interesting fact: No matter how advanced your 3D image is, there's always something cooler. It's all part of the ever-developing nature of computer graphics.

Now that you've gotten the basics out of the way, you can move on to some more advanced modeling and rendering techniques. Keep in mind that advanced techniques are all relative. What's advanced to the newbie doesn't help the seasoned 3D artist.

In this chapter, you'll continue where you left off in Chapter 4, "Creating and Embedding 3D Rendered Images," and explore several miscellaneous topics that may be of interest. This is what you have to look forward to:

- ❑ There are a number of complex modeling techniques, such as sweeping, lathing, and skinning. You'll look at each of these using Ray Dream Studio.

❏ Environment settings are rendering options that don't show up in the image until you actually render it. Settings like reflective backgrounds and fog can give your images a certain ambience.

❏ Just because your rendered image isn't quite what you want doesn't mean you have to throw it away. Tools like Photoshop can be used to touch up images in dramatic ways, if used carefully.

❏ Not all modelers use polygons. Some programs, such as Martin Hash's 3D Animation, use patches and splines to create smooth surfaces. You'll see how this program can be used to create character models.

❏ Another type of modeling that's becoming popular is using metaballs. These sticky spheres are especially good for objects that require smooth surfaces.

❏ A new type of modeling technology is starting to appear that creates 3D models from photographs. You'll look at one implementation called PhotoModeler.

❏ Modeling scenery can be particularly tricky because of its randomness and details. Specialized programs like Virtual Reality Laboratories VistaPro make it easy.

❏ Another tricky modeling item is the human body. Fractal Design Corporation makes a package called Poser that lets you position human figures as you would bendable toys.

❏ Finally, you'll learn about conversion utilities that make it possible to move from one file format to another.

Now that you have your laundry list, get out your pencil and check these topics off as you cover them.

Modeling Complex Objects

Using primitives and borrowed models is definitely the easy way to build a scene. They usually require just pressing a single button or issuing a solitary load command. Deforming models doesn't take much talent either; everyone learned to do that with clay in kindergarten. So how do you go about modeling from scratch? Well, start by learning modeling terms, such as sweep, lathe, and skin.

You'll start this chapter off using Ray Dream Studio. Not that you couldn't use trueSpace, but you want to broaden your skills, and this is a great way to do it. Ray Dream Studio is especially good at modeling from the ground up. First, start with sweeps.

TASK

Modeling Using Sweeps

Many 3D packages are covered in this chapter, but they're still just the tip of the iceberg of what's actually available. Check out Appendix A, "3D Software Resource Guide," for more information.

The sweep function is fairly typical in 3D packages. It's most often used with 2D shapes to introduce them into the 3D world.

By using the sweep function, you could make some interesting 3D fonts.

Remember back in Chapter 3, "Adding Simple 3D Elements to Your Web Page," when extrusions were explained? Well, extrusions don't always have to be along straight lines.

To *sweep* an object is to move its cross section along a path, and an extrusion is the simplest sweep case. In Ray Dream Studio, the Free Form Modeling Window is where most of your custom modeling takes place. Take a look at an example:

1. Open the Free Form Modeling Window by dragging the Free Form icon from the toolbar at the left onto the scene. This will open the modeling environment and present a dialog box where you can name the model.

2. To make the letter *J* with a circular cross section, start with a circle. Select the Draw Oval tool from the toolbar. You might have to hold the mouse button down and drag to the right to select the Oval tool. The Shift key constrains the Oval tool to draw a perfect circle. Draw a circle on the drawing plane (the one that floats free of the others) by dragging the mouse.

3. This action creates a simple cylinder. The pink lines on the left and bottom planes are your sweep lines. Add six more points between the endpoints of the sweep line on the left plane with the Add Point tool. Corresponding points show up on the bottom plane's sweep line at the same time.

4. Click the Selection arrow at the top of the toolbar, then click in the window away from the sweep line to deselect the points just added. Next, move the points one by one to form a new sweep line, as shown in Figure 8.1.

Figure 8.1.
Sweeping the letter J in Ray Dream Studio's Free Form Modeling Window.

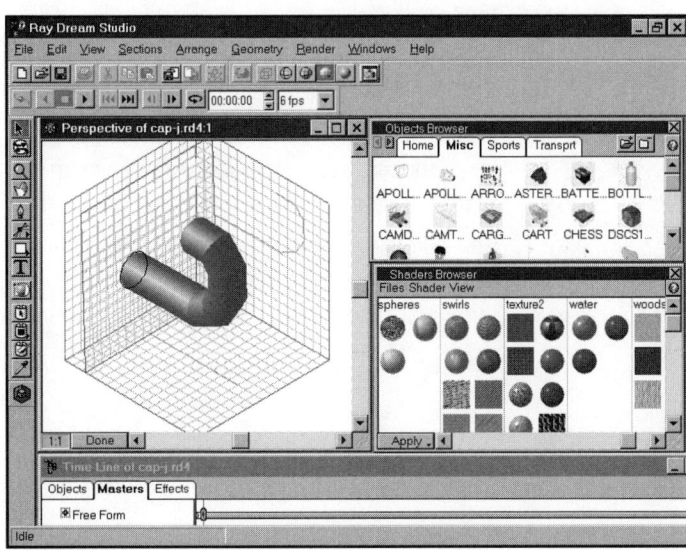

TIP: You can select preset views to look at only one plane at a time by using the View I Preset Position menu command.

Also under the Geometry menu are three preset extrusions: straight, spiral, and torus. The default is straight. Select any of these extrusion options with the Geometry I Extrusion Preset command.

5. Use the Geometry I Extrusion Method I Pipeline setting to make the circular cross section remain perpendicular to the sweep path. The Translation setting sweeps the path while keeping the cross section vertically aligned.

6. When finished, click the Done button in the lower-left corner of the Free Form Modeling Window to return to the Scene Window.

There are a lot of options when sweeping, but they're all based on the same simple concept.

Lathing Models

Lathing creates objects by rotating a profile around the center axis. If you remember how the wood lathe back in shop class worked, you've got the right idea.

Two things are needed to perform a lathe: an outer profile and an axis to rotate around. However, you don't need to rotate the full 360 degrees, as you do with a wood lathe. You can rotate only part of the way, so it's easy to create a full watermelon, half a watermelon, or just one slice.

Try intersecting the profile lines to create some interesting models.

In Ray Dream Studio, you'll use the Free Form Modeling Window again to perform a lathe. The profile is referred to as a Scaling Envelope. Just like wood shop, try creating a baseball bat for old times' sake.

1. Open the Free Form Modeling Window by dragging the Free Form tool into the Scene Window.

2. Draw a circle on the drawing plane by holding the Shift key down while you drag the Oval tool.

If you don't select the symmetrical option, the Extrusion Envelopes can be different to create unique models. For example, to make a surfboard, the Bottom Plane would have a wide rectangle with rounded corners, and the Left Plane would have a thin rectangle to profile the thickness of the surfboard.

3. Select the Sections I Center command to center the circle in the window. Next, choose Geometry I Extrusion Envelope I Symmetrical to enable the Scaling Envelope, which shows up as four blue lines.

4. Add points to the top blue line in the left plane and move them with the Selector tool to form the bat profile. The Symmetrical setting causes the same points to show up on the other envelope lines.

That's all there is to it, and no wood chips. The finished bat is shown in Figure 8.2.

Figure 8.2.

*Your completed lathe—
a baseball bat.*

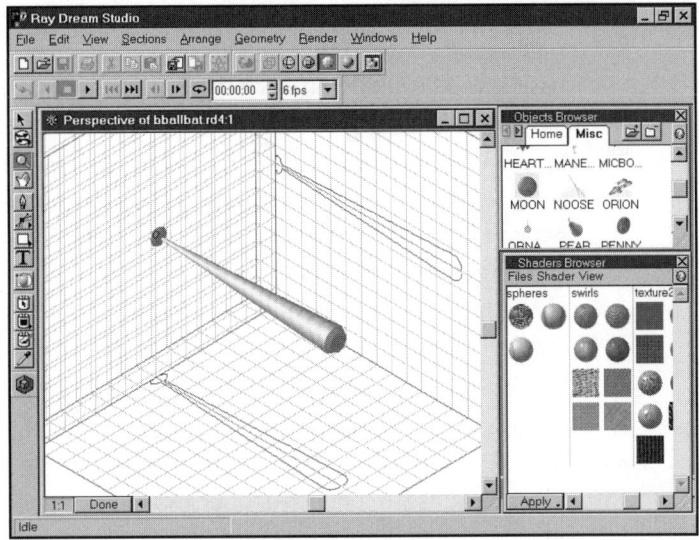

TASK

Skinning: Creating Models with Multiple Cross Sections

If you start to use sweeps and lathes, you'll soon find that they are useful for creating simple models, but many objects don't have a common cross section throughout. Most objects have different cross sections along their length. These types of objects can be modeled using a process called *skinning*.

Skinning is sometimes called *lofting*, after the process used to build ships. Ship builders would arrange the cross sections of the ship along its length and then fasten the ship's surface to these cross sections.

The words *skinning* and *lofting* are used interchangeably. 3D packages typically call the process one or the other.

In Ray Dream Studio's Free Form Modeling Window, you can create several different cross sections and the surface will smoothly move from one to the next. Try creating a screwdriver as an example:

1. Enter the Free Form Modeling Window and name the object Screwdriver.

2. Choose the Sections I Create Multiple command and enter 9 in the dialog box so your screwdriver will have nine cross sections.

3. Click on the back plane to see the first drawing plane. Draw a small circle for the first cross section and choose Sections I Next to move to the next drawing plane. The screwdriver handle cross section was drawn using the Pen tool to place points. Repeat this for each drawing plane until you've drawn all the needed cross sections.

4. Click on one of the sweep paths. All the drawing planes show up as evenly spaced points. With the Selection cursor, move these points until the section has the right length. You will need to place some points on top of one another, such as where the handle connects with the shaft.

5. You can edit the cross sections by clicking on them and moving the points. You can remove the current drawing plane by choosing the Sections I Remove command or by using the Delete Point tool to remove the corresponding sweep path point.

6. For each cross section, you can use the Sections I Cross Section Options command to open a dialog box that will let you set whether the cross section is filled or disconnected from the next cross section.

Drawing planes aren't limited to only one cross section per plane; they can have multiple cross sections. The Sections I Show Shapes Numbering command lets you see which cross sections are connected. Double-click the number to change the association. Figure 8.3 shows two shots of the final screwdriver.

Figure 8.3.
A screwdriver model created with Ray Dream Studio by skinning over several different cross sections.

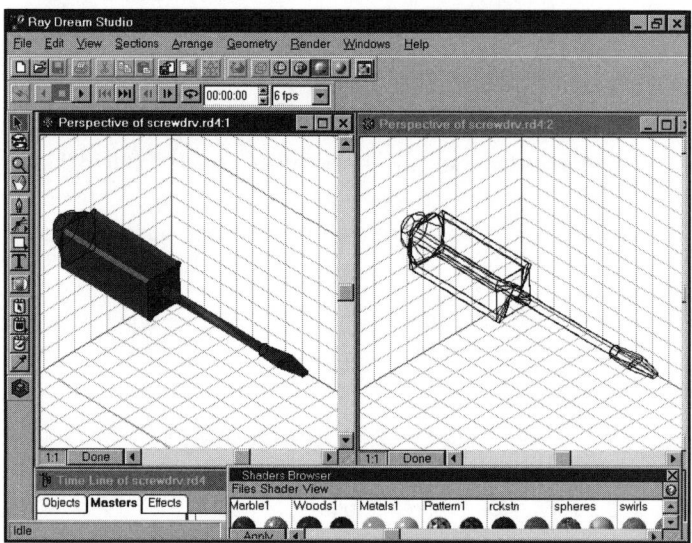

The individual parts that are built using the Free Form Modeling Window can be combined into a hierarchy to create complex models. The windmill, taken from the Ray Dream CD-ROM, shows in Figure 8.4 an example of a complex model created entirely from primitives and free-form modeled parts. By double-clicking on a part or on its name in the hierarchy list, you can launch the part into the Free Form Modeling Window for editing.

Figure 8.4.

This windmill is a fine example of a complex model made from primitives and free-form modeled parts.

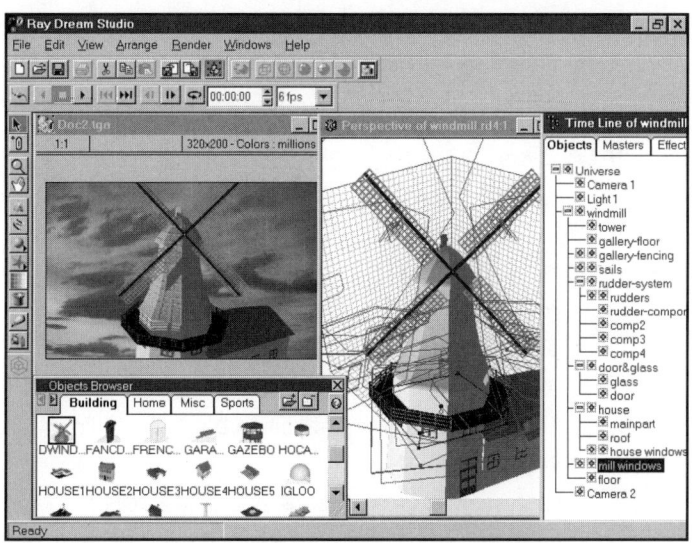

The Ray Dream model collection that comes with the Ray Dream Studio CD-ROM has many good examples of complex models.

There are more ways to model, which are covered later in the chapter, but while you have Ray Dream Studio open, look at some render settings that can add realism to your images.

Using Environmental Settings

No, this section doesn't talk about recycling or how you should use bicycle models instead of cars to save on pollution. In 3D packages, *environmental settings* are special commands you give to the render engine that affect the way the image is rendered. Examples include reflection maps and fog effects. Each package will call these settings something different. Ray Dream Studio refers to reflection maps as *reflected backgrounds*.

Casting Reflected Backgrounds on Your Rendered Images

In Chapter 4, you learned how to add backgrounds to your images. They acted like backdrops that enhanced the image, but didn't really affect the models in the scene. *Reflected backgrounds* are images projected from all sides toward the models and are reflected off any reflective objects within the scene.

Reflected backgrounds are also sometimes called Environment Maps. They can add a great deal to your images without requiring many additional models and can be used as an alternative to ray tracing in some cases. Take a look at how Ray Dream Designer uses reflected backgrounds.

Even though they are called backgrounds in Ray Dream, these maps actually encompass the entire environment and exist as a globe wrapped around the scene.

1. Start by setting up your scene. For the scene in Figure 8.5, I used the Scene Wizard as a start. This gives me a jump on the scene by automatically placing lights and the backdrop.

TIP: Reflected backgrounds show up best when reflected off a model with a large smooth surface area, such as an apple, a car fender, or a window.

2. Once the scene is set up, select Render I Effects to open the Render Effects dialog box. Select the Reflection Background tab and choose Map in the top pull-down menu and open the image you want to use.

3. The other buttons in the dialog box let you flip or rotate the image. You can also tile the image.

4. Next, make sure that renderer is set to RDI Ray Tracer by choosing the Render I Settings command and looking in the Renderer tab.

5. The final step is to render the image with the Render I Render I Use Current Settings command.

TIP: Because of the time it takes to render a scene, you may want to render it using the Low Res Preview option to check the image before it starts the final rendering.

Figure 8.5.
A balloon in the sky showing the cityscape below in a reflected background.

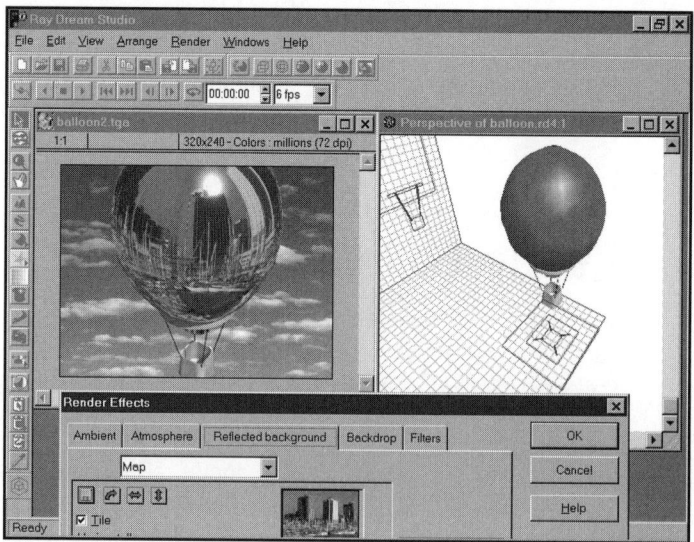

 # Adding Fog Effects to Your Rendered Scenes

There are other environmental settings you can add to your scene. One that frequently shows up in 3D packages is the ability to add fog to your rendered scene.

The fog settings for Ray Dream Studio are also added by using the Render Effects dialog box:

1. Starting from the Scene Wizard once again, position your models and set up the scene.

2. Select Render I Effects to access the Render Effects dialog box and go to the Atmosphere tab. Ray Dream has three types of fog available: normal, cloudy, and laminated. Using the dialog box controls, you can adjust the fog color and its density and lumpiness, among other things.

3. With the scene ready and the render effects set, render the scene to see the fog. The cloudy fog setting was used in Figure 8.6.

Figure 8.6.

A raptor in the early morning forest, complete with misty fog.

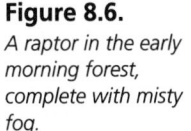

Within the Render Effects dialog box, there are other environment settings, such as Ambient and Backdrop. Other packages have unique features also, but they all work in roughly the same way, by manipulating the settings before rendering.

Using Photoshop to Touch Up Your Rendered Images

A good example of correcting small mistakes is the animation of Bubsy in Chapter 1. When I created Bubsy talking, I previewed several of the frames to check for misaligned models. Everything looked fine until I rendered the final animation. It turned out that as Bubsy's lips were moving, the skin under his bottom lip folded under the mouth interior for a few frames, revealing a bright red mark. It's very unnatural for a model's skin to turn inside out.

To fix the frames, I loaded the problem images into Paint Shop Pro and used the Clone tool to paint over the red areas. Then I saved the images as a new video file; if you look at the animation, you can't even tell.

Keep in mind that if you render your image again, you'll lose any touch-up changes you made to your image.

Notice how the shadow doesn't need to match the actual sticks because the light is coming from a different direction than the camera.

Imagine the following scenario. You've completed your scene, you've got the models in just the right positions, and you've previewed the image a number of times—finally, it's perfect for your Web site. However, after rendering all night, you realize it needs just a little more light in that one area, or you think of another effect that will increase the coolness factor by 14.

This is a common occurrence for 3D artists. Seldom does an image turn out perfectly on the first render. I suggest you do a lot of preview renders, but even those can't see everything. Now for the glimmer of hope. Sometimes you can correct small mistakes and even enhance your image in ways that weren't possible using your 3D package, with help from an image-editing package like Photoshop.

A good example would be in adding some text on top of the rendered image. This can be difficult to line up in the 3D scene, but it's easy to add in Photoshop. Take a look at the following example:

1. Load your rendered image into Photoshop. I'm using a scene created by Ray Dream's Scene Wizard. The original rendered image is seen in the upper-left corner of Figure 8.7.

2. The first enhancement you want to add, using Photoshop's Lens Flare tool, is a specular reflection off the window. Select Filter | Render | Lens Flare to open the dialog box. I used the 50–300 mm zoom lens with 25 percent brightness. The results are shown in the upper-right corner of Figure 8.7.

3. The next enhancement is to add some artistic sticks in the empty flower pot. These sticks would be a lot of needless polygons in the 3D scene, but in Photoshop they are simple black lines painted on in no time.

4. The final enhancement, shown in the lower-right corner, adds some text to the scene.

Figure 8.7.

Your rendered image touched up with Photoshop.

Exploiting the Advantages of Spline and Patch-Based Modeling

Just as you are starting to get the hang of two different 3D packages, you're going to shift gears again. Why, you may ask? Different packages use different modeling paradigms. You've learned about the most popular types, but there are others.

trueSpace and Ray Dream Studio are both polygonal modelers, which means that all their models can be broken down into lines and polygons. This works well and can represent any shape you could want, but there's another way to model—using splines and patches.

Splines were introduced in Chapter 4 when paths were covered. Splines have the unique benefit of being easily controlled. To bend a polygonal line, you need to add more points and create a contour. To bend a spline, you simply need to move the control point handles. Therefore, a curved polygonal line takes many points, but a curvy spline needs only four points, or two points and two handles. This is far fewer points that the computer has to deal with, resulting in simpler models with more curves.

A *patch* is just a grouping of splines forming an element that can be rendered. A line is to a polygon like a spline is to a patch.

Many high-end modelers use spline-based models because of the control it gives them over models, but there's a 3D spline-based package that fits in your price range— Martin Hash's 3D Animation. I will refer to the product from here on as MH3D for simplicity's sake.

You'll use this package to introduce spline-based modeling and to show you how it can help create character models where curves come in handy.

TASK Character Modeling Using Martin Hash's 3D Animation

This product was known as Animation Master, but Hash Inc. developed a newer version—Animation Master 4. The newer product got to keep the popular name, and the older product (still a great tool) was renamed Martin Hash's 3D Animation.

You can model many different things, but modeling characters is perhaps one of the most popular, and difficult, tasks. Most entertainment centers around characters. Whether they're watching TV, cartoons, or sports stars, people like to identify with characters who have a definite personality, whether it's good or bad.

Try smiling at yourself in the mirror. See how your skin smoothly folds back into your cheeks as you grin? This action is very difficult to simulate with polygonal models because the computer has to compute how the polygons smooth from one polygon to the next. For tight curves, like right next to your lips, it's difficult for the renderer to tell whether the edge should be smooth or hard. This is where splines come in. Splines inherently "know" whether an edge is hard or smooth because that's how they are built. This ability means the computer doesn't have to guess how to smooth a polygon, so it's much easier to render and results in a better model.

MH3D excels at creating animations. In fact, to use the modeler, you need to define a path first. You'll get into the animation side of MH3D in the next chapter, but for now, examine the program to see what those splines and patches are all about.

Although the work is done in different windows that act independently, changes made in one window are reproduced in all the windows.

Now you'll create a simple character named Clumgy by using MH3D. I don't know what kind of personality Clumgy will have, but with splines, he'll be able to smile very nicely.

1. Click the New icon to create a New Choreography called Clumgy. MH3D opens the Direction window that shows the top view of your scene. The green box is the camera, and the four projecting purple lines are the camera's scope. The Direction window is where you control the animation.

2. Click the upper-right icon in the floating toolbar, then click in the window to add a path to the scene. Now click the Add a Figure to the Selected Path icon that looks like a little human figure. This brings up a Figure dialog box. Click on New and type in `Clumgy` to open the Character module window.

3. The Character window is where all the parts are assembled and grouped. Click the Add a Child Segment icon in the upper-right corner of the toolbar, then click in the window. Name the new segment "Head." The Sculpture window then opens for you to start modeling.

There are actually four windows in MH3D: *Direction*, where animations are composed; *Action*, where models are animated; *Character*, where models are assembled; and *Sculpture*, where model parts are created. The toolbar icons change with each window.

When working with control points, you can weld points by dragging them and hitting the Enter key when you're on top of the point you want to weld to.

MH3D renders any patches with three or four control points. If your spline has more control points, it won't render. Try breaking the patch into several smaller patches.

In the Sculpture window, use the Edit I Flip I X Axis command to create the left eye.

4. Switch to the Front view by pulling down the View menu from the top toolbar, if you're not already there. Click the Add Mode button in the upper-right corner of the floating toolbar, or just hold down the A key while clicking and dragging in the window to create control points. You'll need about eight points for the head's cross section.

TIP: MH3D is much easier and quicker to use if you learn some of the basic keyboard commands. Almost every command has a single keystroke that invokes an action. For example, holding down the Z key lets you zoom in and out of the scene with the mouse.

5. Click the arrow icon to move into Edit mode, and move the points to create a head profile. You can select several points at once by clicking the Enter Group Mode button (keystroke G) and dragging the box over the control points you want.

6. Once the profile is correct, click the Enter Pivot Placement Mode button (keystroke P) and click in the window at the point you want to lathe the object around.

7. Select all the points in the profile with the Group tool. Remember the Lathe tool? Well, along with the Extrude tool, it followed you here. Click the Lathe tool (keystroke L) to create the lathed head, which you can see in Figure 8.8. Close the Sculpture window to return to the Character window.

TIP: Check out the model by clicking on the Preview tool (keystroke Q) in the top toolbar, then clicking in the window. A shaded view of the head begins to render.

8. In the Character window, click the Add Segment button (keystroke A), then name the segment "Right Eye." Use the Sculpture tools to create an eye, and return to the Character window. Copy and paste the eye to create a segment called "Left Eye."

9. Continue this process for each body feature. In the Character window, the Edit Segment's Attribute button (keystroke F3) brings up the Attributes dialog box where you can specify the material used to render the body parts. When you're finished, save the character; you'll see how to animate it in the next chapter.

Your character's shown in the three different windows of MH3D in Figure 8.8. He isn't really that handsome, but not bad for a spline-modeled character with marshmallows for eyes and a pickle for a nose.

Figure 8.8.

A character modeled in splines and patches with Martin Hash's 3D Animation.

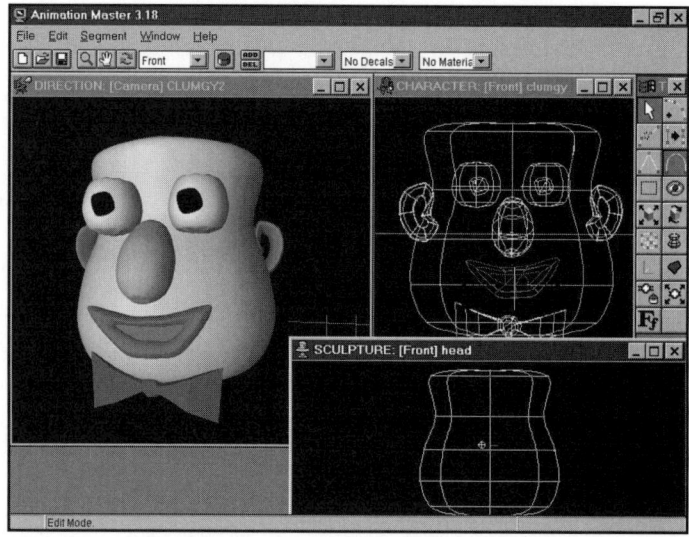

TASK   Using StudioPro's Metaballs

You've learned how to model with polygons and patches, so now look at another fairly new method called *metaballs*. Metaballs are like the equivalent of sticky spheres of clay. They're especially good at modeling rounded surfaces since they're made of spheres.

There are a few shareware metaball modelers available if you want to use metaballs on a PC, such as Blob Sculptor, which is on the CD-ROM.

Isolated metaballs look just like normal spheres, but when they're placed next to one another, the surface of one flows into the surface of the other, much like drops of mercury. You can control the level of attraction between the surfaces.

Several programs, such as StudioPro, are beginning to offer metaballs as a modeling option. Take a look at how metaballs can be used in the following example:

1. Start by placing spheres in your scene; make sure they overlap.

You can also convert existing models into metaballs, but StudioPro changes all parts to spheres before the conversion.

2. Select all the spheres you want to make into metaballs. Then use the Modeling I Metaballs I Join command to open the Metaballs dialog box where you can specify the influence each sphere has on its adjoining spheres.

3. Clicking the OK button causes all joined spheres to exhibit metaball properties. An example of how this works can be seen in Figure 8.9.

Figure 8.9.

Bubble man before and after being converted into metaballs.

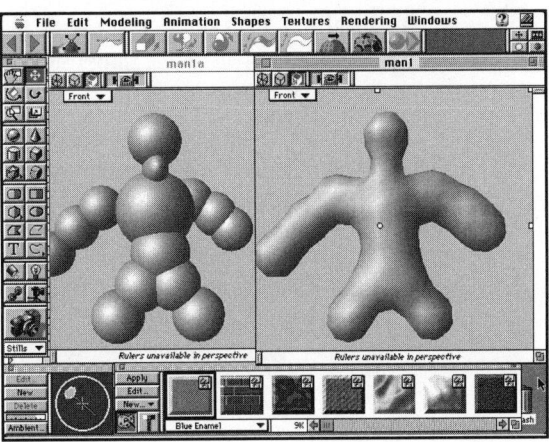

TASK Creating Models from Photographs with PhotoModeler

If all these lines and points and axes are just too confusing, you might want to look into another new modeling technique. PhotoModeler takes regular photographs that have been scanned in and uses visual keymarks to create a model.

The models created with this technique aren't extremely detailed, but by using the photos as texture maps to cover the surfaces, the models end up looking quite good. Because of the low polygon count, these models are especially handy for creating VRML worlds, so remember that when you start to create VRML worlds.

Now look at how PhotoModeler can be used to create a simple model of a computer monitor:

To create effective models, you need to take pictures from all sides of the object, so a single picture from a book or magazine won't help much.

1. Open a new project with the command File I New Project. A dialog box opens where you can give the file a name and approximate dimensions. PhotoModeler uses these dimensions to create a box to help you line up the pictures.

2. Next, click the Photo Import button to open the Photo Import dialog box. Load your scanned photos into the project by changing to the correct directory and clicking the arrows button. Click the OK button when you've got all your photos loaded.

3. With the Project Photographs dialog box open, select one of the photos and click the Position button. To tell the program how the photos fit into the scene, you need to know roughly where the camera was when it took the picture. Drag the camera in each of the three scenes until the cube with the specified dimensions is lined up with the picture.

4. Set the camera position for each photograph in the same manner. Notice how the outline of the dimensioned cube has colors that match the box in the different views.

5. Next, you need to mark specific points as they show up in each photo. Open a photo from the Project Photographs dialog box and enter Marking mode by selecting Marking I Mark Points. The cursor changes to an *X*. Click on recognizable points in the photo, like the corners of the computer monitor.

6. Use the Markings I Mark Lines command to mark lines within the photo. Repeat marking points and lines for each photo. Each point will have its own number, which is visible in the status bar at the bottom of the window.

7. Next, you need to refer to the various points to let the computer know which points match up in the different photos. Select Referencing I Reference Points to enter Reference mode. Open all the photos and select one point, then click on another photo and on the matching point in that photo. Continue until you've matched up all the points.

8. The final step of the process is selecting Project I Process. After some calculations, a 3D model is created. To see the model, choose Project I Open a 3D Viewer. It shows up as a series of points and lines. The final model can be exported as a DXF or VRML file.

There are many more features to this program, such as applying surfaces and checking the accuracy of the model. The finished model for this example is shown in Figure 8.10.

Figure 8.10.

A simple 3D model of a computer monitor created from photographs.

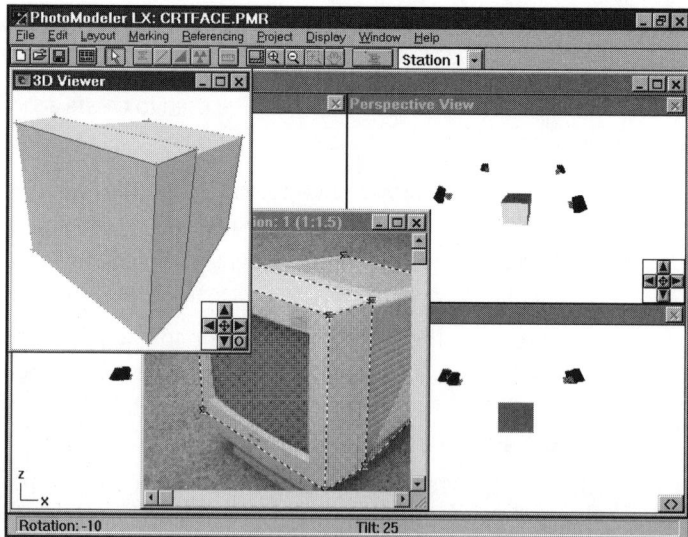

Modeling Complex Scenery with Terrain Generators

As you look into all the 3D packages (see Appendix A, "3D Software Resource Guide"), you'll see that some produce only certain kinds of models. Two good examples are VistaPro, which creates landscapes, and Fractal Design's Poser, which creates only human models. Poser is covered in the next section.

Scenery can be very relaxing and inspiring, and many photo albums are made up of such pictures. So it's only natural for 3D modelers to want to create such images. Lucky for the modeler, there are several good packages especially designed for this type of modeling, such as Virtual Reality Laboratories' VistaPro, Metatools' KPT Bryce, Questar's World Construction Set, and Animatek's World Builder.

These packages usually start with a 2D grayscale image in which the darkness relates to the height, so the blackest areas would be the highest peaks and the white areas would be the lowest. This feature makes it easy to create gradually ascending mountain sides by using a 2D image with a gradual transition from white to black. It also makes it easy to add random peaks.

You'll see this same concept in the VRML world; it's called *LOD*, which stands for *Level of Detail*.

One of the toughest problems with creating scenery is including foliage. It's simple to create desolate moonscapes, but creating a rich, lush mountain scene is much more difficult. Some of these packages include details like trees, shrubs, and flowers that can be added to the terrain. You can further define the range of these details so that they're not visible from far away, but show up with greater clarity as you get closer. An example of the type of images these packages can create is shown in Figure 8.11.

Figure 8.11.
A sample picture created using Animatek's World Builder software.

Positioning Human Figures with Fractal Design's Poser

Think of how the Greeks modeled the human body. Their statues took many months to create, but were detailed and impressive. Today, computer artists find many places to use models of human figures. Whether in an architectural scene or a recreation of a historical event, human models can add a personal touch to any 3D scene, but only if they look realistic.

There are 3D human models available, but they can be difficult to use if you try to reposition them, so you end up getting a human model that's standing, one that's sitting, one that's running, and one that's jumping—or you get Fractal Design's Poser.

Poser lets you choose from several human types—male, female, hero, and manne-quin—and from several different heights, such as baby, toddler, and adult. Once you've selected your model, you can position it by using inverse kinematics. To make your model do aerobic knee lifts, just grab its knee and pull it up. Follow these steps to see how this works:

1. When you start Poser, the default is a male figure standing with his arms out straight. The Tools palette will be open with the Pose mode selected.

2. Start posing your figure by clicking on the man's chest; when you do that, the chest turns white. Then drag the mouse to the right; his upper torso follows, making him lean to the right.

3. You don't want this man to be alone, so introduce a dancing partner. Select Figure I Add Figure I Female Body to add a female figure.

4. Click on the Move icon to change to Move mode, then click on the icon with four arrows, which is the Move icon. Now move the female figure to the left.

5. Return to Pose mode by clicking the Pose button and reposition the female arms, as shown in Figure 8.12.

6. When you're done posing your figures, choose Render I Render to create a rendered image.

Figure 8.12 shows the figures in a ballet step—and don't worry, Poser supports texture mapping, so you can add clothes to your models. If you plan on working with human models often, Poser is a great tool and easy to use. You can also export your models as DXF files to be imported into other 3D packages.

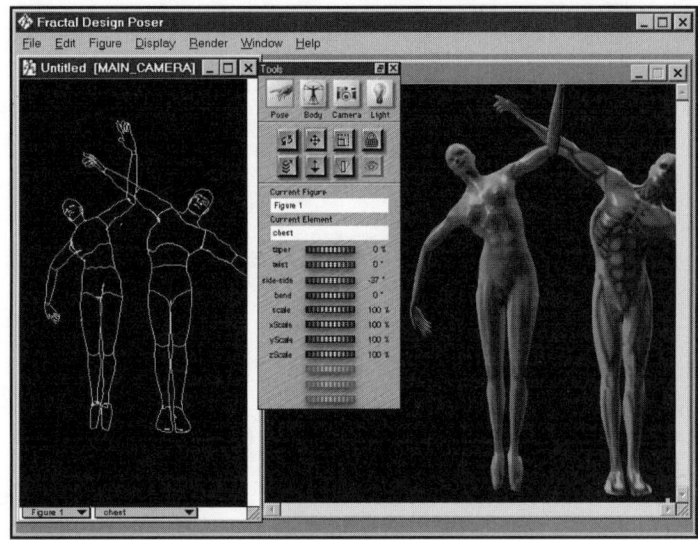

Using Conversion Utilities

You're probably starting to notice that the features of all these different packages vary quite a bit; no one package has exactly the features you want or need. The truth is that 3D artists typically use a variety of tools. This raises the question of how you can load one model into another without losing any of the information—that's where conversion utilities come in.

Almost every 3D package has its own proprietary file format. Each package can import and export several different formats, but it's often difficult to move between packages. Some import and export functions have difficulties with certain formats and may lose material or hierarchy information.

One of the greatest shortcomings of converting scenes is losing lights and cameras. The second great evil is losing materials.

To move a 3D file between formats, you might need to convert it a couple of times. Moving a Ray Dream Studio file to trueSpace requires exporting the Ray Dream file as a DXF or some other generic format and importing it into trueSpace. In Figure 8.13, you can see the results of file conversion. Two images on the left, the top one created in Ray Dream Studio and the bottom in trueSpace, were converted to the other program. You can see that conversion doesn't always give the best results.

With the introduction of VRML as a new file format, many 3D programs are introducing an export feature to VRML. Chapter 13, "Exploring VRML Browsers and Development Tools," covers a number of specific VRML conversion programs.

Several programs are available that handle file conversion. One of the best file-conversion pieces of software is produced by a company called Okino. The product is the NuGraf Rendering System. Not only is it a full-fledged RMA, but it can import and export more file formats than any program I've seen.

Figure 8.13.
Two scenes created in Ray Dream and trueSpace, then converted, loaded, and rendered in the opposite package.

The NuGraf program will be equipped to handle VRML 2.0 conversion by the time you read this book.

Look at how NuGraf's batch conversion feature works:

1. When the program starts, you see a dialog box that lets you start in Beginner or Expert Mode. Select Expert Mode. You can switch back to Beginner Mode using the Options I Switch to Beginner Mode command, but the Batch 3D Convert command is available only in Expert Mode.

2. Open the Batch Convert dialog box by selecting the File I Batch 3D Convert command.

3. Click the Add Files button to select the files you want to convert and select the Export format at the bottom of the screen. When you're ready, click the Convert Files button.

4. The export options for each type of model are in the Options dialog box. Select the options for the conversion process and click OK.

You can check out a demo of the NuGraf Rendering System, along with an excellent conversion utility called PolyTrans, on the book's CD-ROM.

The NuGraf Rendering System also has a fast, efficient renderer and many advanced features, such as a tip-of-the-day box, model optimization commands, and unlimited texture layering. You can see its interface in Figure 8.14.

Figure 8.14.

A screen shot from the NuGraf Rendering System program.

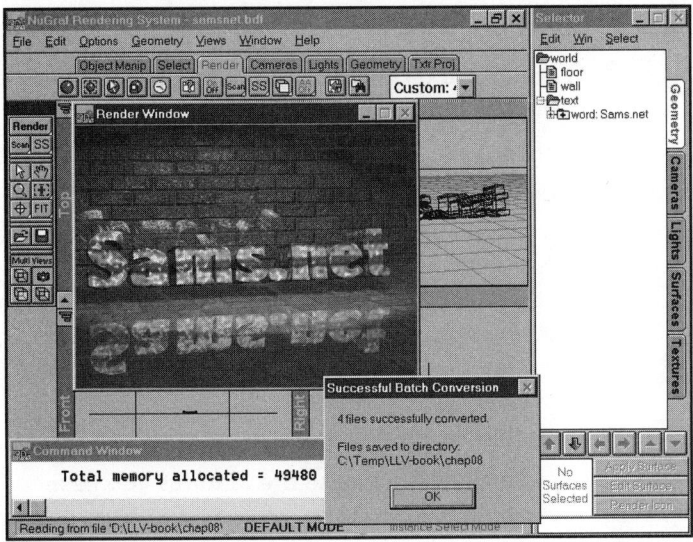

Workshop Wrap-up

The purpose of this chapter wasn't to scare you, but to show you the broad scope of technologies involved in working with 3D graphics. Every year there are new and better techniques introduced that make the process easier and push the envelope of what's possible.

Next Steps

So where do you go after learning about creating advanced rendered images? Actually, anywhere you want, but I would recommend the following:

❏ To make your advanced images move in a sophisticated way, check out Chapter 9, "Creating Advanced 3D Animations for the Web."

❏ Chapter 10, "Using Apple's QuickTime VR," covers an advanced technology for presenting panoramic views that update in real-time. It's not quite VRML, and not quite animation.

❏ A real-world example using many of these advanced techniques can be found in Chapter 12, "Real-Life Examples: Creating a MYST-like Adventure on the Web."

❏ Just beyond that is the VRML introduction in Chapter 13, "Exploring VRML Browsers and Development Tools."

Q&A

Q: If these technologies are changing so much, where can I go to find the latest technologies?

A: There are a variety of books, magazines, and resources on the Web that cover these issues. This book's CD-ROM has a resource guide to get you started.

Perhaps the best forum for keeping up on computer graphics is the annual Siggraph convention held early in the fall. Each year researchers, exhibitors, and artists gather for a week-long conference in which the latest and greatest in computer graphics are presented. If you're interested in computer graphics, don't miss this show. You can find information about the conference at `http://www.siggraph.org`.

Q: I really want to use the features you've mentioned in this chapter, like metaballs, particle systems, and terrain generators. Do I have to buy an entirely new product to get these features?

A: Luckily, you're not alone. Many good shareware programmers have grown weary waiting for the latest features to appear for their favorite modeler, so they've written shareware programs to use some of these features.

Examples of some of these shareware programs are on the CD-ROM. Check out Blob Sculptor for metaball functions and Landscape Maker by Kevin O'Toole for terrains.These tools and many others can be found at the Avalon site at `http://www.viewpoint.com/avalon`. Another good shareware tool is Exploder by Rob Bryerton, which creates particle systems for trueSpace. It can be found on the Caligari site at `http://www.caligari.com`.

Q: You've mentioned splines in this chapter, but I've heard there are different kinds of splines. Is this true?

A: Yes, there are a number of different types of splines, each with its own advantages. The major difference is in how you control the curvature. The mathematics behind the curves cause them to behave differently.

Bezier curves were one of the first types to show up in typefaces and drawing packages like CorelDRAW!. Another type you'll see in the CAD world is *NURBS*, which stands for "non-uniform rational b-spline." Some 3D packages are starting to use NURBS.

NINE

Creating Advanced 3D Animations for the Web

—by Kelly Murdock

During your last look at 3D animations, you covered camera fly-bys, animated models and textures, and keyframes. There are still many ways to enhance your animations, both inside and outside the 3D package. This chapter covers several of these advanced techniques:

❑ Creating animations by warping the surface of models
❑ Using motion blur to make your animations more realistic
❑ Using model constraints and behaviors to control the motion of your models
❑ Using rotoscoping to place video clips in your animation
❑ Creating advanced character animation with inverse kinematics
❑ Using particle systems to create special effects, like explosions and disintegrations
❑ Extending your 3D software with plug-ins, such as 3D Studio IPAS routines

In this chapter, you

❑ Warp the surface of models and use motion blur to create animations
❑ Control your models' motions
❑ Learn about rotoscoping and inverse kinematics
❑ Create special effects with particle systems
❑ Learn how to use plug-ins and video-editing packages
❑ Add post-production special effects to animations

Tasks in this chapter:

❑ Warping the Model's Surface
❑ Showing Relative Speed with Motion Blurs
❑ Using Constrained Animation and Behaviors
❑ Using Rotoscoping
❑ Character Animation Using Inverse Kinematics with Martin Hash's 3D Animation
❑ Using Particle Systems
❑ Combining Several Animation Sequences into One
❑ Adding Sound to Your Animations
❑ Adding Special Effects to Your 3D Animations

❏ Using video-editing packages, such as Adobe's Premiere, to edit your animations and add sound

❏ Adding post-production special effects to animations with products like Strata's MediaPaint

Once again, you'll be introduced to many different products to give you a well-rounded base from which to create.

Warping the Model's Surface

Animation shows how things change over time; it would be pretty boring to have an animation where nothing changes! Most of the time, things change by moving their position or orientation, but another type of movement is when the surface changes. Think of how the ocean surface changes. An animation of the beach scene wouldn't show the ocean model moving back and forth, but the ocean surface rippling along.

To animate surface movement, you create a deformation object or matrix that defines how the surface moves. You can then move the object through this deformation object or move it over the stationary object. Take a look at an example of how trueSpace does this:

1. Open the Primitives Panel and click the Add a Free Standing Pipe for Deformation button. A cylinder appears, along with the Deformation Nav panel that lets you move, rotate, and scale the deformation cylinder.

2. With the cylinder selected, the cursor is in Face Select mode. The light green lines indicate the faces. Click near any of the green lines and select one of the navigation buttons in the Deformation Nav panel. Clicking the Object tool changes the deformation object to light blue and allows you to move, rotate, and scale the deformation object, just as you do with other objects. When the cylinder is deselected, it turns orange. This helps you distinguish deformation objects from other models.

3. Next, load the model you want to deform. When the model is selected, the deformation object turns dark red. Select the Start Deforming by Stand Alone Deformation Object tool in the Model section of the toolbar. When the cursor changes to a glue bottle, click on the deformation object.

4. Click the Animation tool and set it to 30, then move the model through the deformation object. The model will distort to match the shape of the deformation object, which won't be seen in the final rendered image.

By using deformation objects, you can make objects move in different ways without going to the trouble of changing their surfaces. This works by moving the deformation object or moving the model. You can also use the Stop Deforming button, which makes the object unaffected by the deformation object. These two buttons together allow you to turn a deformation on and off as the animation progresses. In Figure 9.1, I've used a deformation object to bend a fish as it moves through the water.

Figure 9.1.

A fish moving through the water is distorted by means of a deformation object that makes it look like it's swimming.

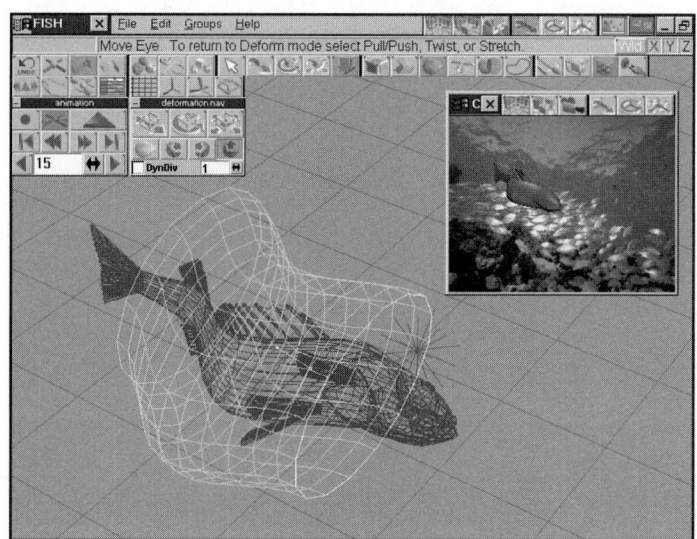

TASK

Showing Relative Speed with Motion Blurs

When a car goes speeding by and you catch it out of the corner of your eye, it looks like a blur whizzing past. *Motion blur* is an advanced animation technique in which you tell the computer to blur objects that are moving quickly in the scene. This blur helps you understand the speed of objects and adds to the movement's realism.

Creating motion blur in trueSpace is very simple. It's a render option that you specify when you render an animation. Here's an example:

The models for this example are all taken from the Viewpoint bundle included on the CD-ROM.

1. Set up your scene. If you plan on using motion blur, then you need to make sure there's some motion in your scene.

2. Set your keyframes to create your animation.

3. When you're ready to render the animation, click the Render to File icon in the View group. The Render to File dialog box will open.

4. Under the Resolution settings are three radio buttons: Motion Blur, Depth of Field, and Field Rendering. Turn motion blur on by clicking the On radio button.

NOTE: Field Rendering is how you set the focus of the rendered image. If you want the nearby and faraway objects blurred, then turn the Field Rendering effect on and change the setting to the focus distance you want.

5. To the right of the radio buttons are the settings. The Blur Length setting controls how long the blur is. The Blur/Depth Frames setting tells the computer how many sequential frames to use to create the blur effect. Click the Render button to start the rendering.

If you plan on using motion blur, then you really don't need to turn on anti-aliasing since the objects will be blurred.

TIP: To create a time-exposure effect, set the Blur Length setting equal to the total number of frames.

In Figure 9.2, one frame of a motion-blurred animation is shown. To really see the effect, you need to run the entire animation. Motion blur applies to all moving items, whether they are models, textures, lights, or reflections.

Figure 9.2.

In a classic animal versus machine race, motion blur is used to give the animation a realistic feel of motion. Any guesses on who wins?

Using Constrained Animation and Behaviors

Have you ever driven a car that suddenly left the road and floated above it, or thrown a ball into the air that never came down, or held a machine that suddenly fell into different parts? Controlling the movements of 3D objects can be difficult because they don't have to obey the laws of nature. That is, not unless you tell them to—that's where constrained motion and behaviors come in.

Constrained motion tells a model the limits of its motion—that it can move this far but no farther or rotate only halfway around. For example, you can make a head turn, but not turn all the way around. After all, it's not very realistic if your human figures have their heads on backwards. You can also link parts together so that they move in relation to one another.

With *defining behaviors*, you can, for example, tell your models to sit, roll over, and beg. By giving your models behaviors, they can interact with other models and the scene without being directed along every step. For example, if you give a ball a bounce behavior, then it automatically bounces off an object when it hits one. In the following example, Ray Dream Studio uses both constrained motion and defined behaviors:

1. Start with a model that requires constrained motion, such as a three-wheeled vehicle. Certain sections of the model, like the front and rear wheel assemblies, need to move together. Group all parts belonging to each of those groups into two different groups.

2. Next, select the Front Wheel Assembly group and bring up the Object Properties dialog box by choosing Edit I Object Properties. Click the Link tab; under this tab are all the different ways you can constrain motion in Ray Dream Studio. Select the Axis menu option, which allows rotation but not movement. Click the Z-axis option and set the rotate option to Limited. This lets the front wheel assembly rotate about 20 degrees in each direction.

NOTE: Here are the other types of constrained motion:

- ❏ **Lock**   locks the object to its parent
- ❏ **Slider**   allows movement along one axis
- ❏ **Axis**   lets an object rotate, but not move
- ❏ **Shaft**   allows movement and rotation along one axis
- ❏ **2D Plane**   lets the object move within a plane
- ❏ **Ball Joint**   allows an object to rotate all around a fixed point

There's also a custom setting for defining your own constraints.

3. Repeat the previous step for the Rear Wheel Assembly, but this time select the Axis link around the X-axis and let the object rotate freely. This option lets the back tires spin.

4. With the Object Properties dialog box still open for the Rear Wheel Assembly, click on the Behaviors tab. You'll see an empty box and four buttons. Click the Add button, and select the Spin behavior. Next, select the X-axis and set the speed to the desired movement per frame. In this example, I set the tires to rotate 10 degrees every frame. This causes the back wheels to rotate throughout the animation.

The constraint settings for each part can be seen in the Time Line window by clicking the green plus sign.

NOTE: Other behaviors include Point At, Bounce, Inverse Kinematics, Track, and Alignment.

With these settings, it becomes much easier to animate your models without worrying about parts flying away from the rest of the model. Behaviors can automate simpler motions to ease the animating process. Figure 9.3 shows the three-wheeler model with these settings.

Figure 9.3.

A three-wheeler model with constrained motion and behavior links for the front and rear wheel assemblies.

Behaviors will become very important when you get to VRML. One strength of the 2.0 specification is the ability to add behaviors to VRML models. Chapter 20, "Interfacing VRML Worlds with Script," covers adding behaviors by using JavaScript, and Chapter 21, "Using Java to Add Behaviors to VRML," shows you how to add behaviors using Java.

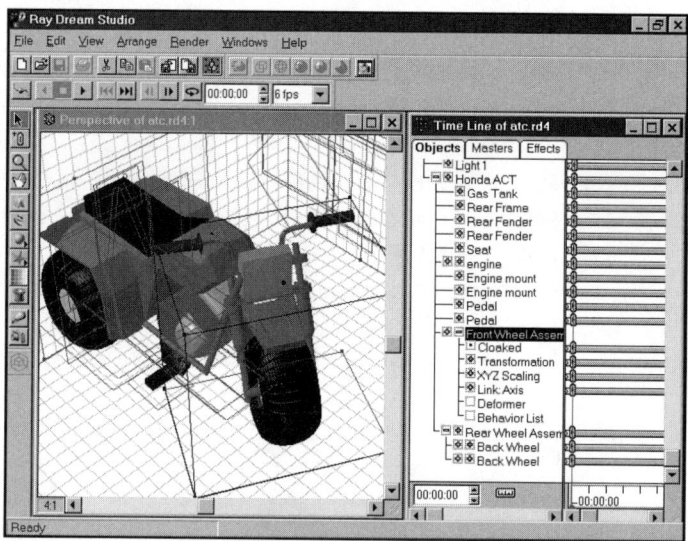

 # Using Rotoscoping

Imagine you want to animate a scene in which a simple 2D animation you've created is playing on a television screen in a 3D scene. The question is—would you have to re-create the simple 2D animation using 3D models, or is there some way to use the existing 2D animation? The answer is, you can use the existing 2D animation—with rotoscoping. *Rotoscoping* is the technique of adding 2D animations into a 3D scene.

Not only will rotoscoping work for the television example, but it's also useful as another way to animate textures. Think of the ocean example; you could rotoscope a simple repeating animation of waves to create a realistic ocean scene.

Rotoscoping isn't limited to models, either. Many packages let you rotoscope background images, which is useful for creating the sense of motion without having to move models. Look at how Ray Dream handles rotoscoping:

1. In the Shader Browser, select a Shader. Then choose the Shader I Duplicate menu option to create a copy of that Shader. Then double-click on the newly created Shader to load it into the Shader Editor dialog window.

2. Click the Color tab in the Shader Editor, then choose Components I Movie from the menu. A File dialog box opens, where you can select the movie file you want to rotoscope.

3. The movie is loaded into the Shader Editor, and several controls are made available that let you rotate the movie's orientation, set the tiling, and play the movie.

4. With the Shader set up, drag the new material onto the model or part that will display the movie, and you're done. The animation sequence includes this movie as the file is rendered.

The example in Figure 9.4 shows how rotoscoping displays an advertising message across a new line of furniture.

Figure 9.4.
Advertising a new furniture line with rotoscoping.

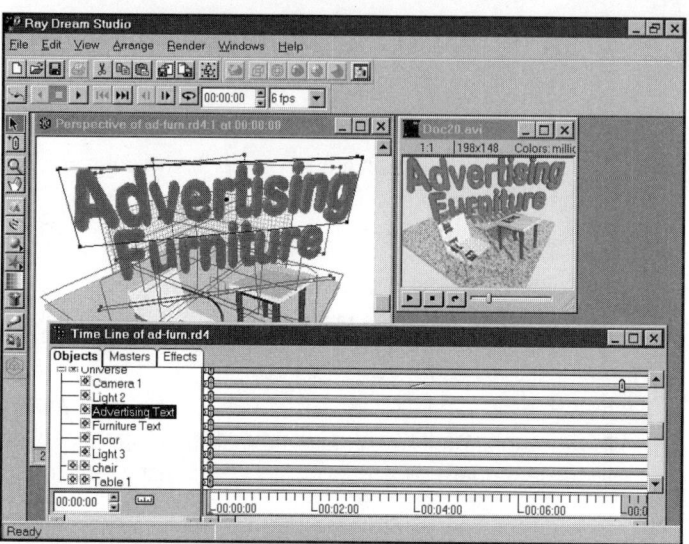

Character Animation Using Inverse Kinematics with Martin Hash's 3D Animation

Inverse kinematics is a buzzword in 3D graphics. A package that supports it can more easily animate complex systems of interrelated parts than a package that doesn't. The human body is an excellent example of a complex system of interrelated parts.

To make a human model do something as simple as walking, these are the steps you'd have to use in a 3D package without inverse kinematics: First move the body forward, then move the thigh forward, then the calf, then the foot, then the toes, then the toenails. Since the 3D package doesn't know the relationship between the different parts, each part has to move independently.

Kinematics helps define how these parts are connected. The connection helps determine how the parts move as a system; therefore, when the leg moves, the foot follows, and when the arm moves, the hand follows. Furthermore, you can apply constraints to these parts so that the system won't move in unnatural ways, like bending a knee backward (unless you're modeling an ostrich).

Any package that supports hierarchy structure has the advantage of kinematics; that is, child parts attached to a parent move along with the parent. The *inverse* part is where inverse kinematics differs. In packages supporting inverse kinematics, the child parts still understand the connections. This means you can pull a character's big toe and its leg will follow. Inverse kinematics makes it very easy to position animation keyframes.

Until recently, inverse kinematics was available only in high-end 3D packages, but now it's common to find it in low-end packages, such as Ray Dream Studio and Martin Hash's 3D Animation (MH3D). Take a look at how MH3D uses inverse kinematics to animate human characters:

Ray Dream Studio supports inverse kinematics, too.

1. Start by creating a new Choreography with the File I New Choreography command. In the dialog box that opens, give the new choreography a name and click OK.

2. The first things you need to add to your new scene are a camera and a light. Click the Add Mode button (or press the *A* key), then click in the Direction window to add a path to the scene. Next, click the Assign a Camera button. Add another path to the scene and click the Assign a Light button to add a light.

NOTE: The scene starts with a default light, camera, and camera target, but these can't be moved. Adding new elements replaces the default ones with ones you can move.

3. Add another path and click the Add a Figure button. A Figure dialog box opens for creating a new figure or selecting an existing figure. I selected the duck figure from the MH3D CD-ROM, as Figure 9.5 shows.

NOTE: The figure will probably be displayed in Bound mode, which makes it look like a group of boxes. This is the fastest draw mode. You can change the draw mode by opening the Attributes panel with the command Window I Attributes Panel. Under the Type box are buttons with a circle, a diamond, and a square—they represent the Curved, Vector, and Bound draw modes.

4. You can add more points to the path by clicking the Add Mode button and dragging the existing path control point to where the new point will be located. Repeat this process to add multiple path points. You can also add multiple path points to the light and camera paths, too. The Edit Mode tool (the arrow tool) lets you select and move individual path control points.

You can delete path control points by selecting the point and pressing the Delete key. For figures and lights, you can delete them by selecting the object and right-clicking its Assign button.

5. Paths control how objects move across the scene, but to move the model parts, you need to build motion scripts. Open the Script window by choosing Edit I Script, then click the Add button. Another dialog box opens where you can select an existing action or build a new one. Click the New button and give the new action a name.

6. This moves you into Skeletal mode. Move to the view on the right and select frame 3 as the current frame number, then drag the lower box representing one of the duck's feet and move it slightly forward. Next, advance the frame to frame 6 and return the feet together. Select frame 9 and move the other foot forward; at frame 12, return them to their starting position. This is inverse kinematics in action. You don't have to worry about moving the legs when positioning the feet. Try moving the wings and the torso around, too.

7. Close the Skeletal window and click through all the frames using the Go to Next Frame button in the upper-right corner (or press the + key). The figure will walk along the path performing the action you just built.

In Figure 9.5, you can see a frame of the duck waddling across the screen. Although this motion is simple, using inverse kinematics is invaluable when you're animating complex motions.

Figure 9.5.
A duck waddling across the screen, produced by using inverse kine-matics.

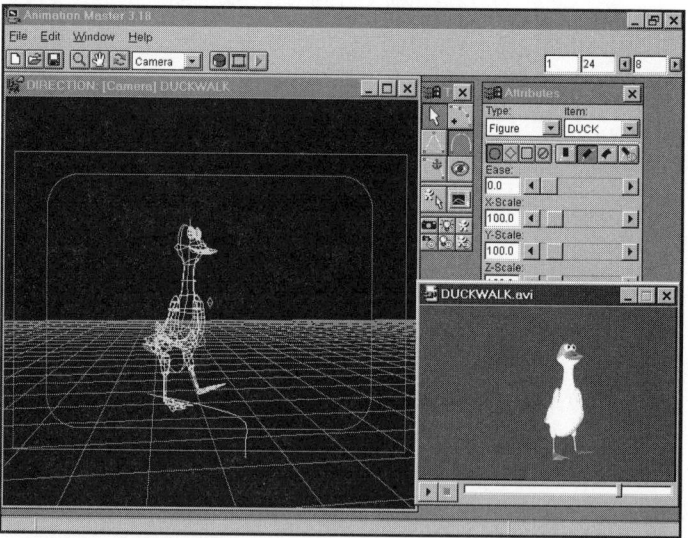

 # Using Particle Systems

Remember a few sections back when you learned how to use constrained motion to link objects together? Well, sometimes you don't want your models to be organized—

you might want to have parts fly off chaotically into millions of pieces. These millions of pieces are called *particles*, and when grouped together are known as a *particle system*. These particle systems can be controlled and given behaviors.

Three common types of particle system movements are shatter, explode, and atomize. These special effects are so common that some 3D packages have them built in, and the results are, well, chaotic.

In Studio Pro, these three particle motions can be used to create some spectacular effects, like the following:

1. Load a model into the Studio Pro workspace and manipulate it to the position where the animation will start.

2. Select a point on the model where the effect will start, then choose Animation I Special Effect I Atomize. This opens a dialog box where several control options are available.

3. The Atomize special effect converts the entire object into small spheres that jump and dance around the screen. In the Control dialog box, you can select the size of the spheres and their instability and energy, which affect how they move and the time for the entire animation.

4. Once you click the OK button in the Control dialog box, Studio Pro begins creating the animation script. These types of animation are quite complex and take some time and memory to complete. Some images from a bowling pin that was atomized are shown in Figure 9.6.

Figure 9.6.

Images from an animation of a bowling pin atomized in Studio Pro.

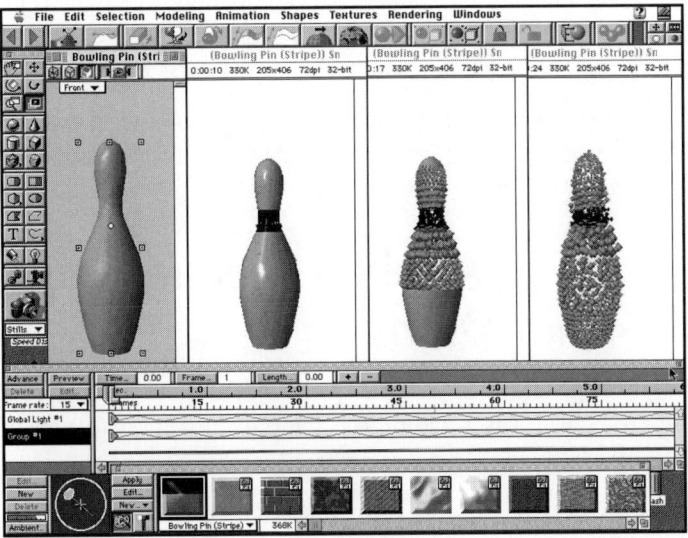

Watch out for out-of-memory errors when using particle systems. Typically, the program breaks simple objects up into hundreds of smaller objects, which can easily bog down even the best outfitted system.

Extending Your 3D Package with Plug-Ins

3D packages sometimes play leapfrog with features, so to get the latest effects and features, you often have to buy the newest product released. To stop this insanity, 3D packages are beginning to support plug-ins. This way, additional functions can be added to a package without buying a whole new version.

In much the same way that Netscape and Photoshop have added functionality to their core products, plug-ins can add special effects or streamline tedious tasks. Although it's a new concept for some 3D packages, others have used plug-ins for a while.

The king of these 3D package plug-ins is the granddaddy of 3D animation for the PC— 3D Studio. 3D Studio uses what are called *IPAS routines*, which exist as different programs that run in the 3D Studio environment.

NOTE: 3D Studio is made by Autodesk, the same people who make AutoCAD, a popular PC-based CAD package. Autodesk recently renamed its multimedia tools group and now calls it Kinetix.

There are several different types of IPAS routines available for 3D Studio; most of them are made by third-party vendors.

3D Studio isn't the only 3D package to support plug-ins. Lightwave and SoftImage also support plug-ins, and even Ray Dream Studio ships with an extension kit that helps third-party vendors build plug-in modules.

Because of the wide variety of plug-ins available, it wouldn't do justice to show one as an example. Over time, you can expect the more popular plug-ins to begin to show up within the actual program.

Using Adobe's Premiere to Edit 3D Animations

Remember in the last chapter how you used Photoshop to touch up some of your 3D images? You could do the same thing with animations if you edited each frame individually, but that would be a lot of work. A better solution is using a video-editing package like Adobe's Premiere; Adobe has created several great editing tools.

So what can you do with video-editing software? You can move the frames around and reorder them, you can add transitions, such as dissolves or fade-outs, and you can add sound to your animations.

Combining Several Animation Sequences into One

Most animations move the camera or objects consistently from start to finish. To produce an animation with several different viewpoints, you need to re-render each animation with a different camera selected. These different segments can then be combined into a single animation by using a video-editing package like Premiere. Take a look at how this is done for an accident reconstruction sequence:

1. Using trueSpace, re-create an accident and render several animations from different viewpoints. I rendered one from the air looking down on the accident, one from the truck driver's perspective, one from the car's perspective, and the last one from a witness's car at the scene.

2. Then, in Paint Shop Pro, make four images to introduce the animations, such as aerial view, truck view, car view, and witness view.

3. Open all four animations and all four text images in Premiere and drag them into the Construction Window in the first Video track. Make sure to align them so that the introduction image comes before its respective animation.

4. Open the Controller by selecting Windows | Controller and click the Play button to see the animation.

5. You can add transitions to the project by dragging them from the Transitions library into the Transitions track under the first Video track.

6. Finally, render the finished movie by selecting Make | Make Movie, and give it a name.

The CD-ROM shows the finished product, and Figure 9.7 shows the Premiere environment with the line-up compiled. There's a lot more you can do with Premiere, such as loading several animations and overlaying them. Before you leave Premiere, you'll look at another valuable addition that can liven up your 3D animations.

Figure 9.7.
An accident-reconstruction animation made from several single animations tied together with Premiere.

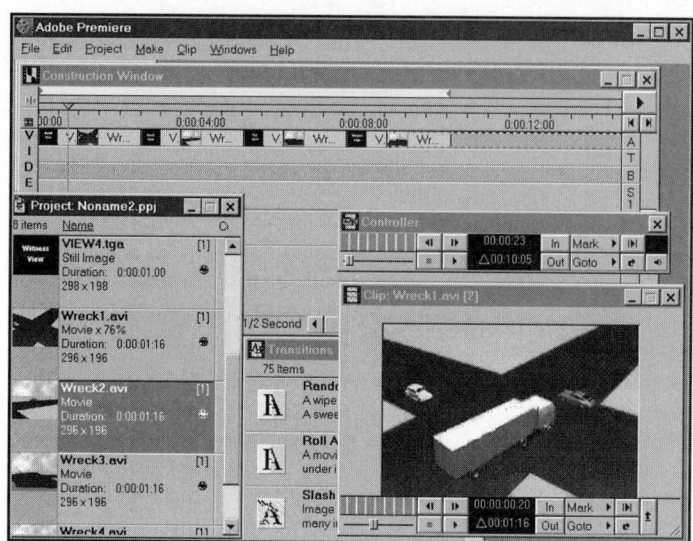

TASK Adding Sound to Your Animations

Adding sound to your animations is more of a requirement these days—nothing makes the experience more real than sound that's well synchronized with the action. Adding a sound track with Premiere is easy:

1. Open the sound file by using the File | Open command. The sound file shows up in the Project window with the other elements.

2. Drag the sound clip onto the Audio portion of the Construction window.

3. In the Construction window, you can move and drag the sound clip around to help synchronize it with the scene.

4. Create the movie with the Make | Make Movie command.

TIP: Because of the size that sound data takes up, limit all sound that will go on the Web to 11 KHz, 8-bit mono sound.

I'd show you the results of this example in a figure, but that wouldn't help much since it's an example of an animation with sound, so go to the CD-ROM to hear it.

 # Adding Special Effects to Your 3D Animations

Premiere lets you draw right on top of the individual frames, but similar packages are beginning to appear that allow you to add special effects like bubbles, fire, and lightning to your animations in what is called *post-production*, or the work done after the animation is rendered.

One such package is Strata's MediaPaint. The core product has functions much like an image-editing package, but add-in packages, such as Special Effects, Volume 1, can easily extend the features of the core product. This special effects pack lets you easily add otherwise difficult effects, such as bubbles, laser beams, fire, fireworks, lens flares, and lightning, among others. Now for an example.

CAUTION: MediaPaint requires that your computer be set to 24-bit true color mode for the program to work properly.

1. Load a pre-rendered animation into MediaPaint with the File | Open command. The first frame of the animation will show up in the Edit window, and the entire animation will be visible in the Filmstrip window.

2. Select a color from the Color Palette window and a brush size from the Brush area. Next, select an effect from the Tools window, such as BabyBoom.

3. Click the Record button in the Movie Controls panel. If this panel isn't visible, choose View | Movie Control Panel. A warning dialog box appears, telling you that you can't undo the operation. Click Proceed to continue.

4. With the Record button pressed, the frames automatically advance once you start to paint in the Edit window.

5. When you're finished, rewind the video and hit the Play button on the Movie Controls panel to see the results.

Adding special effects after an animation is complete offers you another way to enhance your 3D animations for your Web site. For this example, the sparks flying off the Apollo command module as it re-enters the atmosphere would have been difficult to create in a 3D package. Figure 9.8 shows the MediaPaint environment.

Figure 9.8.

Using Strata's MediaPaint to add special effects to your animation.

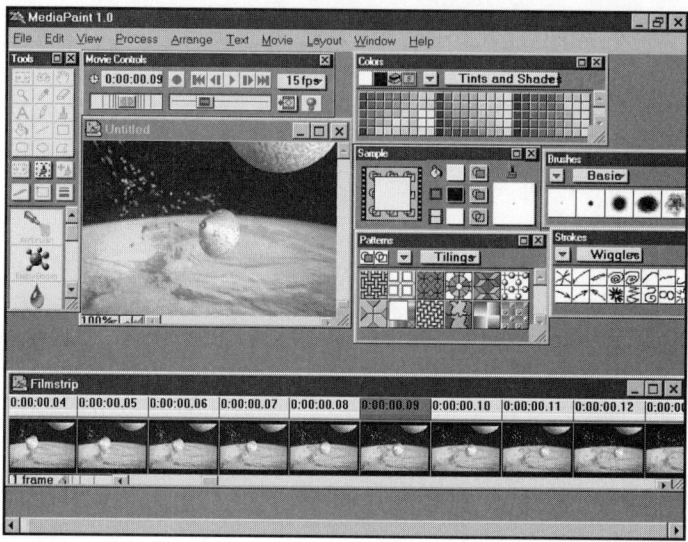

Workshop Wrap-up

You've now expanded on what you've already learned and have seen a sampling of what tools and technologies the real 3D pros use. To create that special scene you see in your mind's eye, you may need to use some of these advanced tricks to unfold your vision to the world. Not everything you need to be a professional 3D animator was covered, but at least now you know where to look.

Next Steps

So where do you go after learning about creating advanced rendered images? Well, anywhere you want actually, but I would recommend the following:

❑ The next chapter, Chapter 10, "Using Apple's QuickTime VR," moves you one step closer to the real-time 3D worlds with an interesting look at Apple's new technology.

❑ For a real-world example, skip over to Chapter 12, "Real-Life Examples: Creating a MYST-like Adventure on the Web."

❑ VRML is still coming up in Chapter 13, "Exploring VRML Browsers and Development Tools."

Q&A

Q: **I used constrained motion and behaviors to animate my models, but their motions still don't look very realistic. Is there any way to improve my models' motions?**

A: Most of the high-end 3D packages support motion capture data. *Motion capture* is the process of placing reflective tape or sensors on an actual person and recording the motions of these sensors as the person performs some motion. The recorded motions are recorded in a format that 3D packages can read. You then line up the points of motion data with your model, and the model is controlled by the motion data.

These systems for recording motion data are very expensive, but the resulting motions are extremely realistic. Viewpoint Datalabs also sells a limited number of motion capture datasets. Contact Viewpoint if you're interested.

Q: **I'm interested in the plug-ins that add more functions to your 3D package. Is it possible to create your own plug-ins?**

A: Several companies make their living from creating IPAS routines. Some of the more popular are 4Division, Pyros Partnership, The Yost Group, and Digimation. These teams have serious graphics programmers, and their products represent the state of the art.

If you're a programmer and would like to try your hand at creating plug-ins, contact the company that produced your 3D package and ask them about an SDK or software developer's kit. These kits have the information you need to begin building your own plug-ins.

Q: **I noticed that you covered video-editing packages as a means of editing 3D animations. Can these products be used to integrate real-life video with 3D-generated models?**

A: Yes, both Premiere and MediaPaint can be used to integrate real-life video with 3D-rendered models, scenes, and elements. Premiere does this by loading the 3D animation into one channel and the video into another, then marking how they overlay one another.

TEN

Using Apple's QuickTime VR

—by Kelly Murdock

In the chapters so far, you've seen a lot of image-creating techniques, from static images to dynamic animations. Before you're introduced to the promised land, where worlds update in real-time, it's time for a short field trip to look at a technology that falls somewhere in between.

Apple's QuickTime VR technology is an extension of their video technology, which enables users to rotate an object or spin about a panoramic scene. The view changes as you move the cursor about the scene, resulting in (for you, the viewer) a feeling of standing in one spot and panning your head back and forth (or even all the way around). How is this done? This chapter answers that question in detail, explaining the following topics:

- ❏ QuickTime VR—what it is and how it works
- ❏ Where to get images to use in creating a QuickTime VR environment
- ❏ How to combine several images to create a panoramic view by stitching images together
- ❏ How to use hotspots to link to other images, sounds, or scenes

In this chapter, you

- ❏ Learn about QuickTime VR
- ❏ Find out where to get images for a QuickTime VR Environment
- ❏ "Stitch".images together to create a panoramic view
- ❏ Learn how to use hotspots
- ❏ Use Studio Pro to render images for QuickTime VR movies
- ❏ Embed QuickTime VR files in your Web page

Tasks in this chapter:

- ❏ Using Strata's Studio Pro to Create Images for a QuickTime VR Scene
- ❏ How to Use QuickTime VR on Your Web Page

❏ How to use Strata's Studio Pro to render images to be used as QuickTime VR movies

❏ How QuickTime VR files can be embedded in your Web pages

Although QuickTime VR is somewhere between 3D graphics and VRML, it definitely can be considered as 3D graphics and it exists all over the Web, so it really belongs in this book.

QuickTime VR—What It Is and How It Works

Stop for a second and turn your head to the left. What do you see? Now look up. Is the view different? Unless you're in a padded room, your view changes as you move your head.

Now try picking up an object and turning it over. The object probably looks different from different angles. QuickTime VR takes images shot from several different positions and combines them to create a file that displays the correct view as you move around the scene.

There are actually two different types of QuickTime VR environments that you can create—panoramic movies and object movies. The first acts like a background and the second like an object you hold in your hand. These two environment types can be combined into one scene.

Apple's Look at 3D: Panoramic Style

Have you ever been so captivated by scenery on vacation that you tried to capture the panoramic view by taking several pictures while rotating? You were probably disappointed that those pictures, when placed side-by-side, didn't quite capture what you saw. QuickTime VR can capture the pictures and give you that panoramic view.

Many 3D packages enable you to render the file as a panoramic scene. This is a great advantage because it doesn't require the extra step of combining the images together.

To create the images, you can use a regular old 35mm film camera, a video camera, or any 3D RMA package. If you use a camera, a tripod helps line up the images. Simply take a picture and rotate the camera, then take another, and another, until you've captured a full revolution. Be sure to overlap the images so that the entire scene is captured without gaps.

You don't have to use a 3D RMA package to create QuickTime VR movies—a simple 3D rendering package would be enough. Any package that can rotate the view and render can be used.

Once you have the images, you need to digitize them into the computer. Users of 3D packages simply need to render and save the various images. Once all the images are ready, you can use the Dicer tool, part of the QuickTime VR Authoring Tools Suite, to stitch the images into a 360-degree environment. The results can be included on your Web page, like the one shown in Figure 10.1.

The QuickTime VR Authoring Tools Suite is currently available only for the Macintosh, but QuickTime VR runtime plug-ins are available for both Macintosh and Windows platforms.

Figure 10.1.

Lightscape created these 3D scenes as an example of QuickTime VR technology.

The view changes as you move the mouse around the image. The view can move left, right, up, or down. The Shift and Ctrl keys can be used to zoom into and out of a scene. Several views of the same room are shown in Figure 10.2.

Figure 10.2.
By moving the cursor to the left of the window, the view updates in real-time.

For more information on LightScape, visit their Web site at http://www.lightscape.com/.

Because QuickTime VR object movies are made from many different images, not all the images have to be identical. For example, the images that make up the back side of the object could have the text "Back Side" printed under them.

Apple's Look at 3D: Object Style

QuickTime VR objects can be manipulated and rotated by moving the mouse, much like picking up a cantaloupe in the supermarket and turning it over to check for soft spots.

To capture images as QuickTime VR objects, you need to capture pictures of the object from several angles—around, above, and below the object. The best way to do this is to take pictures, starting at the top of the object and continuing all the way around until you get back to the top. Repeat the process around the equator of the object.

Once you have photographed the images, use the Dicer tool to stitch them together. A sample QuickTime VR object can be seen in Figure 10.3.

Figure 10.3.

The View360 Web site has many QuickTime VR movies, including these two object movies of a speaker's internals and a Raiders football helmet.

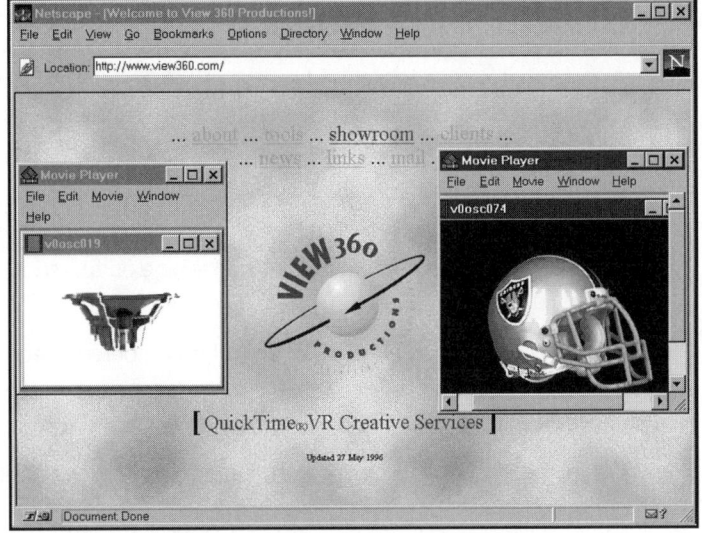

Moving QuickTime VR objects is very natural. The cursor changes to a hand and when the left mouse button is clicked, the object rotates in the direction you move the mouse. In Figure 10.4, the helmet spins to the left as you drag the cursor to the left, and it spins to the right as you drag the cursor to the right.

Figure 10.4.

This QuickTime VR object enables you to view this Raiders helmet from all angles.

Although QuickTime VR object movies can show objects at all angles, some object moves let you rotate around only one axis. Creating these types of object movies is much easier.

Stitching Images

A large majority of QuickTime VR scenes on the Web are made from photographs. However, as newer versions of 3D packages make it easier to output QuickTime VR scenes, you'll probably start to see more rendered movies.

A Dicer tool is based on the Macintosh Programming Workshop and used to stitch images together and compress the final file. It does this by matching the various features in adjacent images.

Many 3D packages offer panoramic rendering, which means you don't have to stitch images together. The final stitched image, or rendered image, is output as a simple PICT file. This file can be loaded into an image editor, such as Photoshop, for some touch-up work before you create the finished QuickTime VR movie.

Figure 10.5 shows an example of a finished rendered image. Notice how the lines in the images bend and warp. This is necessary to map correctly to the 360-degree environment.

When the image is loaded into the QuickTime viewer over the Web, the warp is removed, and the image appears as it would if you looked at it straight on.

Figure 10.5.
The top of this Web page shows the finished image before becoming a QuickTime VR movie.

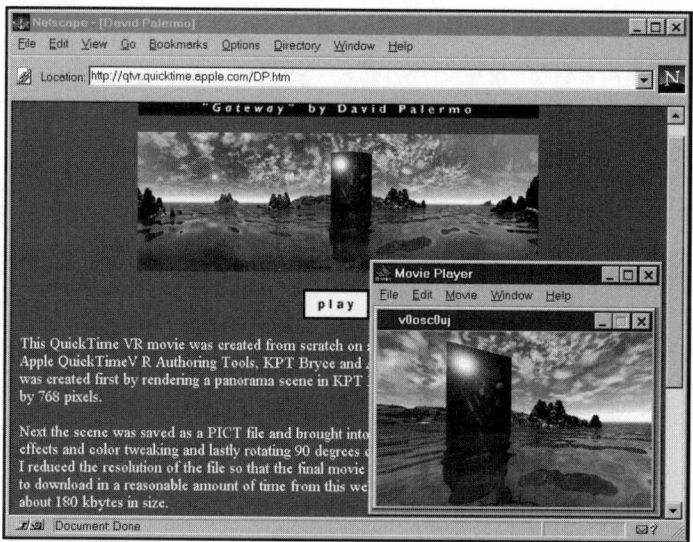

Building Hotspots

QuickTime VR also enables you to specify hotspots throughout the environment. These hotspots let you activate audio clips, display text or images, or even launch another QuickTime VR file. By using hotspots, you can build connected environments called *multi-node scenes*.

Within a scene, you can detect a hotspot by watching how the cursor changes. Double-clicking on such spots loads the associated file.

QuickTime VR 2.0

In May, Apple announced QuickTime VR 2.0, scheduled to be released in August. You can check Apple's QuickTime VR Web site for the latest information and information for developers:

```
http://qtvr.quicktime.apple.com/Home.htm
```

The 2.0 version adds the ability to program how QuickTime VR files play and are controlled. You'll be able to make composite images, such as 3D sprites, so that you can have 3D characters fly around QuickTime VR scenes with 3D sound. You'll also be able to add URL hotspots that link to other Web pages.

Using Strata's Studio Pro to Create Images for a QuickTime VR Scene

Because QuickTime VR authoring is presently available only on the Macintosh, the only 3D packages that offer support for QuickTime VR are Macintosh products. One such product is Strata's Studio Pro.

Strata produces several products, some of which are Windows products, to add special effects to animations. One is Media Paint, used in Chapter 9, "Creating Advanced 3D Animations for the Web."

Studio Pro is one of the first 3D RMA packages to include output options for QuickTime VR. It's a powerful piece of software. Though Studio Pro is currently available only on the Macintosh platform, Strata is working to have a Windows version out by the end of 1996.

One of Studio Pro's chief benefits is the ability to create scripts that automate certain functions. Included in Studio Pro is a scripted camera that creates images that can easily be made into QuickTime VR movies. The following steps show you how Studio Pro can be used to create a QuickTime VR object movie:

1. Start by opening Studio Pro and loading a prescripted camera called "Studio Pro QuickTime VR Object Camera" from the Stationary folder. This camera is programmed to render the object at every 10 degrees, producing 684 frames.

2. This scripted camera file places a cube in the center of the window defining the boundaries of the object movie. Place a model in the cube. Anything outside the cube isn't rendered.

3. Next, add any light sources you want to illuminate the scene and hide the cube by using the Edit I Select I Hide Selected command.

4. Finally, select the camera and open the Render Dialog Box with the Rendering I Render command. Give the file a name and choose QuickTime Movie File as the file format. Figure 10.6 shows the Studio Pro environment with a rendered basketball object file.

5. Studio Pro creates all the frames you need. To finish the process, you need to open the file in Apple's Navigable Movie Player, which is part of the QuickTime VR Authoring Tools Suite, and choose the Edit I Add Navigable Data command.

The basketball model was taken from the Strata Clip SetFree that ships with Studio Pro Blitz.

6. This command opens a Navigable Data dialog box. Select Object and 180 as the Field of View. Enter 19 for the Number of Rows, enter 36 for the Number of Columns, and click OK.

Figure 10.6.
Studio Pro can be used to create images for QuickTime VR object movies and panoramic scenes.

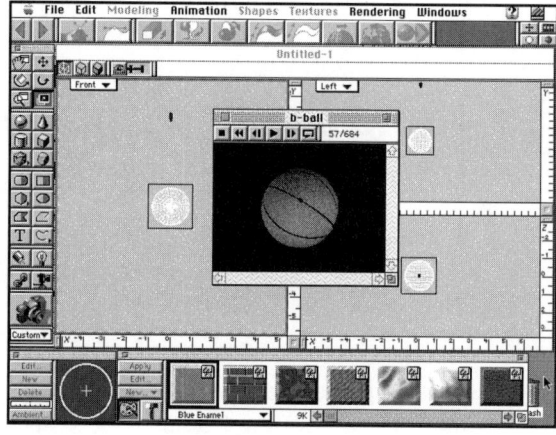

The resulting QuickTime VR object movie is ready to be displayed on your Web page.

Studio Pro also can output VRML files with the Save As command.

NOTE: Studio Pro also can be used to create QuickTime VR panoramic scenes. Select a camera. In the Render Dialog Box, choose QuickTime VR Panoramic as the Renderer setting and either QuickTime VR or QuickTime VR Large as the Size. The rendered PICT file can then be converted into a QuickTime VR movie with the Dicer tool.

 # How to Use QuickTime VR on Your Web Page

Once you've got the QuickTime VR file finished and you're ready to embed it into your HTML file, you'll need to get the QuickTime VR plug-in, available at the Apple QuickTime site:

`http://qtvr.quicktime.apple.com/Install.htm`

Apple has been working with Netscape to include the QuickTime video format within Navigator 3. With this feature, you don't need to download the QuickTime video plug-in.

1. You need to install the video format version of QuickTime first, available for both Windows and Macintosh.

2. Once QuickTime is installed on your system, download the QuickTime VR Player. This player is a plug-in for Netscape Navigator 2.0 or greater. There is no word yet on support for Microsoft's Internet Explorer. The plug-in file should be saved to your Windows directory.

3. You also need to set up a MIME type for the QuickTime files. Select Options | General Preferences, then select the Helpers tab.

4. Click the Create New Type button and enter `video` as the MIME type and `QuickTime` as the MIME subtype. Enter `MOV` and `QT` as the File Extensions, then select the Launch the Application radio button and browse to the PLAYER.EXE helper application, located in the C:\Windows directory.

5. The QuickTime VR Authoring Tools outputs your stitched image as a MOV file. These files can be loaded into the QuickTime helper application by using a standard `<A>` tag:

   `<A HREF="filename.mov"> QuickTime VR scene</A>`

When a Web surfer with the QuickTime VR plug-in installed comes to your site and clicks on this link, the file downloads and plays in the helper application.

CAUTION: The QuickTime VR file must download in its entirety before the movie can be viewed. This can take a long time for large files on computers with low bandwidth connections.

Workshop Wrap-up

This detour into Apple's technology has shown you a valuable technology. QuickTime VR is appearing on many commercial CD products and popping up all over the Web. A natural fit for 3D software packages, it represents yet another way you can display your 3D content on the Web.

Next Steps

Though you need to get back on the beaten path to continue your trip, this section, as always, offers the proverbial fork in the road:

❏ Chapter 11, "Using Microsoft's ActiveVRML," presents another technology. It's not the official VRML, but Microsoft's ActiveVRML adds several interesting capabilities.

❏ After a look at ActiveVRML, Chapter 12, "Real-Life Examples: Creating a MYST-like Adventure on the Web," wraps up this part with a real-life example that ties the advanced section together.

❏ Just beyond is the VRML world you've been waiting for. Skip over to Chapter 13, "Exploring VRML Browsers and Development Tools."

Q&A

Q: Is there any way to embed the QuickTime VR files right in my Web page without relying on a helper application?

A: Apple has teamed up with Netscape to build QuickTime functionality into Navigator 3. This will allow both QuickTime videos and QuickTime VR scenes to be displayed within Navigator without loading the helper application. You'll still need to download the QuickTime VR plug-in, however.

Q: I really like what QuickTime VR can do, but I'm running Microsoft's Internet Explorer browser. Is there any way to access QuickTime VR scenes in Internet Explorer?

A: There has been no official word on support for QuickTime VR for Internet Explorer from either Apple or Microsoft. However, as a helper application, you can set up Internet Explorer to load QuickTime VR programs, just as you would any other helper application. Using helper applications makes them independent of the browser.

You can assume that Microsoft or a third-party company will eventually create an ActiveX control to handle QuickTime VR scenes.

Q: Which 3D packages can I use to create QuickTime VR scenes?

A: Any 3D package that can render an image can be used to create images for a QuickTime VR scene. The QuickTime VR Authoring Tools Suite is required to create the actual file. If QuickTime VR continues its popularity, future versions of 3D packages might be able to produce QuickTime VR scenes directly.

The two packages that have been the tools of choice for working with QuickTime VR scenes are Strata's Studio Pro and Specular's Infini-D. Check out these two products if you plan on creating QuickTime VR scenes from 3D-rendered images.

ELEVEN

Using Microsoft's ActiveVRML

—by Kelly Murdock

Back when VRML 1.0 was starting to show its age, VRML creators decided they needed to start looking toward the future. Rather than going it alone, they decided to ask for proposals on what was to become the 2.0 specification. Well, the response was impressive. Many proposals were presented and discussed; after considerable debate, the Moving Worlds proposal put forward by Mitra, Sony, and SGI was chosen to form the basis of the 2.0 specification.

So what became of the other proposals? Portions were adopted into the 2.0 specification, and others just disappeared. Another proposal made by the people at Microsoft is unique, so it's still being developed. This proposal is known as ActiveVRML.

ActiveVRML scripts can be written using any basic text editor, just as you do with HTML. These scripts are then embedded in an HTML page as an ActiveX control. Because they are ActiveX controls, they aren't limited to just the Web. Any programming language that supports OCX libraries can use ActiveVRML components. ActiveVRML differs from traditional VRML in several distinct ways and is similar in many ways, including:

❏ ActiveVRML can import and control 2D bitmaps.
❏ ActiveVRML supports 2D sprites.
❏ ActiveVRML can detect and act on system events, such as mouse clicks.

In this chapter, you

❏ Use ActiveVRML to support and control 2D bitmaps
❏ Support 2D sprites with ActiveVRML
❏ Use ActiveVRML to import and manipulate 3D objects and worlds
❏ Attach sounds and add interactivity and behaviors to your worlds with ActiveVRML

Tasks in this chapter:

❏ Importing and Controlling 2D Bitmaps
❏ Repositioning 2D Images
❏ Dealing with Sprites and Sounds
❏ Adding Interactivity: Detecting System Events
❏ Working with 3D Elements in ActiveVRML
❏ Creating and Importing 3D Objects
❏ Attaching Spatial 3D Sounds to Objects
❏ Making a Color-Cycling Object
❏ Controlling Behaviors with System Events

❏ ActiveVRML can be used to import and manipulate 3D objects and worlds.

❏ ActiveVRML can attach sounds to objects to create 3D spatial sounds.

❏ ActiveVRML can add interactivity and behaviors to your worlds.

ActiveVRML is *not* the same as VRML 2.0. The basic technologies are different. Although you can create similar worlds in both, they differ in several areas, such as ActiveVRML's ability to handle 2D images. Start comparing them by taking a look at the 2D aspects of using ActiveVRML.

CAUTION: This chapter was written with the pre-beta version of
ActiveVRML, so it has some rough edges. This technology is still in development, but will be fully implemented for Microsoft's Internet Explorer 3.0 in the coming months.

You will notice that the figures for this chapter show the now-old Internet Explorer 2. At the time this chapter was written, ActiveVRML was still being developed. For the latest information on ActiveVRML, check the ActiveVRML Web site:

```
http://www.microsoft.com/developer/tech/internet/avr/avr.htm
```

Working with 2D Elements

ActiveVRML has a lot of power for dealing with multimedia elements. Although VRML defines 3D space, ActiveVRML can be used to create 3D worlds or to present 2D images. In this way, ActiveVRML can also be used to create multimedia presentations, something VRML 2.0 can't easily do.

 # Importing and Controlling 2D Bitmaps

Perhaps the most important multimedia elements are 2D images. ActiveVRML can import most of the standard image formats, as well as text. It can also manipulate these images by using standard programming algorithms. This is how it's done:

Some of the formats ActiveVRML supports are GIF, JPG, WRL, BMP, WAV, and AU.

1. ActiveVRML files have the AVR extension. The first line of an AVR file has the following comment line:

```
// ActiveVRML 1.0 ascii
```

NOTE: Placing two slash marks in front of a line marks the line as a comment, which means it will be ignored when the program runs. This first AVR line is an exception, however. The `//ActiveVRML 1.0 ascii` line must be included at the beginning of the program to identify the type of file to the browser.

2. Next, load the image file into a variable, such as `BackgroundImage`, with the following command:

```
BackgroundImage=first(import("clouds.jpg"));
```

The `import` command returns several values, including the image, the dimensions of the image, and the resolution. The first command indicates that you want only the first value returned, which is the image itself.

Variables can be created and modified on-the-fly without having to declare them. In this way, ActiveVRML is more like a scripting language than a programming language.

3. Now use the same command to load a foreground image, a transparent GIF file:

```
ForegroundImage=first(import("airplane.gif"));
```

4. Finally, use the `model` command to place the image on the page and the `over` command to determine which image is on top:

```
model= ForegroundImage over BackgroundImage;
```

5. To embed the AVR file into an HTML file, the following lines must be included with an HTML file. These lines embed the ActiveVRML file as an ActiveX control into the Internet Explorer browser:

```
<OBJECT
    CLASSID="uuid:{389C2960-3640-11CF-9294-00AA00B8A733}"
    ID="AVView"
    WIDTH=480 HEIGHT=480>
    <PARAM NAME="DataPath" VALUE="hello.avr">
    <PARAM NAME="Expression" VALUE="model">
    <PARAM NAME="Border" VALUE=FALSE>
</OBJECT>
```

The `<PARAM>` tags can be changed to alter the functionality of the ActiveX control. See the documentation for options.

The resulting Web page is shown in Figure 11.1.

Figure 11.1.
Your first ActiveVRML creation shows a GIF image overlaid on a JPG image of clouds.

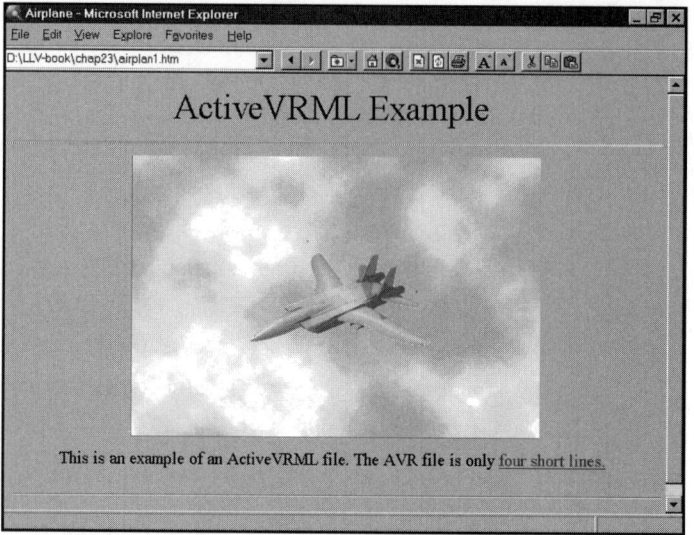

TASK Repositioning 2D Images

Now that you know how to place images on the screen, it's time to learn how you manipulate them. If the image doesn't show up just right, do you have to go back to an image-editing program and change it? The answer is no. In ActiveVRML, you can transform the image to a new location, like this:

1. To rotate the background image, use the `Rotate2` command:

   ```
   RotatedBackgroundImage=transformImage(rotate2(0.5),BackgroundImage);
   ```

   The `2` at the end of the `Rotate2` command tells the browser that it's a 2D command.

Rotation angles in VRML need to be in radians, and 360 degrees equals 2Π radians. Therefore, one degree equals about 0.017 radians, and one radian equals about 57.3 degrees.

CAUTION: ActiveVRML scripts are case-sensitive, so follow the syntax exactly. For example, the command `TransformImage`, instead of `transformImage`, in the previous line would give you an error.

2. You can also scale the airplane image like this:

   ```
   ScaledForegroundImage= transformImage(scale2(0.5),ForegroundImage);
   ```

3. The complete ActiveVRML script would look like this:

   ```
   // ActiveVRML 1.0 ascii
   BackgroundImage=first(import("clouds.jpg"));
   ForegroundImage=first(import("airplane.gif"));
   RotatedBackgroundImage=transformImage(rotate2(0.5),BackgroundImage);
   ScaledForegroundImage= transformImage(scale2(0.5),ForegroundImage);
   model= ScaledForegroundImage over RotatedBackgroundImage;
   ```

4. Save the file as an AVR file and embed it in your HTML file the same way you've done before.

Figure 11.2 shows the results of scaling and rotating the images. There are many other image-manipulation commands in ActiveVRML, such as translate, crop, and tile.

Figure 11.2.

The jet fighter once again, this time scaled to twice its size.

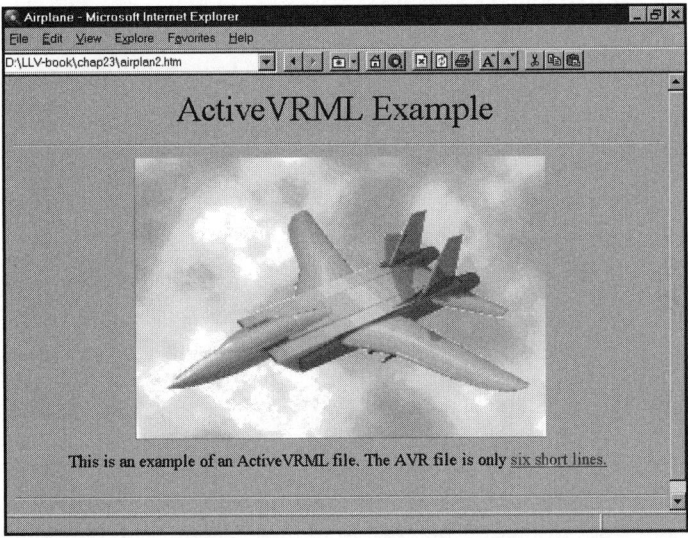

Dealing with Sprites and Sounds

Now you have images placed on top of one another. The airplane in Figure 11.2 just begs to move around the screen. *Sprites* are just that: 2D images that move around the screen. While you're at it, add sound to the file:

1. In ActiveVRML, there's a time element, with the fortunate property of increasing steadily, that can be used to animate your sprites. After loading your images, introduce the time element into a variable called `movement`:

   ```
   movement=time*0.01;
   ```

2. Now use the `movement` variable to move across the screen:

   ```
   Flying=translate(movement,0);
   ```

   Translate requires two numbers, one for the X direction and one for the Y. By leaving the Y set to `0`, you're telling the program you want movement only in the X, or horizontal, direction.

3. Now tell the script which image the translation should be performed on:

   ```
   FlyingForegroundImage=transformImage(Flying,ScaledForegroundImage);
   ```

Here you can see that variables don't always have to contain media types. The `Flying` variable can now be altered as needed. For example, to double the plane's speed, just use this line:

```
DoubleSpeed=
Flying*2;
```

4. Finally, use the `model` command to show the images on the screen:

```
model=FlyingForegroundImage over RotatedBackgroundImage;
```

After embedding the script and viewing the HTML file, you can see the plane moving to the right and off the screen. But what about the sound?

5. Sound is easy. First, load the sound file, just as you did for the images, then use the `union` command for the additional sound. The `union` command should come directly after the `model` command:

```
AirplaneSound=first(import("motor.wav"));
. . .
model=FlyingForegroundImage over RotatedBackgroundImage
  union loop(AirplaneSound);
```

TIP:
Notice how the `union` command is joined to the `model` command. Each ActiveVRML file can only have one `model` command. The `union` command can extend the single `model` command, but a semicolon should appear only after the final `union` statement.

Figure 11.3 shows the airplane flying backward off the right side of the screen. Now that you have images moving around the scene, take a look at the one thing that will separate this technology from the standard Web fare—interactivity.

Figure 11.3.
Here's the ActiveVRML airplane flying off the right side of the screen.

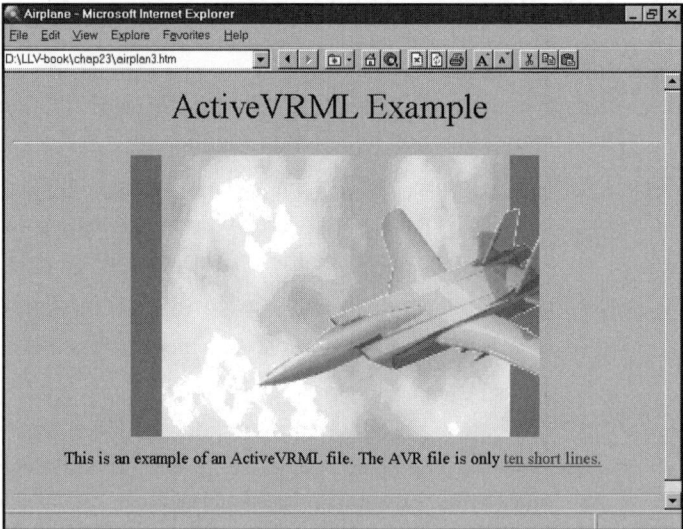

Adding Interactivity: Detecting System Events

ActiveVRML can detect and react to system events, such as keystrokes or mouse clicks. Detecting such events is essential when you're creating multimedia applications. So how do these system events work?

1. Start by loading a couple of images, one of Jack and another of Jumping Jack:

   ```
   Jack1=first(import("jack1.jpg"));
   Jack2=first(import("jack2.jpg"));
   ```

2. Next, overlay some text telling the user how to make Jack jump by using the `renderedText` and `simpleText` commands:

   ```
   JackText=first(renderedText(simpleText("Click to make Jack jump.")));
   ```

   The `simpleText` command loads a text string, and the `renderedText` command converts the text string into an image.

3. Then combine the images of Jack with the text:

   ```
   JackState1= JackText over Jack1;
   JackState2= JackText over Jack2;
   ```

4. Close the program with a check for the `leftButtonDown` system event; if the event takes place, you move to JackState2. If the event is triggered a second time, then you return to JackState1.

   ```
   model=JackState1 until leftButtonDown => (JackState2 until
   ➥leftButtonDown => JackState1);
   ```

Figure 11.4 shows one of the Jack states. Another common system event is the `keyboardButtonPress` command, which is triggered when a key on the keyboard is pressed.

ActiveVRML deals with images, so any text used in a scene must be converted to an image with the `renderedText` command to be seen.

Figure 11.4.
Jumping Jack getting ready to jump. When a user clicks on the window, another image of Jack jumping loads.

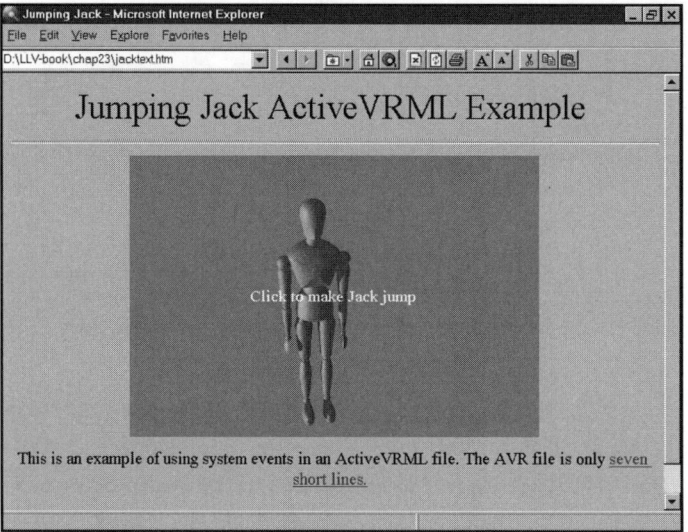

Working with 3D Elements in ActiveVRML

When moving into the 3D world from the 2D world, many of the commands change only by getting a third value to represent the Z axis. However, there's so much more to the 3D world than just adding another direction. It's a whole new way of looking at objects. The 3D world involves more than just images moving in front of the screen. The object's location in space is known and can be controlled. For example, 3D sound can be heard even if the object isn't visible (if it's behind the camera, for instance).

TIP: Certain commands, such as `rotate2`, become `rotate3` when you're using 3D objects. The `rotate3` command takes input for all three axes.

Creating and Importing 3D Objects

When you started learning about 3D models back in Chapter 4, "Creating and Embedding Rendered Images," you began with primitives. When you get to VRML 2.0 in a couple of chapters, you'll see primitives again. However, in ActiveVRML there aren't any primitives to start with, but you can import existing VRML 1.0 models and scenes.

When ActiveVRML detects a VRML scene, it automatically presents some navigation options. As you move the cursor around the screen, it changes to an arrow. Clicking and dragging the button moves the scene in the direction of the arrow. When the cursor is in the center of the screen, it changes to crosshairs. By clicking on these crosshairs, you can rotate the object around.

Once a VRML object is loaded, you can define its color, textures, lights, and movements, as you'll see in this example:

In the lower-right corner of a 3D ActiveVRML world is a control that lets you toggle between Object and Walk mode.

1. Using the standard `import` command, you can import VRML 1.0 worlds and objects:

   ```
   Soda=first(import("soda.wrl"));
   ```

2. With the VRML object imported, you can then control all the attributes of the object, such as material properties:

   ```
   SodaCan= diffuseColor(colorRgb(255, 0, 0), Soda)
   ```

   This paints the soda can red with a diffuse color setting. Other available color settings include ambient, specular, and emissive attributes. The diffuse setting doesn't glow like the emissive attribute; that's why the can in Figure 11.5 looks black instead of red.

   # TIP:
   ActiveVRML has several primary colors built into the language that don't need to be specified as values. They include red, green, blue, cyan, magenta, yellow, white, and black.

   Another way to add materials to your objects is to use the `texture` command to wrap 2D images around your models:

   ```
   Soda= first(import("soda.wrl"));
   SodaMap= first(import("textureMap.jpg"));
   SodaCan= texture(SodaMap, Soda);
   ```

3. Next, reposition the soda can and give it some movement. With the `transformGeometry` command, you can combine several positioning commands into one line. The `o` is a concatenation operator that links commands.

   ```
   SpinningCan= transformGeometry(translate(0,-1.5,0) o
      scale3(0.5) o rotate(yVector3,time*0.1),SodaCan);
   ```

4. Now you're ready to use the `model` command, but how about a little light on the subject? ActiveVRML can specify four types of lights: ambient, directional, point, and spot. Illuminate your 3D scene with the `directionalLight` command:

Lights have additional parameters for controlling their brightness, color, and falloff rate.

   ```
   model= SpinningCan
      union directionalLight;
   ```

The `union` command combines the light effect with the rest of the scene.

Figure 11.5 shows the VRML model. The can is slowly rotating around the Y axis. There are many more commands you could use to enhance this scene, such as placing cameras and adding the ability to select objects.

Figure 11.5.
In ActiveVRML, you can view this soda can from any angle.

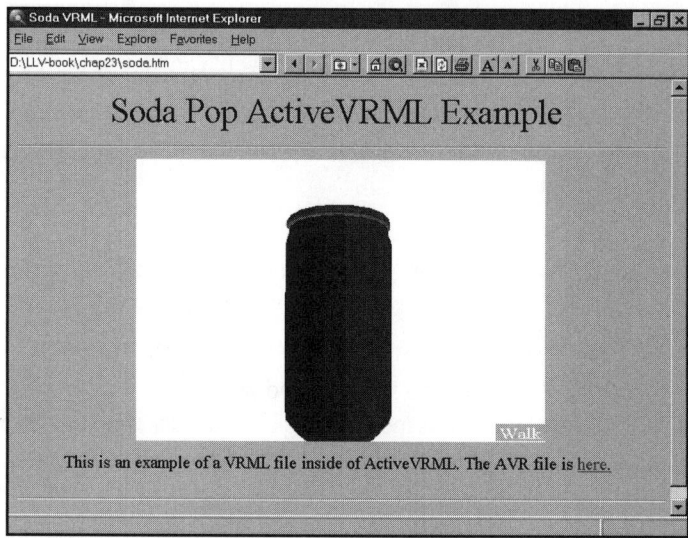

TASK Attaching Spatial 3D Sound to Objects

When 3D sound is attached to an object, as the user approaches the object in 3D space, the sound gets louder; as the user moves away, the sound gets fainter. Any object in the scene can get its own sound.

1. First load your VRML object and a sound. This time you'll use a toy jack:

```
Jack=first(import("jack.wrl"));
JackSound=first(import("whirl.wav"));
```

2. Then apply materials (this time, you'll use blue) and perform the transformation on the object. You want the jack to spin as the soda can did in the previous example.

```
BlueJack=diffuseColor(colorRgb(0, 0, 255), Jack);
SpinningJack= transformGeometry(scale3(0.1) o
   rotate(yVector3,time*0.1),BlueJack);
```

You could have replaced the `diffuseColor` (`colorRgb(0, 0, 255)`) command with the single word `blue` since it's a defined color, but leaving it in this form makes it easy to go back later and change the color.

3. To introduce the spatialized sound, simply use the `union` statement to join the sound to the model with the `soundSource` command:

```
model= SpinningJack
    union directionalLight
    union soundSource(loop(JackSound));
```

Several options can be joined to the `model` command with a `union` statement. Here you see lights and sound added; the `loop` command makes the sound continuous.

That's it. Now as you move around the world, the sound changes depending on your distance from the 3D object. Take a look at the scene in Figure 11.6.

Figure 11.6.

The toy jack spins around the scene; the sound associated with the model changes volume as you get closer or farther away from the object.

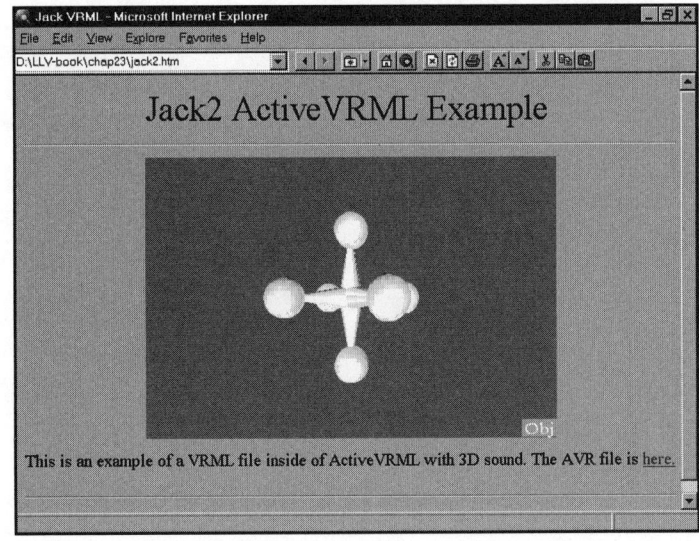

Object Behaviors

The `rotate` command covered previously is an example of a behavior. Behaviors can be instilled in objects that perform actions and respond to events. Because ActiveVRML has the mathematical capabilities of a programming language, you can outfit objects with complex behaviors. Take a brief look at two behaviors that manipulate color.

Making a Color-Cycling Object

One behavior that's easy to use is *color cycling*. This behavior simply changes the color of the object over time.

1. Start by loading an object; any 2D or 3D object will work:

   ```
   Star=first(import("star.wrl"));
   ```

2. Then introduce the color of the star as a result of time:

   ```
   SparkleStar= emissiveColor(colorRgb(time,time*2,time/3),Star);
   ```

3. Finally, model the star with the color-cycling behavior:

   ```
   Model SparkleStar;
   ```

This is a simple example for a simple behavior. Figure 11.7 shows how it looks on the page.

Figure 11.7.
The star object has the behavior of changing its color over time.

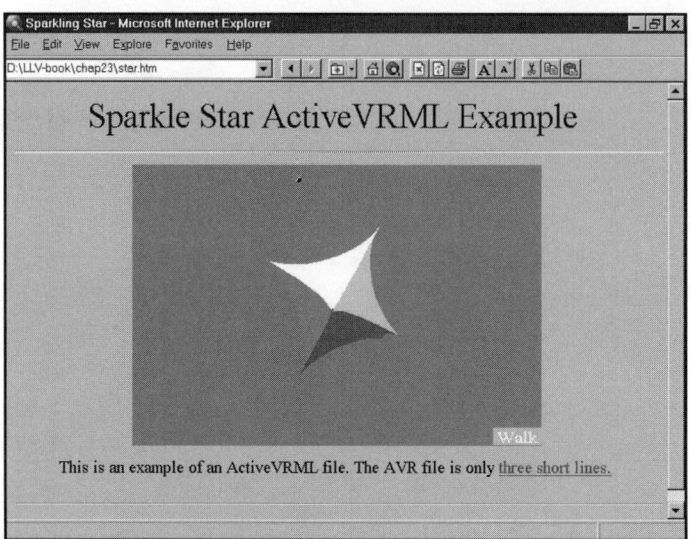

 **Controlling Behaviors with System Events**

Once you have behaviors built into your objects, you can control them with system events. In this way, users can turn certain behaviors on or off whenever they want. Look at an example of how an object's color can be controlled by a mouse click:

1. Working from the same star object used in the last example, simply add a system event check that changes the object's color when the left mouse button is clicked:

   ```
   ColorStar= diffuseColor(red until leftButtonDown => green,Star);
   ```

2. This new object is then modeled, along with a light command:

   ```
   model= ColorStar union directionalLight;
   ```

These sample behaviors are very simple, but they demonstrate how ActiveVRML can be used to make scenes interactive.

Workshop Wrap-up

Although the VRML Architecture Group has decided that the Moving Worlds specification is recognized as VRML 2.0, Microsoft is still supporting its proposal as a way of creating multimedia content and VRML worlds on the Web.

Next Steps

I hope ActiveVRML has whet your appetite for the real VRML, or maybe you're confused because there really weren't enough pages to cover ActiveVRML in depth. In either case, many of the chapters ahead will get you into the nitty-gritty of VRML 2.0:

- ❏ Before getting to VRML, this part concludes with a real-life workshop in Chapter 12, "Real-Life Examples: Creating a MYST-like Adventure on the Web."
- ❏ Chapter 13 starts off the whole VRML section with "Exploring VRML Browsers and Development Tools."
- ❏ To see a real-world use of VRML, jump over to Chapter 17, "Real-Life Examples: The VRML Art Gallery: A VRML World by Hand."
- ❏ To learn some more tricks to make your VRML worlds run more quickly and smoothly, check out Chapter 18, "Tricks to Optimize Your VRML Worlds for the Web."

Q&A

Q: I understand that this chapter was completed using the pre-beta release of ActiveVRML. When will a beta version be available?

A: This pre-beta version was used as part of the proposal Microsoft made to the VRML Architecture Group. Since its creation, the Microsoft team has re-evaluated ActiveVRML's position. Microsoft has been working on a beta release that will build on ActiveVRML's strong points while fulfilling Microsoft's goal for the technology.

Although there hasn't been any formal announcement, Microsoft plans to release a beta version about the same time the VRML 2.0 specification is ratified.

Q: If this book is about VRML 2.0, why is Microsoft's ActiveVRML even being covered?

A: Although ActiveVRML wasn't chosen to become the VRML 2.0 specification, the technology has much to offer, and Microsoft has the resources to develop ActiveVRML in a way that few companies can.

I believe that, in time, ActiveVRML will distinguish itself from the 2.0 specification and offer a simple solution for creating and publishing multimedia presentations and VRML worlds on the Web.

Q: Microsoft has a lot of different programming languages. How does this one differ from its other languages?

A: The goal of VRML is to create 3D worlds that will be available on the Web. To do this, the VRML specification was created. Microsoft believes that VRML 2.0 will be too complicated for most Web users to work with, so it's continuing to develop ActiveVRML as an alternative.

ActiveVRML is a programming language, but it's simple to use and effective for creating VRML worlds and multimedia pages.

Another distinct advantage of ActiveVRML is that it will integrate with Microsoft's other languages as an ActiveX control. This advantage gives developers a unique tool for creating VRML worlds that integrate seamlessly with other development tools, such as VBScript.

TWELVE

Creating a MYST-like Adventure on the Web

—by Kelly Murdock

It's time to put the skills you've gained in this part of the book to practical use. To conclude Part III, "Advanced 3D Graphics on the Web," you'll apply the techniques you've learned to create an interactive Web adventure. This is what you'll need to do to pull it off:

❑ Build a storyboard to get an organized look at how the adventure will progress.

❑ Use the 3D package techniques you've learned throughout this part of the book to create the images for the adventure.

❑ Create Web pages with the necessary links.

❑ Enhance the adventure with embedded animations and other 3D elements.

In this chapter, you

❑ Learn how to build a storyboard

❑ Create images for the adventure with 3D package techniques

❑ Create Web pages with links

❑ Embed animations and 3D elements to enhance the adventure

Tasks in this chapter:

❑ Storyboarding the Volcano Treasure Adventure

❑ Creating the Images

❑ Building the Web Links

❑ Enhancing the Web Pages with 3D Elements

Because there's no new techniques to present, you can move pretty swiftly through this example. The real test is to actually experience the adventure, which can be found on the book's CD-ROM. Forward all—adventure awaits!

Step 1: Storyboarding the Volcano Treasure Adventure

Because of its popularity, you have no doubt seen and probably played the game MYST. Robin and Rand Miller, the creators of MYST, didn't just throw together a bunch of cool-looking pictures to produce a major hit. They started with a detailed plan and story. It was the story that pulled you in and made the game so popular.

For this adventure, too, you need to start with a plan. When the plan for unfolding the adventure scene-by-scene is illustrated, it's called a *storyboard*, a tool often used by directors of movies and commercials. Storyboards often end up resembling complicated flowcharts.

Software for creating storyboards is available, but it's expensive. The easiest way to create storyboards for Web projects is to just get out a pen and paper and start drawing.

I created the storyboard for this adventure by sketching the images, then connecting them with lines showing which images were attached to each other through links. Part of the finished storyboard is shown in Figure 12.1.

Figure 12.1.
Part of the Volcano Treasure Adventure storyboard.

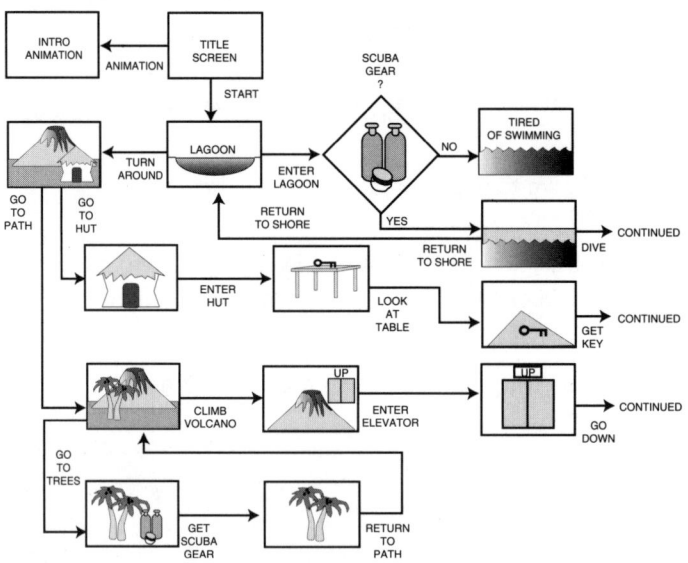

The buttons at the bottom of each scene are the links that move you through the adventure. By making the correct decisions, you move through the adventure until you finally enjoy the spoils of the treasure.

Step 2: Creating the Images

The Miller brothers used Strata's StudioPro for their breathtaking images. A demo of StudioPro can be found on the book's CD-ROM, but you'll use several different tools that you've worked with already in this book. You'll also get some help from other supporting products.

The bulk of the work is in setting up the scene. Because the scene would be too big to handle as only one scene, I broke the adventure down into several scenes:

- ❏ **Island scene**   This is the largest scene, where all the island shots are taken.
- ❏ **Volcano Interior scene**   This is a simple scene showing the volcano's origin; an elevator provides access to the interior of the volcano.
- ❏ **Undersea scene**   Being underwater introduces some interesting challenges with lights.
- ❏ **Treasure Cave scene**   A closed environment where lots of lights are needed to give the treasure a glow.
- ❏ **Hut Interior scene**   A simple mapped image shows the landscape outside the window.

Once the scenes looked right, I started capturing the individual images by moving a camera around the scene and rendering the images to file as JPG images. A few of the images can be seen in Figure 12.2.

There's an assortment of models in these scenes. Some were borrowed from collections, like the palm trees; others were modified from existing models, like the island and the hut; and others, like the elevator and the key, were created from scratch.

Figure 12.2.
Rendered 3D images taken from the Volcano Treasure Adventure.

Step 3: Building the Web Links

With high-resolution 3D images, the file sizes will be fairly large. To make the adventure's file size reasonable, you should eliminate what's not needed. My Web pages for this adventure weigh in at about 50KB per scene. That's 45KB for a highly compressed JPEG image, 5KB for each button, and about 1KB for the HTML page.

Once you have all the images, you need to build the Web pages to display them on. The Web pages should use an unobtrusive interface that doesn't detract from the adventure's look and feel. Also, you don't want to increase your file size with unnecessary elements.

The first element to consider is the background image. Since the images are quite detailed, you don't want the background to steal any of the thunder. That's why I opted for a simple colored background, but I changed the color depending on the location in the adventure. Therefore, a light blue background is used for the undersea portion, tan for the island images, and fiery red for the volcano section, as Figure 12.3 shows.

Figure 12.3.

Descending into the volcano pit during the Volcano Treasure Adventure.

The next elements to consider are the user interface buttons. The navigation buttons underneath the image represent choices you can make based on the image. They are clearly marked and, coupled with the image, make it clear where each choice leads you.

The images tell the main story, but some text pages are used occasionally to fill in the gaps. The story text isn't really necessary and is added just to enhance the adventure. I designed the interface so that a text page can fit on one 800 × 600 resolution screen without any scrolling required.

Another way to navigate through the adventure is to use image maps. Within the adventure is a scroll item you can use to hyperjump to different parts of the island. This shows another navigation method, as shown in Figure 12.4.

Figure 12.4.

Use the overview image map to navigate in the adventure.

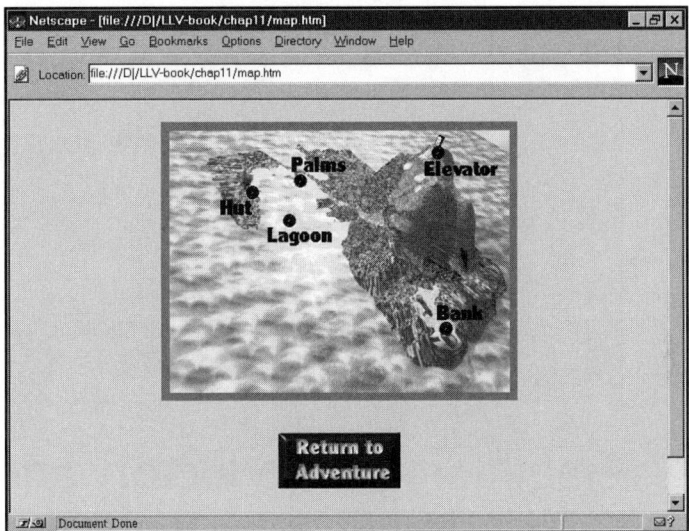

With the interface fixed, you can work on enhancing the page with additional elements, such as a title page and animations.

Step 4: Enhancing the Web Pages with 3D Elements

The tough work is done, but there are subtle ways to enhance the experience. The home page should have a unique look with a 3D title. After that, you can spice up the adventure with some 3D animations, but place the animations out of the normal Web path so that viewers who don't have the correct plug-ins won't get frustrated.

The Title Page

Title creation is easier than creating the images you just finished. I used some 2D tools to touch up the title page, shown in Figure 12.5. You'll notice that since this figure is reproduced in black and white, the effects used for the letters don't show up that well. For example, to see the "lava" texture map used on the word *Volcano* and the swirled jungle leaves on the background, check out the Adventure on the CD-ROM to see the title screen in all its glory. Notice how a thumbnail image shows a scene from the introductory animation.

Figure 12.5.
Title page for the Volcano Treasure Adventure.

It's common courtesy to explain on the title page what's required in the way of plug-ins and what kind of download time visitors are facing.

Embedding Introductory and Conclusion Shockwave Animations

Animations can add a great deal to your adventure. They can give visitors a sense of how the entire island fits together. I can see two logical places where animations would help. One is at the start to introduce the adventure and convince visitors to take the time to participate. The second one is a final animation at the end of the adventure, where an animation can be a reward for finishing the adventure. Creating the animations is really quite easy once the scene is set up. All you have to do is to plan the motions.

Make sure your visitors know what they're getting before they go through the download process. Thumbnails are a good peek at the animation. I used the Shockwave plug-in to handle the animation sequence because it's widely available and provides probably the best playback quality. GIF animations and streaming animations can be choppy because their playback quality is influenced by Internet traffic. Shockwave, on the other hand, downloads the entire sequence before playing the animation. Frames from the introductory animation are shown in Figure 12.6.

Figure 12.6.

This animation is located at the beginning of the adventure and gives visitors a look at the island from above.

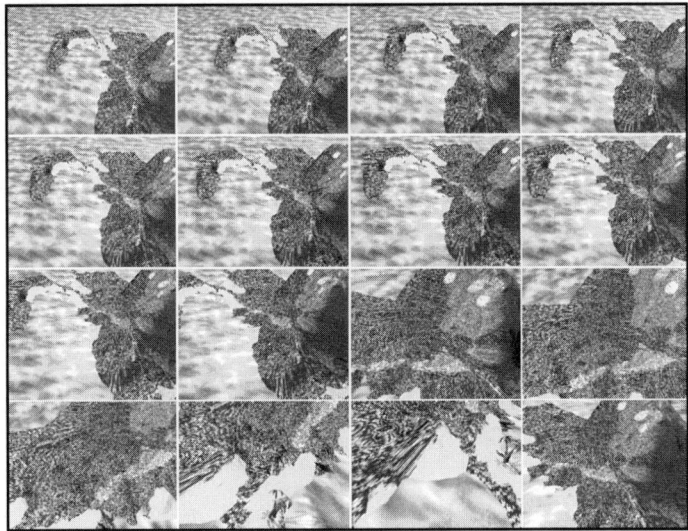

The concluding animation is more of a reward for having completed the adventure. It also uses the Shockwave plug-in.

Be sure to check out the adventure on the book's CD-ROM. The example in this chapter is really meant to give you a glimpse of what's possible.

Sneaky Inline Animations

On some of the pages, you'll notice a simple animation within the scene. These "sneaky" animations would take a lot of bandwidth if they were made up of different images. However, most of the images for one of these inline animations don't move, so you can get away with overlaying GIF animations. The trick is to make the unchanging portion of the image a non-tiled background and to center the animated portion, like a bird flying in the sky, on top of the background as a transparent GIF image. (See Figure 12.7.)

CAUTION: The problem with this technique is that images line up only if the screen is exactly 800 × 600. If the screen is any other size, the background becomes tiled and the GIF animations don't line up.

Figure 12.7.

In this scene, the image was made part of the background so that the small bird in the sky could be included as a GIF animation.

Workshop Wrap-up

This is more than the workshop wrap-up; it's also the part wrap-up. You've covered a lot of ground in these short chapters. You can use your 2D graphics packages to create interesting 3D graphics; you've learned the basic concepts of 3D rendering, modeling, and animation; and you've learned how to use this content to enliven and enhance your Web pages. I hope you take the lessons learned in this book and develop wonderful, rich games, such as MYST, for the Web.

Next Steps

Before you say ciao to this chapter, take a look at what's up ahead:

- ❏ If you're eager to learn about VRML, the wait is over. The next chapter moves into real-time 3D for the Web. See Chapter 13, "Exploring VRML Browsers and Development Tools."

- ❏ In Chapter 14, "Starting with Models," you get back into the modeling scene, but this time it's modeling for VRML.

- ❏ If you liked this workshop, be sure to check out Chapter 17, "Real-Life Example: The VRML Art Gallery: A VRML World by Hand."

Q&A

Q: What kind of machine did you use to create the images in this adventure?

A: 3D packages usually require the fastest machines available. I used a 133 MHz Pentium with 16MB of RAM. My Matrox Millenium video card with 3D acceleration also helped.

The place I was really hurting was in my PC's memory. For large-scale scenes like this one, you really should consider 48MB or more. With prices for RAM dropping, this is becoming more reasonable.

Q: In the game MYST, you navigate around the scene by simply clicking on the image. Why didn't you just make all your images into image maps and do away with the buttons?

A: The honest reason is that I was lazy. There are several simple programs that automate the task of creating image maps, but since this example usually had only two choices per scene, the button interface was easier. The buttons also made it clear what the choices were without having to include a lot of text.

For more complex and detailed scenes, images maps would be a good option. I leave it to you to include them in your next adventure.

P A R T

IV

Basic VRML Techniques

THIRTEEN

Exploring VRML Browsers and Development Tools

—by Justin Couch

So you liked what you saw in Chapter 2, "Up and Running: First VRML Creation," and think that this real-time 3D stuff is worth checking out. VRML can be tricky, and you're going to need some help getting started. That first look at VRML only touched on how to create a quick and dirty VRML scene. Now you'll be introduced to VRML properly.

This is an introductory chapter to get you up and running with VRML, both from the browsing and creating points of view. It should also familiarize you with some of VRML's background. This chapter has three main parts:

❑ First, you see what VRML is, how it fits in with HTML, and what the third dimension has to offer.

❑ You'll then get a quick overview of VRML's history, examining the different versions and what the differences mean to you.

In this chapter, you

❑ Learn what VRML is and how it fits in with HTML
❑ Review VRML's history briefly
❑ Discover what types of browsers are available
❑ Learn how to navigate in three dimensions
❑ See how to overcome obstacles to designing a new world
❑ Learn how non-VRML tools can be used when creating a VRML world
❑ Get a preview of new modeling tools for creating VRML worlds

Tasks in this chapter:

❑ Navigating in Walk Mode
❑ Using Mouse-Driven Navigation
❑ VRML Exports from Traditional Tools
❑ IDS Software's VRealm Builder
❑ Caligari's Pioneer

The second part looks at how you go about viewing somebody else's VRML worlds:

❏ You'll be shown the different types of browsers that are available.

❏ One of the most important things to know about VRML is how to navigate in 3 dimensions—you'll look at navigating with Netscape's Live3D browser.

The last part of the chapter deals with the issues involved in designing your own VRML world:

❏ As with HTML, you need to know what you're up against when you're designing a new world, so you'll learn about some of the obstacles you'll have to overcome.

❏ You may be used to using other non-VRML tools, like the ones covered in the first half of the book, so you'll learn how to use these tools to get a jump on your VRML world creation.

❏ Finally, you'll see a few of the new modeling tools specifically designed to create VRML worlds.

Now it's time to roll up your sleeves and get into VRML.

What Is a VRML File?

VRML acts in many ways, the same way HTML files can produce many different effects on the screen. A VRML file is composed of a series of text commands that are interpreted by the VRML browser and displayed on the screen, but the file's objects are all three-dimensional. This content is referred to as a *world* or *scene*.

In HTML, you place text and images on the screen using tags. Similar to tags, VRML files have nodes that define 3D objects such as cubes, spheres, and other shapes in a real 3D coordinate system. With the browser, you can navigate around these worlds at your own pleasure, examining the world from whatever angle you want. Basic worlds can be enhanced by adding lights, colors, textures, and motion to the scene.

To navigate around the scene, you move the mouse—the scene changes in real-time. So, by moving the mouse forward, the objects in the world become larger, as if you're approaching them. If you pull the mouse back, the scene recedes. If you click and drag the right mouse button, the entire scene rotates around its center.

How VRML Is Similar to HTML

Just as HTML is designed purely for document formatting, VRML is designed for 3D VR scenes. Most of the rules of creating Web pages also apply to creating 3D worlds. If you create a 3D scene, make sure it's interesting and offers the user something to do. Similarly, if you create a plain HTML page with no headings—just pure text—it too will be boring, ensuring that visitors don't return.

Say you create a Web page that looks absolutely stunning with lots of graphics, but it takes twenty minutes to download—how often do you expect people to visit? You must apply the same rules to creating VRML worlds that you do to creating Web pages. By its nature, VRML creates larger files than HTML does, but you can keep the file sizes to a reasonable level. Limiting the use of large images (textures), sticking to using color only, and using simple primitives are some techniques. Chapter 18, "Tricks to Optimize Your VRML Worlds for the Web," covers some of the common methods for optimizing your creations to keep people coming back.

An outstanding Web page can be put together in a couple of hours, if you have all your resources ready to go. Because VRML is more complex, it takes more time, even when you're using a GUI construction tool. However, it always pays to spend some time planning what your new world will look like in all three dimensions.

Once you add in that third dimension, VRML starts to diverge from its 2D "relation." HTML pages can be viewed in only one way, defined by the page writer, but users can explore VR worlds by looking at them in whatever way they like.

The similarities between the two technologies stretch further than just the method of creating them. Many HTML pages are designed much as magazine pages are, with lots of pretty graphics and links, and some cutting-edge pages seek to break this mold by stretching technology to do something unique. VRML is no different. A vast majority of VR worlds use traditional earthbound paradigms, such as the shop and art gallery examples presented in this book. However, a few stretch the limits as they seek to explore the possibilites of virtual reality. VRML offers a whole system for artists to create with, but HTML only allows them to display one of their creations.

When creating a Web page, you can do it in several ways. You could use a plug-in to common word processing packages (Internet Assistant for MS Word), a standalone application (Sausage Software's Hotdog or MS FrontPage), or the text editor of your choice. Equivalents exist for VRML world builders. You can export files from packages like AutoCAD and 3D Studio, use standalone dedicated applications like VRealm Builder, or use a text editor. However, with the pace at which VRML is developing, you should get familiar with a text editor. The best worlds are still created by hand, particularly when it comes to creating behaviors in VRML 2.0.

Working in Three Dimensions

One of the most important differences between VRML and HTML is that with VRML you have a whole extra dimension to worry about. This added dimension gives the visitor to your VRML world the chance to go inside, behind, and around your scene. This can be used to your advantage, but it also presents some difficulties. The next section examines some of the advantages and disadvantages to working with this third dimension.

Advantages

First, you have more freedom. All those 3D effects you've been producing in earlier sections of this book can now be done in real-time. Instead of just looking at a picture of a car, you can walk around it, kicking virtual tires if you like. The images and animations created up until now are all canned. You can play the animation a thousand times and it always looks the same. A VRML world, on the other hand, presents infinite ways to view the animation, all at the viewer's discretion.

VRML has a second advantage: control. Users can view the scene from any angle (if they can effectively navigate), so they aren't stuck viewing the same image every time.

A third advantage to VRML is the ability to obscure items. By using the third dimension, you can hide items behind other items, something tricky to do on HTML pages. This enables you play some interesting hide-and-seek games.

Perhaps the greatest advantage to using the third dimension is the realism you achieve. Moving a user through an architectural structure gives them a much better feeling of spatial relationships for the building than pictures do.

One of the intended uses of VRML is in the remote visualization of data. This might take the form of a VR world that mimics the environment a remote-controlled vehicle is operating in, or it might even act as mock-ups of designs. Now, there are several other languages and file formats that could do this, but VRML was born with the Internet firmly in mind. Anyone should be able to view any VRML world without needing proprietary software. VRML has the same benefits for users in the 3D arena that HTML has for people working in 2D environments and document publishing.

Disadvantages

Probably the most challenging aspect of working in 3D is trying to manipulate a 3D model in 2D. Input devices like the mouse are two-dimensional, so moving them in 3D can be difficult. Even with 3D-based interfaces like Caligari's Pioneer, or the split view approach of 3D Studio, it's still difficult to keep track of exactly how things look until you get to see them in the final environment.

Not only are computer input devices 2D, so are output devices, such as the monitor. Moving around the world helps the viewer understand the relative positions of objects, but it's still difficult to determine depth on 2D monitors. In the future, *head-mounted displays* will help. Head-mounted displays are worn like glasses; the scene changes as you move your head. To see the object behind you, you turn around.

The main disadvantage to working with real-time 3D is the computing time involved. The poor little processor really has to work hard to calculate how the scene looks as you move. The more complex the scene, the more it taxes the processor. Because of the huge calculations involved, the details of VRML worlds are purposely kept simple. You may have noticed that the images in the first half of the book don't really compare with images created in a VRML world. The scenes in the first half are drawn only once, but in VRML, the world may be redrawn as often as 30 times a second. Complex scenes take longer to draw, so to keep users happy, the world is much less detailed.

Many companies are developing and introducing 3D accelerator boards that can help the overloaded processor with 3D calculations. These boards range from $200 on up and can increase your rendering capability by two to four times.

Complex pre-rendered animation can take all night to produce just a single frame of the animation, but when the animation's complete, you can play it as fast as you want. VRML worlds have less than a second to compute and render the scene before your eyes detect that the motion isn't fluid. So until processors get much more powerful, you're stuck with the simple-looking worlds.

Where Did VRML Come From?

The idea for distributing 3D graphics across the Internet was the result of a meeting at the First International Conference on the World Wide Web. Mark Pesce and Tony Parisi had developed a demo program called Labyrinth that showed the use of a platform-independent graphics format. At this same conference, Tim Berners-Lee and David Ragget (the inventors of HTML and HTTP) held a discussion forum about what was then termed the Virtual Reality Markup Language, or just VRML.

Sometimes VRML has been pronounced as "vermel." Those who've been in VRML for a long time always cringe when they hear this, because the pronunciation connotes small, furry rodents (you certainly don't hear HTML pronounced as "hutmel!").

VRML's designers wanted to create a platform-independent way to send 3D worlds across the Internet. For this to work, the file format had to describe where objects were placed in 3D space and what their attributes were, such as color. VRML browsers would be running on everything from powerful UNIX workstations to humble desktop PCs. Silicon Graphics offered the Open Inventor file format for use, which was greatly accepted. A number of changes were made to make it compatible with the Internet and World Wide Web. This was released in May 1995. Following a number of different interpretations, a clarified version called 1.0c was then issued in January 1996.

In December 1995 it was proposed that the next version of VRML incorporate simple behaviors. Like everything else in the development of VRML, new pieces were being done bits at a time. VRML 1.0 described only static scenes. VRML 2.0 was to include programmable behavior but not the multi-user virtual environments of Gibson's cyberspace. They could be built on top of VRML 2.0, but multi-user virtual environments are not part of the language specification.

There was an ill-fated attempt to produce a 1.1 version of the VRML standard. This included a change to the syntax being used in 2.0 and some even simpler (non-programmable) canned behaviors. All work on a 1.1 version was dropped when it became apparent that everyone was interested in 2.0.

The examples presented in this book are based on the Draft 3 version of the VRML 2.0 specification. Apart from clarifications in wording, nothing changed between that and the final version. The official VRML 2.0 specification was released on August 4, 1996—the opening day of SIGGRAPH, one of the most important conferences for the international graphics community.

VRML 1.0 Versus VRML 2.0

By the time you read this, there will be two official versions of VRML, and you may be wondering what the difference is. The first version was deliberately limited to creating static scenes. In this way it was not much better than a standard Web page. A user could wander about, clicking on links to other worlds or pages and enjoying the scenery, but that was all. The second version of VRML introduced programmable behaviors—meaning that things are really starting to live up to that virtual reality tag.

Along with the addition of behaviors, VRML 2.0 added many other things. The most important for general world design is the ability to incorporate real 3D sound and video file formats. From a world creator's point of view, however, other changes are even more significant.

The major difference between versions is the completely different approach to creating VR worlds. To incorporate behaviors into the version 1.0 file format would have required a lot of messy additions. Worlds that were created in the version 1.0 format couldn't simply have extra information added to put in the behaviors. A whole new system needed to be drawn up. At the file level, everything—even the header—is different.

Chapter 1, "Building a 3D Enhanced Web Site," presented a model built with commonly available software. VRML 2.0 is so new that there are no tools available yet to create worlds with. Already two converters are available to change between the file formats. However, if you're interested in pursuing VRML worlds at the present, then you'll have to roll up your virtual sleeves, delve into the mechanics of VRML, and create it all by hand.

You'll see the problems of using the file converters in the next chapter—as well as a demonstration in Chapter 17, "Real-Life Examples: The VRML Art Gallery: A VRML World by Hand," about how to use them.

The rest of this chapter looks at both 1.0 and 2.0 VRML software. To the viewer, the difference in what they see will probably be slight. What they may notice is that some worlds have more responsiveness than others. (After this chapter, this book deals exclusively with VRML 2.0.)

If you're new to VRML, you shouldn't worry about learning version 1.0—head straight for version 2.0. At this stage version 2.0 may be a little more work because everything has to be created by hand, but over the next few months a number of dedicated VRML creation programs will be on their way. Besides, being at the leading edge of virtual reality on the Internet will help give your site that look of high technology.

NOTE: Although there are type-different versions of VRML, they aren't interchangeable. VRML 1.0 browsers can't view VRML 2.0 worlds, and vice versa. Given this fact, most people predict that VRML 1.0 browsers and tools will eventually become obsolete.

Types of Browsers

VRML browsers come in two types: standalone and plug-ins for HTML browsers. With the speed at which Netscape is currently moving, your latest version of Navigator will include Live3D, a VRML plug-in, as standard. This is good news, because you will be able to assume that most people have VRML capabilities. However, the Live3D plug-in is capable only of displaying VRML 1.0 files, so you will need to find an alternative to view 2.0 worlds.

If you're only going to view your VRML world, then a standalone browser will work satisfactorily. However, if you're planning to create mixed HTML and VRML worlds, particularly using Frames, then you will need to have a plug-in browser. Standalone browsers do offer one advantage—you can run your VRML browser and your HTML browser at the same time. A frames-based approach does limit the user's ability to go wandering—looking at full sized documents—particularly if the user wants the 3D world to be a constant reference point he or she explores various documents.

CAUTION: VRML worlds may look different depending on what browser you use, just as HTML pages look different when running on two different browsers. For example, one of the biggest problems with the first-generation browsers was that the colors seemed different between them. Where one browser made the world look very bright, another, even running on the same machine, made it look a lot darker.

Netscape and Live3D

One of the most common VRML browsers on the desktop is Live3D, Netscape's own VRML browser. Live3D is distributed as a standard part of browsers from Navigator version 3 onwards. It offers most of the standard features that you will find in the other browsers. The browser with Navigator 3 is capable of viewing only VRML 1.0 worlds, so to view VRML 2.0 worlds, you need to get one of the browsers mentioned later in the chapter. Netscape will no doubt update their browser to be 2.0 compliant in the future. The following sections look at how to navigate VRML worlds with the Live3D browser.

Microsoft and ActiveVRML

When the VRML development community was looking to move to the second version of the VRML specification, a call was sent out to all interested parties for their proposals. Six submissions were received from Silicon Graphics/Sony, Apple, Microsoft, Sun, IBM, and the German National Research Center for Information Technology (GMD). Of these, the Moving Worlds proposal by SGI and Sony was accepted by popular vote to be the starting point for version 2. As a result, Microsoft took their proposal, which was called ActiveVRML, and started marketing it against VRML 2.0.

Microsoft is currently developing ActiveVRML and is planning to release it to beta about the same time as the VRML 2.0 specification is ratified.

Although it did have the potential to read VRML 1.0 files, ActiveVRML is no longer true VRML, as decided by the VRML Architecture Group (VAG)—the controlling body of the VRML standards development group. Microsoft released an alpha version of their ActiveVRML browser in January 1996, but little has been seen of them since then. Chapter 11 takes a closer look at ActiveVRML technology, if you want more information.

Learning to Navigate VRML Worlds

If you've ever played the game Descent, you probably realize how quickly a newcomer to a 3D environment can get completely disoriented. For those who haven't, Descent is based on a 3D world in tunnels that leaves you with almost no idea of which way is up, or even exactly where you are. This section gives you a quick overview about navigating in 3D worlds.

When you're first learning to get around, stick with just one navigation method. VRML browsers offer at least two different ways of exploring the world, and many offer more. Until you're familiar with one, it's wise not to chop and change. Changing is one of the quickest ways to get disoriented. There is quite a difference between being lost and being disoriented in VR worlds. Being lost means that you have absolutely no idea about where you are; being disoriented means you can't work out which way is up, or worse still, have no idea how to adjust your view so that you could work out where you are.

Most browsers now offer a DOOM-style navigation method as a default. This is often known as Walk mode. The up/down cursor keys move you forward and backward, and the left and right cursor keys turn you in the respective direction. For newcomers, this option is probably the best. Most existing 3D worlds are based on the familiar real world, where you walk along the ground. Tunnel traveling, where you move forward and backwards in a tunnel that can spin, or flying navigation, requires the use of another mode.

The other mode that is commonly available is Examine. This allows you to spin an object, looking at it from any angle. Where would this be useful? If you're running a virtual shop then it allows you to examine any particular item, just as you would in real life: by holding it in your hand and turning it around to look at it. This mode rotates the entire world around its center.

VRML allows the world builder to build up a world from a collection of files—which is called *inlining*. Inlining isn't restricted to files located on the one server. Virtual worlds may be composed of many files from all over the real world. This leads to the familiar problems of servers and files not being available. When the browser is first building the scene, it may let you wander about before all the parts have been retrieved. When this is the case, inlined files are specifying by a wireframe cube specifying the dimensions of the file to be inlined at that location. When you come across one of these, it either means that the file is not available or the browser is still downloading it. Figure 13.1 shows a world still in the process of downloading.

TIP: A quick check to see whether the entire world has finished downloading is to look at the Stop button. If it's still active, then the world hasn't finished downloading.

Figure 13.1.
A partially loaded world showing the bounding boxes of objects to be inlined. The world is George Towne from Terra Vista.

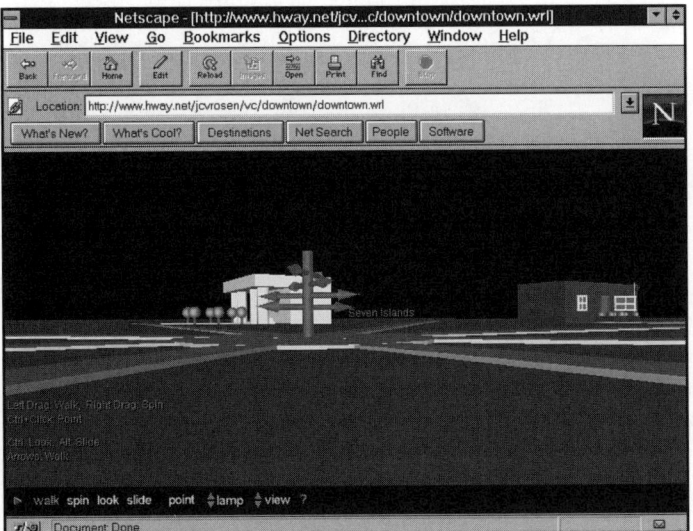

 # Navigating in Walk Mode

Live3D offers the standard Walk mode as its default. The cursor keys always move you forward, backward, left, and right in relation to the direction you are facing, similar to DOOM's controls. If you have managed to view the world upside down, then you have to switch mode to right the world. Walk mode is what you will be using most of the time to explore worlds. A good practice drill is to turn the world upside-down, literally.

Live3D is similar to DOOM. If you come across a set of stairs, you can climb them. Recently a designer— in a house he'd created— discovered that if you accidentally went off the side of the stairs you'd fall to the floor. His friends said that it was a great stress relief to throw themselves off the third story and walk away when they landed.

1. Start by moving around the world, using the arrow keys, to get familiar with the controls. You will soon find that you can't move off the plane that you are on.

2. Try clicking on the Examine button to switch to Examine mode. This causes the world to spin about its center. Rotate the world 180 degrees by pressing the up/down keys until the world is upside down. You will probably find yourself beneath the floor.

3. Click the Walk button onscreen to switch back to Walk mode and move about the now upside-down world.

You don't have to use the keyboard to navigate. In many ways, the mouse is better because it can give you better feedback.

Using Mouse-Driven Navigation

The following steps should give you some practice moving around a VRML world in Live3D with the mouse.

1. In the screen shot in Figure 13.2, you will notice a menu bar at the bottom of the screen. The first four words offer the choice of navigation mode when you're using the mouse. These refer to the actions that occur when you drag with the left mouse button down. The other modes are available by using either the right mouse button or a combination of the Ctrl or Alt key with the left mouse button. In the following steps, only the default left button actions are described.

Figure 13.2.

Netscape 3.0 running Live3D under Windows NT. The browser is currently in Walk mode, with the Navigation Help option turned on from the default starting position.

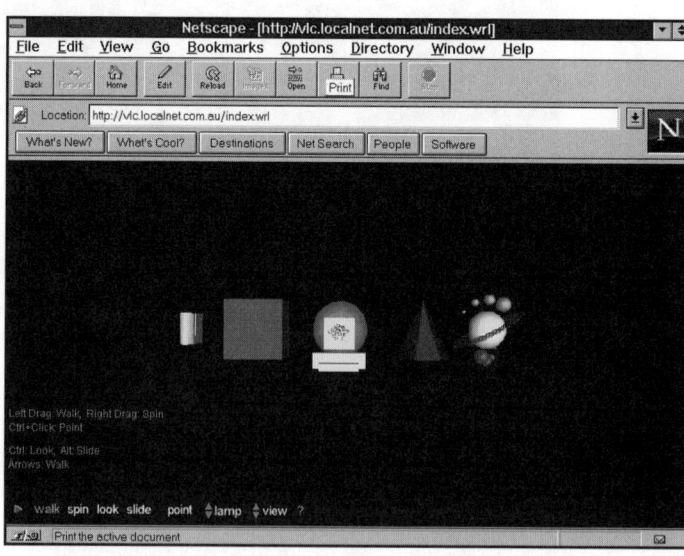

2. Walk mode enables you to navigate in the same way as the cursor controls. Holding down the left mouse button and dragging up moves you forwards, as Figure 13.3 shows. Drag down to move backward and drag left and right to revolve around the current point.

Figure 13.3.

The resulting view of walking forward to the center, then turning left to look at the planet in back.

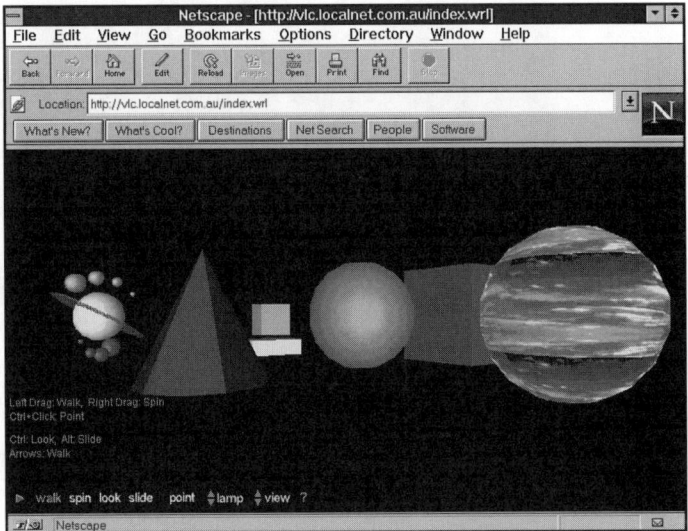

3. Spin mode rotates the world around the current center of the screen. A left/right drag of the mouse rotates the world left or right in relation to the current window. An up/down drag rotates it vertically in relation to the current orientation. If you took the world and rotated it up 90 degrees and then dragged it left 90 degrees, you would be looking at it from the side. Figures 13.4 and 13.5 illustrate the resulting views.

4. Look moves an object as though you were moving your head to look at it. The scene moves in a sphere around the user's current viewpoint, as shown in Figure 13.6. In a large world, Look is handy for looking up to the roof or down to the floor.

5. Slide mode slides you left, right, up, or down while keeping you pointed in the same direction. This is handy for looking around corners or dodging objects.

There is also a menu that controls the default settings of the VRML world.

Figure 13.4.
The result of a vertical spin starting at the default position.

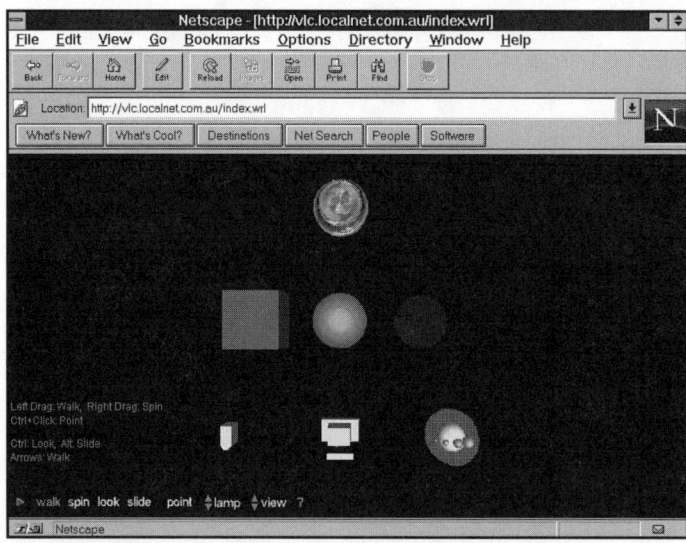

Figure 13.5.
The result of spinning Figure 13.4 horizontally.

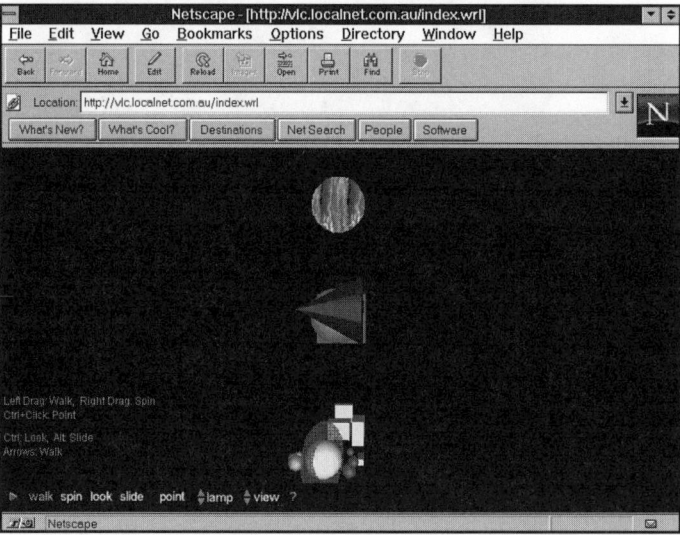

Figure 13.6.

Figure 13.6.
Starting from the default position looking left. Notice that the objects have rotated not only in the horizontal direction, but also in the vertical.

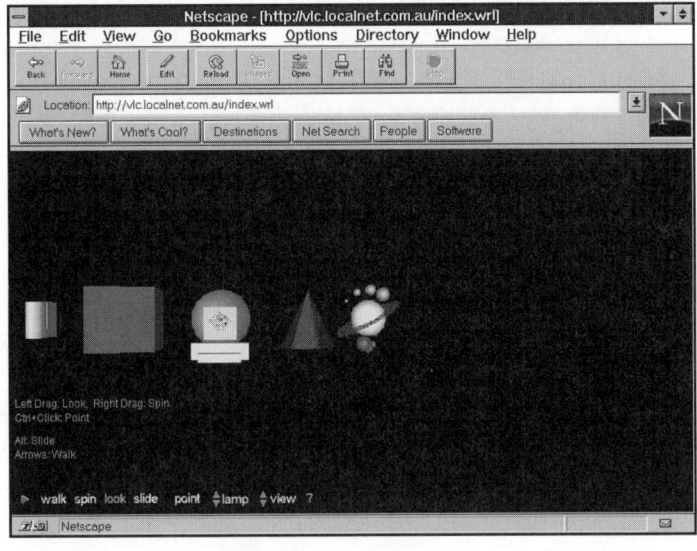

Using the Options Menu

The right mouse button is also used for Examine mode. To see the Options menu, just click and let go quickly, or hold the button down to access Examine mode.

The last part of the Live3D interface that you regularly use is the Options menu, which you get by clicking the right mouse button. The Options menu has all the options for customizing your viewing preference.

Viewpoints

At the top of the Options menu are four items dealing with viewpoints. These are predefined points that you can visit in a VRML world. The first item contains a list of all the viewpoints in this world that you can select. Upon selecting one, the browser takes you to that position. Once there, you're free to navigate around as normal. Should you get lost or disoriented, then selecting the Current Viewpoint option takes you back to the last visited viewpoint. You can check out each of the views in order by selecting the Next and Previous Viewpoint options.

Navigation

Next on the list is the Navigation menu. The submenu lets you control how you move around the world. The first five items are the same as the menu bar options outlined in the previous sections, except that they control what the cursor keys do. The previous sections outlined what the effect of the mouse did—these same navigation methods can be achieved using cursor keys. The menu also adds one more: Fly. Fly enables you to navigate just like a flight simulator, with the same key setup as Descent. A and Z move you forward and backward while Q and E roll you right and left, respectively. Straighten returns you to the normal relationship to the ground and usually back to the starting point.

One of the things that VRML 1.0 did not specify was physical effects. The next 3 options control how to make the system feel more real. Stay On Ground makes your view follow the terrain. This can be used to climb stairs, follow mountainous terrain, and do all sorts of neat tricks. When you're in Fly mode you may want to have the scene feel like you're in a real aircraft, so select Bank When Flying. One enhancement that has gained popularity in all the VRML browsers is the Collision Detection option. This stops you from walking through objects as you otherwise would.

In VRML, the X-Z plane is defined as being the ground (Y points up). Watch for this because it may cause confusion when you start creating your own models.

The last pair of options control how you move between points. If neither of these options are selected then you always jump to a point. However, it's a much nicer effect when you select the animation option, because the browser flys you to the selected point. The end result is like being carried on a tour bus through the scene to the next viewpoint.

Lighting

Sometimes you need to adjust the lighting within the world. The browser defines a headlamp for you. This headlamp is a directional light that always points in the direction that you're facing. In dark or dimly lit worlds this is really handy—it gives you a miner-in-a-cave perspective on things. The first option enables you to turn the lamp on or off, while Dimmer and Brighter enable you to control the amount of light.

Besides controlling your own light, you also can control how objects in the world are lit. Smooth Shading makes rounded objects look round rather than tessellated, but it also makes the rendering slower, particularly on slower machines. If you have lots of processing grunt, then turning on Texture Lighting makes everything look even better when texture mapping is used on objects.

Detail

If you're having problems with computer speed (particularly in large worlds), then the Detail submenu is where you should head. This submenu enables you to define how the world looks, either as Solid objects, where you can't see through them, Wireframe, or as a Point Cloud of the vertices. Point Cloud is not normally very useful and can get you disoriented very quickly. In a highly detailed model with lots of polygons, you can usually just make out the shape of the object from the points. The points are just the individual vertices that make up an object, so in a low-detail world all you end up with is an apparent mass of random points.

Heads Up Display

HUD enables you to control what information is overlaid on the viewing screen. While you're still learning to navigate, the Navigation Help option turns on hints that are printed in the lower-left corner, giving you details about what the keys are for the current navigation mode. The other helpful item is the Download Status. This presents a little blue and yellow bar across the top of the navigation menu bar, indicating the status of the world download. The blue section indicates how much of the download is complete and the yellow section indicates the progress of the internal processing of the file.

Options

In this submenu, you'll find the miscellaneous options for controlling the general behavior. Fast Rendering allows Live3D to take shortcuts to produce a better frame rate. This means a loss in quality of the picture while you're traveling around. In big worlds it is a much-needed option.

Providing you're sober, the Motion Blur option is great fun. This is the same effect as motion blurring in Magic Carpet, and gives that extra effect of speed as you travel through worlds. It does, however, slow up the responsiveness of the browser considerably.

If you're lucky enough to have a head-mounted display like the VFX-1 or Virtual i/o Glasses, then select the Stereo Camera option when using it. On a normal 2D display this option is disabled. Another option that you might want to include is Generate Back Faces. This option is used when you have worlds full of polygon meshes. Normally, only one side of the polygon mesh is visible—the front face. When you go behind it, you can no longer see it because there is no face defined for you to see. This option makes sure you can see it from both sides.

The Navigation Bars option turns the bar across the bottom of the window on and off, while Optimize Window Size controls the size of the viewing window to get the best rendering speed. The Save Settings As Default option is self-explanatory.

Other VRML Browsers

After such a long introduction to Live3D, it's time to introduce a few of the other available browsers. The first pair are VRML 1.0 browsers that are knocking on the door of Live3D in terms of quality, and are better in some respects. The second pair are the only two VRML 2.0 browsers at the time of writing. They are what have been used to test the examples in this book.

There was some difficulty in finding good examples of VRML 2.0 that didn't use scripting because both of the browsers were very early in development (first release of beta). The main problem was that they supported two different languages for scripting (see Chapters 20 and 21 for more details), and the small number of worlds meant that cross-browser support was nonexistent. There should be many more worlds that can handle more browsers by the time you're reading this.

One of the interesting things about browsers is that even on the same machine the coloring and lighting can be completely different for the same scene. To demonstrate this, the same scene has been used for each pairing of Objects. The VRML 1.0 scene comes from Jeremy Leader's Airlink Zone (`http://www.softronics.com/users/jeremy/world.wrl`). There is a larger problem in VRML 2.0 because the current browsers support different languages for scripting, so some of the sample files supplied with each of the products had to be used.

Intervista's WorldView

The first browser comes from Intervista. WorldView is available either as a standalone program or as a plug-in to Netscape 1.x and above, as well as for Microsoft's Internet Explorer. WorldView has one advantage over Live3D in that it can run with whatever your favorite browser environment is. The screen shot presented in Figure 13.7 shows the standalone version.

One of WorldView's nice features is its ability to nominate your own camera positions while navigating a world and then return back to them. The rendering is very smooth, but it isn't very accurate for handling mesh objects.

Figure 13.7.
InterVista's WorldView Browser.

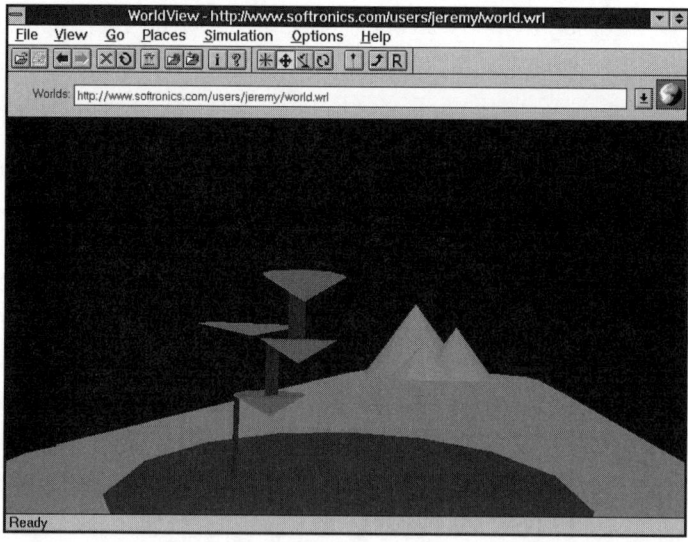

Chaco Communications VR Scout

VR Scout was the first browser released that didn't belong to Silicon Graphics. As a result, it's one of the most developed and stable browsers of the current crop. (See Figure 13.8.) It is also one of the strictest browsers in terms of compliance with the VRML 2.0 specification. If your file doesn't pass this test then you should definitely go back and fix it up until it does.

The rendering of objects with VR Scout is more accurate than WorldView—particularly large mesh objects, but this means that the performance is not as good—even though both programs have the same underlying rendering library. In my general experience, it seems to be about half the speed, although it will be different for each person. Accurate measurement is really not possible.

Figure 13.8.

Chaco's VR Scout.

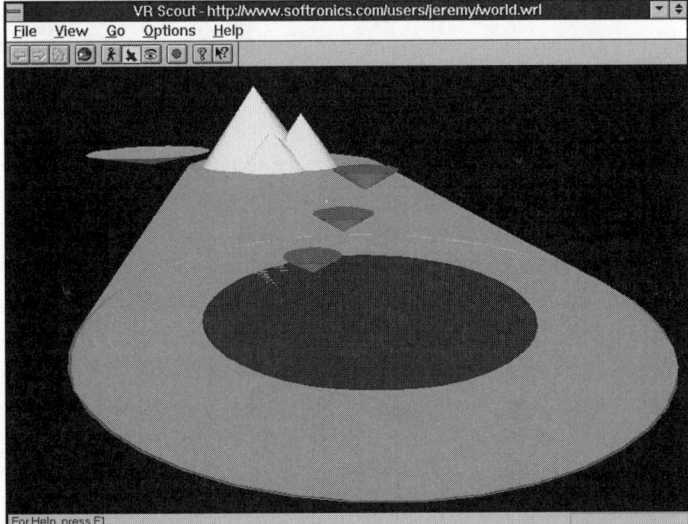

SGI's CosmoPlayer

When VRML changed file format so radically from version 1.0, it meant that its Open Inventor-based browser, WebSpace, was no longer able to support VRML 2.0. So they started from scratch.

CosmoPlayer comes with its own standalone converter so that it can be used for VRML 1.0 files. (See Figure 13.9.) This sometimes causes problems with files that aren't quite VRML 1.0-compliant because it won't display them or, even worse, only half displays them. The converter supports Netscape's Spin and SpinGroup extension nodes and turns them into legal VRML 2.0 files using the standard nodes.

Figure 13.9.
*Silicon Graphics'
CosmoPlayer. This early
beta contains a different
dashboard from what
you will see in the final
product.*

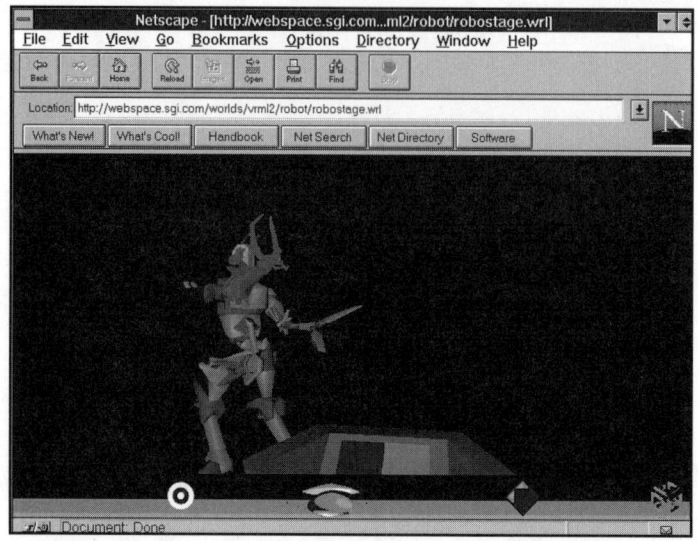

CosmoPlayer supports JavaScript for programming simple behaviors. While this does limit some of the potential functionality, all your common behavioral tasks can be constructed. Only if you are doing some very complex worlds using networking will you need to use something else. It is available only as a Netscape plug-in.

Sony's CyberPassage

The range of browsers for the Macintosh is much more limited. The main one is Live3D included with the Netscape Navigator. Live3D is VRML 1.0 only at the time of this writing. There are rumors of a couple of 2.0 browsers being released in beta form around the time of SIGGRAPH '96.

CyberPassage was the first VRML 2.0 browser to be available. (Yes, Sony does produce things other than TVs and stereo systems.) In the second version, it now supports VRML 2.0 and retains the same svelte interface of the first version. CyberPassage operates only as a standalone product, which is a bit of a pity, but its very fast rendering puts it ahead of CosmoPlayer on most aspects. (See Figure 13.10.)

CyberPassage supports Java for scripting, which makes it much more extensible when you need to do that little something extra, such as talking to a network or running multithreaded behaviors within a script. It still retains its multiuser capabilities from the first version, allowing you to participate in virtual worlds with people from around the globe in real-time. Current multiuser-capable browsers are discussed in further detail in Chapter 22, "Adding Interactivity: The Future of VRML."

Figure 13.10.

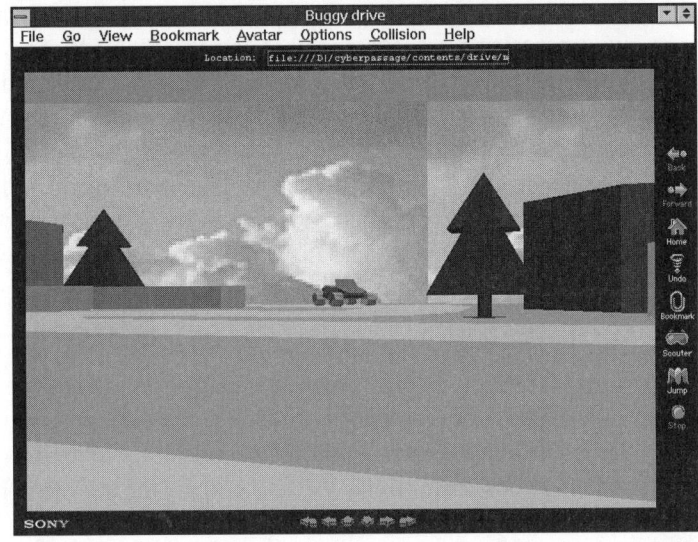

Figure 13.10.
The black interface of Sony's CyberPassage makes it fit in with the rest of Sony's electronic products.

Designing VRML Worlds

As HTML is designed purely for document formatting, VRML is designed for 3D VR scenes. Most of the rules for creating Web pages also apply to creating 3D worlds. If you create a 3D scene, make sure that it's interesting and offers the user something to do. Similarly, if you create a plain HTML page with no headings, just pure text, it too will be boring—ensuring that visitors only visit once.

Suppose that you create a Web page that looks absolutely stunning, but it takes twenty minutes to download. How often do you expect people to visit? You must apply the same rules to VRML worlds that you create. By its nature, VRML creates larger files than HTML, but you can keep things to a reasonable level. Keeping down the use of large images (textures), sticking to using color only, and using simple primitives are some techniques. Chapter 18, "Tricks to Optimize Your VRML Worlds for the Web," presents some of the more frequently used methods to optimize your creations and keep people coming back.

An outstanding HTML Web page can be put together in a few hours—if you have all your resources ready to go. Because VRML is more complex, this is not usually the case, even when using a GUI construction tool. It always pays to spend some time planning what your new world will look like in all three dimensions.

You can create a Web page in a number of ways. You can use a plug-in to common word processing packages (Internet Assistant for MS Word), a standalone application (Sausage Software's HotDog or MS FrontPage), or create it all by hand in the text editor of your choice. Equivalents exist for the VRML world builders. You can export files from packages like AutoCAD and 3D Studio, use standalone dedicated applications like VRealm Builder, or use a text editor. However, with the pace at which VRML is developing, you'd better become comfortable with the text editor. The best worlds are still created by hand, particularly when it comes to creating behaviors in VRML 2.0.

Simplest First: Using a Text Editor

You thought you could throw out Notepad because some great HTML editors are now available and now you're being told to get it back out again! Just as with HTML, you can create VRML worlds with nothing more than a simple text editor. Indeed, if you're seriously considering using VRML 2.0, then for the moment it is the only way of creating worlds.

Even once some modeling tools become available it has been the experience of most current VRML developers that you need to get into hand-editing the file after finishing with the modeling tool. This is particularly true with VRML 2.0, because the first generation tools only output static scenes which need to be added to your own behaviors.

The next chapter discusses the creation of basic VRML files from scratch. For the moment, you can put the editor away as you look at a few of the current VRML 1.0-based software available.

VRML Exports from Traditional Tools

One of the first ways that complex VRML models were constructed was with non-VRML modeling tools like AutoDesk's 3D Studio and Caligari's trueSpace. These tools exported to a standard format like DXF, which then had a third-party converter like WCTV2POV change that into VRML. This provided a very quick working base for many VRML worlds because they could leverage existing knowledge to get going.

Today a number of these tools contain plug-in exporters that can automatically produce VRML output files. One of the most widely used is Syndesis Corporation's Interchange, which acts as a plug-in file exporter for most popular modeling tools.

One of the more interesting results of VRML is the number of software companies that have released separate, dedicated VRML authoring tools, which are based on their non-VRML modeling tools. The next section looks at several of these.

Another approach that many of these companies are taking is to build VRML export options right into their modeler. One example of this is Ray Dream Studio, whose 4.1

release offers the ability to save your file as a VRML 1.0 file. The following steps illustrate how this is done:

1. Set up your scene by positioning your objects, lights, cameras, and such.

2. Save the file as a VRML 1.0 file by selecting the File | Save As command. Select VRML as the file type and give the project a name. Ray Dream responds with a message box that warns that some elements will be lost if not saved in Ray Dream's native format, which is true. Compare the images in Figure 13.11 and 13.12.

Figure 13.11.

An image rendered with Ray Dream Studio.

Figure 13.12.

The same scene exported and viewed as a VRML 1.0 file.

3. Load the VRML file into a browser to view it. Notice how many of the details have been lost. When converted, the resulting file was 206KB and included fifty 2KB material images used to map textures.

Judging from the size of the resulting VRML file, you need to use caution when exporting VRML files with traditional modeling tools. Some of these issues are covered in the following sections.

Export Issues with trueSpace, 3D Studio, and Other Tools

The problem with many non-VRML tools is that they don't understand VRML. They export everything as high-detail, large polygon count models, rather than take advantage of the basic primitives like square, cone, and cylinder to produce much smaller file sizes. Reduction of polygons has been known to cut file sizes by a factor of five and more when edited to use VRML primitives.

Before exporting, you really need to strip the scene down. Replace any texture maps that you really don't need with basic colors, and throw away any modeling details that don't really add to the scene. For example, the Viper model that you saw earlier included an elaborately detailed engine underneath the hood. This would have been worthless in the VRML world, because for anyone to see it they would have to go inside the car—and at that close range they wouldn't be able to tell what it was anyway.

The other major problem is that some programs produce incorrect normals for polygon meshes, particularly when exporting to DXF format. One of the suggested workarounds is to load the DXF file into a CAD-type program, get it to regenerate the face normals, and then resave it as DXF before conversion to VRML.

The next chapter looks a little more deeply into the export and conversion issues.

World Builders: Tools from the VR Community

Like all things, the best way to produce a product is to use a tool designed for the job. There are a wide range of tools available, ranging from those that barely hide VRML from you to those that could create any sort of file format. This section examines three of the most popular tools used in the VRML community today. They are all VRML 1.0 tools, but you should expect their companies to come out with upgraded versions that export to VRML 2.0 any time now.

Each of the tools presented has a different perspective and frequently many people use all three products to produce the final scene. The strengths and weaknesses of each product are presented so that you have a good understanding of how to combine them to produce the required result.

IDS Software's VRealm Builder

If you really want to learn VRML while you're creating a scene, then VRealm Builder is the software for you. It presents a four-view layout on the right side while you see the structure of the VRML file being graphically produced on the left. (See Figure 13.13.)

The best part about using VRealm Builder is the real-time updates of the objects in the viewing windows. As you adjust the numbers in the dialog boxes, the objects change in response to your input. This enables you to fine-tune the look of objects accurately and quickly, without having to go through the save/reload cycle every time you make a change.

VRealm Builder is very good at ensuring strict file syntax so you know that the output files will be correct. It won't enable you to insert things in the wrong order, or where they are not supposed to be. For the newbie learning VRML, this is a very handy thing.

Figure 13.13.
VRealm Builder, used to construct the basics of my homeworld.

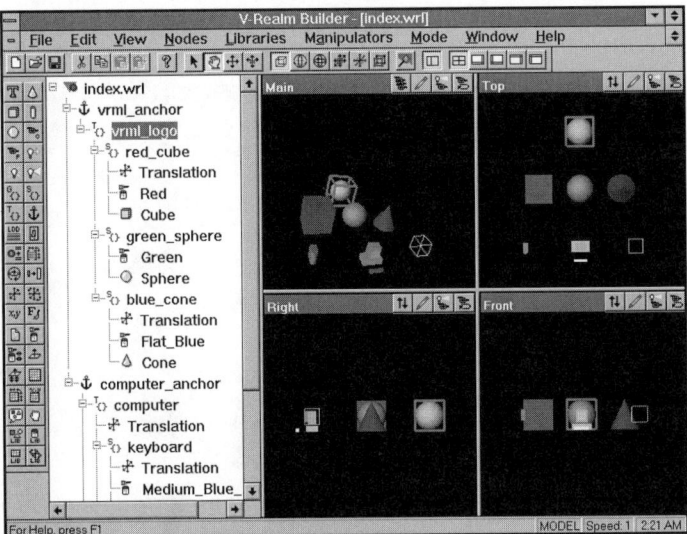

In the beta 3 version that was available for testing, VRealm Builder had a number of key features missing, such as mesh objects and reuse of pre-existing objects in the scene. When it comes to building very large files, node reuse is critical to maintaining small file sizes. The other problem of significance to the world builder is that it defines names for every node, even when they're not needed, which is also responsible for file size bloat and can contribute to other problems. VRealm Builder can read standard VRML 1.0 files, providing they don't contain meshes and node reuse.

Another small issue with VRealm Builder's beta version was the lack of drag-and-drop node editing. As is demonstrated in the next chapter, VRML contains a hierarchy of nodes. It would be nice to be able to pick up and redistribute the node organization within the scene graph.

Caligari's Pioneer

Pioneer is a spin-off from Caligari's trueSpace product, which was demonstrated in the first part of this book. It contains the same user interface, but has been modified to handle the VRML way of doing things. Pioneer used to be known as Fountain but not much else has changed about it. An example of Pioneer in action is shown in Figure 13.14.

Where Pioneer really excels is in the production of free-form shapes based on polygon meshes. You can play with these with so much ease it's a wonder that many other tools haven't done a similar thing. Another good thing about Pioneer is its ability to produce extruded text. It's amazing how often you come across 3D text just floating in space in a VR world.

Figure 13.14.
Caligari's Pioneer in action, producing Bubsy's showroom from the second chapter.

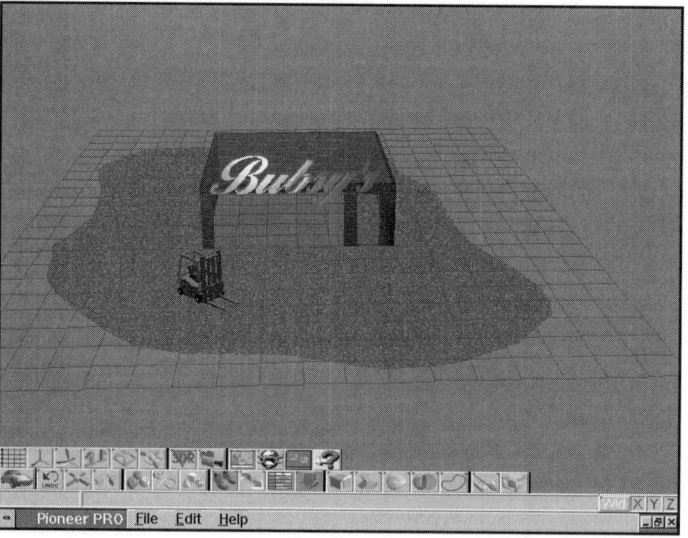

What's not so good about Pioneer is the standard scene that Home Space Builder is good at. Generally, what most people seem to do is create the individual objects using Pioneer, the core of the scene with HSB or VRealm Builder, and then stitch everything together in a text editor.

Workshop Wrap-up

By now you should have a reasonably good idea of what you can do with VRML, and how it looks and feels. The CD-ROM contains a list of links to places where you can find VRML software. Now it's time to learn VRML 2.0. Apart from occasionally mentioning version 1.0, the rest of the book doesn't look at it any more. The bridges have well and truly been burned.

The next two parts of this book examine a lot of different areas:

- ❏ Chapter 14, "Starting with Models," guides you through an introduction to many of the basic concepts in VRML 2.0. It shows you where things are different as well as introducing you to many little tricks for producing your first VRML world.

- ❏ Once you have finished learning the basics, you can pretty up the scene by adding other images as textures, as shown in Chapter 15, "Sprucing Up Models with Textures and Materials."

- ❏ Until now, you could create any sort of world you wanted. Chapter 16, "Adding a Dash of Reality," is about adding realistic effects to your newly created worlds.

Part V contains advanced topics in VRML. In the previous sections you could have easily created the same thing in VRML 1.0, which is not the point of VRML 2.0. Version 2.0 is all about adding interactivity to your world. Things move and respond to your presence.

- ❏ Beyond basic animation, you'll no doubt want to create your own. Chapter 19, "Using Built-in Animation Techniques," introduces you to incorporating your own behaviors into VRML.

- ❏ Chapter 20, "Interfacing VRML Worlds with Scripts," is for the hard-core world designer. This chapter looks at using Java for programming behaviors and really digs into VRML to look at producing top-class worlds.

- ❏ If you're a future gazer, then have a look at Chapter 22, "Adding Interactivity: The Future of VRML." The crystal ball is dusted off and examined for a look at some of the issues facing the VRML designers and users in the coming years.

- ❏ To see what you can really can do with VRML 2.0, check out the workshop in Chapter 23, "Real-Life Examples: A 3D Gallery: An Advanced VRML World," where a full guided tour of a VR gallery is presented.

Q&A

Q: What sort of computer do I need to play with VRML?

A: In the days of VRML 1.0, a 486 DX2/66 with 8MB of RAM was considered the minimum system. However, with the advent of Windows 95 and Java, VRML 2.0 browsers are now saying that a minimal system should be a Pentium with 12MB RAM, so you should consider a Pentium 100 with 16MB of RAM the target. RAM makes a very big difference in performance when running VRML 2.0 worlds, so you should aim to have as much as you can afford. The computer used to develop the examples in this book is a Pentium 90 with 32MB RAM and a 3D accelerator card and runs Windows NT.

Q: Which pieces of software do you recommend for creating VRML worlds?

A: If you're looking only at VRML 1.0, then the three products mentioned in the previous section are your best bet. Trial copies of these are included on this book's CD-ROM—along with the VRML 2.0 browsers (in their beta form at the time of publishing) to get you started. The tool you're most likely to use you're no doubt already familiar with—a text editor. All the sample code displayed in this book is handwritten, except where models have been included from companies like Syndesis.

Q: Where should I start looking for good worlds to visit?

A: The VRML repository (`http://www.sdsc.edu/vrml/`) contains a list of many VRML sites. You also can try searching on VRML in one of the many Internet search engines. The third place to look is at Terra Vista. Terra Vista is a group that grew from the VRML development list, where people gather to learn how to apply their knowledge of VRML in a practical sense. There you'll find many of the people involved in the standards development also testing what they're writing. You'll find many varied worlds, from ancient Wessex to fantasy space sites, so it should give you a wide range of ideas to start from. You can even come and build your own house in cyberspace. Terra Vista's homepage can be found at `http://www.terravista.org/`.

FOURTEEN

Starting with Models

—by Justin Couch

You've looked at a few browsers, tried a few of the creation tools in the previous chapter, and now would like to start creating your own. Where do you start? Well, the best place is to look at what makes up a VRML file. In this chapter, you'll start creating your own scene without the help of a modeling tool. After all, that's how most people started Web publishing with HTML—with just a handy old text editor.

To get you started, this chapter covers the following topics:

- ❏ Learn what makes up a VRML file
- ❏ Introduce some of the available primitives
- ❏ Give the primitives materials, like color
- ❏ Find out how to modify primitives by scaling, rotating, and moving them around
- ❏ Finally, see how to import models from other 3D file formats, such as DXF

Once you understand the basics, then you'll look at some slightly more advanced areas:

- ❏ Look at the advanced VRML shape primitives
- ❏ Link your world to others
- ❏ Take a quick look at some factors you need to consider when creating a world

In this chapter, you

- ❏ Learn what makes up a VRML file
- ❏ Give primitives color and modify them by scaling, rotating, and moving them around
- ❏ Import models from other 3D file formats
- ❏ Look at advanced VRML shape primitives
- ❏ Link your world to others

Tasks in this chapter:

- ❏ Using Primitives to Create a VRML Scene
- ❏ Adding Color to a VRML Object
- ❏ Moving Your Objects with the Transform Node
- ❏ Using the SFRotation Field Type
- ❏ Using Scale and ScaleOrientation to Shear an Object
- ❏ Using Multiple Transform Nodes Together
- ❏ Constructing an IndexedFaceSet Node
- ❏ Linking VRML Objects to Web Pages and Other VRML Worlds
- ❏ Converting Other File Formats to VRML
- ❏ Converting VRML 1.0 to 2.0

By the end of this chapter, you'll be able to build your own VRML worlds with the same text editor you used to make your first Web pages, but don't abandon the other chapters in a burst of creative passion. There's still a lot to learn.

Throughout this chapter, you will develop a VRML world of a simple virtual tree. If this is your first VRML 2.0 file or even your first VRML file, don't worry—this chapter starts slowly and illustrates some of the common mistakes to watch out for.

After this chapter, things will speed up. If you've seen VRML before and already know something about it, then I suggest you still look through this chapter to see how much things have really changed with the 2.0 specification. You'll also find several important design tips that will help you when building VRML worlds.

What's Needed to Create VRML Worlds?

VRML is similar to HTML in many ways. For the "backyard operator," it costs nothing to start creating—all you need is a text editor. In fact, even after you've used a modeling tool, you'll probably need to go back and hand-edit the file. Many of the worlds you see on the Web today were created with simple editors like Notepad or vi. Just like HTML, the VRML code can be viewed with the View Source command available in most browsers.

This isn't to suggest that you shouldn't use the modeling tools, but it's important to understand the details underneath the interface. The modeling tools were presented first in the previous chapter because that's where you spend most of your time, but get your text editors ready to take a look at the code at its base level for now.

What Makes Up a VRML 2.0 File?

The first line is known as the header for VRML files and must follow a fixed format for it to be recognized by the browser. Your header will always look like the following:

```
#VRML V2.0 utf8
```

Unlike HTML, VRML is case sensitive, which means you must follow the capitalization as shown.

What does it all mean? #VRML says to the browser that it's about to start looking at a VRML-type file; VRML uses #VRML to distinguish this sort of text file from an HTML file. The next bit tells the browser that it's about to deal with a Version 2 VRML file, which is important because the two versions aren't compatible. The last part tells the browser what sort of character set to use.

NOTE: Utf8 is an encoding that allows the file to be written with non-ASCII characters. This is all part of the internationalization of computing systems. For example, a site aimed at Russians has the text descriptions in Cyrillic characters rather than English. You might have heard of the term "Unicode characters." Unicode and Utf8 are similar animals. The International Standards Organization has defined a set of characters that need to be represented, which is known as ISO 10646. Utf8 is one method of encoding these, and Unicode is another. HTML requires using special escape sequences to get non-ASCII characters, but VRML does not. If you're Danish, then you just type away in Danish to create your VRML file.

VRML 1.0 files were allowed to be in standard ASCII text only. You can tell the difference between the versions by looking at the first line. The Version 1.0 header looks like this:

`#VRML V1.0 ascii`

Except for the first line of a file, you can place comments by using the # character; anything after that character on the line is ignored by the browser. Comments are helpful when you're trying to debug one of your files and also when others are looking at your source code and trying to understand how you have achieved those amazing effects.

Nodes, Fields, and Things

One term you'll see frequently throughout this section is *node*. Almost everything is a node, which is a predefined word describing a bit of the VRML scene. Nodes take many forms—from simple shapes to complex scripts—that are referred to as their *type*. You're probably familiar with the term *tag* to refer to the formatting code instructions in HTML; the VRML equivalent is called a node. To identify a node, notice that it's written in the file with the first letter of every word in uppercase characters, such as Cube, Material, IndexedFaceSet, and so forth.

Because you're writing this in a text editor—that is, "by hand"—rather than a modeling tool, you will no doubt spend a lot of time in the specifications reading up on what properties a particular node type has. Therefore, it's worth a bit of time to understand how a node type's definition is put together.

A node type has a number of fields to describe its characteristics. At this point, VRML starts to look a little bit more like a programming language, but don't be concerned. This is where VRML 2.0 gets its power. Each field must have a basic type, like MFString or SFFloat; a name, like url or speed; a default value, like 0 or FALSE; and some set of access privileges, like exposedfield or eventOut. (Access privileges will be discussed in depth in Chapter 19, "Using Built-in Animation Techniques.")

The basic field types help define the characteristics of the node. Types can be any kind of data, from integer numbers, strings, and booleans to time or even color values. You can learn more about these by dissecting the MovieTexture node definition, which looks like the following in the VRML 2.0 specification:

```
MovieTexture {
    exposedfield MFString url []
    exposedfield SFFloat speed 0
    exposedfield SFBool loop FALSE
    exposedfield SFTime startTime 0
    exposedfield SFTime stop'Time 0
    field SFBool repeatS TRUE
    field SFBool repeatT TRUE
    eventOut SFFloat duration_changed
}
```

The curly brackets are used to delimit the scope of the node in the same way that the angle brackets (< >) are used in HTML, but the name lies outside the brackets, rather than inside. The name for this node is MovieTexture. The other major difference is that VRML nodes can be nested inside other nodes. Everything that helps define this node is contained in a set of curly brackets; some nodes are longer and some are shorter, but everything within the brackets belongs to the node.

Notice that some types start with *SF* and others with *MF*. What's the difference? The first two letters of the field type specify how many of that type to look for. SF types can take only one value—so you can give an SFFloat only one floating point value. MF types can take any number of values.

If you're specifying more than one value, you need to enclose it in square brackets. Take the string field type, for example: An SFString could contain the value "Hello World", which is one value, but an MFString can contain "Hello" and "World" as two separate strings. The values are separated by commas inside the square brackets. The following are all legal declarations of the value 1 for a multiple-valued field:

```
1
[1,]
[ 1 ]
```

The default values are just that—values that are there by default. When coding VRML, you don't need to include all the fields, only the fields you need. Any fields that aren't listed assume the default value.

Group and Leaf Nodes

The 2.0 specification defines two groups of nodes (as compared to node types): group and leaf. A *group node* can contain any number of other nodes called child nodes, but a *leaf node* can include only specified nodes.

By using group nodes, you can eliminate duplicate code. Since you're specifying a material once, you can apply it to several shapes simultaneously.

For example, the Transform node, which has a field called Children, is of type MFNode, meaning it can contain many other nodes. All nodes contained within this group node get the transform applied to it. The Shape node, on the other hand, has only two SFNode types in its definition: one that contains the appearance node and another for the geometry node. These are the only nodes that can be placed in the Shape node.

Planning Your VRML World: Establishing a Hierarchy

Now that you have enough knowledge to work out what's happening in somebody else's file, you want to start thinking about your own. But you haven't even seen how to write VRML yet? Good, because it pays to think first, then create. In the 1.0 version, it didn't matter so much, but now, with the ability to add programmable behaviors, the wrong method of structuring your nodes could lead to a lot of unnecessary work.

When designing a scene, the best way to think about how the nodes go together is to visualize how the individual parts fit. On the small scale, a hand is part of an arm. A body has two arms and two legs, but the body also exists within the world. From this, you get an idea of how to create a hierarchy of nodes for the scene. For those unfamiliar with 3D graphics, this is called a *scene graph*. A scene can be deconstructed into a series of elements with links showing how the parts relate together, as Figure 14.1 shows.

Inverse kinematics are currently not supported in VRML, but they should be in the future.

In VRML 1.0, you could get away with a simple flat model in which every node existed at the same level, but this is definitely not the case for VRML 2.0. Remember the problem that inverse kinematics helped you out with back in Chapter 9, "Creating Advanced 3D Animations for the Web"? Well, the same problem exists in VRML. Take the simple case presented in the preceding paragraph. Each finger can move individually on the hand, but when the hand moves, the fingers move with it. If you use a flat object structure, then when you move the hand, you also have to make sure you move the fingers to stay with it. However, if you use a hierarchical structure, when you move the hand, the fingers automatically follow. This is particularly important in the later stages when you're involved in behavior programming—where the less you have to do the better.

There's no such thing as a correct hierarchy system or even some sort of system you could use to make one; it comes down to the individual situation and experience. For the example of the hand and fingers, it would be silly to make the fingers an object that wasn't a child of the hand, but in another case, you might want a model, such as a shaky car, in which all the parts jiggle whenever the horn is honked.

Figure 14.1.

Scene graph for a simplified car.

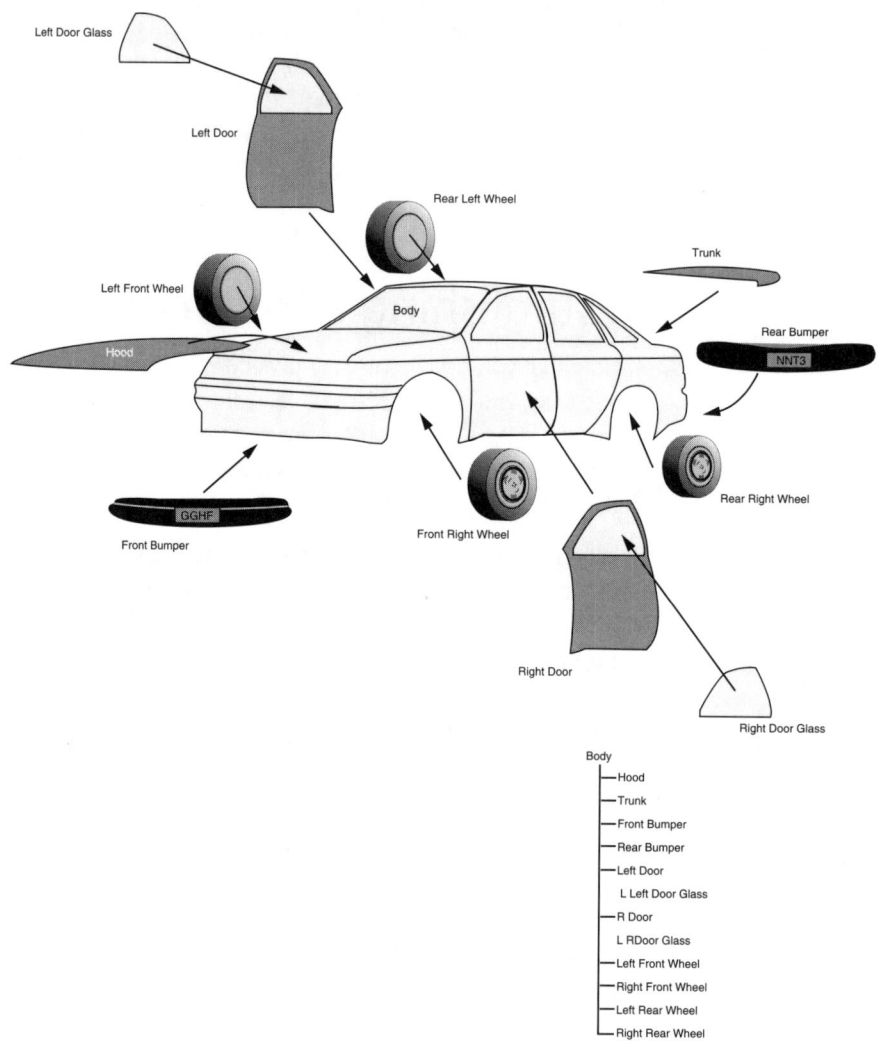

Body
- Hood
- Trunk
- Front Bumper
- Rear Bumper
- Left Door
  - L Left Door Glass
- R Door
  - L RDoor Glass
- Left Front Wheel
- Right Front Wheel
- Left Rear Wheel
- Right Rear Wheel

Formatting Your VRML Files

One last thing to consider before you start writing VRML files is the formatting. As in any other text document, formatting can make the difference between a readable file and an incomprehensible one. Similarly, there's no correct way to format a file, but the following guidelines should help you understand not only what's being written here, but also how to figure out what's wrong with your own file. These are only suggestions; you should use whatever works best for you.

❏ Indent each level of the hierarchy from the previous level. Usually, this is either one tab stop or two spaces.

- When dealing with lists of values, such as coordinate lists in face sets, put each item on a separate line. This is fairly flexible. If you're creating a grid style of structure, then values in rows and columns obviously make more sense.
- Place the closing bracket at the same level of indent as the node it's associated with.
- Put a comment at the start of major blocks of nodes.

In the final production version of my VRML files, I use one space for indents and strip most of my comments out, leaving only the bare essentials for someone else reading my file. However, while I'm creating them, I comment just about every line and use four spaces for indenting. As a result, the final file is about half the size of the developmental one.

Compared to HTML, VRML usually creates large files, and the actual contents of a VRML file are never directly viewed. These two factors mean that any excess formatting won't be to your advantage and will cause longer download times. A good example of this is using spaces for indenting. The code in this book uses four spaces of indenting for readability, but you shouldn't in your file. In a typical file, using four instead of two spaces can lead to a 30 percent difference in file size. Using tabs is better, but you usually end up having nodes written way off the right margin of your page—so use one or two spaces.

VRML Primitives: Box, Sphere, Cylinder, Cone

Whether you're creating scenes with a text editor or with a scene builder, there are always some basics you need to know. The first is the basic shapes. VRML offers a number of basic primitives, such as Cone, Box, Cylinder, and Sphere. There are also more complex primitives, such as Extrusion and the IndexedFace/Line/PointSet nodes.

It's best to use a collection of the basic primitives to form the bulk of your scene. The basic primitives, like the sphere and cone, are normally provided as part of the renderer at the heart of the VRML browser. This makes drawing them go more quickly than if you had created them as a big collection of polygons because the browser can control the amount of detail to get the best performance.

TIP: You should strive to use the basic primitives whenever possible, instead of the more complex ones. This always leads to better performance.

These primitives provide the basic complete shapes. If you want to create your own, then you should look at the section called "Advanced Primitives" later on in this chapter. All the VRML primitives are based on distances from the origin or center. A given height extends for half that value above and below the origin, so a cube with a width, height, and length values all equal to 1 would actually be $2 \times 2 \times 2$.

❏ Box—width, length, and height (X, Y, and Z). This is the same as the VRML 1.0 Cube.

❏ Sphere—requires radius. From this, you can stretch it to get football-shaped objects.

❏ Cone—radius of the base and height with height aligned on the Y axis.

❏ Cylinder—height and radius with height aligned on the Y axis.

OK, enough about definitions—time to build that tree.

Using Primitives to Create a VRML Scene

This is really quite simple. You use nodes to define what you want to appear, and they appear in the browser when you load the file. The browser takes care of all the rendering and navigation.

1. Start your VRML 2.0 file with the VRML header line mentioned earlier:

   ```
   #VRML V2.0 utf8
   ```

2. Now, the objects. The first thing you need for the scene is a tree trunk, which you can make out of a cylinder. It will be a small tree, so make it only a meter high and quarter of a meter in diameter. To do this, you need the Cylinder node with values set for the radius and height. The code looks like this:

The units in VRML are non-specific; however, the specification says that generally you should treat one unit as being equivalent to one meter.

Listing 14.1. A first attempt.

```
#VRML V2.0 utf8
Cylinder {
     radius 0.25
     height 1
}
```

3. Now add a sphere to represent the leaves (I said it was a simple tree; you'll get to complex models soon enough). The sphere node looks like this:

   ```
   Sphere { radius 0.5 }
   ```

   This section of code can be appended to the end of the cylinder code.

4. That's it. Pretty simple. Save the file with a WRL file extension and load it into a VRML browser.

If you load this file into a VRML browser, it will complain. That's because you've forgotten something fundamental about VRML: A geometry node cannot exist on its own; there needs to be some node it belongs to. If you read the VRML specification closely, you will notice it says that the geometry nodes must exist as a child of the Shape node—specifically in the geometry field. Here's how you would represent Step 2 from above:

```
Shape {
    geometry Sphere { radius 0.5 }
}
```

Even when you do try to load it now, it doesn't look very much like a tree. In fact, you won't see anything. Hmmmm, where's the cylinder and sphere? Lesson number one for VRML. The background color and the object color both default to black—not very helpful. If you can't see an object, usually it's because you haven't given it a color. You need to figure out how to add materials to your objects, but you're in luck! That's the next example.

Most VRML browsers support a feature known as *headlights*, which cast default lights on the scene. If the headlights are turned on, then you can see the objects.

Adding Color to a VRML Object

If you were to sit down with just the VRML specification, then adding color wouldn't be immediately obvious. VRML primitive nodes do not include color as part of the definition because your cube doesn't have to just be a plain color. The color-applying command is contained in the Material node, which is far more powerful. With the Material node, you could do things like applying texture maps or even a rotoscoped movie. These material properties are defined in a general node called Shape.

The Shape node has only two fields: the *appearance* and something called *geometry*. The appearance field can take only one type of node: an Appearance node, one of those nodes that's always surprising you with something new it can do. For the moment, limit youself to just making it color your cylinder. To do this, you need to use the material field, which takes only one type of node—the Material node. Hey, this is pretty logical.

1. To color the tree trunk, start with the Shape node. Within that node are the appearance field, where you specify the materials, and the geometry field, which contains the primitive you want to color—this case, the cylinder.

2. Once you know where you're putting the color, you need to define the material properties. Several different material fields can add color to objects, but you will use emissiveColor, which gives objects a nice glow (the tree isn't radioactive; it just looks good against a black background). The color is specified as the amount of red, green, and blue, ranging from 0 to 1. The mixture of .41, .40, and .1 gives you a nice brown, perfect for the bark on your tree trunk. The VRML tree file now looks like the code shown in Listing 14.2.

Listing 14.2. The tree trunk VRML source code with color added.

```
#VRML V2.0 utf8
#
# A Virtual Tree
Shape {
    appearance Appearance {
        material Material { emissiveColor   .41 .40 .1 }
    }
    geometry Cylinder {
        radius .25
        height 1
    }
}
```

Notice how this all takes place within the Shape node brackets. The resulting colored tree trunk is shown in Figure 14.2; now, what about the leaves?

Figure 14.2.

The basic tree trunk colored in brown.

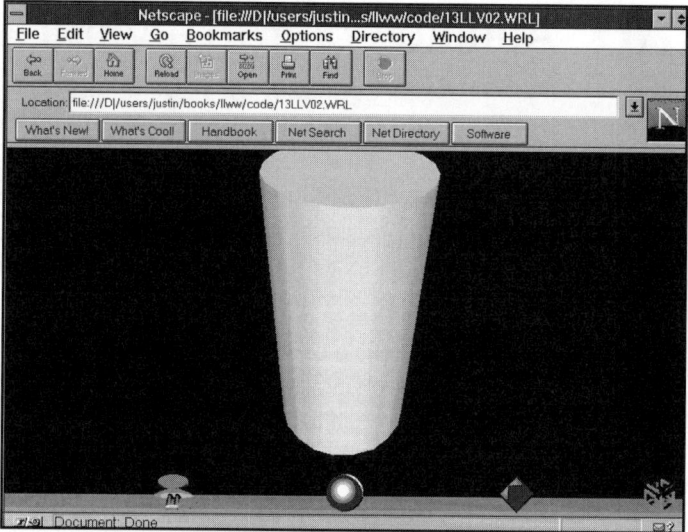

3. Below the tree trunk code, place a similar definition for the sphere that makes up the leaves. Looking at the set of values for the emissiveColor property below, you can see that the leaves will be green because the middle value, which represents green, is larger than the other two.

```
Shape {
    appearance Appearance {
        material Material { emissiveColor .1 .6 .1 }
    }
    geometry Sphere { radius 0.5 }
}
```

If you view this file in a VRML browser now, you get what you see in Figure 14.3. However, it still doesn't look much like a tree. Ooops. Looks like you need to do something else, like move the sphere above the trunk. The next example shows you how to move objects around, so you can position the leaves above the trunk where they belong.

Figure 14.3.

The trunk and leaves centered on top of one another.

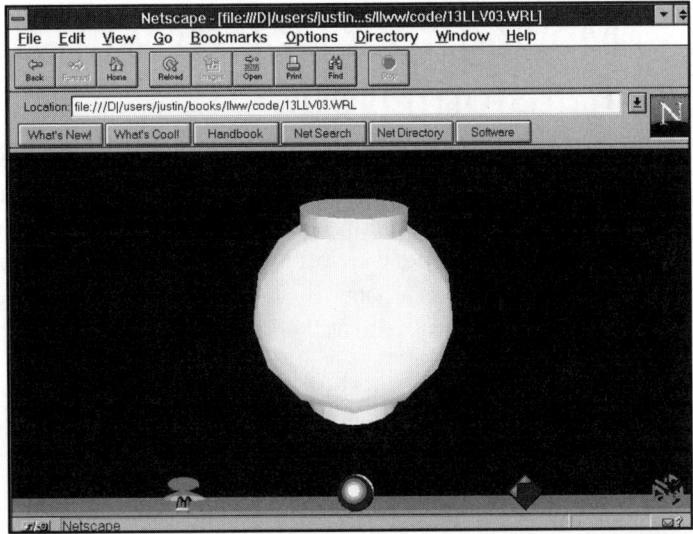

Color Field Options

So which of the color fields should you specify? There are so many of them! For general purposes, all you usually need is the emissiveColor field. The color fields are defined in the following list:

❏ **diffuseColor**   Reflects all VRML light sources, depending on the angle of the surface in relation to the light source. The more directly the surface faces the light, the more diffuse light reflects.

❏ **ambientIntensity**   Specifies how much ambient light this surface should reflect. Ambient light comes from all directions and depends only on the number of light sources, not their positions in relation to the surface.

❏ **specularColor and shininess**   Determines the specular highlights—for example, the shiny spots on an apple. When the angle from the light to the surface is close to the angle from the surface to the viewer, specularColor is added to the diffuse and ambient color calculations. Lower shininess values produce soft glows, and higher values result in sharper, smaller highlights.

❑ **emissiveColor**   Models "glowing" objects. This can be useful for displaying radiosity-based models (where the light energy of the room is computed explicitly) or scientific data.

❑ **transparency**   Determines how "clear" the object is, with 1.0 being completely transparent and 0.0 completely opaque.

Moving Your Objects with the Transform Node

As you just discovered in the previous example, all new objects are positioned at the origin. Therefore, to create a world with several objects, you need to move some of them. Enter the Transform node. Like the Appearance node, this is one of those multifunctional nodes with lots of surprises. To start with, you'll use it just to move some of the objects around. The Transform node has the following definition in the specification; it shows you all the fields that can be contained in the Transform node:

```
Transform {
  eventIn       MFNode      add_children
  eventIn       MFNode      remove_children
  exposedField SFVec3f      center          0 0 0
  exposedField MFNode       children        []
  exposedField SFRotation   rotation        0 0 1 0
  exposedField SFVec3f      scale           1 1 1
  exposedField SFRotation   scaleOrientation 0 0 1 0
  exposedField SFVec3f      translation     0 0 0
  field         SFVec3f     bboxCenter      0 0 0
  field         SFVec3f     bboxSize        -1 -1 -1
}
```

The eventIn, exposedField, and field fields can be ignored for now. They will be covered in Chapter 19, when adding animation to your world is discussed.

Transform is one of the grouping nodes discussed earlier. The children field is where you locate your child nodes, such as the Sphere. For the moment, look just at the *translation*. To move the sphere, just set the values of the translation to where you want to put the center of your collection of nodes specified in the children field. When nesting Transform nodes, the effects are in relation to the parent; this will be illustrated later when you produce the tree with the cone type top. Now, fix that tree:

1. To get the sphere to the top of the trunk, you could move it by half the height of the trunk plus half the height of the sphere making up the top. However, that would be too far—the sphere would only just touch the top of the trunk, so just reduce the number a bit until it overlaps the trunk. A value of 0.9 in the Y direction should be about right.

2. Next, within the children field, put the Shape node you used in the previous example. Notice that the radius of the sphere has been increased to 1 for better proportions.

```
Transform {
    translation    0 .9 0
    children [
        Shape {
            appearance Appearance {
            material Material { emissiveColor .1 .6 .1 }
            }
            geometry Sphere { radius 1 }
        }
    ]
}
```

3. This new Transform node is placed right after the Shape node for the cylinder in the previous example. Save the file and load it into your browser.

The tree top now looks like Figure 14.4. However, the Transform node can do a lot more than just translation. Who wants to just move around, when you can rotate and scale, also?

Figure 14.4.

The complete tree (finally).

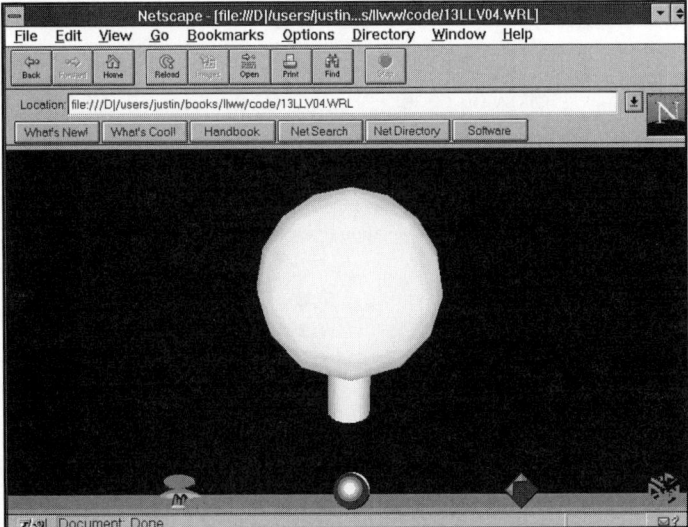

Using the Rest of the Transform Node

Several other fields in the Transform node were not covered in the previous section, but most of them are fairly self explanatory. A *rotation* rotates the object around the point that is defined as the center. *Scale* multiplies the values on each axis by the specified value. The scaleOrientation field is a little more confusing—it specifies an axis that the scale values then align themselves with. Once mastered, this is a very powerful tool because it allows you to do shears and other effects. However, first you need to understand how the SFRotation field type works.

Using the SFRotation Field Type

When using scales, one of the most confusing aspects to understand is how the SFRotation field works. To examine how it works, first look at its use in the Transform node, which has the following partial definition:

```
Transform {
    exposedField SFRotation rotation          0 0 1 0
    exposedField SFVec3f     scale             1 1 1
    exposedField SFRotation  scaleOrientation  0 0 1 0
}
```

The SFRotation field type requires four numbers. The first three are the axis around which the rotation takes place, and the fourth is the angle, in radians, of the rotation. Specify the single axis by placing a 1 in one of the first three values, which represent X, Y, and Z. Try rotating a red cone object:

1. If you wanted to rotate it 45 degrees around the Z axis, you would use the following code:

```
Transform {
        rotation  0 0 1 .707
        children [
            Shape {
                appearance Appearance {
                material Material { emissiveColor 1 0 0 }
                }
                geometry Cone {
                    bottomRadius 1
                    height 2
                }
            }
        ]
}
```

This rotated cone can be seen in Figure 14.5.

2. If you wanted to do something more complex, like a 45-degree rotation along the line running between two diagonally opposite corners, then just nominate the axis around which the rotation takes place—in this case, the positive vector (1, 2, 1), which are the bounding dimensions for the cone.

```
rotation 1 2 1 .707
```

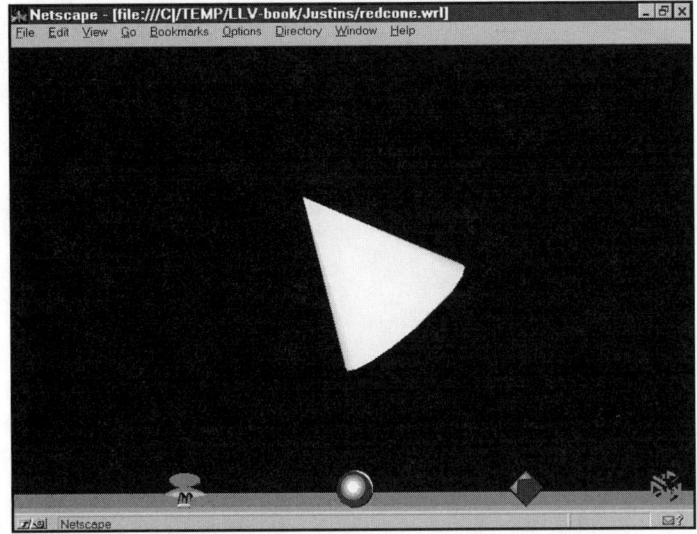

Figure 14.5.

A cone rotated around a diagonally defined vector.

Notice how easy it is to reuse sections of code and change a few numbers to get new results. As you edit your VRML worlds, keep track of similar functions so that the code can be copied and modified.

Using this format, you can perform several quite complex rotations in a single line. There are many ways you could specify the same amount of rotation; for example, the following two rotations achieve the same effect:

```
rotation 3 5 2 1.57
rotation -3 -5 -2 -1.57
```

Which one to use depends on the context. Normally, you would choose the first option because it contains four fewer characters—a factor not usually that important, but in a large file with hundreds of rotations and objects, the difference in the resulting file size could be quite large.

Using Scale and ScaleOrientation to Shear an Object

Now that you've mastered using SFRotation, you can start using it in more complex situations, such as creating shears. The scaleOrientation field uses the SFRotation type to specify an axis along which the scale is then applied. Take a look at an example of how a simple box can be sheared:

A *shear* means that one side of an object is held still while the opposite side is moved, thus distorting the entire surface between the two sides.

1. To get a shear, specify a diagonal axis and the amount of scale you need. The following code produces a shear along the X, Y axis:

```
Transform {
    scaleOrientation    1 1 0 0
    scale               2 2 1
}
```

2. Once the Transform node is applied, you need to specify a Shape node that receives the effects of the transform, as in the previous examples. For this example, use the Box primitive. The following code can simply replace the Cone node used in the previous example of the rotated cone:

```
Shape {
    appearance Appearance {
        material Material { emissiveColor 1 0 0 }
    }
    geometry Box {
        size 1 1 1
    }
}
```

The scale values work as multiples of the original values. A scale of 1 1 1 leaves the object unchanged. Scale 2 2 2 produces a uniform doubling of size in all directions.

3. With the Transform and Shape nodes included, save the file and load it in your browser.

Figure 14.6 shows the original cube to the left and the sheared cube to the right.

Figure 14.6.

The original cube and its resulting shear.

TASK Using Multiple Transform Nodes Together

Now you have everything you need to create some complex objects just from the basic primitives. In the next example, you'll build another tree that will use multiple levels of Transform nodes.

1. Start with the same cylinder trunk from the previous tree example.

2. Instead of using the sphere for leaves, substitute a cone. To compensate for this new primitive, you'll need to readjust the Transform values a little:

```
Transform {
    translation 0 1.5 0
    children [
        Shape {
            appearance Appearance {
                material Material { emissiveColor .1 .6 .1 }
            }
            # Default cone values look good
            geometry Cone {}
        }
    ]
}
```

3. To spruce it up a bit and make it look more like a pine tree, add a second cone to the top with another Shape node. There are two ways you could do this. You could place another Transform node in the file after the first one, copying the first one and then adjusting the translation value. However, when you come to more complex scenes and interactions later, this might not be such a smart move. You'll try using a second method and demonstrate how to create a proper hierarchy by placing the second cone in the same Transform group node as the first one.

Why create a hierarchy? Remember the hand and arm combination mentioned earlier in this chapter? A *nested hierarchy* means that by moving the arm, you're also moving the hand without any extra effort. With the hierarchy, everything stays properly aligned.

4. To create this hierarchy, all you do is place the Transform for the top cone in the children field of the original Transform. Order is not important. It can be placed below the Shape node for the first cone or in front of it. Next, adjust the translation values in relation to the first cone so that the second cone in the file moves upward in the Y direction 0.75 meters from the first cone. The resulting file looks like this:

```
Transform {
    translation 0 1.5 0
    children [
        Shape {
            appearance Appearance {
                material Material { emissiveColor .1 .6 .1 }
            }
            # Default cone values look good
            geometry Cone {}
        }

        # Now put in the second cone
        Transform {
            translation 0 .75 0
            children [
                Shape {
                    appearance Appearance {
                        material Material { emissiveColor .1 .6 .1 }
                    }
                    geometry Cone {
                        bottomRadius .8
                        height 1.5
                    }
                }
            ]
        }
    ]
}
```

Figure 14.7 shows the results of this VRML file in the CosmoPlayer browser.

Figure 14.7.

The pine tree standing too perfectly straight.

Okay, the tree is looking pretty good, but what if the wind is blowing? Trees don't tend to stand straight up most of the time because in nature, wind makes trees sway. To produce a little sway at the top, add a small rotation to the top cone. This illustrates a good reason for creating a hierarchy of objects.

5. To get a lean in the top cone, all you need to do is add a single rotation field in the Transform node, rather than specify some complex series of translations and rotations. If you just added the following line to the code shown in Step 4,

   ```
   rotation 0 1 0 0.1
   ```

   then things would still look a little strange. This is because the rotation is based on the center of the object. What you really want to do is locate the rotation around the base of the cone.

6. Use the center field to move the point of rotation to the bottom of the cone. To make it even more realistic, add a bit of sway to both cones, which results in the final tree shown in Figure 14.8. The final swaying tree is shown in Listing 14.3. Make sure you keep this code because it will be used again in later chapters.

Listing 14.3. The code to produce a swaying tree.

```
#VRML V2.0 utf8
#
# A Virtual Tree
Shape {
    appearance Appearance {
        material Material { emissiveColor   .41 .40 .1 }
    }
    geometry Cylinder {
        radius .25
        height 1
    }
}
Transform {
    translation 0 1.5 0
    rotation 0 0 1 0.1
    center 0 -0.75 0
    children [
        Shape {
            appearance Appearance {
                material Material { emissiveColor .1 .6 .1 }
            }
            # Default cone values look good
            geometry Cone {}
        }

        # Now put in the second cone
        Transform {
            translation 0 .75 0
            rotation 0 0 1 .1
            center 0 -.375 0
            children [
                Shape {
                    appearance Appearance {
                        material Material { emissiveColor .1 .6 .1 }
                    }
                    geometry Cone {
                        bottomRadius .8
                        height 1.5
                    }
                }
            ]
        }
    ]
}
```

Figure 14.8.

The final pine tree swaying in the breeze.

Advanced Primitives

Besides the basic primitives, VRML also has capabilities for defining your own models by using sets of points and connecting them to form faces. This is how modeling tools convert models into VRML models—by outputting a list of point coordinates and a list of which points are connected to form all the faces within the model. Coordinates can be connected to form faces, connected to form lines, or left as a group of points.

Advanced primitives also include the ability to specify different colors or textures for each vertex or face within the node. This makes it possible to create some interesting models. Look at some of the nodes used to create these advanced primitives:

- ❏ **IndexedFaceSet**   Provides a set of faces by connecting together points in any order.

- ❏ **IndexedLineSet**   A series of 3D lines joining points; typical uses are to make wireframe objects, such as fences.

- ❏ **PointSet**   Provides a point cloud; sometimes used to simulate stars.

- ❏ **Extrusion**   Forms a pipe-like extrusion that can be bent and twisted as required.

- ❏ **ElevationGrid**   Given the dimensions and number of points for each side, it then takes a series of heights and makes it into a terrain.

A special feature of the ElevationGrid node is that when the browser is in WALK mode, the eye position automatically adjusts to follow the terrain underfoot.

Using these advanced primitives, you can combine models you've created yourself with lines to create unique worlds, like the one shown in Figure 14.9.

Figure 14.9.

Uses of advanced VRML nodes—IndexedLineSets are used in the spire; the roof is formed from an IndexedFaceSet. From Michael St. Hippolyte's 7 Islands world in Terra Vista.

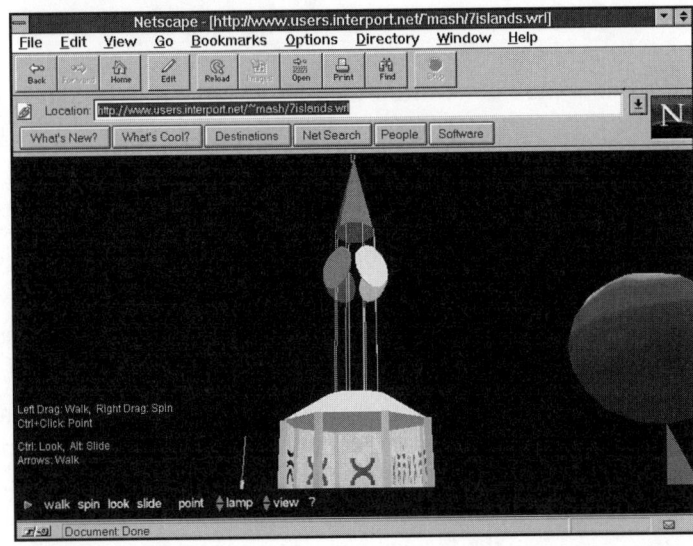

The advanced primitives are fairly simple to create by hand, but when creating a complex shape, they become unwieldy to maintain in a handwritten file. Normally, they're generated by some modeling package. For this reason, take just a brief look at how to construct a simple square and triangle with the IndexedFaceSet node.

Constructing an IndexedFaceSet Node

At the heart of the face set, it really just consists of a list of 3D points and a series of connections through them. Here's the definition of the IndexedFaceSet node:

```
IndexedFaceSet {
  eventIn        MFInt32 set_colorIndex
  eventIn        MFInt32 set_coordIndex
  eventIn        MFInt32 set_normalIndex
  eventIn        MFInt32 set_texCoordIndex
  exposedField   SFNode  color              NULL
  exposedField   SFNode  coord              NULL
  exposedField   SFNode  normal             NULL
  exposedField   SFNode  texCoord           NULL
  field          SFBool  ccw                TRUE
  field          MFInt32 colorIndex         []
  field          SFBool  colorPerVertex     TRUE
  field          SFBool  convex             TRUE
  field          MFInt32 coordIndex         []
  field          SFFloat creaseAngle        0
  field          MFInt32 normalIndex        []
  field          SFBool  normalPerVertex    TRUE
  field          SFBool  solid              TRUE
  field          MFInt32 texCoordIndex      []
}
```

The list of points goes into the coord field, and the coordIndex field contains the list of connections. To specify a face, list the index of each point to be used in order, then terminate the list with the value of -1. The same set of points can produce two different figures, as demonstrated in the following steps:

1. First, build the structure for your file, using the familiar Transform and Shape nodes.

2. This time, instead of a primitive defined in the geometry field of the Shape node, include the IndexedFaceSet node.

3. In the IndexedFaceSet node, fill up the Coordinate node with point values separated by commas.

4. Finally, in the coordIndex field, list the points in the order you want them connected. Notice that the first point (0,0,0) is point number 0. When you're finished connecting the dots, place a -1 to tell the program you're finished. The completed program will look like the code given in Listing 14.4. Figure 14.10 shows what happens when you connect points in different orders.

When counting in VRML, remember to always start with 0. The first index in any multivalue field is always 0. When you come to scripting later, these fields are represented by an array, which has its first index as 0 as well.

Listing 14.4. VRML code to illustrate how the same vertices can be connected differently.

```
#VRML V2.0 utf8
#
# Example of Two IndexedFaceSets
Transform {
    translation -1.5 0 0
    children [
        Shape {
            appearance Appearance {
                material Material { emissiveColor 0.3 0.2 0.1 }
            }
            geometry IndexedFaceSet {
                coord Coordinate {
                    point [
                        0 0 0, 1 0 0, 1 1 0, 0 1 0
                    ]
                }
                coordIndex [ 0, 1, 2, 3, 0, -1 ]
            }
        }
    ]
}
Transform {
    translation 1.5 0 0
    children [
        Shape {
            appearance Appearance {
                material Material { emissiveColor 0.1 0.2 0.3 }
            }
            geometry IndexedFaceSet {
```

```
coord Coordinate {
    point [
        0 0 0, 1 0 0, 1 1 0, 0 1 0
    ]
}
coordIndex [ 0, 1, 3, 2, 0, -1 ]
            }
        }
    ]
}
```

Figure 14.10.
Two sets of identical coordinates but with different ordering of vertices.

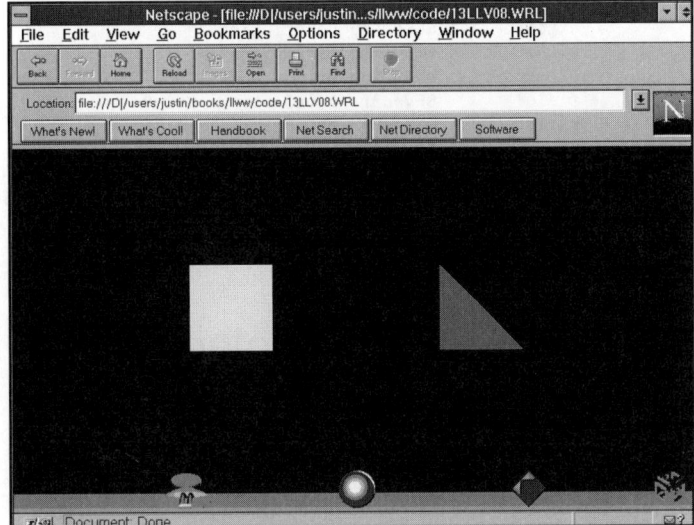

The ordering of vertices is very important. The list you define in the coordIndex field is the order in which the points are joined together. Joining points 0 1 2 3 0 produces a square shape, but the ordering of 0 1 3 2 produces a bowtie shape. Also, if you don't define the normals for each face, then the browser calculates them from these points. When you are behind a face, then it won't be visible to you. Effects like walls inside an object can be produced by using the forward and reverse ordering of points within the same coordIndex field.

Linking to Other Worlds and Pages

VRML, like HTML, is a hypermedia system. Not only can you display 3D objects, but you can also include video and streamed 3D sound. However, you know the advantages of linking to other Web pages; VRML supports this and goes one step further. You can also link to other VRML worlds. All this magic is done with the Anchor node.

The VRML Anchor Node

The VRML Anchor node works in a similar fashion to the anchor <A> tag in HTML. The Anchor is a grouping node, so it can contain objects like the good old Shape node with its primitives. When a user clicks on the primitive, the browser is sent to the URL that's linked. This is how the Anchor definition looks in the specification:

```
Anchor {
    eventIn       MFNode    addChildren
    eventIn       MFNode    removeChildren
    exposedField  MFNode    children       [ ]
    exposedField  SFString  description    ""
    exposedField  MFString  parameters     [ ]
    exposedField  MFString  url            [ ]
    field         SFVec3f   bboxCenter     0 0 0
    field         SFVec3f   bboxSize       -1 -1 -1
}
```

One of the handy fields is the description field. It was added so that a Text string could be used to describe what the link was to. When the user moves the mouse over the top of the object with a link, the text listed in the description field shows up.

In some browsers, the description text shows up above the object in the air, but in the CosmoPlayer browser, only the URL shows up in the status bar at the bottom of the screen.

TASK

Linking VRML Objects to Web Pages and Other VRML Worlds

In VRML, the URL includes support for the # anchor. This can refer to several different things, depending on the context. See the sections on defining viewpoints in Chapter 16, "Adding a Dash of Reality," and on object reuse in Chapter 17, "Real-Life Examples: The VRML Art Gallery: A VRML World by Hand."

The parameters field is covered in Chapter 22, "Adding Interactivity: The Future of VRML," when multi-framed documents are introduced.

First, start with a simple world made of two basic primitives. Each of these primitives will contain links, one to another VRML world and the other to a HTML document. Because you have two separate links, you need two Anchor nodes to contain the objects.

1. Starting with the first Anchor node, define the text for describing the linked world; you'll also include the world's URL.

2. Then, within the children field, specify your translation and, eventually, the Shape node with its sphere primitive.

3. Immediately below the first Anchor node, place a second. This code can be copied directly from the first. The only changes are the Anchor URL and description fields, the translation field (so that your objects don't end up on top of one another), and the material color and primitive shape. For the second primitive, I chose to use a plain old box and colored it red. Here is the completed code in Listing 14.5:

Listing 14.5. Linking your world to other VRML worlds and HTML pages.

```
#VRML V2.0 utf8
#
# Using Anchors
Anchor {
    url      "another.wrl"
    description "A Link to another VRML world"
    children [
        Transform {
            translation 1.5 0 0
            children [
                Shape {
                    appearance Appearance {
                        material Material { emissiveColor 0.1 0.1 0.6 }
                    }
                    geometry Sphere {}
                }
            ]
        }
    ]
}
Anchor {
    url      "another.html"
    description "A Link to another HTML Document"
    children [
        Transform {
            translation -1.5 0 0
            children [
                Shape {
                    appearance Appearance {
                        material Material { emissiveColor 0.6 0.1 0.1 }
                    }
                    geometry Box {}
                }
            ]
        }
    ]
}
```

The two target files are very simple; both offer links back to the original VRML file to show you examples of how to link VRML and HTML together. Figure 14.11 shows the final VRML file in a browser.

Figure 14.11.

Two primitives in this simple VRML world show how links can be attached to objects connecting HTML pages and other VRML worlds.

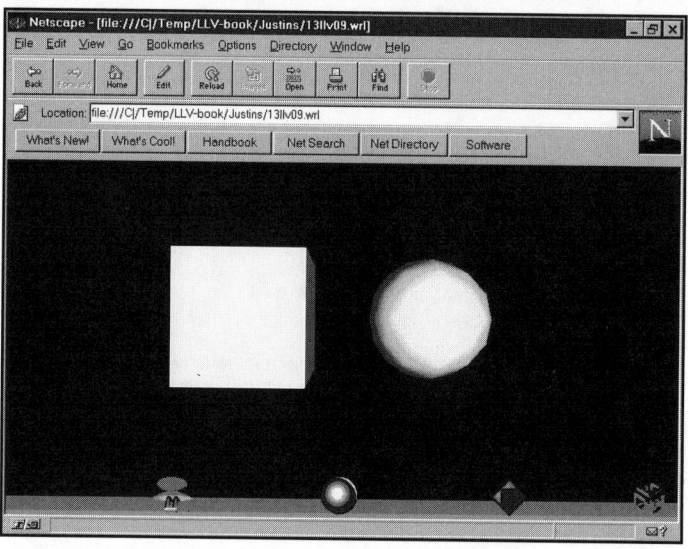

Designing for Easy Navigation

Now you have enough knowledge to design some interesting worlds. It's time to take a step back and look at what you are about to create. Navigating VR worlds provides quite a different challenge compared to moving around a collection of 2D Web pages, so consider several of these tips when you're creating VRML worlds.

First, VRML worlds take a lot longer to download than most HTML pages. Therefore, users are likely to want to spend more time exploring before moving on to the next place. On the other hand, they don't want to have to explore too much to find what they are after. A clear concise world with objects that are easy to identify as having links should be the aim.

A good VR world should offer a series of readily identifiable landmarks to help navigation and also act as reference points in the initial exploration. In small worlds, this doesn't generally present a problem because all the available information is given within the current viewing area. However, with VRML 2.0 comes the capability to create giant seamless worlds that aren't displayed all at once, so the need for landmarks becomes more important.

Using VRML Conversion Programs

There are two types of VRML conversion programs. The first, and largest group, is the type for converting other file formats to VRML, and the second type is the 1.0 to 2.0 converters.

Converting Other File Formats to VRML

Right from the very beginning, it seemed that VRML was destined to become popular. Within months of the start of the VRML development process, conversion programs for most of the major 3D graphics file formats were available.

Keith is working on updating WCTV2POV so that it can convert directly to VRML 2.0.

One of the most used programs is Keith Rule's WCTV2POV. This shareware MS Windows–based program is capable of importing and exporting just about all the current common file formats and then exporting them to VRML 1.0 format. It has a simple, easy-to-use interface that makes file conversion as simple as two commands to open the file and then save it as a given format; specifically, this is how it's done:

1. To convert a DXF file, all you need to do is open the DXF file using the File | Open command.

2. Then select the File | Save As command and the destination file type (VRML), and it's done. No more effort is required—you now have a VRML 1.0 file.

Converting VRML 1.0 to 2.0

Because VRML 2.0 is so new (still in draft at the time of this writing) and so different from VRML 1.0, the browsers being released also come with their own converters. When the browsers are used to view 1.0 files, they operate seamlessly but can also be used separately as a command-line program. The converters are included as part of their respective browsers, so you don't need to download them separately. Both follow this syntax:

```
vrml1to2 <VRML1.0 filename> <Output filename>
```

Currently, it would be wise to use only the converter that came with the browser because the browsers have varying levels of capability, and the converter is usually designed for that level. In the previous chapter, you looked at the two current VRML 2.0 browsers: Sony's CyberPassage 2.0 and Silicon Graphics CosmoPlayer. For either of these browsers, the process goes like this:

1. The CosmoPlayer installation places this file with its examples in a separate directory. Locate where the installation placed this file.

2. You can use the Windows 95 Start | Run button, but the easiest way to do this is to run the MS-DOS prompt and enter the following line:

```
vrml1to2 tree.wrl tree2.wrl
```

Then, hit the return key. The program will work on the conversion and come back with a message saying that the conversion was successful.

3. You can then test the VRML 2.0 file by opening it in the browser you're using.

If you're using a non-VRML modeling package, then you need to first save the output in a common format like DXF, convert that to VRML 1.0, then use the browser's converter to change it to VRML 2.0 format.

Conversion and Importing "Gotchas"

One of the major problems with using modeling tools that aren't wise to VRML is that they don't take advantage of its primitives, which can lead to massive file bloating. If you're using 3D Studio, it doesn't save a sphere as a sphere but rather as a big collection of polygons. If you have the detail turned up high, you end up with a VRML file containing a few thousand more polygons than are really needed. In these cases, you need to hand-edit the file to remove the polygon mesh and replace it with the appropriate VRML primitives. If you have many of these objects, then it would probably be quicker to create the whole lot by hand.

Another major problem is the differences in color models used. This is not necessarily the conversion program's fault, but that of the software packages. The rendering libraries the programs are based on all use different color models. An attempt was made to fix this in the ill-fated VRML 1.1 specification, and work is underway to specify algorithms from the VRML color model to that of the major rendering libraries. Even at this early stage, it would be a good idea to check what your world looks like on as many different browsers as possible to ensure a reasonably good-looking world. Recently, it was reported that a color that looked gold on one browser turned out a very dark red on another running on the same machine.

The final problem is that many programs don't export to DXF properly, which often means missing object normals. If you're using a DXF model, you should first load it into a CAD program to make sure everything is correct, then resave it before trying to convert it to VRML.

Workshop Wrap-up

Now you have a fairly good understanding of the basic concepts of VRML and how it works. Don't be surprised if a lot of it has gone over your head on the first reading. VRML is a large and relatively complex language that takes some time to learn. You can avoid some of this initial learning pain by using existing modeling tools and then running them through conversion programs. This introduction has gone fairly slowly, but from now on, it's assumed that you can create some basic worlds and would like to spruce them up a bit by using some of VRML's features.

Next Steps

So you've gone as far as you can with basic colors and links, even tried a few IndexedLineSets. What's left?

- ❏ To find out how to liven up that basic color with texture maps, go to the next chapter, Chapter 15, "Sprucing Up Models with Textures and Materials."

- ❏ More advanced effects can be created by using light sources, presented in Chapter 16, "Adding a Dash of Reality."

- ❏ If you just want to get on with creating VRML worlds, then check out Chapter 17, "Real-Life Examples: The VRML Art Gallery: A VRML World by Hand," where you'll see how to mix static VRML scenes with HTML pages.

- ❏ So you're really keen to see how far you can push VRML? Well, Part V, "Advanced VRML Techniques," is for you. In that section, you'll discover techniques to optimize your VRML worlds and learn about the huge world of behavior programming.

Q&A

Q: I've been looking around the Web and some of the VRML files have something about a draft number in the header. What's this about?

A: The draft #*n* in the header was used to differentiate files that conformed to the draft standards of VRML 2.0. At the time of this writing, Draft 2b was current, but by the time this book reaches the shelves, VRML 2.0 will be complete so you don't need to worry about this line. Your VRML browser should be able to understand its meaning.

Q: Which is the best browser to view these examples in?

A: All the examples in this chapter and in the rest of Part IV were tested with Silicon Graphics's CosmoPlayer. At the time of this writing, the only other browser was Sony's CyberPassage, which came out before CosmoPlayer and supported only Draft 1 of the VRML 2.0 specifications. There were enough differences between the drafts that it couldn't be used for testing.

FIFTEEN

Sprucing Up Models with Textures and Materials

—by Justin Couch

Chapter 14, "Starting with Models," introduced you to the concept of the Material node, which allowed you to define some pretty colorful worlds. However, in the real world, no object is ever just one color. Therefore, this chapter introduces texture mapping to make your 3D world more interesting. *Textures* involve applying a picture to an object. In VRML, a texture could be anything from a plain image to an MPEG video.

Putting textures in VRML worlds is easy. However, getting them all to line up is another story. In this chapter, you'll see how to add that extra bit to your images with some of the following techniques:

- ❏ Learning how the various VRML nodes hang together to produce the color and look of objects
- ❏ Applying textures to any object you like, first in an example using a simple object and then with a more complex primitive
- ❏ Producing a texture map to add to objects

In this chapter, you

- ❏ Learn how VRML nodes are used to produce the color and look of objects
- ❏ Apply textures and create a texture map for objects
- ❏ Use transparency for interesting effects
- ❏ Add movie textures to an object

Tasks in this chapter:

- ❏ Using the Texture Field
- ❏ Working with Texture Coordinates
- ❏ Building Texture Maps
- ❏ Using Transparency
- ❏ Adding Movies

❑ After mastering the basics, learning more complex techniques, like transparency, to create some interesting effects

❑ Adding movie textures to your object

The chapter finishes on a theoretical note to show you when to use, or not use,
textures.

Beyond Color

In the previous chapter, I introduced the Appearance node as a way to get some color
into your world. Now you'll take a more in-depth look at it to see all its capabilities.
Here's how the Appearance node is defined:

```
Appearance {
    exposedField SFNode material          NULL
    exposedField SFNode texture           NULL
    exposedField SFNode textureTransform  NULL
}
```

In the previous chapter, you used just the material field, but now you'll get to play with
everything. You'll start with the texture field.

TASK Using the Texture Field

The texture field is where you put a reference to the type of texture node you'll be
using. VRML defines three types of textures: ImageTexture, MovieTexture, and
PixelTexture. All three are nodes that can be placed here, but you can't place just any
type of node. Usually, you will see this rule referred to as using a *legal node*, as opposed
to adding a node that's not allowed. For example, a Shape node would be an *illegal
node* because it's not allowed in this context.

PixelTextures are covered after this section and MovieTexture is covered later in the
chapter; this is how ImageTexture is defined:

```
ImageTexture {
    exposedField MFString url       []
    field        SFBool   repeatS TRUE
    field        SFBool   repeatT TRUE
}
```

ImageTexture looks somewhat like the HTML <IMG> tag. To use an image as an texture
map, simply supply the URL to the image in the url field. Once you have the geometry
defined in the Shape node, you have an instant texture map. The VRML 2.0
specification requires that JPEG and PNG image formats be supported, but GIF is

You have a great deal of flexibility when defining specific textures, since you can use any of the supported image file formats. The specification allows the image to be any size, but the size is usually limited in most browsers. Most PC-based VRML browsers limit or scale the image into 128 × 128 pixel blocks. The actual content of the texture is limited only by your imagination.

recommended. Both VRML 2.0 browsers supported GIF and JPEG images from their first beta release.

Any image can be used as a texture. It can be something simple, like the wood grain used in the example in Chapter 17, "Real Life Examples: The VRML Art Gallery: A VRML World by Hand," or more complex, such as a photo of your favorite basketball player. The first texture model will be a basic marble column; you'll wrap a marble texture around a basic column constructed out of a group of cylinders:

```
Shape {
    appearance Appearance {
        texture ImageTexture { url "marble.jpg" }
    }
    geometry Cylinder {}
}
```

Not much has changed from the example of using color in the previous chapter; you just substitute the ImageTexture field for the Material field and give it a filename to use. The browser takes care of the rest. By applying a collection of Transforms and cylinders, you can create a whole Greek-style marble column, shown in Listing 15.1.

Listing 15.1. A basic texture-mapped marble column.

```
#VRML V2.0 utf8
#
# Example 1 Chapter 15
# A simple texture-mapped column
Group {
    children [
        Transform {
            translation 0 1.45 0
            scale 0.6 0.15 0.6
            children [
                DEF marblecylinder Shape {
                    appearance Appearance {
                        texture ImageTexture {
                            url "marble.jpg"
                        }
                    }
                    geometry Cylinder {}
                }
            ]
        }
        Transform {
            translation 0 1.15 0
            scale 0.4 0.15 0.4
            children [ USE marblecylinder ]
        }
        Transform {
            scale 0.3 1 0.3
            children [ USE marblecylinder ]
        }
        Transform {
```

continued

I've used the DEF/USE syntax to cut down the file size and save me lots of cut-and-paste work. You should be able to work out how to use it from the example in Listing 15.1. A real explanation of how to use it isn't given until Chapter 17.

Listing 15.1. continued

```
            translation 0 -1.15 0
            scale 0.4 0.15 0.4
            children [ USE marblecylinder ]
        }
        Transform {
            translation 0 -1.45 0
            scale 0.5 0.15 0.5
            children [ USE marblecylinder ]
        }
    ]
}
```

Now try applying texture mapping to a box, using a picture this time so you can tell what's happening. Notice as you play with the size of the box that the picture expands or shrinks to fit the object's size. For simple primitives, this is really handy.

Figure 15.1.

A finished scene, with texture-mapped columns and a floating picture.

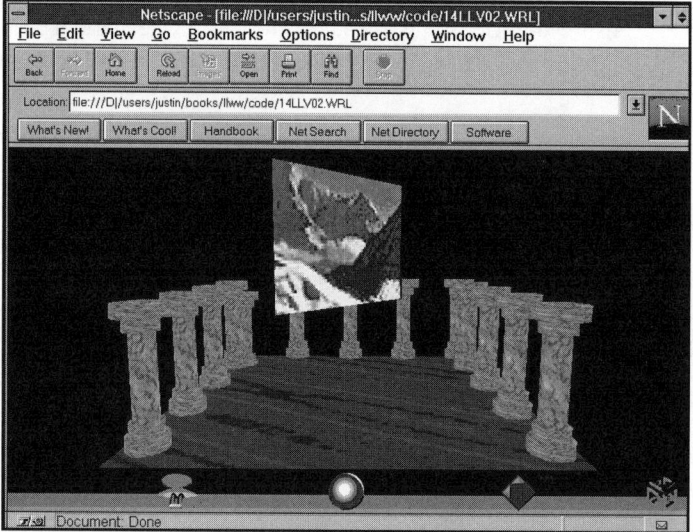

The textureTransform Field and TextureTransform Node

Sometimes you don't want the picture filling the whole face of the object you're applying it to. Like the rest of the VRML system, you start with a collection of basic nodes, then add a modifying node. The textureTransform field allows you to add a TextureTransform node, which can be used only in the Appearance node. You can use it to scale and rotate an image to fit the object as you please. Here's how the TextureTransform node is defined:

```
TextureTransform {
    exposedField SFVec2f center       0 0
    exposedField SFFloat rotation     0
    exposedField SFVec2f scale        1 1
    exposedField SFVec2f translation 0 0
}
```

By using this node in the Appearance node, you can control exactly how the texture looks. If you look at the floating picture in Figure 15.1, you can see the effects of the different fields, whose names are fairly self-explanatory. Center, for example, is used to specify a point that all the other fields act in relation to. A texture is a 2D image, which means the fields are much simpler. Each of the actions relate only to the picture itself. Therefore, a rotation rotates the picture around the point defined in the center field by the given angle, but doesn't rotate the whole primitive.

Figure 15.2 illustrates the effects of the different fields. On the far left, a rotation of 45 degrees (0.707 radians) is applied. Next is a scale in both dimensions of 0.5, then a translation by 0.5, and finally a rotation of 45 degrees around the point 0.5,0.5. An arrow image is used that points up so you know what's going on.

Figure 15.2.

Illustrating the effects of TextureTransform's different fields.

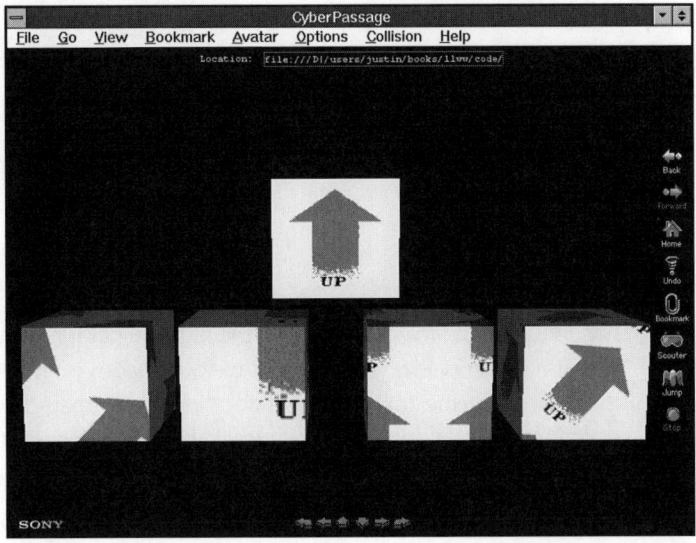

The top figure is the reference image. Along the bottom row, from left to right, you see examples of rotation, scale, translation, and rotation around a point other than 0,0.

Remember that all angles specified are in radians, not degrees.

The end results aren't exactly what you were expecting, are they? The right-hand image probably illustrates what you were expecting the left-hand image to do. Read on for more about how textures work.

Working with Texture Coordinates

Unlike the rest of VRML, textures use their own special coordinate system. The coordinates of textures are relative to the size of the texture itself. Therefore, a value of 1 is equivalent to the length of that side of the image. In graphics terminology, there are two axes: S is the vertical part, and T is the horizontal. They actually measure how the graph is applied to the object itself.

A coordinate of 2,2 would be the upper-right corner of the rightmost image in the top row, shown in the image on the right in Figure 15.3.

Figure 15.3.
The S,T coordinate system of VRML textures. The figure on the left is the basic system for one image; the figure on the right shows how it fits with multiple images.

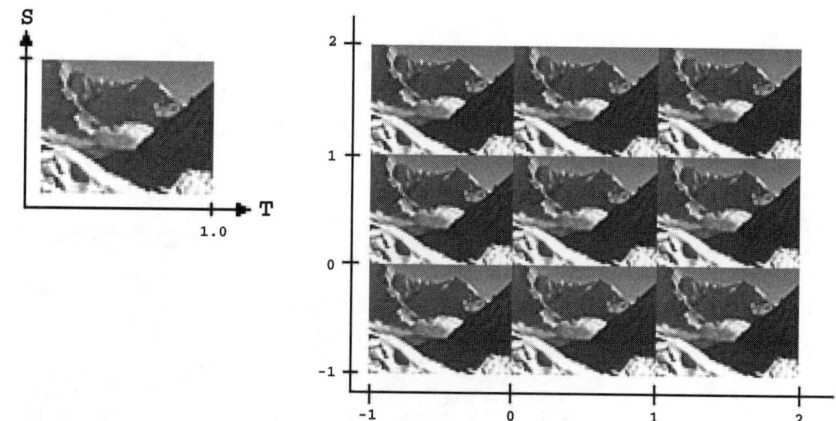

VRML 1.0 had a much more complex texture-mapping scheme, in which there were three coordinate systems. The first dealt with the flat image, the second with the image as it was shaped to fit the object, and the last was the standard x,y,z system of the geometry. This scheme caused a lot of confusion, so it was simplified to the current system.

Going back to the images presented in Figure 15.2, you can now figure out what happened. In the rotated figure on the left, the default center is 0,0—the lower-left corner—which is why you get parts of four images on it. (Why you get four images is explained in the following section, "Including Images with PixelTextures.") The scaled image was doubled in size (scale by 0.5). Because it increased out from the default center, you got only the lower-left corner of the image.

With this in mind, the effect of a translation by 0.5,0.5 is easy to understand. The translation simply moved the origin into the middle of what the old picture used to be (the middle of the object's face). Because of the texture's wrapping effect, you end up with all four quadrants of the picture, just reversed. The last box probably showed the effect you were expecting to see from the first rotation. Since you specified a center of 0.5,0.5, which is really the center of the image, the image rotated around its own center.

By combining all these fields, you can get any effect of stretching and rotation to fit any object.

Including Images with PixelTextures

Apart from importing external files for images, you might want to include those pictures directly in the VRML source file. This saves the overhead of establishing extra HTTP connections for each file. However, adding pictures results in the file being much larger, slowing down the initial load times.

These texture images may be grayscale or color, with or without transparency.

The PixelTexture node lets you use VRML's built-in format to include images in the source file. Naturally, this isn't usually done by hand, so you need to learn only the basic concepts of working with the `SFImage` field type. However, you might need to use this method of including images when you want to create a small grayscale or color image used as a tile, which would be too much work to add as an external file. Here's how the PixelTexture node is defined:

```
PixelTexture {
    exposedField SFImage   image     0 0 0
    field        SFBool    repeatS   TRUE
    field        SFBool    repeatT   TRUE
}
```

The first three values of the image define the height, width, and number of components in the image. A component value of 1 is grayscale, 2 is grayscale plus transparency, 3 is color represented in RGB space, and 4 is RGB images plus transparency.

The following declaration is a one-pixel–wide grayscale image, with the top pixel white and the bottom pixel black:

```
texture PixelTexture {
    image 1 2 1 0xFF 0x00
}
```

If you want to create a small grayscale tile, such as a herringbone pattern, then this method would be ideal. However, this is an uncompressed image format; for anything larger than a basic pattern, a normal compressed format like GIF, JPEG, or PNG should be used.

Wrapping Up Textures

You might have noticed in the introduction to ImageTexture that I didn't explain the repeatS and repeatT fields, but you needed the information in the previous section to understand what these fields do.

In a nutshell, they tell the browser whether it should repeat the texture map to fill up the blank space on the surface. By default, they're set to TRUE. Setting them to FALSE means you end up with just a single image scaled, rotated, or translated on that particular face. Using a single image is especially handy if you want to put a small version of the image on the face, leaving a blank border around it. This can be done easily by transforming it to the middle of the face and scaling it to the size you want.

Textures on IndexedFaceSets

Many of your worlds will consist not of primitives, but of the more complex IndexedFaceSet that was introduced at the end of Chapter 13, "Exploring VRML Browsers and Development Tools." IndexFaceSets present a different problem than using a standard primitive for texture mapping does. Because you have many different sizes of sides and logical relationships between them (that is, how they are located in 3D space), mapping texture coordinates is also complex. To add a texture map image to an IndexedFaceSet, use the same method you do for the other geometry nodes, using the Shape node. Instead of a box or cylinder, you put the IndexedFaceSet declaration in the geometry field. The textureTransform field is also used if you have it defined in the Appearance node.

Start with a basic shape that has four faces. So you can see where the edges of the faces are, they'll be arranged so they aren't in a plane. Three of the four faces have common edges, but the fourth is offset so that it doesn't touch them. Apart from that, everything else is the same as the previous examples—just a Shape node with a texture and the IndexedFaceSet as the geometry.

To illustrate a few points, the simple picture of the arrow on a couple of faces works better than a real-world object having a few hundred faces. Most of the applying textures to individual faces will eventually be done in a proper GUI VRML editor, rather than being done by hand. However, if you know the principles behind it, then you can create some wonderful worlds very quickly.

Listing 15.2. The test file for using textures and IndexedFaceSets.

```
#VRML V2.0 utf8
#
# Texture mapping an IndexedFaceSet
Shape {
    appearance Appearance {
        texture ImageTexture { url "picture.jpg" }
    }
    geometry IndexedFaceSet {
        coord Coordinate {
            point [
                0 0 0, 1 0 0 , 1 1 0, 0 1 0,
                -1 1 -.5, -1 0 -.5,
                0 -1 -.5, -1 -1 -.5,
```

```
                    0 0 -1, 1 0 -1, 1 -1 -1, 0 -1 -1
                ]
            }
        coordIndex [
            0, 1, 2, 3, -1,
            0, 3, 4, 5, -1,
            0, 5, 7, 6, -1,
            11, 10, 9, 8, -1
        ]
    }
}
```

When you load the example in Listing 15.2, notice that the picture is spread across all the faces. If you want to spread an image to fit some underlying framework without lining up vertices with strategic parts of the model, then this method is very handy; however, for many purposes it isn't satisfactory. Sometimes you might want to control the exact positioning of the texture on the faces. To do this, you need to define in texture coordinates how the image is mapped onto the individual faces.

As an experiment, declare a face that lies directly behind the first face (coordinates 0 0 -1, 1 0 -1, 1 1 -1, 0 1 -1). Have a look at the resulting texture that's applied and compare it to the face in front. Notice that the image behind is identical in coordinates to the image on the front face.

Texture coordinates mirror what happens with the standard coordinate system used to define a face. The texCoord field contains a list of the texture coordinates you want to use. TexCoordIndex is then used to gather these texture coordinates into the correct relationships, much as the coordIndex field is used to associate relationships of points to form a series of faces. Each entry in this field corresponds exactly to that vertex in the coordIndex field. Each face must end with the value of -1, again, just like the coordIndex field.

To map a section of an image to an IndexedFaceSet, do the following:

1. Declare the Shape node and put the IndexedFaceSet in the geometry field.

2. Put the list of vertices and faces in the coord and coordIndex fields respectively. Assume the face has the following coordIndexes:

    ```
    coord Coordinate { point [ .... 20 25 10, 19 25 10, .... 19 20 10, 20 20
    ➥10, .... ] }
    coordIndex [ .... 35, 36, 45, 44, -1, ......]
    ```

3. Declare a list of texture coordinates that you want to map to individual vertices on the IndexedFaceSet in the texCoord field:

    ```
    texCoord TextureCoordinate { point [ .... 0.4 0.5, 0.6 0.6, 0.6 0.5, 0.5
    ➥0.5, ....] }
    ```

4. Match the indices of the just-declared texture coordinates of the image to the vertices by declaring the texCoordIndex field with the coordinates corresponding to each of the faces:

    ```
    texCoordIndex [ .... 10, 11, 12, 13, -1, .... ]
    ```

The end result is to place the texture coordinate 0.4,0.5 on the vertex defined as 20, 25, 10.

If you leave the texCoordIndex field empty, then the browser matches each vertex in coordIndex to the texCoord values by using each one for the vertices of each face, as declared in the coordIndex field. You must have one more texCoordIndex value than the number of texCoord values. This matches the definition for the coord and coordIndex fields. As you can see from the result, it's not very useful most of the time. What you want to do is control the way each face is rendered individually.

If the texCoordIndex field isn't empty, then it's used to define the texture coordinates that belong to each face. The values you put in will correspond to each vertex for the corresponding face. Likewise, you must end each face with the value of -1. The order in which you declare the faces must be the same order you used for the texture values.

Figure 15.4.
The full use of textures on IndexedFaceSets.

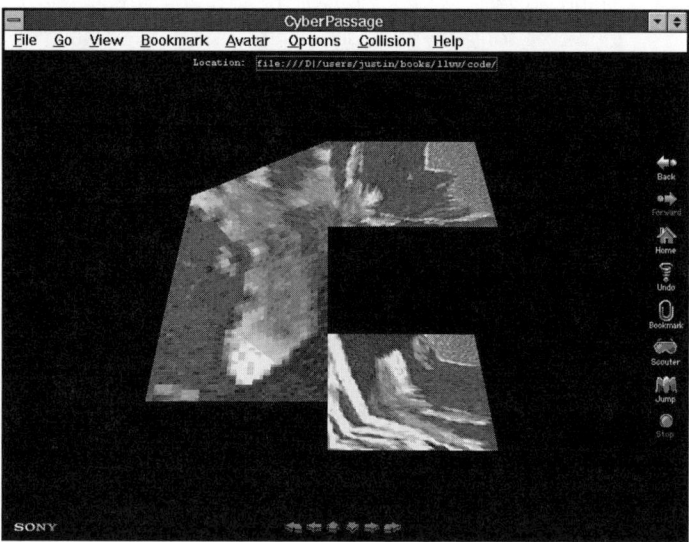

TASK # Building Texture Maps

As you've seen, a texture map can be anything you want. The marble columns used a standard background available from the Internet, the picture was just one I had lying around from an old Web page, and the arrow I created myself in Paint Shop Pro. What makes a good texture?

Producing a texture for VRML uses the same techniques as producing a texture for any other type of 3D graphics, so if you have a collection of textures from previous examples in this book or from a ray-tracing program like POVRay, then you can use them here. In Chapter 17, you'll start developing an art gallery that shows off many of the pictures Kelly developed in the first half of this book. You will find that I use the terms *picture*, *image*, and *texture* interchangeably throughout the book. In terms of VRML, there's very little difference among them.

If you're planning to hang your picture up as a photo, then it doesn't really matter what size or type of primitive you use. You won't even need to worry about using a TextureTransform. The picture always stretches to fit the object. As long as you have the proportion of each dimension the same for the image and object, it will work out.

If you're using a texture map that will be tiled across a surface, rather than just a single image used to produce a photo, then you might run into another problem. VRML is the same as any other 3D or 2D image production with tiled images—getting the edges of the tile's texture to line up can be quite frustrating. As any 3D model maker will confirm, this is one of the most time-consuming tasks you'll face. Usually, you're modifying other textures and background images rather than building your own.

If you decide to build your own images—as Mr. Bubsy wanted you to do for his shop—then you should already have the tools you need from the first part of this book.

1. Importing image formats and converting them to a supported format is the first requirement.

2. Next, you want to manipulate the images in some way, such as adding extra detail or cutting and pasting montages.

3. Finally, map that image to the surface by using an IndexedFaceSet.

For most general-purpose work, you can't beat Paint Shop Pro for the first two steps. Applying textures to models then falls into the realm of the VRML modeling tool. Software like Pioneer and V-Realm Builder do this work for you in a nice GUI environment.

TIP: If you want to create more stunning texture maps, then use trueSpace to produce a 3D image. Import the resulting Targa file into Paint Shop Pro, and save it as a JPEG file. This method gives you some attractive effects when you use the 3D image to replace VRML geometry.

Using Transparency

Once you've created a few standard images, then try experimenting more. Most of today's standard image formats include more than just the basic image. Interlacing, transparency, and multiple-image files (for example, animated GIFs) can be used. Interlacing works the same way as it's used on 2D pages, and the animated formats are covered in the next section, "Adding Movies."

Transparency has several different uses, depending on the combination of image transparency and the underlying primitive's transparency. Follow these steps to use transparency:

1. Start with the basic arrow again, but this time make the white background transparent.

2. Place the arrow on a box with the normal texture declaration—no TextureTransform nodes.

3. To add some flair, I've placed it on a green floor.

Notice that the whole primitive seems to have disappeared except for the texture map; the picture looks like arrows just floating in space. The effect is shown in Figure 15.5. You can use transparency for all sorts of things, such as creating floating signs in space; it can save you the work of trying to build the geometry of a sign.

Figure 15.5.

A set of arrows hanging in space, courtesy of the transparency effect.

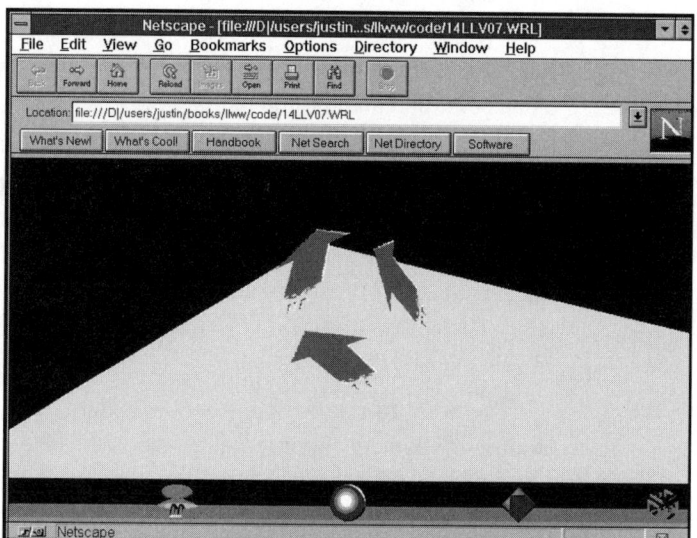

TIP: Always put your signs on a box rather than an IndexedFaceSet. This way, you have to declare the image only once, and it's displayed on both sides of the sign. Watch out for arrow-type signs, however. The one on the back will point the wrong way!

I mentioned before that you could declare both a texture and a material for one Appearance node, and here's how you do it:

1. Create an Appearance node that has a material with a blue color.

2. To the texture field, add the arrow you've been using for the previous examples in this chapter.

3. Now view the end result. Notice that the image is still the same as before—the material node has no effect.

When you define both a material and a texture, the texture has priority. Normally, the object is created with the material color, and once the texture has been downloaded, then the texture is displayed instead of the color. You could use this effect when creating a grass surface, for example:

1. Create the basic outline of the surface by using an IndexedFaceSet.

2. Add the Material node to the Apperance node with the colors set to be reasonably close to the final texture's color.

3. Finally, add the ImageTexture and TextureTransform nodes, which specify the grass image used to finish the scene.

 # Adding Movies

One of the nice features of VRML is the ability to add animated textures just as easily as you can add ordinary ones. You can also put a movie wherever you can have a standard image. This means you could wrap your favorite MPEG movie around a sphere or hang it on a floating flat screen.

To start with a familiar example, take a flat face formed from an IndexedFaceSet and apply a movie to it so it looks like an ordinary movie screen. Instead of the ImageTexture node used in the previous examples, now you'll use the MovieTexture node:

```
MovieTexture {
    exposedField SFBool    loop          FALSE
    exposedField SFFloat   speed         1
    exposedField SFTime    startTime     0
    exposedField SFTime    stopTime      0
    exposedField MFString url            []
    field        SFBool    repeatS       TRUE
    field        SFBool    repeatT       TRUE
    eventOut     SFFloat   duration_changed
    eventOut     SFBool    isActive
}
```

The MovieTexture url field is a pointer to the movie file. VRML requires that MPEG1-Video and MPEG1-Systems be supported. Animated file formats, such as GIF89a, are not specifically mentioned in the specification, but it would be reasonably safe to assume that when GIF is supported, these animated formats will be too, under the standard ImageTexture node. However, this isn't enough to play the movie; you need to set the start and stop times.

To get sound from MPEG1-Systems files, see Chapter 23, "Real-Life Examples: A 3D Gallery: An Advanced VRML World," which covers introducing audio into your 3D world.

RepeatS and repeatT are the same as the ImageTexture fields. The speed field controls the relative speed of the movie compared to its original speed. This relative speed setting is handy for doing fast forwards, once you learn how to control the film from external input with scripting and from user input through sensors.

A full discussion of how time runs in VRML isn't presented until Chapter 19, "Using Built-in Animation Techniques," so I don't want to tread on my own toes. For the moment, to play a movie, just set the loop field to TRUE and the startTime field to 1. These settings give you a continuously looping movie. To add a movie into your scene, all you need to do is declare the following:

Listing 15.3. Adding an MPEG movie to the scene.

```
Shape {
    appearance Appearance {
        texture MovieTexture {
            url "mymovie.mpg"
            loop TRUE
            startTime 1
        }
    }
    geometry IndexedFaceSet {
        coords Coordinate {
            point [ -1 0 0, -1 1 0, 1 1 0, 1 0 0 ]
        }
        coordIndex [ 0, 1, 2, 3, -1 ]
    }
}
```

Optimizing Worlds with Textures for the Web

Earlier in this chapter, I mentioned that you can use textures to replace parts of the scene graph's geometry. This is a fairly common tactic in VR systems. By using 3D textures like the ones my co-author has created in the first half of this book, you can save yourself a lot of work. In a VR world, not everything must conform to reality.

Buildings are a good example of using textures to replace geometry. A simple box wrapped with the texture of the building's exterior is much simpler than actually modeling the whole building. Although textures make the world slower to navigate in, the same highly detailed building made by using geometry would have exactly the same effect. For a good example of using textures to replace geometry, have a look at Planet9's Jackson Square world at http://www.planet9.com/worlds/jacksq.wrl. It has many good examples of how a cool world can be built with very little effort.

Modeling realistic-looking trees is another good use of textures. I will be the first to admit that the trees developed in the previous chapter didn't look very realistic. If you want realism, then have another look at the trees in the Jackson Square site. They're made from a pair of faces that mimic the outline of the tree texture on them. By placing these two faces at right angles, it's very difficult to tell they're not real, highly detailed trees until you get up close and look at the bases of the trunks, where you notice the cross shape of two planes rather than a properly modeled tree.

You need to be careful where you use textures and where you use colored geometry. As a good rule of thumb, textures should be used when you have a highly detailed object that would be time-consuming to model properly. Small items, like doorknobs, are another good use for textures. It's really up to your judgement, but be careful about overusing them because they slow the VRML world down considerably. Colored geometry is better when you need to show the detail structure of an object the user may walk around in. You could summarize this as saying: Use textures for small objects and geometry for large objects.

Workshop Wrap-up

By combining primitives and textures, you can get some very realistic worlds—the Jackson Square example being one of them. You can also use textures to create some fantastic-looking places that look far from real. Textures are a common technique in VRML worlds for creating anything from tiled floors to movies hanging in space.

Next Steps

The previous chapter and this one is where you'll spend a good portion of your time when developing VRML worlds, so it's important you understand the basics before you head into more advanced topics.

- ❏ In Chapter 16, "Adding a Dash of Reality," you'll learn about putting in light sources and defining positions to view the world from.

- ❏ If you want to see the use of textures in action, go to Chapter 17, "Real-Life Examples: The VRML Art Gallery: A VRML World by Hand." Here, you'll start developing a VRML art gallery featuring the pictures created in the first part of this book.

- ❏ Chapter 19, "Using Built-in Animation Techniques," introduces basic animation techniques for VRML 2.0, so you can learn how to control those movies you've just added.

Q&A

Q: Apart from creating my own, where can I find predefined textures?

A: Many Internet sites offer large collections of predefined textures. One of the Internet search engines, like Yahoo!, will give you a list of sites to visit. Netscape has quite a selection of them at its site, which you're free to use. Also, just about every modeling package now comes with a smaller collection of textures.

Q: Is it possible to use streamed video with the MovieTexture node?

A: The VRML 2.0 specification doesn't say anything about streamed video. However, if the browser of your choice does support it, then you should be able to use it. With the use of streamed audio and video increasing on the Internet, I expect it won't be long before browsers support streamed video by default.

Q: How can I put a different texture on each face of my box?

A: You can't. To do this, you must declare a collection of individual faces and give each one a separate texture.

SIXTEEN

Adding a Dash of Reality

—by Justin Couch

So far, you've learned to populate your VRML worlds with primitives and models. You've also learned some tricks for painting objects, but using basic colors is just the first step. With textures, you can make your VRML objects much more visually appealing, but there's still a lot to do to make your worlds realistic. What's missing? Well, there are no lighting effects. Another effect that's missing is not being able to walk through walls, and you also need a way to show details when you get close to an object. Luckily, VRML addresses each of these problems.

This chapter introduces the basic techniques for adding that extra touch of realism to your world:

❏ Start with the basic lighting types provided in VRML.

❏ Make walls and objects you can no longer walk through.

❏ Show how to change the amount of detail on an object as you get closer to it.

❏ Find out how to set up different cameras to give you several viewpoints.

By the time you've finished this chapter, you should be able to create some very believable worlds. Just remember that the more detail you put in, the longer it will take to download and the slower the world will run.

In this chapter, you

❏ Use VRML's basic lighting types

❏ Create walls and objects you can't walk through

❏ Change an object's details as you get closer to it

❏ Set up cameras to get different viewpoints

Tasks in this chapter:

❏ Adding Directional Light to a VRML Scene

❏ Controlling Spot Lights

❏ Using PointLights

❏ Stopping Visitors from Walking Through Walls

❏ Using Level of Detail Nodes for Effective VRML Worlds

❏ Setting Different Views

Lights in the VRML World

If you have spent any time ray-tracing images for your Web pages, you will have no problems with the VRML light source models. However, you might notice some other differences. Unlike ray-tracing, there are no ambient light settings. If you don't specify an emissive or diffuse color value for your objects, you can't see them.

VRML defines three types of light sources: SpotLight, DirectionalLight, and PointLight. Their names are pretty self-explanatory. You'll look at examples of each, using a basic test scene that's shown in Figure 16.1 without any lights except the headlight.

NOTE: To show the effects of the light sources, define only diffuseColor values on all your objects. Chapter 13 briefly outlines the effects of the various color types used in the Material nodes. For this example, you'll define only diffuseColor values because emissiveColor would ruin some of the lighting effects. Emissive light sources emit their color even without other light sources in the scene. To see the effects of external lights, you need to make sure that the only lighting effects are produced by the lights themselves.

Figure 16.1.
The basic test scene with the headlight turned on.

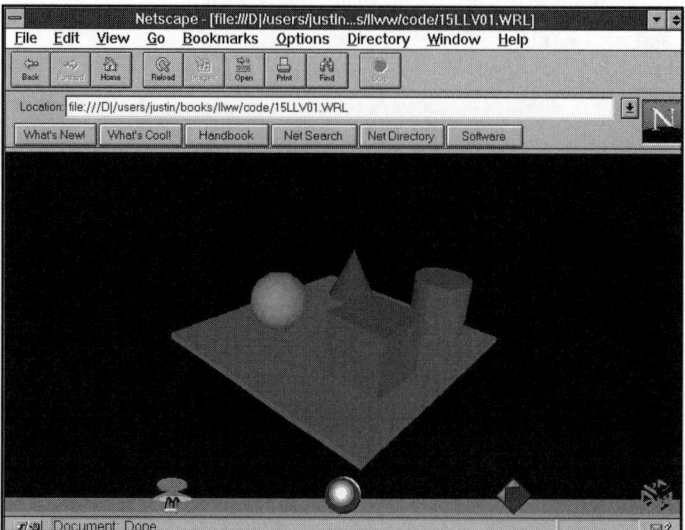

Within the test scene are four objects; each is a different color. In the figures that follow, some objects will look brighter, probably because of their color rather than the lighting effects.

Although I mentioned that there were no ambient light sources, this isn't completely correct. There are no *separate* ambient light sources, but within each light node, there's a field value that can control the ambient light intensity. The resulting ambient light is the sum of all the values defined in the light nodes.

For each of the examples, you'll see what the light looks like in the scene, as well as commentary on the effects.

 # Adding Directional Light to a VRML Scene

DirectionalLight specifies a direction along which the given light color travels; it's the equivalent of a distant light like the sun. All the rays of a directional light are parallel.

1. Start by specifying a node called the DirectionalLight node. One of the fields within this node is the direction field.

2. Now, set the direction field values to -1 -1 -1. This should get the sun shining over your shoulder toward the objects. Place this node at the top of the file, as shown in Listing 16.1.

Listing 16.1. Extract from the file illustrating DirectionalLights.

```
#VRML V2.0 utf8
#
# A world to show the effects of various light sources
# The directional light sources
DirectionalLight {
    direction  -1 -1 -1
}
```

3. The DirectionalLight node also has a field that sets the intensity of the light, but leave this at the default value for this example.

4. After the light is set, you need something for it to illuminate, so create a scene. You will show only the box portion of your test scene. Remember to use the diffuseColor field to set the color of the box.

```
# The basic scene
Transform {
    translation 1 .5 1
    children [
        Shape {
            appearance Appearance {
                material Material { diffuseColor 0.7 0.1 0.1 }
            }
            geometry Box { size 1 1 1 }
        }
    ]
}
etc....
```

The same scene is shown again, this time with the DirectionalLight added, in Figure 16.2.

Figure 16.2.

Directional lighting for the entire scene. The headlight has been turned off.

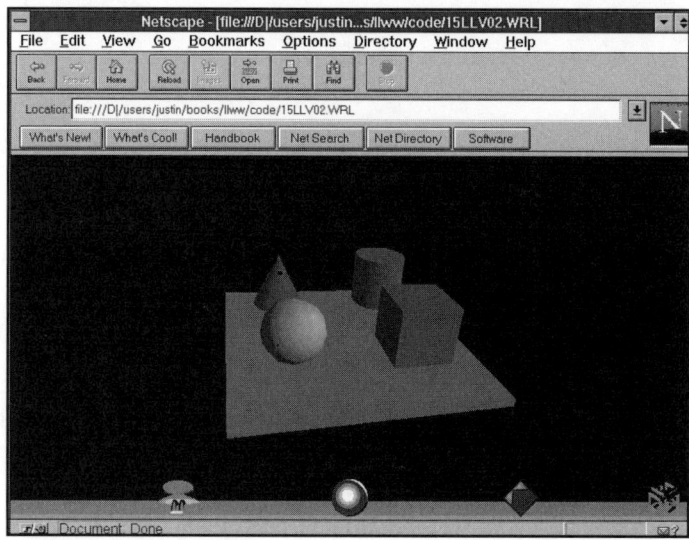

Now look closely at the scene, particularly at the floor. What do you notice? That's right—there are no shadows. In VRML, everything is lit equally, regardless of whether there's another object between it and the light source.

OK, try experimenting a little bit. Add another directional light, this time coming from over your other shoulder, but place it within the Transform node that holds the sphere. To increase the effect, the intensity of the first light is turned down to 0.2. If you're using the CosmoPlayer browser, it will light up all the objects, but if you look at the world with the CyberPassage browser, it will light up none of them. Which one is correct? Strictly speaking, neither of them.

According to the VRML specification, the DirectionalLights are limited in scope to the parent grouping node. In this case, there should be light only on the sphere, nowhere else. The VRML specification has a small rider saying that some low-end rendering engines won't support lighting on a per object basis, so lights should be placed as high as possible in the scene graph.

Controlling SpotLights

If you want to highlight a particular object, then DirectionalLights aren't the technique to use. You should be using a SpotLight to provide a focused beam of light aimed at a particular direction from a given point. In this example, you want to highlight the sphere, so add the SpotLight node into the Transform node where the sphere is located:

1. Start by adding a SpotLight within the children field of the sphere's Transform node. This will highlight only the sphere.

2. Then add values for the direction field, so that your light knows where to point, and the coordinates of the location where your spotlight will be placed.

Now if you look at the world, it's very dark. The SpotLight doesn't seem to have taken effect. If you look closely at the SpotLight definition, it has a default radius of 1. You have placed the light at a distance of more than 10 meters from the object, so the objects aren't within the SpotLight's radius. Anything outside this radius results in no light, so you need to increase the radius a bit:

3. Add the radius field and give it a value of 30 to ensure that the sphere is within this radius.

4. The final fields you specify are the beamWidth and cutOffAngle fields. To get the feel of how spotlights work, you should experiment with these field values. They control how focused the light is. The wider these angles, the more diffuse the effects become. This section of the scene should look like the code in Listing 16.2.

To control your SpotLights, you should also look at the attenuation field, which controls the amount of attenuation between the location and the radius. *Attentuation* means how quickly the light decreases with distance. The default value is set so that there's no attenuation. Many of the low-end rendering engines used in the PC-based browsers don't support light attenuation, so it's not really useful for most work put on the Web.

Listing 16.2. Using a SpotLight in place of a DirectionalLight.

```
Transform {
    translation -1 .5 1
    children [
        SpotLight {
            direction 1 -1 -1
            location -5 5 5
            radius    30
            beamWidth 1.57
            cutOffAngle 1.57
        }
        Shape {
            appearance Appearance {
                material Material { diffuseColor 0.1 0.7 0.1 }
            }
            geometry Sphere { radius 0.5 }
        }
    ]
}
```

Figure 16.3 shows the results of the SpotLight on the sphere. Remember that different browsers have different rendering engines, so there may be some difference in the image quality between browsers.

Figure 16.3.
Using a SpotLight instead of a DirectionalLight; this time, Sony's CyberPassage is used as the browser.

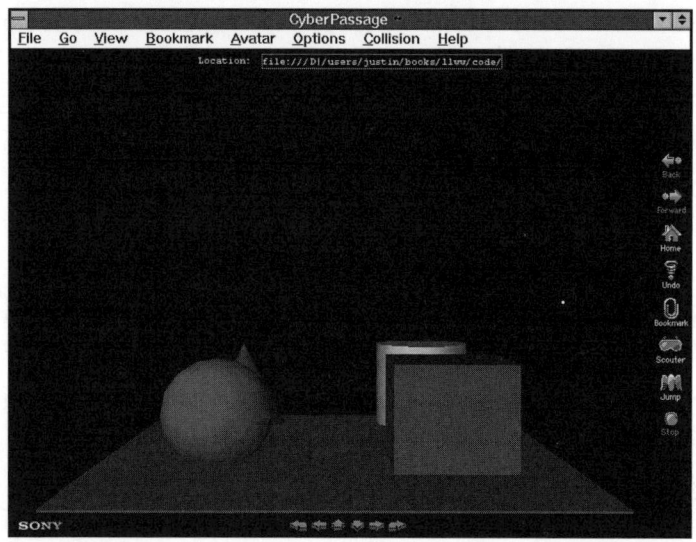

At the time of this writing, SpotLights were implemented as PointLights in CosmoPlayer.

SpotLights are one of those tricky nodes that need a bit of playing with to get the right effect. Generally, you won't use a SpotLight without any other lighting source. While testing the examples for this book, you've discovered that SpotLights aren't completely implemented.

The world seen in Figure 16.3 included a directional light, but with no headlight. Notice how dark the picture is. What really needs to be added to the scene is some ambient light to brighten the whole scene. The SpotLight can then be used to create highlights.

The last item of note about using SpotLights is that they aren't constrained by the parent nodes. Normally, you would place a SpotLight within a Transform if you wanted to keep it relative to some object. If this isn't necessary, then you should place them at the top of the file with the rest of the light sources.

Using PointLights

When you're trying to create a scene normally, you want to model a lightbulb that sends light in all directions. To do this, you would use the PointLight node. Try placing a PointLight in the middle of the four objects to show its effect:

1. The best place for the PointLight node is at the top of the file, so begin there.

2. The PointLight node has many of the same fields as the other lights, but you need to set only two for this example: radius and location. The code is as simple as this:

```
PointLight {
    radius 10
    location 0 1 0
}
```

Figure 16.4 shows the results of the PointLight placed in the middle of all the objects in your scene; notice that again, no headlight is used.

Figure 16.4.

A PointLight placed in the middle of the objects. Note the graded shadowing on the side of the cylinder and cube.

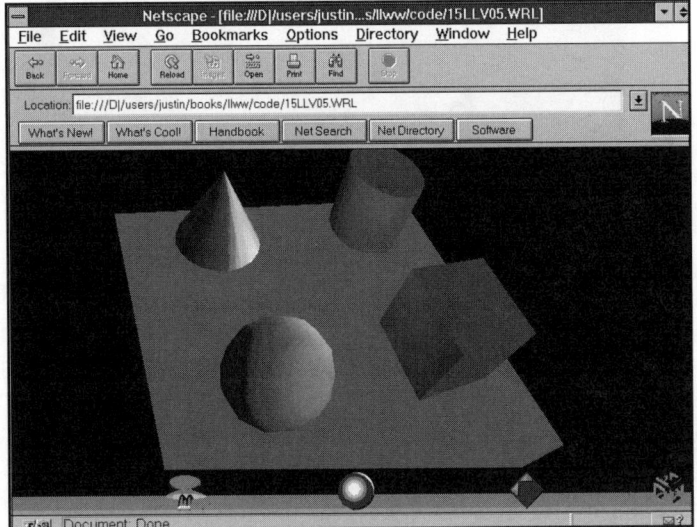

A radius of 10 is used to make sure the lighting effect is used over the whole scene. You should experiment with the radius to see how it affects the lighting. As with the SpotLight, there's also an attenuation field to control the drop-off of light intensity. The same comment about its use also applies; that is, attenuation is not really usable because most PC browsers aren't supporting it.

Putting Them All Together

Now that you've explored the various light source types, this would be a good time to try combining them all into a single scene. Using the same sample scene, put all the lights in; the results are shown in Figure 16.5.

Figure 16.5.

The result of turning on all the lights.

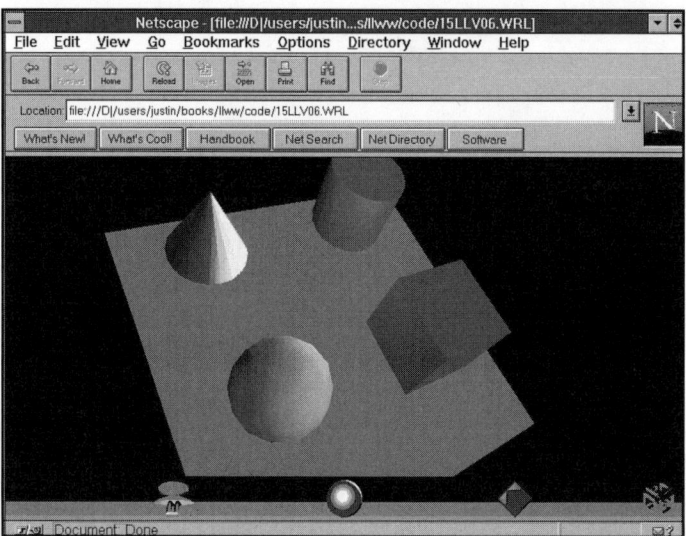

The differences in these scenes can be difficult to see in the black and white figures used in this chapter. Check the CD-ROM to see these examples in actual VRML color.

Note that the effects of the SpotLight are hardly visible; directional lights contribute the majority of lighting to the scene. Look at the cube for the best illustration of the two lighting sources. The sphere, which showed most of the SpotLight effect, has had this all but removed by the domination of the DirectionalLight.

Stopping Visitors from Walking Through Walls

One of the biggest problems in VRML 1.0 was that you couldn't stop people from wandering through objects. This really became a problem when you were building houses. There was no need to put a front door in because people could walk straight through the wall! This had to be fixed, so in Version 2.0 a Collision node was added. It works like any of the other grouping nodes. By simply adding the Collision node as a parent, you get instant solid walls.

1. Start with a simple object, such as a cylinder. You have already added a bit of color to make it pretty, but that's it. Now try walking toward it—you go straight through it!

2. Add a Collision node, which works like all the other group nodes. To turn on collision detection for the cylinder, just put it in the children field of the Collision node. This is what the code looks like:

Listing 16.3. The simple cylinder you can no longer walk through.

```
#VRML V2.0 utf8
#
# Using Collision Detection
Collision {
    children [
        Shape {
            appearance Appearance {
                material Material { emissiveColor 1 0 0 }
            }
            geometry Cylinder {}
        }
    ]
}
```

TIP: You can create collision detection on a group of separate objects by putting them all in the children field. You won't be able to walk through the objects, but you can walk around them. This effect can be used to create doorways, so that you can walk through the doorway, but not the walls.

3. The Collision node also has some extra little tricks you can use. The definition contains a field called *proxy* that takes a single node for its value. Put a sphere in as the node for this field. This proxy field builds an invisible "force field." Its code is simple:

Listing 16.4. An expanded collision detection field, with a sphere added around the cylinder.

```
#VRML V2.0 utf8
#
# Using Collision Detection
Collision {
    children [
        Shape {
            appearance Appearance {
                material Material { emissiveColor 1 0 0 }
            }
            geometry Cylinder {}
        }
    ]
    proxy Sphere { radius 2 }
}
```

Now you can no longer get anywhere near the cylinder. In the previous example, you could walk up and touch it, but now you can't get anywhere near it. This is because the proxy field defines the shape of the collision detection field. Any drawing node can

Another node, called NavigationInfo, might affect how close you can get to the cylinder. It contains the avatarSize field, which determines the radius around your viewpoint that will trigger collision detection. The default distance is 1 unit, so you may not be able to get very close to the cylinder.

be specified here, but obviously it makes no sense to define a complicated shape since it has no visible geometry. The idea is to create a simplified detection radius, not a more complex one.

TIP: The proxy field can contain any type of node, allowing you to create any sort of collision boundary around your objects. For example, you could place a Group node around the object and put a collection of IndexedFaceSets in it to get exactly the behavior you want.

Using Level of Detail Nodes for Effective VRML Worlds

One thing guaranteed to slow down your VRML world is excessively high levels of detail. However, when you're close to an object, you want to see some detail. The problem is deciding what to put in and what to leave out. By using the Level Of Detail (LOD) node, you can get the best of both worlds.

LOD allows you to define a set of ranges and what you want the object to look like in each range. In a way, this approximates reality, as you gradually discern more detail the closer you get to an object. This technique is helpful when you're using textures. Texture mapping always slows down a world, so it's a good idea not to use it until you're close to an object. Start with a simple model: a cube that turns into a sphere.

1. First, place the LOD node at the beginning of the file. Within the LOD node, you can specify the range, which is the distance at which the details show up, and a level field, where the details are defined.

2. With the LOD node in place, declare the range. Several ranges can be specified. If the range field has two numbers, then there are three levels of detail. You made the range value 5, so there are only two levels: a cube and a sphere.

3. The level field contains the details and starts with the highest level of detail first. The final VRML file looks like this:

Listing 16.5. A quick LOD demo: A cube that turns into a sphere.

```
#VRML V2.0 utf8
#
# A simple LOD
LOD {
    range [ 5 ]
    levels [
        # first level for greatest detail - a sphere
```

```
Shape {
    appearance Appearance {
        material Material { emissiveColor 0 0 1 }
    }
    geometry Sphere { radius .5 }
}
# second level minimum detail
Shape {
    appearance Appearance {
        material Material { emissiveColor 0 0 1 }
    }
    geometry Box { size .5 .5 .5 }
}
    ]
}
```

WARNING: When you view this file in a browser, you might notice that it always stays a cube—it never swaps to being a sphere. This is because the specifications allow the browser writers a lot of leeway to optimize the rendering speed. If the browser thinks it can handle a higher level of detail, then it will use that. The situation you get is that the cube is simpler to render than the sphere, so it gets used all the time.

Just because a VRML file contains a LOD node doesn't mean the browser will use it. The browser can decide whether it wants to use the LOD node, based on performance reasons.

Detail levels are always defined as being the most detailed first, then fewer details as you go down the file. This doesn't stop you from declaring the most detailed as the last item, but it would sure confuse both your visitors and the browser. The specification suggests you should declare as many levels as you need to get smooth transitions, but this can create an awfully large source file just for a simple smooth change. However, there are ways around this; they will be covered in Chapter 18, "Tricks to Optimize Your VRML Worlds for the Web."

Because of their internal implementation, many browsers that run scenes with LODs actually run slower than those scenes that use no LODs at all and are kept at a reasonably high detail level. They also tend to use more resources because browsers try to load all the details before choosing the best one.

Another way of getting the same effect is to create nested LOD systems. A building might consist of one overall LOD, but within the highest detail setting, there would be another LOD node controlling the details of the windows and doors. A nested LOD structure uses the same syntax as before. In each child, instead of putting a grouping node like Shape in the previous one, you put in another LOD node, as shown in Listing 16.6. Just because you have a nested LOD at one range doesn't mean it needs to be in all of them.

Listing 16.6. Nested LOD outline example.

```
LOD {
    range [ 5 ]
    levels [
        # first level for greatest detail - a sphere
```

continued

Listing 16.6. continued

```
Shape {
    appearance Appearance {
        material Material { emissiveColor 0 0 1 }
    }
    geometry Sphere { radius .5 }
}
# second level minimum detail
LOD {
    levels [2.5]
    # first level in nested LOD
    Shape {
        appearance Appearance {
            material Material { emissiveColor 0 0 1 }
        }
        geometry Box { size .5 .5 .5 }
    }
    #Seconnd level in nested LOD
    Shape {
        appearance Appearance {
            material Material { emissiveColor 0 0 1 }
        }
        geometry Cone {
            bottomRadius .5
            height 1
        }
    }
}
]
}
```

TASK # Setting Different Views

So far, you're viewing every file from the default position the browser gives you. Often, this isn't convenient, so you might like to define your own viewpoints; at other times, you might want to offer a collection of different places to view the world from. Using the Viewpoint node, you can do this and more.

1. Your first task is to provide a different default viewing position. Use the same model from the section on lighting to illustrate this.

2. The Viewpoint node uses the SFRotation field type, the same one you saw in the rotation Transform node, but this time it's combined with a position. This pair of values defines where you are located and in what direction you are looking. For your example, place the camera at (0,3,3) and then rotate it down 45 degrees.

3. You aren't limited in the number of viewpoints you can add to a file, but the first one defined becomes the default viewpoint you see when the file is first loaded. To distinguish all the viewpoints in a file, the description field allows you to give names to the different viewpoints:

```
Viewpoint {
    position 0 3 3
    orientation 1 0 0 -.785
    description "default camera"
}
```

The world seen from the default viewpoint you set up is shown in Figures 16.6a and 16.6b. The browser recognizes these extra viewpoints and allows you to change the predefined viewpoint, typically by clicking the right mouse button. In the CosmoPlayer browser, click the right mouse button and select the Next Viewpoint option from the pop-up menu to move to the next viewpoint position, or you can use the Page Up/Page Down keys.

Figure 16.6a.

The default entry view of your earlier model.

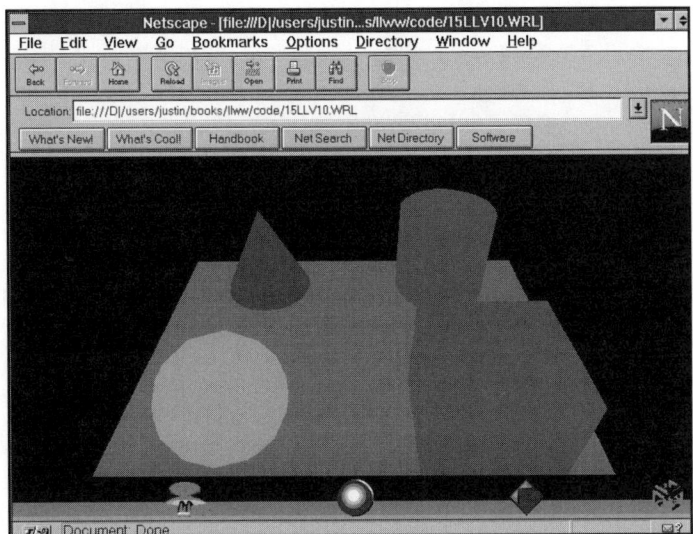

Figure 16.6b.

The same scene now viewed from the second viewpoint.

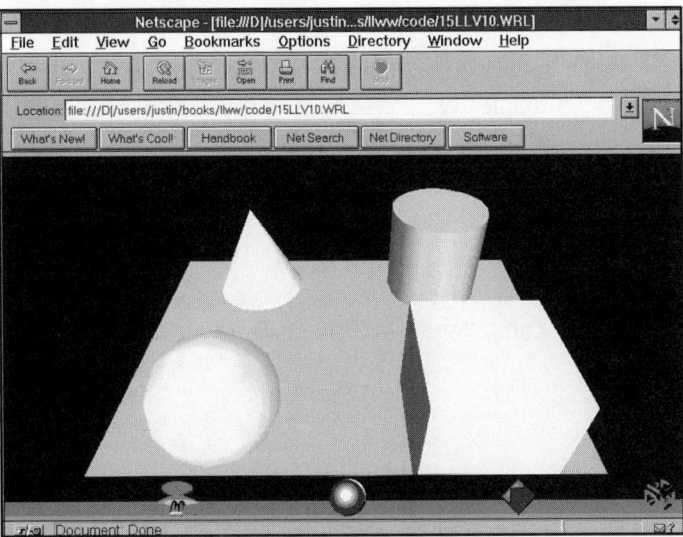

Another handy field in the Viewpoint node is the jump field. If the jump field is specified as false, the browser gives you an animated sequence from your current position to the next viewpoint. This is especially effective when you're giving guided tours.

The last field to experiment with is fieldOfView, which lets you control the amount of the world that's visible at once. A small value acts like a telephoto lens; a large value produces a wide-angle lens effect. Most of the time, you use only the default value because it gives a fairly good view of things.

TIP:
From this first view, you will notice quite a pronounced perspective on the objects. If you want to create an orthographic (that is, no perspective) camera effect, you can set the fieldOfView to a very small, almost non-zero, value (but definitely not zero) and set the distance fairly far away.

Workshop Wrap-up

You've now been introduced to many of the effects used in VRML worlds to make them more believable. Using them depends on what sort of machine you expect people to be viewing your file with. In the experience of the Terra Vista community, using the LOD node had too many problems, both with its implementation (it didn't like being used as a child of Transform) and also the performance penalty it imposed.

Next Steps

You now have some reasonable-looking worlds, but there's still a lot more for you to learn:

- ❏ To see a full demonstration of how to use VRML, go to the next chapter, Chapter 17, "Real-Life Examples: The VRML Art Gallery: A VRML World by Hand."

- ❏ If your world files are starting to get very large and slow, head to Chapter 18, "Tricks to Optimize Your VRML Worlds for the Web."

- ❏ Even more advanced VRML, with material on adding behaviors to your world, can be found in Chapters 20, "Interfacing VRML Worlds with Scripts," and 21, "Using Java to Add Behaviors to VRML."

Q&A

Q: I tried loading some of the examples in this chapter, but they look completely different, especially the ones on the lighting model.

A: Usually this is because you have the headlight turned on. The headlight is a spotlight mounted just above where your virtual head should be and always points in front of you. This can be turned off either by clicking the right mouse button to get a pop-up menu in CosmoPlayer or using the View menu in CyberPassage.

Q: What happens if I nest collision nodes?

A: You've jumped ahead of everybody else! Nested collision nodes are allowed and are very useful when it comes to behavior programming in a later chapter. When you collide with something, each collision node produces its own event notification to the system, so it's useful and sometimes necessary to have nested collision nodes.

Q: When I have multiple child primitives within a Collision node, what defines what can and cannot be collided with?

A: Only the primitives themselves can be collided with. If you have two cylinders located some distance apart, then you can walk between them with no problems, but you still can't walk *through* the individual cylinders.

SEVENTEEN

The VRML Art Gallery: A VRML World by Hand

—by Justin Couch

You now have enough information to start creating your first large VRML 2.0 world. In Chapter 2, "Up and Running: First VRML Creation," you created everything using readily available tools, which limited you to generating 1.0 worlds. Now that you've gotten this far, it's time to dust off your favorite text editor because this VRML world is going to be done all by hand.

One of the best things about virtual reality is that you don't need to conform to traditional earthbound construction—you can do whatever you want. I'm the sort of person who likes to experiment with things, so this creation is going to be a virtual art gallery. What am I going to put in this gallery? Well, my co-author has been good enough to create the content for me:

❏ First, you need to plan what the gallery will look like, then construct the basic outlines.

❏ After the gallery is constructed, add the content. You'll collect the pictures, organize them, and offer a virtual tour.

❏ The basic gallery is still a little boring, so you can spice it up with some extra links and scenery.

If you've been reading the preceding few chapters, many of the pieces will look familiar to you. Once you've created a few worlds, you will find that you've built up a library of parts you use over and over. Now you'll see the reason for doing what seemed like trivial examples in previous chapters; when you combine them, you get quite a stunning scene.

Designing the Gallery

So far in your collection of parts, you have a marble column, a tree, an arrow floating in space, and a few lights and cameras. Not much, but it's really all you need. It's amazing what you can do with just a few basic parts. I also have eight images from my co-author in my collection of pictures that I want to display.

A series of islands sounds like fun to me. Of course, since this is virtual reality, they will have to float in space, too. The islands will be connected by a series of wooden bridges, and the marble columns can be used to act as a gateway.

Constructing the Islands

Each island will be made from an IndexedFaceSet. You could have used the ElevationGrid to create the islands, but to get a real 3D look, I didn't want all the islands to be the same height. Using IndexedFaceSets allows you to create a floating island that can be viewed from all angles.

The first island is easy. It's almost a cone, but if you use a face set, you can control some of the properties.

1. Declare the list of vertices that you want to make the island from. The island will have an octagonal base and a single-point vertex at the top in the center.

2. Next, join the vertices so you get a triangular face that has the base as one side of the octagon and the top as the single center point. There should be eight of these.

3. Create the base by making a single large face that has the edges of the octagon as the face's edges.

4. Put this all into a Shape node and make the material color green—the islands must be grass-covered, after all.

5. Load the single island and move around it, checking that each face is visible. If not, then reverse the order of the vertices declared in the coordIndex field. Don't forget to check the base as well.

The island declaration is given in Listing 17.1.

TIP: Make note of the order that the vertices are declared in the coordIndex field. If they were declared in the opposite order (for example, 8, 0, 1, 0), the island would become invisible when you moved over the top of it. Normals aren't specified for the face, so the renderer works it out. If you have problems with the face not appearing when you expect it to, then try reversing the order.

Listing 17.1. The basic island.

```
#VRML V2.0 utf8
#
# A simple island constructed from an IndexedFaceSet
Shape {
    appearance Appearance {
        material Material {
            diffuseColor 0.1 0.5 0.2
            emissiveColor 0.05 0.1 0.05
        }
    }
    geometry IndexedFaceSet {
        coord Coordinate {
            point [
                20 0 0, 15 0 15, 0 0 20, -15 0 15, -20 0 0, -15 0 -15, 0 0 -20,
➡15 0 -15,
                0 10 0
            ]
        }
        coordIndex [
            8, 1, 0, 8, -1,
            8, 2, 1, 8, -1,
            8, 3, 2, 8, -1,
            8, 4, 3, 8, -1,
            8, 5, 4, 8, -1,
            8, 6, 5, 8, -1,
            8, 7, 6, 8, -1,
            8, 0, 7, 8, -1,
            0, 1, 2, 3, 4, 5, 6, 7, 0, -1,
        ]
    }
}
```

Creating More Islands by Reusing Objects

If you wrote out all the code for the object every single time you used the file, it would soon get out of hand. With VRML, you can reuse an object in the file by naming it, then using that name when you need the object again. This method applies to any node in the scene, which could be anything from a material to a script.

To name a node, place the keyword DEF and the name in front of the node you want to reuse. To use it somewhere else, insert the keyword USE and that same name. Yes, you've seen these keywords before. In Chapter 15, "Sprucing Up Models with Textures and Materials," when you texture-mapped the cylinders to make the marble column, you reused a single cylinder and scaled it to fit with the other cylinders.

Now create four more islands to go into the scene. The first island was based around the origin, so move it by placing a Transform node around it. You'll do the same thing when you clone the island, so that means you need to use the DEF keyword on the Shape node, then insert the USE keyword in the children of the other Transform nodes. Listing 17.2 shows how to do this:

Listing 17.2. Reusing parts of the scene graph with the DEF and USE keywords.

```
Transfrom {
    translation 0 -20 0
    children [
        DEF island Shape { # rest of shape definition
        }
    ]
}
transform {
    translation 50 0 0
    children [ USE island ]
}
```

When you use the keyword USE on an object, you're creating a reference to the original, not a copy of it. This can be both bad and good. By creating a reference, if any properties of the original change, every other version with the USE keyword will change as well. If you've declared many instances of the one object and you want them all to change color together, then this is an effective technique. Change one, and you change the rest. Of course, creating a reference has its bad points, too, because this method might cause unwanted side effects. Basically, keep use of the USE keyword to the minimum you need to get the effect you want. In the previous example, you used the DEF keyword on just the Shape node, rather than the whole Transform node, because that was all that was necessary.

 Connecting the Islands

If you've seen the basic layout of the world already, you'll notice that I have placed four islands at one level and a fifth one at a different level. How should they be connected? I think a set of stairs would work nicely between them. Sticking to the theme, these stairs should just be floating in space. Make the stairs from boxes, and use the texture Bubsy used on the background of his pages to give them that surreal industrial look.

To construct the stairs, follow these steps:

1. Create a very thin single box.

2. Add the texture of the safety metal to the box, using the ImageTexture node in the appearance field.

3. Create a series of boxes with each one offset from the next one below it to produce a single staircase.

4. Take copies of the completed staircase and place them on each of the four sides that lead from the central island to the elevated ones.

Each one must be offset from the previous one, which you can declare in two different ways. The first method is to create several individual Transform nodes, putting the stairs at a fixed offset in relation to the origin or some other point in space. The second method is to position the first stair, then offset each subsequent one in relation to the one below it (assuming you build the staircase from the bottom up). I prefer the second method, because if you move the second stair, for example, then the rest automatically move to stay in the same relative position.

Once you've created the first staircase, then you want to copy it for the other staircases between the islands. Here's what I did:

```
Transform {
  translation 21 -20 0
  children [
    DEF stair_group Group {
      children [
        DEF a_stair Shape {
          appearance Appearance {
            texture ImageTexture { url "safety_metal.jpg" }
          }
          geometry Box { size 2 0.1 6 }
        }
        Transform {
          translation 2 2 0
          children [
            USE a_stair
            Transform {
            # etc etc for the stairs
```

```
                }
            ]
        }
    }
    ]
}
Transform {
    translation 0 -20 -21
    rotation 0 1 0 1.57
    children [ USE stair_group ]
}
```

The stairs opposite the first set were not rotated; rather, they were scaled with a factor of -1 in the X axis (that is, scale -1 1 1) to get the same effect. Sometimes that's easier to do than rotating the objects through 180 degrees.

The tricky part to copying this staircase is that you need to use both the first untransformed step (as the base point) and the rest of the staircase. To do this, you must put a wrapper around both of them. Use the Group node as this wrapper; it has no function other than to collect a group of nodes together so you can use the DEF keyword on them. See how much cleaner the code has become when you get ready to add the stairs to the other islands?

Now connect the top islands with some wooden planks. By now you should know what to do—first, declare a single box with a wood texture, use the DEF keyword, then translate it into position.

Adding the Gallery Contents

Now that you have a basic world up and running, you need to put some pictures in it. I've chosen eight pictures from the first part of the book that I want to put in the upper levels of the islands. For now, I'm going to leave the bottom level empty.

Putting in the Pictures

Each of the pictures is a different size, so this time you can't use the DEF and USE keywords to save file space. Each image requires a box of its own. I used boxes rather than face sets to get the image on both sides without any effort. Later, you'll use this effect when doing guided tours.

To create an individual picture, you need to do the following:

1. Create a thin vertical box.
2. Apply the appropriate image as a texture, using ImageTexture.
3. Adjust the size of the box to maintain the correct aspect ratio of the image.
4. Place it on an island by using a Transform node. At the same time, you want to add a rotation so that the viewer needs a separate viewing position for each image in the world.

Creating separate boxes for each picture makes it even more "fun" when you're writing files by hand. It's a continual process of adjusting and reloading the files so that everything looks right. One of the many tasks involved was readjusting the boxes so that the corners weren't sticking into the island's hills. You'll discover similar problems when creating your own worlds.

Adding the Basic Guided Tour

If you don't specify a default viewpoint, then the browser puts you quite a distance away. To avoid this, add a viewpoint to the file. The first one declared is the default entry; in this case, it starts you off in the middle of the center island.

This is an art gallery, so everyone wants to view the pictures. In a real-life tour of an art gallery, people stop to look at the pictures, so you should, too, in your virtual gallery. For each picture, I created a viewpoint about 4 meters away looking straight at it. It's worth the planning effort to make sure you're facing in the correct direction. The amount of time you spend adjusting everything to get that right look can be huge, so a little planning never hurts.

Once you have these viewpoints, put them in a logical order so that the tour makes sense. You don't want visitors to your gallery jumping randomly around the scene. In Chapter 23, "Real-Life Examples: A 3D Gallery: An Advanced VRML World," when you continue developing this scene, you'll offer an automated guided tour. Having the viewpoints logically defined already will make automating the tour easier.

Adding Links to Other VRML Worlds and Pages

Although developing this world has been fun, remember that you need to make it a worthwhile place to visit, too. Since I've used my co-author's pictures in the gallery, it makes sense to link the pictures back to some description. In this case, I've set the links up to point to the corresponding file on the CD-ROM where that image was created.

1. Create the basic image and box in the scene, as you normally would.
2. Decide which page you're going to be linking it to.
3. Build the Web pages.
4. Place an Anchor node around the geometry you built in Step 1.

I found one of the images on the POVRay site, so I've supplied a link back to its home page so you can see where it came from. In Chapter 13, "Exploring VRML Browsers and Development Tools," you learned about the Anchor node; now you get to use it properly for the first time. Surround each of the pictures' Transform nodes with an Anchor—that's all you need to do to provide links. For example, the Anchor declaration for the picture linking back to the POVRay site looks like the following:

```
Anchor {
    url "http://www.povray.org/"
    children [
        # place the code to produce the picture here
    ]
}
```

For this chapter, all the links are to other HTML files. You could make the links point to another VRML file, as demonstrated in a previous chapter. There's no need to use the parameters field, either, because this is just a pure VRML document. It is possible to create worlds that use HTML frames. The next workshop, in Chapter 23, explores the use of multi-framed documents combining VRML and HTML.

Adding a Background

A few things are still missing in your VRML world. Every world you've created so far has had a black background. For some people, this is fine, but basic black can get a bit boring. Try spicing up the background a bit with the Background node.

The Background node is very handy; by using it, you can specify pictures or a color gradient for sky colors. You can even use a combination of colors and pictures. I like the idea of those islands up in space, so I found a star picture I'm going to use as the background. To do this, put the URL of the image file in the Background node, as shown here:

```
Background {
    eventIn        SFBool    set_bind
    exposedField   MFFloat   groundAngle   []
    exposedfield   MFColor   groundColor   []
    exposedField   MFString  backUrl       []
    exposedField   MFString  bottomUrl     []
    exposedField   MFString  frontUrl      []
    exposedField   MFString  leftUrl       []
    exposedField   MFString  rightUrl      []
    exposedField   MFString  topUrl        []
    exposedField   MFFloat   skyAngle      []
    exposedField   MFColor   skyColor      [ 0 0 0 ]
    eventOut       SFBool    isBound
}
```

The sides are relative to the background's local coordinates. If you're looking down the Z axis toward -z, then the front side is directly in front of you. To get some funky effects, you can put the background under a Transform node and spin it around with the rotation. The background is always a fixed distance away, so you can't translate it, but you can use rotation. Using the Transform above the Background node allows you to keep the background's up direction the same as the user's up direction, regardless of his or her orientation.

Which one of the six fields for holding image file URLs do you pick? Usually, you choose the ones defining the sides. The background pictures are mapped onto a box surrounding the world, with each URL referring to one side of the box. If you want, you can specify a different image for each side. In this world, I wanted the whole lot to appear in a star field, so I put the same image file URL in all the url fields.

The other method of putting in a background is specifying a collection of colors and angles. You need to supply one more color than the number of angles because the colors go between a pair of angles, giving a ring effect. There are two fields: one for the ground and the other for the sky. You can combine the images and colors together. If you don't specify an image, then the color is used. Therefore, a common tactic is specifying the images around the sides but letting the sky/ground color show through on the other two—the top and bottom for the box that defines the background.

You want the star background to totally envelop the world, so the same declaration goes in each of the URL fields and nothing goes in the color field.

Making the User Fit the Scene

Sometimes you want to create your model in a scale that's different from what's normal. For example, a chemical model would be no good drawn at real scale. However, you need to consider the problem of fitting the user to the scene. The NavigationInfo node is used to give the browser some basic information about the properties of the user in the scene:

```
NavigationInfo {
    eventIn      SFBool    set_bind
    exposedField MFFloat   avatarSize       1.0
    exposedField SFBool    headlight        TRUE
    exposedField SFFloat   speed            1.0
    exposedField MFString  type             "WALK"
    exposedField SFFloat   visibilityLimit  0.0
    eventOut     SFBool    isBound
}
```

The user can set the size, as well as other basic properties. By now, you've probably discovered the options available by clicking the right mouse button. Several of these options can be predefined when the scene is loaded by specifying the values in the NavigationInfo node. A detailed description of all the options is given in Chapter 13.

When you start talking about virtual reality, you'll see the word *avatar* pop up quite frequently; it refers to the user's representation in the virtual world. The avatar is what other people in the world see and also how the world reacts to your presence as you navigate through it.

The avatarSize field is particularly important in most VRML files. It contains several values that specify how the avatar will behave. The first value is your collision radius— how close you can get to objects. The second value defines how high your "eyes" sit above the terrain. VRML 2.0 allows you to define a terrain by using the ElevationGrid node. As you wander over one of these nodes, the browser maintains the specified distance above the ground.

If you have collision detection running, then the third value defines what the maximum step height is that the user can negotiate. Anything higher than this value and you will have to make the avatar negotiate (fly?) the obstacle. In the world you designed, the steps are 2 meters apart, so the step height needs to be more than 2 meters so you can "walk" up the stairs without any extra effort. However, in this scene I didn't add collision nodes to the stairs. Feel free to do this and experiment with the results.

Any values specified after the first three in the avatarSize field are browser dependent. You need to check what they mean and whether the browser supports this information. The only way to tell what extra values the browser supports is to read the accompanying documentation.

Visibility limit, specified in the visibilityLimit field, defines how far you can see. If you have a very large world, then the value supplied in this field is important. If it's too small, then the visibility limit would cut out a lot of the scene that might need to be rendered. The headlight field sets the default state for its use, and the type field specifies what sort of navigation you want to do. The types of navigation available were defined in Chapter 13 and include the types Walk, Examine, and Fly.

The Final Touches

The island in the middle is still a little blank, so to spice it up a bit I'm going to drag out the tree and marble columns from previous chapters and place them on the island. The columns will form archways leading to the stairs, and I'll add a block across the top of the columns to complete the arch. For consistency, the blocks use the same marble texture.

Now I get to have a bit of fun. For each staircase, I'm going to put a message up as well. VRML does have a 3D text function, but getting the text to line up can be tricky. The most reliable method is to create the individual signs as transparent GIF images, using all the 3D effects you've learned from my co-author, and then place them on a plane that sits very close to the top block. One of the benefits of taking this approach is that you can create shadowed highlights you wouldn't normally get from creating the scene in VRML 3D text.

Adding Information to the Scene with WorldInfo

The final node covered in this chapter is WorldInfo. This one doesn't display anything on the screen; it just contains a series of text strings. The title field is the world title that normally appears in the browser's title bar. It has the same effect as the <TITLE> HTML tag.

If you want to store other information, like copyright notices, in the scene, then you put this in the info field. The browser might take this information and display it in a separate dialog box, like the infamous About box. A proposal has been put forward to place meta information in the info field, as well. The proposal uses essentially the same fields and names as the <META> tag. At this stage, it's not a recommended use of the info field, but it is valid nonetheless.

Workshop Wrap-up

There you have it—your first fairly large VRML world. The sample file was created all by hand; not a single modeling tool was used. Most of the file is consumed by the definition of each object type. Once you have the definition, then it's repeatedly cloned with the USE command. Imagine how much bigger the file would be if you had to declare each object explicitly.

With a bit of effort and time, you can create very cool worlds like the one presented in this chapter. Apart from the face sets for the islands, the rest of the scene was constructed using just the basic primitives with some color and textures thrown in. Careful design in the first place means you can spend more time playing around with things later. Also notice how I've used the viewpoints to act as a guided tour in a logical sequence around the art gallery, rather than use random ordering. Details like this are what make the difference between an average world and a good one.

Next Steps

Now that you've mastered the basics of VRML, it's time to move on to the more advanced topics covered in Part V, "Advanced VRML Techniques":

❏ The next chapter takes a look at optimizing your worlds for use on the Internet.

❏ Then the fun and games begin. Chapter 19, "Using Built-in Animation Techniques," starts the ball rolling, literally. You learn how to create basic animations in a scene by using the built-in VRML animation techniques.

❏ When the built-in techniques aren't enough, then you need to create your own. Chapter 20, "Interfacing VRML Worlds with Scripts," introduces the concept of the Script node and also looks at one language to write behaviors in.

❏ If you're really keen to see what can be done, then head straight to Chapter 23, "Real-Life Examples: A 3D Gallery: An Advanced VRML World," where I continue to develop this scene to include behaviors and other interesting features.

Q&A

Q: Did you really write that whole scene by hand?

A: Yes. All I used was Notepad with Netscape 2.02 with CosmoPlayer beta 1a. There were some serious memory leaks that resulted in having to shut down Netscape and restart it; however, they were the only two tools used. A lot of the pieces I just pinched from other files—like the columns and trees—so this makes the development time much shorter. Once you're happy with the basic design, then it's just a matter of using a Transform node to move copies around the scene graph.

Q: Where did you get the textures from?

A: Apart from the sign textures—which were created in Paint Shop Pro—everything can be done just by using standard textures and pictures straight from the Internet. As you can see, all the big pictures came straight from my co-author without any modifications. These days most of the modeling tools come with a collection of textures and images that can be used to create your worlds with. Also check out places like Netscape's background texture page or one of the Internet search engines for other places.

Q: What other sorts of things can I do with VRML? This 2.0 stuff looks just like the 1.0 worlds. Why do I need to upgrade?

A: VRML 1.0 is designed only for static scenes. So far, what you've covered is the equivalent functioning of 1.0, but with the 2.0 syntax. In the next part of the book, you get into what this latest version is all about: creating moving worlds.

PART

V

Advanced VRML Techniques

EIGHTEEN

Tricks to Optimize Your VRML Worlds for the Web

—by Justin Couch

When you first start creating worlds, you can get quite carried away with detail. A texture here and a mesh there—it all makes the world look nicer. Everything looks pretty, but as soon as you put it up for public consumption, you notice that it takes forever to download. What can you do about it?

Many of the basic tricks come straight from the high-end simulation market; after all, they've been trying to cope with this sort of problem for years. Making the world run faster also means it will download faster, too, so you win on both counts. The following topics are covered in this chapter:

❏ One of the prime candidates for slowing things down is meshes. You'll see how to keep an object looking the same but make it run much faster.

❏ The other great resource waster is texturing and coloring models; you'll explore where textures and colors are best used.

In this chapter, you

❏ See how meshes make your world run slower

❏ Learn where textures and colors are best used

❏ See how to compress a file

❏ Discover how inlining files can decrease load times

❏ Use built-in VRML techniques, like Billboard, to make worlds run faster

Tasks in this chapter:

❏ Simplifying Models with Pioneer Pro

❏ Compressing Those Models

❏ Inlining Your World Using Billboards

❏ Once you've got your world running faster, you'll see how to get it to the end user faster by compressing the file and eliminating unnecessary white space.

❏ When you have huge files, people might not wait for the whole batch to load. To entice users into exploring your worlds, you'll learn about inlining files.

❏ You can also make worlds run faster by using some of the built-in VRML features, such as Billboard.

I'm into flying, so I'll start with the P51 model from the Syndesis collection included on the book's CD-ROM. The file size is 93K before you convert it into VRML 2.0. There's no color or texture or even any scenery. Once you start adding those things, you can quite easily blow the file size up to 200K or more, which is way too big for the Web.

Reducing the Polygon Count of Your Models

When you first create a lovely model of a plane in 3D Studio or AutoCAD, you want it to look professional, so you make every little detail perfect. The result is a perfect rendition with over 10,000 polygons. The rule of thumb for current hardware is that you can have an upper limit of 3,000 on polygon count if you want to keep the world operating smoothly. If you use this plane model in a VRML file, it will be a huge file that will take forever to download.

One of the problems is that you often generate complex models with some sort of authoring tool. If you try to edit complex models by hand, then all I can say is good luck—even this intrepid hacker isn't that game! The models you created in trueSpace for generating 3D effects in the first part of this book are much too detailed for a VRML world.

VRML modeling tools, to various degrees, allow you to control the amount of detail in the object. Each tool is different, but to reduce the object's complexity, look somewhere under the Options menu. Sometimes the ability to control detail comes in the form of an accuracy setting; at other times, it's found in a high/medium/low detail setting.

 ## Simplifying Models with Pioneer Pro

If you're planning to buy a VRML modeling tool, then Caligari's Pioneer Pro would be a safe bet, particularly if you have already settled on trueSpace2. In the Pioneer Pro version, there's an option to automatically reduce the polygon count of imported objects. If you create something in trueSpace2, save the object in its native format (.scn or .obj), then import it into Pioneer Pro to finish the job. An example of a model that's been imported into Pioneer is shown in Figure 18.1.

Figure 18.1.

The original high-detail Viper model loaded into Pioneer.

If you have been suckered into producing polygon meshes by hand, you already have an automatic polygon-reduction mechanism happening!

TIP: Reducing your model's polygon count doesn't necessarily mean reducing the quality. With proper lighting and smooth shading, you can create similar effects. It's amazing what you can find when you spend a bit of time digging around in the specifications. For example, the IndexedFaceSet node has a creaseAngle field that specifies the maximum angle between faces that a browser should try applying smooth shading to. If you set this to a very small value, then the object takes on a faceted look, but a large value produces smoothing across even large angles.

To reduce the polygon count of a model, you need to follow these steps:

1. Start with a new scene with nothing in it.
2. Use the Load Object or Load World menu options from the File menu.
3. Correct anything you want to (like deleting extra bits of useless detail).
4. Save the model. At this point, you get the Export VRML file dialog box, which gives you a number of options. You want the Precision value; the larger the value in this field, the more precise your object will be. Less precision means fewer polygons are produced in the final model. A value

around 2 should produce acceptable models; a precision value of 1 tends to make the object look very square.

5. Click OK to save the new, lower detail model.

When producing the models for this book, Kelly first trimmed out most of the detail in trueSpace, then passed them to me. I did a little more trimming, using Pioneer Pro, then exported the files with a precision value of 1. You saw the "before" shot in Figure 18.1; now take a look at the "after" shot in Figure 18.2.

Figure 18.2.

The model after the polygon reduction; since a precision value of 1 was used, the model came out looking somewhat "blocky."

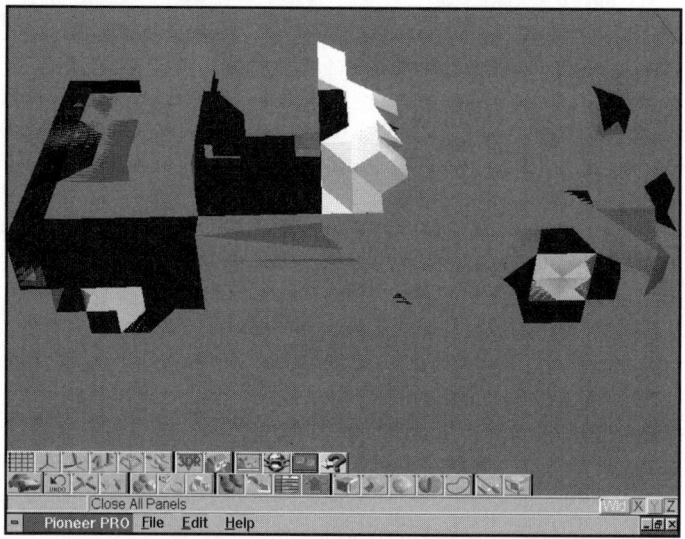

TASK

Compressing Those Models

Another big waster of space in a VRML file is formatting. When you're hand-coding, formatting is essential for working out relationships between the file's parts. Once you have finished with the file, there's no need to keep the formatting.

One of the problems with converting other file formats to VRML is that other formats are unnecessarily precise. Unless you're building a very small-scale world, there's no point in being any more specific than three or four decimal places. Inaccuracy in the browser's rendering engine will often cause more problems than your lack of precision does. Many examples in this book with numbers like 0.5 have the leading zero missing; a file containing many points can save quite a bit of space this way.

Almost since the beginning of VRML, there have been several programs that allow you to remove all the formatting, reduce the precision, remove leading zeros, and other things to save file space. Recently, Alex Aveenendaal released a Java version of a utility called Cruncher. Since it's Java, you can run it on any platform to compress a VRML 1.0 or 2.0 file.

After running the original P51 model through the VRML 1.0 to 2.0 converter, the file size goes from 93K to 118K. If you use Cruncher on it, the file shrinks to 83K, so you save 35K just by removing a few tab characters and zeros.

Alex has also produced a Java applet called Hier, which produces a plan view of your VRML file to use as a map. The utilities can be found at `http:// www.wessex.co.uk/ vrml/utilities.html`.

Real File Compression

Besides removing the file formatting, the other option is compressing the file with a compression utility. During the original specification work for 1.0, it was suggested that files be compressed with a UNIX utility called gzip. This utility caught on very quickly; now, large files can be compressed to reasonable sizes for transmission across the Internet. You can tell a gzipped file because its file extension is .wrl.gz.

To view compressed files, you don't need to do anything because browsers now come with an uncompression program. To compress your own files, you need to get a copy of a program that compresses files. Some programs, such as CosmoPlayer, come with the command-line version or you can get WinPack to do it graphically for you, from the following site:

`http://www.winsite.com/info/pc/win95/miscutil/wpack32d.exe`

Compressing the P51 file now results in a file size of a tiny 19K, a big difference from the original 118K.

Binary File Format

During the proposal stage for developing VRML 2.0, Apple submitted a version of its 3DMF file format (used in QTVR and QT movies) for VRML 2.0. After some discussion on the development list, it was agreed that Apple's version would be a good format to have, along with the standard text format, as a binary file format.

Because of problems during the VRML 2.0 specification, the binary file format probably won't be released at the same time as the official 2.0 release. However, it should be released with the upgraded 2.1 specification a few months later.

Inlining Your World

When you start creating large worlds, it's difficult to maintain a single large file. It's much easier to split the world up into lots of manageable chunks. To do this, the Inline node lets you specify a URL to a file you want to include. You can, for instance, include files located on different servers. In Terra Vista, almost every world contains a small yellow globe with green and red planets flying around it (it can be seen in Figure 13.3 in my homeworld). It's always the same file, but it has been inlined into other worlds.

Inlined worlds allow you to create a small skeleton file, then tell the browser to download a number of other files and place those in the scene at a specific location. For example, you might create a basic world consisting of just a green plane and a whole series of inlined files representing each building.

Inlining has many advantages over having a single large file. Apart from being able to build your world piece by piece, it also means a user can start wandering around in your world much sooner. The common tendency among browsers is to load the main file, placing it on the screen, and then go look for inlined files. Once the basic outline is up, the user can move around and explore while the rest of the world loads, particularly if he or she is already familiar with the world. Any currently unresolved inlined files are usually represented by a wireframe box indicating the missing file.

Here's the definition for the Inline node:

```
Inline {
  exposedField MFString url        []
  field        SFVec3f  bboxCenter 0 0 0
  field        SFVec3f  bboxSize   -1 -1 -1
}
```

The size of the bounding box is specified in the bboxSize field. The *bounding box* is a box covering the maximum size in each dimension that the contents will take up. There's no checking to see whether the bounding box is the same size as the node to be inlined. The center field indicates where to position the inlined field in relation to the current local coordinates. You could also control this position as a child of a Transform node by setting the translation field.

TIP: A number of times I have been caught by inlining someone else's world that was a completely different scale from mine, and it just filled up everything. If you run across this problem, then just put a Transform node above it and set the scale field to make it the correct proportions for your world.

To use inlines, you need to do the following:

1. Create the object to be inlined and save it to a VRML file.
2. Create the target world.
3. Put the Inline node into the world, determining its position either by setting the position field or by making the Inline node a child of the Transform node. The url field then contains the filename of the object created in Step 1.

Combining LOD and Inline nodes is quite common. The browser gets the list of inlined files and then loads them from the lowest detail first. This way you can be guaranteed to get a nice quick load and a world that runs very quickly because the initial loads are the lowest in detail. This method combats the problem of the browser chewing lots of memory because it keeps the browser from loading everything right from the start.

 # Using Billboards

The Billboard node is a handy node included in the new version of VRML. This grouping node turns its children so that they're always facing the camera. A simple but fairly common use of the Billboard node is simulating a tree.

By combining a single-face polygon mesh, a transparent GIF of a tree, and the Billboard node, you can get a pretty effective tree that doesn't require a set of transformations and primitives:

1. Start off with a Shape node and add a tree texture map. The geometry field contains an IndexedFaceSet with a single face defined as standing upright. On this face, you can put your tree texture or whatever you like; using a texture with a transparent background makes the tree look more realistic.

2. The Billboard node works for any sort of child. You could add a collection of objects to form a robot so that whenever you turned something around, the robot would be facing you waiting for instructions. The Billboard node is easy to use because it contains the same fields as the other grouping nodes:

```
Billboard {
    eventIn       MFNode    add_children
    eventIn       MFNode    remove_children
    exposedField  SFVec3f   axisOfRotation   0 1 0
    exposedField  MFNode    children         []
    field         SFVec3f   bboxCenter       0 0 0
    field         SFVec3f   bboxSize         -1 -1 -1
}
```

The bboxSize, bboxCenter, and children fields all do what you normally expect in a grouping node. The axisOfRotation field allows you to specify an arbitrary axis for the Billboard node to rotate around. This field is useful if, for example, you have a tree on the side of a hill because you can specify an axis perpendicular to the hill to make the tree behave properly.

3. So you want to be a bit tricky and specify an axis of 0 0 0? Try it…. Got you on this one! This particular axis tells the browser to rotate the object so that it's always facing the viewer, no matter what direction the viewer is looking at it from.

When you specify an axis of rotation, it's the only axis the object rotates around to face the viewer. You can fly over the "top" of the object and look down on its edge, watching it rotate underneath you as you fly over, but not when you specify an axis of 0 0 0.

Other Nodes to Speed Up the World

There are other nodes that come in handy for speeding up your world. Chapter 14, "Starting with Models," had a quick introduction to the IndexedLineSet, and in Figure 14.7, you saw how this node was used to simulate a larger real-world type of structure. For example, a browser is slow at rendering a long, narrow pipe but renders a line very quickly. IndexedLineSets are useful anywhere you might need to display a long, narrow object, such as framework and fencing.

You can use an IndexedFaceSet in the same way to represent a very thin surface rather than using a very flat box. In Figure 14.7 you can see how face sets are used in the roof. There is no thickness to the roof; it's just a double-sided face. Double-siding faces can save you lots of computing power.

CAUTION: Some browsers ignore options to turn double-siding on or off. One workaround solution is to declare two faces but with the edge order opposite, so that it looks like there's two distinct faces occupying the same set of coordinates, as shown in the following example:

```
points [ 1 0 1, -1 0 1, -1 0 -1, 1 0 -1 ]
coordIndex [ 0, 1, 2, 3, -1,
             0, 3, 2, 1, -1 ]
```

Dividing a World of Faces

Apart from being able to reduce the number of polygons in an object you also need to think how they are located in relationship not only to each other but also the rest of the world.

Take an L-shaped room, for example. If you examine both edges, you'll notice that most of the time you can't see both of them. If you declared them as being two faces within the one face set, then the browser must check both faces for redrawing every frame. If they were declared in separate faces, then for each frame, the browser needs to do only a single check for the overall visibility of that face set, rather than a whole heap of single face calculations.

In a simple example like the L-shaped room, there's really no need for this sort of detail. Where a complex object comes into it, such as a statue, then you should think about the arrangement of face sets. You'll see only one side of the statue, so breaking it into four sections (one for each quadrant) would make sense and help in the rendering.

Workshop Wrap-up

You should be able to put up some pretty compact, high-performance worlds now. There are a range of techniques you can apply to do this. The biggest killer in most VRML files is overusing the IndexedFaceSet. Care should be taken when you're using this node to make sure that face bloat doesn't happen.

This part of the book covers some of the more advanced topics in generating VRML worlds. From now on, you'll start digging deeper and deeper into the underlying parts of VRML to see how it works. Worlds stop standing still as you examine the exciting realm of VRML 2.0.

- ❏ In Chapter 19, "Using Built-in Animation Techniques," you'll look at adding basic behaviors and animation to the world just by using what VRML provides. As part of this discussion, you'll start digging into how VRML creates behaviors with an event-driven system.
- ❏ Chapter 20, "Interfacing VRML Worlds with Scripts," builds on this by showing you how to add programmable behaviors using the Script node and VRML's scripting language, VRMLScript.
- ❏ If you're a hard-core kind of person, head to Chapter 21, "Using Java to Add Behaviors to VRML," which examines using Java in scripting behaviors.
- ❏ If all this programming stuff is too much for you, then take a look at Appendix A, "3D Software Resource Guide," where Kelly looks at other 3D technologies out there.

Q&A

Q: Is there any commercial software that can be used to automate these tasks?

A: There are no standalone applications designed just for optimizing a VRML world. They either get packaged as part of another VRML program (for example, Pioneer Pro's reduce polygon count feature) or are do-it-yourself jobs.

Q: When should I use these optimization techniques?

A: It's a good idea to get into the habit of optimizing every file. Every byte less that your world takes, the better, because it means the end users' download time is shorter, which increases your chances of them coming back.

NINETEEN

Using Built-in Animation Techniques

—by Justin Couch

So far, all the worlds you've been developing are static; apart from clicking on links, nothing else changes as you wander around. However, now you'll explore some of the built-in animation techniques that VRML offers. Animation can be almost anything, from moving position to changing color. This chapter will cover the following areas:

❏ Looking at events and how they affect a VRML world

❏ Giving a scene a sense of time

❏ Learning how to connect parts of the scene with ROUTEs

❏ Using time to modify objects, such as changing color and position with Interpolators

❏ Learning how to control the scene by responding to user input

In this chapter, you

❏ See how events affect a VRML world

❏ Give your scene a sense of time

❏ Connect scene parts with ROUTEs

❏ Use time to modify objects

❏ Control the scene by responding to user input

Tasks in this chapter:

❏ Building Your First Animation

❏ Creating a Smooth Animation

❏ Changing the Animation Path

❏ Using the TouchSensor Node to Control Animations

Animation requires addressing many separate issues before you actually get to anything that will appear onscreen. So sit tight for a few pages of hand-waving discussions, until you have enough information to start creating worlds that move.

As you get into animations, you'll start working with constructs that look like a programming language. The real programming doesn't start until the next chapter, but many of the core issues for understanding the programming come from this basic introduction. Hold on and enjoy the ride!

If you're serious about getting into behaviors in a VRML world, then it's worth the time to read these first two sections on VRML events and the TimeSensor node a couple of times. They throw some tricky situations at you that can cause all sorts of strange unwanted effects.

Events Are Happening

Once you introduce motion into a previously static system, the main question is how to control the animations. In VRML, you do this by using events. An event is like a dialog box—the program is telling you that something has happened, forcing you to respond. Think of it as one part of your scene telling another part that something has changed, so it needs to respond.

VRML contains many nodes; some can generate events and others receive them. Some nodes can do both, and, as you'll see in the next two chapters, you can even create your own nodes that receive *and* generate events. Where do VRML events show up? Events are used as a way of passing data between two different nodes; this data takes the form of the field types you're now familiar with. Take a step back and have another look at the definition of the Transform node:

```
Transform {
  eventIn       MFNode       add_children
  eventIn       MFNode       remove_children
  exposedField SFVec3f      center          0 0 0
  exposedField MFNode       children        []
  exposedField SFRotation   rotation        0 0 1 0
  exposedField SFVec3f      scale           1 1 1
  exposedField SFRotation   scaleOrientation 0 0 1 0
  exposedField SFVec3f      translation     0 0 0
  field         SFVec3f      bboxCenter      0 0 0
  field         SFVec3f      bboxSize        -1 -1 -1
}
```

Remember the last time you saw this definition? I told you then not to worry about the first column. Well, now it's time to look at it. Notice that many of the fields are declared as exposedField. There are also eventIns, EventOuts, and ones called just field. Up to now, you've ignored the eventIn and eventOut fields, but you'll be dealing with them almost exclusively now.

Understanding Field Interfaces

The first column in all node definitions is referred to as the *interface type*. It controls what access the other nodes have to the contents of that field. They can be broadly classified into these categories:

- ❑ **field**   No access.
- ❑ **eventIn**   Write access; a node can pass values into this field but not read them back.
- ❑ **eventOut**   Read access; a node can read values from this field but not write to it.
- ❑ **exposedField**   Read and write access for all nodes.

Animation is all about changing the properties of nodes, which means that any field declared as having a field interface isn't much use to you when talking about animation. If you want to update a value in a node, then you have to pass an event to that node. You can pass events only to fields with either the eventIn or exposedField interface, and you can get events only from fields with eventOut or exposedField interfaces.

This is roughly how animation works: You translate objects with the translation field in the Transform node. The translation field has an exposedField interface, which means it can send and receive events. Later in the file, you have a timer that sends regular events. The last piece needed to produce animation is a connector that sends new translation values to the translation field when the event is signaled. These new translation values update the position of the object and it moves around as time passes. Voilà—animation!

The Passing Event

So far, the discussion has been about passing events, not actually creating them; that's because there is no way to just "create" events. They must come from some other node in the scene graph. A single event may start a long chain of cascading events that eventually causes a change across the whole scene. But what causes the first event?

It's possible to create event loops, but VRML defines a set of rules in the execution model that enforces a break in the event loop after processing each event connection (**ROUTE**) exactly once.

The first event is always caused by some external influence, since there's no method for directly generating events within the scene graph. An external influence can be anything from the passing of time to a user clicking on an object. These nodes are embedded in the scene graph, but they generate new events only when something changes. Once the initial event has been generated, it can trigger other events, causing a domino effect.

Time on Your Hands

As mentioned previously, the scenes created so far in this book are very static. In a static scene, there's no need for any notion of time. Once you start to add motion that you don't control, however, then you need to give the scenes some sense of time.

Unlike many of the other proposals for VRML 2.0, the original Moving Worlds didn't have any implicit sense of time, but it's since been added.

One of the most valuable event generators is a timer node called the TimeSensor. It "senses" that some amount of time has passed, then passes this value on to other nodes. If you need time, then it is just another node you add to the scene graph. The TimeSensor node is defined like this:

```
TimeSensor {
  exposedField  SFTime   cycleInterval 1
  exposedField  SFBool   enabled       TRUE
  exposedField  SFBool   loop          FALSE
  exposedField  SFTime   startTime     0
  exposedField  SFTime   stopTime      0
  eventOut      SFTime   cycleTime
  eventOut      SFFloat  fraction_changed
  eventOut      SFBool   isActive
  eventOut      SFTime   time
}
```

This node is the heart of any VR animated behavior, so first you'll learn the basics. You'll see an example later as you progress through the chapter.

You can see from the definition that you can specify the interval cycle, start and stop times, and whether the event loops. This gives you a lot of control over how events are generated.

Time 0 is defined as midnight GMT January 1, 1970. This is the time that most computer systems are calculated in relation to, but for most of your work, you won't need to worry about this. When you might need to use it is if you're creating an alarm at some definite point in time—say at 2:00 p.m. on March 19, 1998.

The current time is available from the time field. StartTime and stopTime are also absolute values from the same point. They allow you to specify an alarm event to be set to happen at some point.

The TimeSensor node represents the way most of the sensor nodes work. Other sensor nodes covered later in the chapter include ProximitySensor and TouchSensor. Sensor nodes contain several fields that control its behavior and a collection of eventOut fields that define its behavior. EventOuts usually act in a group. For example, the isActive field says that this TimeSensor is currently active, so the values available from the time field are valid.

Getting Connected with the ROUTE Command

Now you have nodes like TimeSensor to generate events and nodes like Transform to receive them. How do you get them talking to each other? You use an explicit connection method defined by VRML. If you want to connect the output of one node to the input of another, then you must define this connection with the ROUTE command, which tells the browser how to pass events between nodes. If an event interface on a node isn't connected to anything, then the browser doesn't generate events for it.

This is the syntax for connecting two event handlers:

```
ROUTE node1.eventOutName_changed TO node2.set_eventInName
```

The node names are those defined with the DEF keyword, as discussed in the workshop in Chapter 17, "Real-Life Examples: The VRML Art Gallery: A VRML World by Hand." Naturally you can only connect an eventOut to an eventIn, and they must be of the same type. This is a very strict rule; you cannot, for example, connect a SFNode eventOut to an MFNode eventIn, even though they're both based on the Node type.

You do, however, have more leeway with exposedFields. They act as both eventIns and eventOuts, so if you had an eventOut connected to an exposedField, you could also have an eventIn from another node (or even the same one) connected simultaneously. For example, you can construct a chain of events and ROUTE commands so that if you tell a sphere to move when clicked by the user, then a box will rotate when the sphere moves, and a cone will change color when the box rotates...well, you get the idea.

Figure 19.1 shows how this would be constructed. An alternative is connecting the one eventOut to two eventIns. In engineering terms, this is known as *fan-out*—one node's output can feed the inputs of many other inputs. The opposite of this is called *fan-in*. These techniques are useful for doing things like having a light switch turn on many lights simultaneously. Creating fan-in and fan-out is as simple as using the ROUTE command to declare a path between the nodes.

Figure 19.1.
How eventIns, eventOuts, and exposedFields relate to each other.

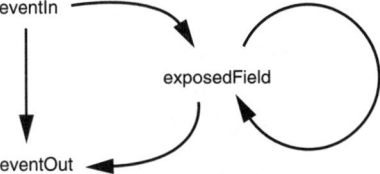

Unlike the rest of VRML, ROUTE commands are independent of the scene graph structure. A ROUTE can be placed at any point in the file as long as it's declared after the nodes where the DEFs are declared. There are two common strategies for using ROUTE commands: declare them just after they're needed (within the nests of Transforms and other nodes), or place them all at the end of the file. How you do it is a matter of preference, but in this chapter the first option is used for clarity in the examples. In very large files, you might have well over one hundred of them.

Interpolators: VRML Glue

When you start digging into how VRML functions (you've made it this far, so you must be interested), you'll notice that none of the objects seems to be aware of anything outside itself. Take the shape primitives, for example; they know only their shape attributes. They know nothing about what color they are or where they're placed in the scene. If you continue to dig, you notice they have no knowledge of time or motion, either. If a sphere is to move in a scene, then something higher up the hierarchy must cause it to move to a different position. But how does a Transform node know it's supposed to change the position of its children? It must have something else set the value of the new position.

On one side of the fence, you have a Transform node placing the sphere at a location; on the other side, you have a TimeSensor node saying that time is passing, so that sphere should be going round in a circle. You need a translator in the middle to facilitate communication between the nodes—enter the Interpolator nodes.

At last, no more theory—you finally get to develop some code. The Interpolator nodes are the glue in the scene graph; they translate the notion of time passing to actually make it look like that's what is happening. Interpolators come in many different forms and can be used to perform several tasks, anything from changing color to changing positions. Take a look at a simple example of moving a sphere across the floor.

Building Your First Animation

As you start building this example, you'll use many of the concepts you've already learned. First, you build the basic file, then modify it to get some specific animation motion:

1. Begin by defining the basic file. First, use a standard white floor as a reference point:

   ```
   # First the floor
   Shape {
       appearance Appearance {
           material Material { emissiveColor .7 .7 .7 }
       }
       geometry Box { size 10 0.1 10 }
   }
   ```

It's important to have a reference such as the floor, or the object would just zip by. Without the floor, you would see movement but wouldn't recognize it with the camera out of position.

2. You want the sphere to show up against the floor, so a bright shade of red will do.

3. To animate an object, you need to move its position, and to position an object in a scene, you need to place a Transform node before it:

```
# now the red sphere.
DEF transform Transform {
    translation 4 0.5 0
    children [
        Shape {
            appearance Appearance {
                material Material { emissiveColor .8 0 0  }
            }
            geometry Sphere { radius .4 }
        }
    ]
}
```

Actually, the default values for the startTime, stopTime, and loop fields are **0**, **0**, and **false**, respectively, which means that the TimeSensor node is effectively turned off.

4. You want to see what the object is doing, so say it will need eight seconds to travel across the floor. Looking at the definition of the TimeSensor, it seems sensible to set the cycleTime field to this value. This field defines the total time for one cycle of the output. You also need to specify the loop and the startTime fields:

```
# put in a timesensor
DEF time TimeSensor {
    cycleInterval 8
    loop TRUE
    startTime 1
}
```

5. Next, you need to add an Interpolator node, but which one should you use? If you're causing animations by changing an object's position, use a PositionInterpolator. The keys and values fields are already supplied in the following code; they will be explained in the next section, "Interpolator and TimeSensor Internals."

```
# Finally the interpolator
DEF position PositionInterpolator {
    keys [ 0  1 ]
    keyvValue [ 4 .5 0, -4 .5 0 ]
}
```

6. The last thing to do is tie them all together with the ROUTE command:

```
# now connect everything together
ROUTE time.fraction_changed TO position.set_fraction
ROUTE position.keyValue_changed TO transform.translation
```

Figure 19.2 shows the resulting scene, even though you can't see the sphere actually move in the figure. See the CD-ROM for the actual file.

Figure 19.2.
The sphere is animated in this scene with the help of event nodes.

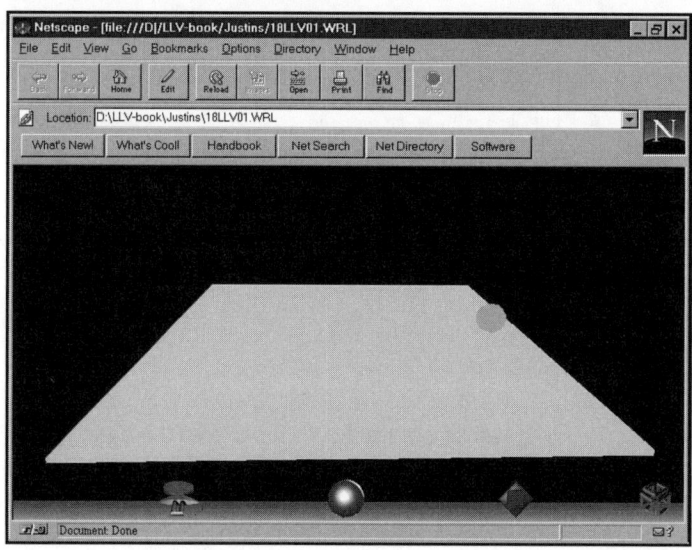

Interpolator and TimeSensor Internals

Just like the sensor nodes, there are several different Interpolator nodes, such as ColorInterpolator, CoordinateInterpolator, and PositionInterpolator, among others. All the interpolators follow a very simple scheme: You give it a set of points defined in the keys field and a set of matching values belonging to these keys in the value field. The interpolator receives a value from the set_fraction field, and a value is returned from the value_changed field. The actual type of value returned depends on the type of interpolator used.

Another way to start the animation is setting startTime to some value in the recent past and setting stopTime to a value in the future. However, once you reach this future time, there's no way of setting things back in motion again without editing the VRML file. Don't write this method off yet, though; it comes in handy when you combine it with scripting, in which you can dynamically set time values.

Keys can lie in any range, but you need to look at what is passing the data. Reviewing the TimeSensor definition shows that it displays the time by using the `fraction_changed` eventOut. This ranges in value from 0 to 1, so you must set up your keys values to fall in this range.

Next, you need to define a set of matching values for the keys. Since the start position in the previous example is (4 0.5 0), then it was made to match the value for 0. To make it nice and even, set the other key to be the opposite side of the floor at (-4 0.5 0).

Now you're getting into more detail about the time model used in VRML 2.0. If stopTime is set to be less than startTime, and the loop field is set to `false` (the default settings), then nothing will happen. The simplest solution to this problem seems to be setting the loop field to `true`; that should give you continuous animation that loops indefinitely. Wrong! There's something you've missed—that happens only when startTime is greater than stopTime, not equal to it. Therefore, you need to set startTime to some value other than 0. Since you're not likely to be visiting the 1970s again, the value of 1 used in the previous example does the trick (remember, a time of 0 is midnight GMT on January 1, 1970).

Creating a Smooth Animation

Besides the animation, what else did you notice about the sphere's behavior? That's right—when the sphere got to the left side of the floor, it jumped back to the right, which isn't particularly helpful behavior because you wanted it to travel backward and forward smoothly.

Have a look at Figure 19.3. The fraction_changed field goes only from 0 to 1, but never the other way. When the Interpolator receives values, it just sends the value out depending on what it receives. At the end of cycleTime, the fraction field jumps from 1 back to 0 again, which causes the jumping behavior. In animation, you want the jumps to be as small as possible, so why not set them to 0? If the Interpolator sends out the same endpoint as the start point, then there will be no jump. Here's the solution:

Figure 19.3.

In the animation sequence, the motion returns to the position for 0 at the end of every cycle interval.

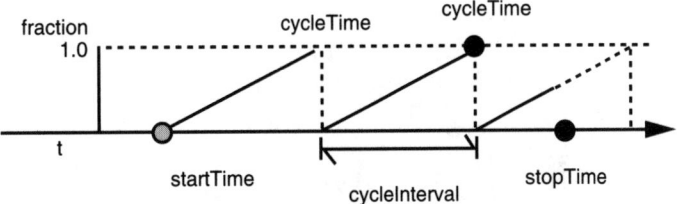

1. The keys and value fields should be changed so that they still range from 0 to 1, but the jumping problem is solved by introducing an intermediate step of 0.5:

   ```
   key [ 0 0.5 1 ]
   ```

2. If the number of values in the keys field changes, then the number of values in the value field should change to match:

   ```
   keyvValue [ 4 .5 0, -4 .5 0, 4 .5 0 ]
   ```

With these changes, the sphere moves back and forth across the screen like a boring ping-pong game—still not a very exciting motion. What can you do to liven it up?

 # Changing the Animation Path

Applying a little bit of lateral thinking, you notice that the sphere is moving only backward and forward—that's because those are the only positions you defined. To make the sphere travel a square path, just add more points in positions outlining a square path.

1. Try increasing the number of points from three to five and see what happens. First, add addition values in the keys field.

2. Corresponding values need to be placed in the values field. The PositionInterpolator node is now defined as this:

```
DEF position PositionInterpolator {
    key [ 0 .25 .5 .75 1 ]
    keyvValue [   4 .5  0,
               0 .5  4,   # new value added here
              -4 .5  0,
               0 .5 -4,   # new value as well
               4 .5  0 ]
}
```

Yes, the object is now moving in a square, which illustrates that the values are a linear interpolation between the defined points. If you specify a value halfway between two keys, then you get the middle value of the two corresponding value field items. Therefore, to get more accuracy, you need to have more points so that the linear bits between points aren't too long.

TIP:
Time to dig out those pocket calculators. To calculate a circular path, take the number of points you want to use in the circle and divide that number into 360. The x and y value of each position is given in this formula:

x = radius * sin(angle) y = radius * cos(angle)

Keep doing this for each angle you need and place it in the values field with the corresponding number of entries in the keys field. Don't forget to put in the extra point that returns you to the original position.

Using this combination of keys and values, you can define whatever path you choose. For example, by a simple rearrangement of the current points, you end up with a bowtie-shaped path.

TIP:
You can create different speeds on the path by simply compressing or expanding the range between 0 and 1 that you devote to a particular part of the track. The object traveling a greater distance in the same time as one going a shorter distance moves more quickly.

Sensors for Control

So far, so good. You have this red sphere that travels around in circles forever, consuming memory and valuable CPU time. Now you're going to add the ability to start and stop the animation on demand. To do this, you just need to click on something to tell the animation to stop; you can also use the reverse position of what you click on to make it start.

Earlier in this chapter, you learned that sensors are the only nodes capable of generating new events. You have a collection of seven sensor types to play with, and you've already seen how TimeSensor works. The Cylinder, Plane, and Sphere sensors are used to translate drag motions into a particular geometry. The three other sensors are Proximity, Touch, and Visibility.

Visibility sensors activate when something becomes visible. Proximity sensors activate when you get within a defined bounding box, which could be very useful. For example, the ball does nothing until you get near it. When the ProximitySensor is tripped, the ball scurries away until it's out of the proximity range; then ProximitySensor returns `false`, and the sphere stops moving. The final sensor, TouchSensor, is used in the next example.

Using the TouchSensor Node to Control Animations

TouchSensors relate any sort of touch-type input to an event. To add a TouchSensor to a scene, place it at the same level in the hierarchy as the objects you want to detect touches on. TouchSensor looks at the children of its parent node but doesn't contain children itself, which is unusual. In your current scene, you could place a TouchSensor directly into the Transform node containing the sphere. However, you don't want to try hitting a moving object with a mouse.

Originally, TouchSensors were called ClickSensors, but since people will likely be navigating in the future with non-mouse devices, like datagloves and wands, the more generic name was used.

1. Since it's difficult to click on a moving object, you'll create a new cone primitive that can take the TouchSensor and position it in the corner of your scene.

2. Once the primitive is in the scene, the TouchSensor can be added in the same Transform node. Listing 19.1 shows the code for the entire file; notice that a Viewpoint and a bowtie path for the animation have been added.

Listing 19.1. The finished file with animation and user-controlled actions.

```
#VRML V2.0 utf8
#
# Animating a sphere - now with 5 points
# forming a bowtie path.

# Introduce a Viewpoint looking down from above
Viewpoint {
    position 0 5 5
    orientation 1 0 0 -.707
}
# First, the floor
Shape {
    appearance Appearance {
        material Material { emissiveColor .7 .7 .7 }
    }
    geometry Box { size 10 0.1 10 }
}
# Now, the red sphere
DEF transform Transform {
    translation 4 0.5 0
    children [
        Shape {
            appearance Appearance {
                material Material { emissiveColor .8 0 0 }
            }
            geometry Sphere { radius .4 }
        }
    ]
}

# Put in a TimeSensor
DEF time TimeSensor {
    cycleInterval 8
    loop    TRUE
    enabled FALSE
    startTime 1
}

# Finally, the Interpolator
DEF position PositionInterpolator {
    key [ 0 .25 .5 .75 1 ]
    keyVvalue [   4 .5  4,
                  4 .5 -4,
                 -4 .5  4,
                 -4 .5 -4,
                  4 .5  4
             ]
}

# Add the TouchSensor on a blue cone
Transform {
    translation 4.5 0.5 4.5
    children [
        Shape {
            appearance Appearance {
                material Material { emissiveColor 0 .8 0 }
```

```
            }
            geometry Cone {
                bottomRadius .4
                height 1
            }
        }
        DEF touch TouchSensor {}
    ]
}

# Now connect everything together
ROUTE time.fraction_changed TO position.set_fraction
ROUTE position.keyValue_changed TO transform.translation
ROUTE touch.isActive TO time.enabled
```

Figure 19.4 shows the finished file. When you run this file, you'll find that the object moves only while the mouse button is held down over the cone. This is because TouchSensor doesn't have a toggle action. Therefore, the isActive field is held `true` only while the mouse button is held down over the object. If you want to use a toggle action, you need to use scripts, which are covered in the next two chapters.

Figure 19.4.

The sphere is animated and moves when the cone primitive in the corner is clicked.

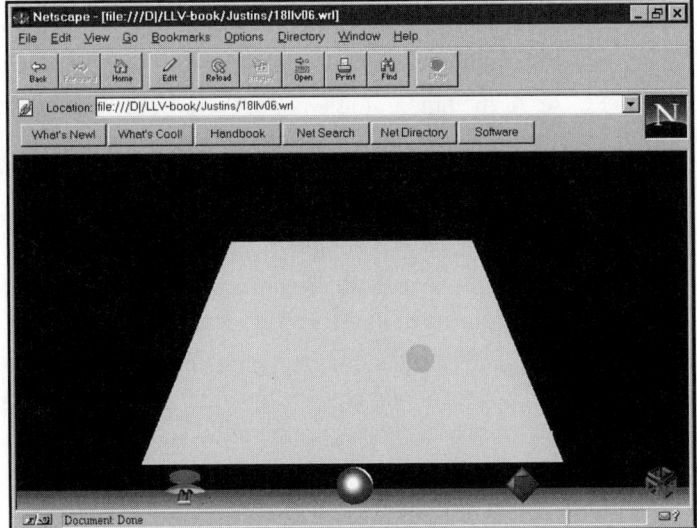

Workshop Wrap-up

Welcome to Moving Worlds. What you have seen here is only a small part of adding behaviors to VRML worlds. The topic is so large that a whole book could be devoted to the subject, but you got a chapter instead. However, you've learned almost everything there is to know about VRML nodes—there's only a few left. A few of these get covered in the next workshop in Chapter 23, "Real-Life Examples: A 3D Gallery: An Advanced VRML World."

Next Steps

In the rest of this book, you'll be looking at the following:

❏ Create simple programmable behaviors using CGI and JavaScript in Chapter 20, "Interfacing VRML Worlds with Scripts."

❏ If you're a real hard-core content creator and want to stretch your wings a bit, then go to Chapter 21, "Using Java to Add Behaviors to VRML."

❏ Chapter 22, "Adding Interactivity: The Future of VRML," discusses where VRML is likely to head and some other interactivity issues, like multi-user VRML worlds and online personalities.

❏ You'll go completely over the top in the final workshop. Here, you'll use all the multimedia features of VRML and develop a guided tour of the gallery you've been developing in the previous two workshops, Chapter 23, "Real-Life Examples: A 3D Gallery: An Advanced VRML World."

Q&A

Q: All these behaviors are interesting, but they seem complex. Is there some way they can be automatically produced?

A: At the time of this writing, there were no automated VRML 2.0 static scene creators, let alone one capable of doing behaviors. For the time being, learn to love your favorite text editor. Ideally, a good tool would consist of a GUI front-end, like Caligari's Pioneer or IDS-Software VRealm, and the point and click interface of Kinetix's Hyperwire.

Q: Simple interpolations are fine, but how do I create more complex interpolations, like turning effects for corners?

A: Complex situations can be modelled either statically at creation time by getting lots of points that simulate the curve or by creating a script that dynamically calculates these position values. Scripting is covered in the next two chapters.

TWENTY

Interfacing VRML Worlds with Scripts

—by Justin Couch

Once you've started using the built-in animation techniques you learned in the last chapter, you'll soon find yourself wishing for more functionality. For instance, in the last example in Chapter 19, "Using Built-in Animation Techniques," (when you controlled behaviors in response to mouse clicks on an object) there was no way to toggle the button click event. However, these limits can be overcome by building your own behaviors. If you've never programmed before, then here is a chance to jump in feet first. Scripting is a simple technique to understand. If you've ever written a macro for MS Word or a DOS batch file, then you're almost there.

Scripting can be considered a subsection of behaviors program-ming. On one side, you have the simple built-in system described in the previous chapter, and on the other, you can create your own behaviors. If you felt like it, you could write your own scripts that do the same job as the interpolators, but this is a waste of time because the language for built-in systems has already done that work for you. Generally, you use scripting to add more complex behaviors on top of the ones provided for VRML. In this chapter, you'll explore the following topics:

❑ Using CGI with VRML

❑ Seeing how VRML incorporates programmable behaviors with the Script node

❑ Adding some simple behaviors by using JavaScript

❑ Seeing how scripts can control browser behavior

As in the rest of the book to this point, you still need only a basic text editor to create interesting VRML worlds.

If you're interested in just using Java for the scripting, then you should still read the section on the browser interface and the basic introduction to the Script node. These two sections describe the generic interface for controlling the scene graph itself through the browser. In Chapter 21, "Using Java to Add Behaviors to VRML," it will be assumed that you already understand these browser interface basics.

 # Combining VRML and CGI

As you already know, CGI produces documents read in by the browser that are built dynamically in response to user input. CGI can be used several ways under VRML 2.0. If you're responsible for writing C or Perl scripts, then you also need to be familiar with how VRML works, which is why you're reading this book in the first place. Explaining how to develop a CGI script to produce a VRML model is beyond the scope of this book, but there are a few pointers provided to help you on your way.

The first method of producing dynamic worlds is to use the standard HTML/CGI form input, which then generates a VRML output file. If you're familiar with writing CGI programs, then you should have no trouble producing output. For VRML files, you need to send the MIME type as the following:

```
x-world/x-vrml
```

There are many examples of this style of work. A good one to look at is The VRML Roller Skater by GraphComp's Bob Free, which is shown in Figure 20.1. If you take a look at `http://www.graphcomp.com/vrml/`, you'll see an example of combining a number of Web technologies. This site combines VRML and HTML with frames and CGI input. Using standard frames, you can keep the form on frame, then have the CGI script deliver the contents to another frame by using the TARGET field in your anchor tag. The end result of the query is then shown in Figure 20.2. See how the output of the CGI script is kept in the left-hand frame, instead of taking over the whole page?

Figure 20.1.

The introductory page, including the CGI form interface.

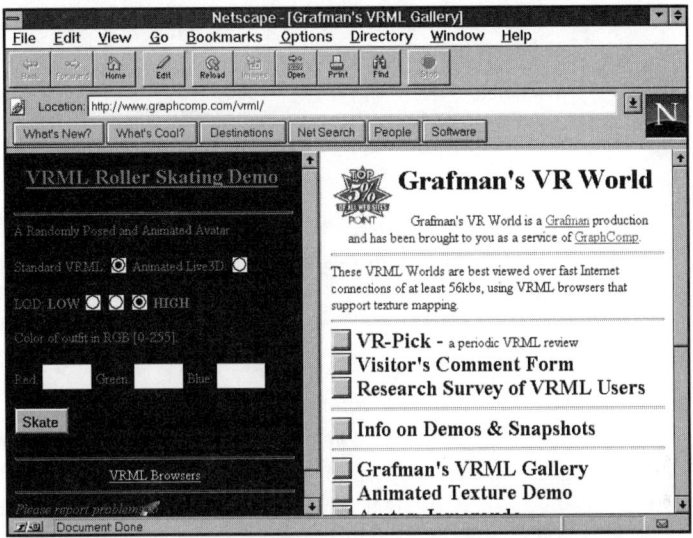

Figure 20.2.

The result of the CGI query; now you have your own customized roller skater.

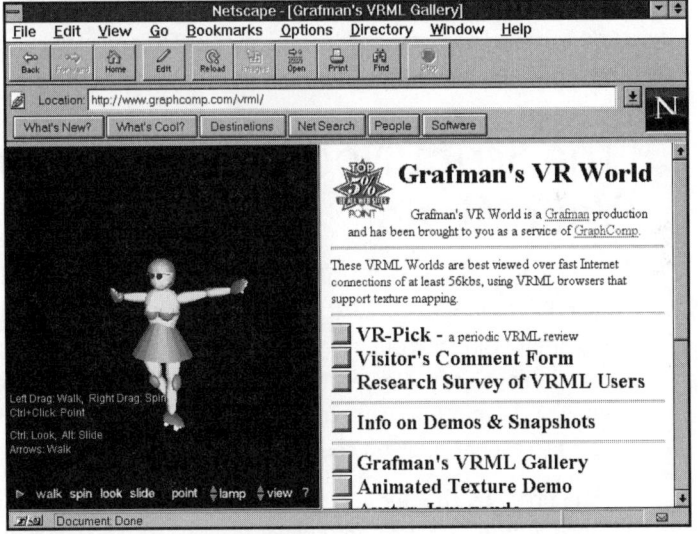

A second option is using CGI within the VRML world. Besjon Alavandi's Outland part of Terra Vista (`http://www.webking.com/outland`) dynamically generates a world on-the-fly, using values for the lengths of the world's sides. It also encodes that information into the VRML file itself so that a single script can be used to generate any part of the world. This is particularly handy for large worlds, when you don't want to give the user the whole world at once because downloading would be too slow. Take a look at how this is done:

1. To use CGI within the VRML world, just add the URL to the CGI script in the url field of an Anchor node, like this:

```
Anchor {
    url "/cgi-bin/myworld.cgi LENGTH=50,WIDTH=35"
    children [ # child list here
    ]
}
```

2. When you click the Anchor node, it will load the world given in the url field. When the browser has finished fetching the file, it replaces the current world you're in.

The URL must contain a blank after the main path description and before the parameters. No question mark is used to act as a separator. This method is different from the way most HTML-based forms would submit the information to the server.

TIP: You can use the parameters field to send the output to another frame. To do this, set the field value to `"TARGET=destination_frame"`. You'll see how this is done in Chapter 21, when you produce a frames-based document with both VRML and HTML static content, rather than CGI scripts.

In the last section of this chapter, you'll look at another method of using CGI, in which CGI is used as part of the scripts themselves to control the world. However, before you can do that, you need to learn about using scripts first.

The Script Node: Internal Control of Your World

The biggest problem with using CGI is that your whole world gets replaced when you use it. For example, if you're just trying to control the state of a button, then there's no point to using it. Your users won't bother using your world just to change the color of a single object. However, with the Script node, you can add programmable behaviors within the scene graph. By placing them within the scene, you get direct access to every node you could place a ROUTE command to.

In the previous chapter's last example, you could run the animation only while the mouse button was held down over the switch. To start with a basic examination of how to use scripting, you'll add a toggle switch in the section "Creating a Toggle Behavior with Scripts."

Outline of the Script Node

Script nodes are a little different from the rest of the nodes in VRML. When you're using them, you have the ability to specify your own fields and event interfaces. The basic Script node is defined as the following:

```
Script {
  exposedField MFString url                []
  field        SFBool    directOutputs FALSE
  field        SFBool    mustEvaluate  FALSE
  # And any number of:
  eventIn      eventTypeName eventName
  field        fieldTypeName fieldName initialValue
  eventOut     eventTypeName eventName
}
```

NOTE:
Note that exposedFields are not permitted in Script nodes. If you want to create the equivalent of exposedFields, then you need to provide an eventIn and an eventOut field, as well as some scripting.

The url field is used for specifying where your scripts are located. Currently, there's support only for Java and a derivative of Netscape's JavaScript with some of the functionality cut out. The url field will be a reference to the Java .class file or the JavaScript file. JavaScript is dealt with in more depth in the next chapter.

The other two fields are directions to the browser on how this script interacts with the world. Normally, you won't need to change the values for these fields. The mustEvaluate field is used to tell the browser that as soon as it receives an event for this node, it must evaluate the event. Set this field if you are writing scripts that deal with hard real-time constraints. If you aren't, then you don't need to worry about changing the default value. The directOutputs field is used to tell the browser whether this Script node is writing directly to the inputs of another node. Until now, you've been told that the way to pass events is through the node's event interface. The browser API section in this chapter explains how it is possible to pass information directly to a node from within a script.

Apart from these three fields, the rest of the node definition is up to you. You can place whatever combination of fields you like. You can add ROUTE commands to them just as you would to any other predefined node, pass events to them, and do anything else that's legal.

Script nodes, because they don't affect the drawing of any node, can be placed anywhere you want in the scene. They don't need to be located in the same place as the nodes they communicate with. There's no rule as to where they should be placed in your file, but usually they're placed at the end so they can have access to every other node that has been defined with the DEF keyword.

Creating a Toggle Behavior with Scripts

Adding the toggle behavior is as simple as slotting a Script node between the TouchSensor and the TimeSensor. The behavior you need to add is toggling the TimeSensor for each click of the mouse button. The first step is designing a script to work out what inputs (eventIns) you're going to take and what outputs (eventOuts) the script will deliver to other parts of the scene. Although the majority of scripts have both inputs and outputs, not all do. In the next chapter, you'll see how to use Java to act as a gateway with the outside world.

You can refer to scripts circularly, with the events of script 1 fed to script 2, which in turn sends more events back to script 1, but this can get messy. Leaving them at the end of the file is a good idea because you can keep track of how all the behaviors act together. For moderately complex behaviors, you will find yourself routing events between scripts, as well as to the nodes.

1. The TouchSensor outputs an SFBool and the TimeSensor takes an SFBool, so that means you need one eventIn and one eventOut of the same types. Pretty simple.

2. To create a toggle behavior, you also need to keep track of what the current state is—that is, has the button been pressed already or is it unpressed? That means you need another SFBool. This time SFBool is a field because it's holding information but not giving it out for public display. Your Script node outline looks like this now:

```
DEF toggle Script {
    field SFBool active FALSE
    eventIn SFBool isClicked
    eventOut SFBool click_changed
    url  # not done yet
}
```

The scripting part is explained in the following section, but the framework shown in the preceding paragraphs illustrates how the script connects with the VRML fields.

3. The final step is to include your ROUTE statements:

```
ROUTE touch.isActive TO toggle.isClicked
ROUTE toggle.click_changed TO time.enabled
```

> **TIP:** Leave the url field to last if you're using JavaScript to do your behaviors. JavaScript is embedded within this field, and it makes the code much easier to read if all the field definitions are first, then the code to deal with them is presented later.

Start with a FALSE value for the internal value of the button state. When the user clicks the mouse button, it toggles the output to the TimeSensor, thereby starting and stopping the animation. In the examples from Chapter 19 that this code is based on, you have already set the TimeSensor-enabled field's default to FALSE, so everything is in sync.

Behaviors Made Easy with JavaScript

Once you have the outline for the Script node done, the rest becomes easy. What language do you write it in? Obviously, VRML has no built-in scripting language, so you need to use another language. The specification allows you to write behavior using JavaScript, which gives you some flexibility. Chapter 21 deals with the Java issues, so you'll focus on JavaScript here. All you need to do is learn how JavaScript fits with the VRML scripting environment.

Thirty-Second Introduction to JavaScript

If you haven't used JavaScript before (just another language like Visual Basic), then here's a quick overview. If you haven't done any programming before, the overview won't be much help. It's in no way a comprehensive guide but should be enough to get you up and running so that you can understand the rest of this chapter. There are several good books on JavaScript, such as Sams.net Publishing's *Teach Yourself JavaScript in 21 Days*, or you can check out the Netscape site at http:// home.netscape.com/comprod/products/navigator/version_2.0/script/ script_info/.

The standard operators +, -, *, and / all have their usual meanings. A single equal sign (=) is used for assigning values. JavaScript also borrows heavily from C for a few extras. By putting the operator just in front of the equal sign, you can adjust that variable by the value afterward. For example, the following line means that you add the value of 5 to that of a and leave the result in a:

```
a += 5;
```

Conditional operators are represented by double characters. For example, a logical AND is && and OR is ¦¦. As always, there's an exception to every rule, so NOT is a single !. To compare two values for equality, use a double equal sign (==). Be careful, though, because many a programmer has become stuck by using a single equal sign, rather than a double equal sign, in a conditional statement. When you assign one value to another, it's always evaluated to mean TRUE.

There are no types in JavaScript, so a variable just takes the type of when it's first assigned something. This is very handy when playing with the defined types from the VRML fields. You don't need to do anything special to incorporate specific types from VRML.

JavaScript is somewhat object-oriented in nature. When you want to access functionality declared outside the current script, use the object name and the function name

In JavaScript, the VRML SFBool and MFBool types are interpreted as being numbers. A value of 0 is FALSE and a value of 1 is TRUE.

separated by a dot. For example, to assign the sine of 30 degrees to the value z, use this:

```
z = math.sin(30);
```

To create your own function, just enter the function name followed by a list of parameters enclosed in brackets. Because there are no object types, you need to put in just the variable names. This is normally very useful, but you must remember to make sure that the types of values you're passing are the same as what you're interpreting within that function.

Using JavaScript in Script Nodes

JavaScript is embedded within the VRML source file, this time in the url field of the Script node. Instead of putting in the normal URL-style reference, you're giving the browser the MIME type directly. To start your url field, you need the following:

```
url "javascript: "
```

For each eventIn you've declared in the VRML declaration of the script, you must also have a corresponding function. You can have any number of parameters you want; however, only the first two are used when the function is called by the browser. The first parameter is of the same type as the field type, and the second is the timestamp value (a floating point number indicating the number of seconds since midnight GMT, January 1, 1970).

Sending values to eventOuts is as simple as assigning values to them. Naturally, the value should be the same type as that of the eventOut.

1. Now you have enough to complete your Script node. All you need is one short function; the Script node definition now looks like this:

```
DEF toggle Script {
    field SFBool active FALSE
    eventIn SFBool isClicked
    eventOut SFBool click_changed
    url  "vrmlscript:
        function isClicked() {
            if (active == 0)
                active = 1;
            else
                active = 0;
            click_changed = active;
        }
        "
}
```

What happens when you try this? The behavior is still the same! Ooops. What did you do wrong?

Looking back at the definition of the TouchSensor node, notice that the isActive field is TRUE when the mouse button is pressed down and FALSE when the mouse button is released. The script is receiving two events for each button click. What really needs to happen is to have the script look at only one of these two events, and then look at alternating mouse button ups or downs.

2. To do this, the function needs to incorporate a parameter for the actual button position; then a check for the button position is added to eliminate one of the two events. Use the button up event to toggle on:

```
function isClicked(button_pos) {
   if(button_pos == 0)   // button up so exec
   {
       if (active == 0)
           active = 1;
       else
           active = 0;
       click_changed = active;
   }
}
```

The code can be placed wherever you like in the javascript: section. Order is not important.

There is one last bug you need to fix. If you click down on the cone, then drag the mouse sideways and let go, it still triggers the behavior. This isn't how a button should behave. You might not have taken much notice of how buttons behave in a GUI environment. If you click down and drag your mouse away from the button, it becomes "unclicked." You want to replicate this behavior, so you need to add another eventIn to tell the script when the mouse is actually over the object.

3. The isOver field of the TouchSensor node indicates when the pointer is over the sensor but not necessarily clicked on it. When you click the mouse button and then drag away, as the pointer moves off the sensor, this field goes FALSE. Using the combination of these two events, change the behavior so that it requires both isOver and isClicked to be TRUE on a button up event before you can start and stop the animation. The final code is shown in Listing 20.1.

This code can be placed wherever you like in the VRML file as long as both the Script and the TouchSensor and TimeSensor nodes are declared before the ROUTE statements at the bottom.

Listing 20.1. The final script for toggling behavior.

```
DEF toggle Script {
    field SFBool active FALSE
    field SFBool pointer_over FALSE
    eventIn SFBool isClicked
    eventIn SFBool isOver
    eventOut SFBool click_changed
    url  "javascript:
        function isClicked(button_pos) {
            // the following two if statements should be combined
            // together with && but CosmoPlayer did not like it -bug
            if(button_pos == 0)
            {
                if(pointer_over == 1)
                {
                    if (active == 0)
                        active = 1;
                    else
                        active = 0;
                    click_changed = active;
                }
            }
        }
        function isOver(value) {
            if(value == 0)
                pointer_over = 0;
            else
                pointer_over = 1;
        }
    "
}

ROUTE touch.isActive TO toggle.isClicked
ROUTE touch.isOver TO toggle.isOver
```

Controlling the Scene Through the Browser

The simple scripting introduced in the previous section gives you the ability to do many things. The problem is that objects must already be existing in the scene, so although you can control the actions of a robot within the scene, you can't add more robots. To add more robots, you need to be able to get inside the scene graph by telling the browser to perform some action. In this section, you'll look at the browser interface that allows scripts to control the contents of the scene graph.

The browser interface is defined in a language-neutral approach, which then allows individual languages to produce a binding to the interface. At the time of this writing, bindings were available for JavaScript and Java in the form of a class called, appropriately, Browser. In the next few paragraphs, I will outline how the different available functions work; you can get more detailed descriptions from the VRML 2.0 specification.

Sometimes you might want to include browser-specific behavior. HTML doesn't allow you to do this, but the `getName()` and `getVersion()` functions return strings with information about the browser environment. There is no defined format, so you need to find out what each browser returns.

In heavily loaded scenes, you might want to adjust the behavior so that it doesn't load down the computer too much. You can use the `getCurrentSpeed()` function to return what speed the user is moving at to control the actions of other objects. There is no point in having fine-tuned behavior control when the user is screaming by at 100 units per second. Heavy behavior calculations mean that less time is spent doing the rendering, so that affects the updating of the screen image. You can modify behavior depending on what the current frame rate is by looking at the return value of `getCurrentFrameRate()`.

The `getWorldURL()` function returns a string holding the URL of the currently loaded world. If you want to load in a new world, then pass a list of URL strings to the `loadURL()` function, which will try to load one of them. The order they appear in the string defines the loading order preference.

TIP:

Because `loadURL()` replaces the whole world with the new one, it may or may not return. Don't count on it returning in your behavior.

The function `loadURL()` is more flexible than just being limited to loading VRML worlds. With this function, you can call any valid URL, which could be a CGI script call, a normal HTML page, or even things like FTP or news.

 # Building VRML Scenes On-the-Fly

One of the features of VR programming is the ability to build the scene graph on-the-fly. Two functions do this in the browser interface. The first, `CreateVRMLFromString()`, takes a string that's the equivalent of what you would write in the .wrl file and returns a node. You don't need to put in the header, though.

1. To create a box on-the-fly, write the following:

   ```
   node = Browser.createVRMLFromString("Box { size 2 3 1 }");
   ```

2. You can then add the returned node to any part of the scene graph you want. In your script definition, include a reference to a Group or Transform node, where you could then add the node as a child by passing the returned node reference to the add_children eventIn field.

The other way to add new nodes to the scene is to grab the values from some predefined VRML scene by using the `createVRMLFromURL()` function. It's different from the string function because, for arguments, it takes a node reference and a string that refers to an eventIn. As you know, fetching something with an http call isn't instantaneous. To alleviate this problem, `createVRMLFromURL()` starts the call and then returns right away. When the file has been retrieved and converted into the internal format, the nominated eventIn is then called with a list of the nodes (`MFNode`).

If you want a delayed loading of the world, then you can call one of the create functions and pass the list of nodes to `replaceWorld()` at your own convenience. This function performs the same task as `loadURL()` of replacing the entire world with the given contents but adds the ability for you to control when this happens.

Once you have a list of nodes, you might also want to adjust the event handling, too. The functions `addRoute()` and `deleteRoute()` let you add and delete event routes between nodes. You pass the node instance and a string referring to the event field name for each end of the route.

Creating Objects On-the-Fly

Building on the previous scene using the animation, you'll delve into using behaviors. Using the browser interface in JavaScript, a series of controls will be added across the front of the test world from Chapter 19 to show the various actions. The same things can be done with the Java version, too.

The first new control will use the `createVRMLFromString()` function. Touching the control will add a new box to the system. Each additional box you create will pile on top of the previous ones. To do this, you need to add another script, a few more objects, and routes.

1. The first thing you need is a Transform node containing the box primitive and the TouchSensor node. To make it easier, define a Transform node that locates the stack of boxes in relation to the whole scene; then each time you add a box, it's just stacked in relation to the previous box. The script acts in the same way as defined earlier in this chapter for working with the mouse. A few of the DEF names have been rearranged so that things are a little more clear:

```
# A purple box to produce the stacked cubes when clicked on
Transform {
    translation 3 0.5 4.5
    children [
        Shape {
            appearance Appearance {
                material Material { emissiveColor .5 .4 .5 }
            }
            geometry Box { size 1 1 1 }
```

```
        }
        DEF box_touch TouchSensor {}
    ]
}

DEF box_stack Transform {
    translation 0 0 -4.5
}
```

2. Following that comes the Script node. Basically the actions of the script are fairly simple. When a box is defined, you need to give it not only a parent Transform but also some color. Most of the script is taken up with just putting together the string that defines the shape. You could substitute whatever sort of shape you wanted here, but defining a complex IndexedFaceSet would be a waste of time. For the moment, just stick to plain old boring boxes.

This isn't the only way to define the text to be created. Instead, you could define each item separately with a createVRMLFromString() call for each, then assemble it using the event interfaces. For example, you can create the top Transform node as node1 and the Shape node as node2, then set the Shape node as the child of the Transform by using node1.add_children = node2. This method lets you build objects in a much cleaner way, particularly if you won't always be generating identical shapes.

Listing 20.2. Code portion showing the script to dynamically add a box to the scene in response to user input.

```
DEF add_box Script {
    field SFBool pointer_over FALSE
    field SFVec3f position .5 0 0
    eventIn SFBool isClicked
    eventIn SFBool isOver
    eventOut MFNode new_child
    url "javascript:
        function isClicked(button_pos) {
            // the following two if statements should be combined
            // together with && but CosmopPlayer did not like it.- bug
            if(button_pos == 0)
            {
                if(pointer_over == 1)
                {
                    box_string = "transform { children [ ";
                    box_string += "Shape { appearance Appearance { ";
                    box_string += "material Material { diffuseColor";
                    box_string += "0 0 .6 } }";
                    box_string += "geometry Box { size 1 1 1 } }";
                    box_string += "] }";

                    node = Browser.createVRMLFromString(box_string);
                    node.set_translation = position;
                    new_child = node;

                    postion[1] += 1;
                }
            }
        }
        function isOver(value) {
            if(value == 0)
                pointer_over = 0;
            else
                pointer_over = 1;
        }
    "
}
```

3. The final step is the ROUTE statements:

```
# The box addition routes
ROUTE box_touch.isActive TO add_box.isClicked
ROUTE box_touch.isOver TO add_box.isOver
ROUTE add_box.new_child TO box_stack.add_children
```

 # Adding Other Worlds

The second way to modify the scene graph is to load in other files. If you go back to the workshop from Chapter 2, "Up and Running: First VRML Creation," you'll see that all the cars were in the scene right from the beginning. Now, by using scripts, you can load one car at a time whenever you want. In this case, loading the cars will be a one-shot affair. After you've loaded the car a first time, you won't allow it to be loaded again.

1. Again, the script is very simple. Take the same code for the isOver event from the previous sections and the basic outline for the isClicked event. In the spirit of VRML, add a field to the Script node that contains the URL strings for the car you'll be loading.

2. You'll use the createVRMLFromURL() function to retrieve external files, which requires an eventIn field and a node reference.

3. You want to be able to place the car somewhere besides its default position. Since you don't need to do any other processing, create an ordinary Transform node and place the child directly into it. If extra processing were needed, then you could have created an extra eventIn to pass to the Script node. The complete script is shown in Listing 20.3.

Listing 20.3. Code portion for adding an external file to the scene.

```
DEF car_position Transform {
    translation -4 2 0
}
Transform {
    translation -1.5 .5 4.5
    children [
        Shape {
            appearance Appearance {
                material Material { emissiveColor 0 0 .6 }
            }
            geometry Cylinder {
                heigth 1
                bottomRadius 0.5
            }
        }
        DEF car_touch TouchSensor {}
    ]
}

DEF add_car Script {
    field SFBool pointer_over FALSE
```

When you want to include a node reference, you can take advantage of the DEF and USE keywords by adding USE to a node in the script definition, which can then be included in the function calls in the script. When you add USE to a node, essentially you're creating another reference to the original DEF, rather than creating a copy of it. If you want to refer to your Script node, then you can use first DEF, then USE, without any problems, as shown here:

DEF myscript Script { field SFNode myself USE myscript .... etc }

```
      field SFBool done FALSE
      field MFString car_url "p51.wrl"
      field SFNode car_pos USE car_position
      eventIn SFBool isClicked
      eventIn SFBool isOver
      url "javascript:
          function isClicked(button_pos) {
              // the following two if statements should be combined
              // together with && but cosmoplayer did not like it -bug
              if(button_pos == 0)
              {
                  if((pointer_over == 1) && (done == 0))
                  {
                      Browser.createVRMLFromURL(car_url,
                                        car_pos, "add_children");
                      done = 1;
                  }
              }
          }
          function isOver(value) {
              if(value == 0)
                  pointer_over = 0;
              else
                  pointer_over = 1;
          }
      "
}

# The car addition routes
ROUTE car_touch.isActive TO add_car.isClicked
ROUTE car_touch.isOver TO add_car.isOver
```

Fast Loading of a New World on Demand

The final example for this chapter shows how to load a new world on demand by using the combination of createVRMLFromURL() and replaceWorld(). They will respond to two separate objects in the scene that are clicked on. After clicking on the first object, it will start to load in a world. When the world has finished loading, it will be indicated by a new object being added to the world. When this object has been added, then you can click on it to replace the current world with the new one. In this example, you'll use all the features of the previous sections plus the last few calls left from the browser interface.

1. Preloading the world is easy. You'll use another eventIn within the script because you want to do some more processing of the returned values.

2. When the event is received, you'll create another boring cube on-the-fly, a TouchSensor node to go with it, and a Transform node to contain them.

3. Because you've just created these nodes, there aren't any ROUTE commands to connect the TouchSensor to a script to do the final part. Even though it's cheating a little, you'll use the one script that will also include another eventIn to signal that the world should now be replaced. Put it all together, then look at the results in Listing 20.4.

Listing 20.4. Code fragment to produce a dynamically created and loaded world in two stages.

This task section illustrates the ability to create separate smaller nodes by using createVRMLFromString() and the JavaScript capabilities to manage children. As you can see, it makes for simpler, easier to read code. You also needed to use this method so you could get the node instance of TouchSensor to create routes to it. This way, you don't need to give the node a DEF name because the node pointer gives you a reference to the node.

```
# the final example using replaceWorld()
Transform {
    translation -4.5 .5 4.5
    children [
        Shape {
            appearance Appearance {
                material Material { emissiveColor 0 0 .6 }
            }
            geometry Sphere { radius 0.5 }
        }
        DEF replace_touch TouchSensor {}
    ]
}

# this is the Transform where you will put the new object
DEF new_object Transform {
    translation 4.5 0.5 0
}

DEF replace_script Script {
    field SFBool pointerOver          FALSE
    field SFBool pointerOver_new      FALSE
    field SFBool done                 FALSE
    field SFNode myself               USE replace_script
    field SFNode secondObject         USE new_object
    field MFNode new_world            NULL
    field MFString externalFile       "p51.wrl"
    eventIn SFBool isClicked
    eventIn SFBool isOver
    eventIn SFBool isClicked_new
    eventIn SFBool isOver_new
    eventIn MFNode newNodesReady
    url "javascript:
        function isClicked(button_pos) {
            // the following two if statements should be combined
            // together with && but CosmoPlayer did not like it -bug
            if(button_pos == 0) {
                if(pointer_over == 1) (
                    if(done == 0) {  // same problem as above :(
                        // call create the external file
                        Browser.createVRMLFromURL(externalFile,
                                                  myself,
                                                  "newNodesReady");
                        done = 1;
                    }
                }
            }
        }

        function isOver(value) {
```

```
            if(value == 0)
                pointerOver = 0;
            else
                pointerOver = 1;
    }

    // when the final click comes, then replace the world
    function isClicked_new(button_pos) {
        // the following two if statements should be combined
        // together with && but CosmoPlayer did not like it. ????
        if(button_pos == 0) {
            if(pointer_over == 1) {
                Browser.replaceWorld(new_world);
            }
        }
    }

    // same as the ordinary isOver but just for your new object.
    function isOver_new(value) {
        if(value == 0)
            pointerOver_new = 0;
        else
            pointerOver_new = 1;
    }

    // the function that really does all the work. Now that the
    // new world has been loaded, you need to create another object
    // with a TouchSensor and place that in the scene
    function newNodesReady(node_list) {
        shape = "Shape { appearance Appearance {} }"
        material = "Material { emissiveColor .2 .2 .2 }"
        box = "Box { size 0.5 0.5 0.5 }"
        sensor = "TouchSensor {}"

        shape_node = Browser.createVRMLFromString(shape);
        shape_node.material =
                        Browser.createVRMLFromString(material);
        shape_node.geometry = Browser.createVRMLFromString(box);
        sensor_node = Browser.createVRMLFromString(sensor);

        // update the internal field with the newly created
        // list of nodes
        new_world = value;

        // now add the nodes to the scene
        secondObject.add_children = s_node;
        secondObject.add_children = sensor_node;

        // finally add routes between the newly formed
        // TouchSensor and the inputs to this script
        Browser.addRoute(sensor_node, "isActive",
                        myself, "isClicked_new");
        Browser.addRoute(sensor_node, "isOver",
                        myself, "isOver_new");
    }
            "
}

# The replaceWorld script routes
ROUTE replace_touch.isActive TO replace_script.isClicked
ROUTE replace_touch.isOver TO replace_script.isOver
```

Workshop Wrap-up

So how did it go? Did I lose you? For the non-programmer, it can be easy to get bogged down in scripting. The last example is probably one of the more complex scripts you will ever have to write. If you ever need to do anything more than this, you will need to learn a full programming language like Java. Now, where do you go from here?

❏ If you understood the last example without any trouble and would like to try something even heavier, head on over to the next chapter on Java, Chapter 21, "Using Java to Add Behaviors to VRML."

❏ So I have lost you totally? Don't give up yet. Go to Chapter 22, "Adding Interactivity: The Future of VRML," which plays a bit of future forecasting, looking at where VRML is heading in future versions and some of the fun parts of using VRML.

❏ Chapter 23, "Real-Life Examples: A 3D Gallery: An Advanced VRML World," is also a good place to visit. Here you're guided through the second phase of developing the VRML art gallery. This shows you how far you can stretch even the current versions of VRML to provide that true VR feeling.

Q&A

Q: It seems like scripting is very powerful—what can't you do with it?

A: JavaScript is limited to working with objects already in the scene or added after a VRML file has been retrieved across the network using HTTP. There's no way of writing your own functionality to deal with the network, so you couldn't build a real-time external information feed into your world with JavaScript. If you switch to Java, then you can do things like that.

Q: If there is no networking, what other functionality is available to JavaScript?

A: JavaScript also includes the JavaScript date and math objects. With these, you can create some very complex behaviors. Using the date object, you could, for example, load a file depending on what the phase of the moon is. With the math object, you could define a complex path or shape using Bézier curves to model the real world.

Q: Where can I learn more about JavaScript?

A: There's not much more to learn. I have deliberately left out the description of the event processing and execution model because they can get highly complex. When you're dealing with scripting, it's a good idea not to change them. If you believe you need to look at understanding and using these, then you should probably look at using a proper programming language like Java for adding behaviors. The event-processing model is covered briefly in the next chapter.

Q: Sometimes I see references to VRMLScript. What is that?

A: VRMLScript was the working name for the JavaScript section when VRML 2.0 was being developed. At the time, there was some debate about whether VRML could use the name JavaScript for copyright reasons. This has since been cleared, and the name has returned to JavaScript.

TWENTY-ONE

Using Java to Add Behaviors to VRML

—by Justin Couch

In the previous chapter, you were introduced to scripting and the basics of JavaScript. Once you start playing with it, you'll realize some of its limitations. It's fine for doing basic mathematical work and input response, but it can't do any of the more juicy bits you need for doing really interesting things. So you need to use something that's designed for the task: Enter Java.

The VRML 2.0 specification deliberately did not require support for any one language for VRML scripting. At the time of Draft 3's release, there were two language bindings for the VRML API: JavaScript and Java. If you've made it this far into the chapter, then I expect you either already know Java or have enough interest that you want to learn it. Compared to the rest of the book, this chapter will really start to dig into the heart of VRML. Java isn't a scripting language, so you really want to know the effects of your code on what the world does.

You'll start by taking up where the last chapter left off and cover the following topics:

❏ First, you'll see how to create scripts in Java by transforming the example from the previous chapter into Java.

❑ Once you have the basics down, then you'll see where you should use Java and where you should JavaScript, examining their strengths and weaknesses.

❑ The final section looks at using other Java classes to produce exciting, dynamic, moving worlds.

Setting Up to Use Java

The first thing that's assumed here is that you're already set up to use Java. You have either the JDK from Sun Microsystems (`http://www.javasoft.com/`) or you have another implementation that comes with a Java compiler, like Borland C++ 5.0 or Symantec Cafe.

1. You need to get hold of the Java classes for VRML; they're found with your browser. Start with Sony's CyberPassage. You've been using CosmoPlayer for most of the examples, but it doesn't support Java for the scripting.

2. Add the directory path to the VRML class files to the CLASSPATH variable so that the Java compiler can find them. Assuming you have installed it in the directory C:\Program Files\Cyberpassage, then you need to add C:\Program Files\Cyberpassage\vrml to CLASSPATH. Now you should be able to compile your Java scripts with no problems.

CAUTION: Early versions of CyberPassage put classes in a PKZipped file called classes.zip. This required you to create a directory called vrml and unzip the class files into that directory for it to work. Check the information with the latest version of the software.

3. Start to write and compile your Java scripts in your favorite environment.

The difference between Java and JavaScript is that you can't write Java source code directly in the file, which means you must compile every single script, too. Compared to JavaScript, this does slow down the development cycle a bit, but the end result is scripts that execute much faster than the interpreted JavaScript. Each class will be a separate file to be downloaded, but if you're using the same script many times in the world, then it needs to be downloaded only once.

Using Java in Scripts

Assuming you understood what was happening in the scripting in the last chapter, you'll now convert it to Java. To start with, you need to change the url to point to the Java class file. The VRML specification says only that the Java byte code needs to be supported. In this case, you'll call the source file `replace_script.java` to match with the name used in the DEF keyword.

The vrml Packages

In VRML, Java does not run as an applet; it runs as a special Java class called Script. Script is a class that's extended for the individual scripts. VRML-specific Java classes are available in the vrml packages, which have three main parts: vrml, vrml.node, and vrml.field. There's also a class specifically for the browser, which is in the vrml package.

The Field class is empty so that individual classes can be created that mimic the VRML field types. There are two types of Field classes: read-only and unlimited access. The read-only versions start with Const<*fieldtype*>, and the unlimited access versions have the same name as the field type. The types returned by these classes are standard Java types, with a few exceptions. MF types return an array of that type, so the call to the getValue() method of an MFString would return an array of type String. The basic outline of a Field type class is demonstrated by the MFString class:

```
public class MFString extends MField
{
    public MFString(String s[]);

    public void getValue(String s[]);

    public void setValue(String s[]);
    public void setValue(int size, String s[]);
    public void setValue(ConstMFString s);

    public String get1Value(int index);

    public void set1Value(int index, String s);
    public void set1Value(int index, ConstSFString s);
    public void set1Value(int index, SFString s);

    public void addValue(String s);
    public void addValue(ConstSFString s);
    public void addValue(SFString s);

    public void insertValue(int index, String s);
    public void insertValue(int index, ConstSFString s);
    public void insertValue(int index, SFString s);
}
```

The method names are pretty straightforward. You can set values using both the standard VRML type as well as the read-only field value, which comes in handy when you're setting values based on the arguments presented.

The other half of the vrml Java API is the Script itself. Script is based on the Node interface, which is defined only for VRML scripts. This interface serves as the basis for representing the individual nodes. VRML 2.0 defines Script class as the only implementation of the Node interface, which is shown below:

In later versions of VRML, there should be individual classes for each node type, just as there are individual field classes now.

```
public abstract class Script extends BaseNode {
    // This method is called before any event is generated
    public void initialize();
    // Get a Field by name.
    //    Throws an InvalidFieldException if fieldName isn't a valid
    //    event in name for a node of this type.
    protected final Field getField(String fieldName);
    // Get an EventOut by name.
    //    Throws an InvalidEventOutException if eventOutName isn't a valid
    //    event out name for a node of this type.
    protected final Field getEventOut(String fieldName);
    // processEvents() is called automatically when the script receives
    //    some set of events. It should not be called directly except by its
subclass.
    //    count indicates the number of events delivered.
    public void processEvents(int count, Event events[]);
    // processEvent() is called automatically when the script receives
    // an event.
    public void processEvent(Event event);
    // eventsProcessed() is called after every invocation of processEvents().
    public void eventsProcessed()
    // shutdown() is called when this Script node is deleted.
    public void shutdown();
}
```

Every script is a subclass of the Script class. However, you can't just go out and write your own script now. You need some more introduction to how it works.

TASK Outlining the Script

1. Since you must use the vrml packages to write scripts, then you have to tell the compiler to use it by importing it. Most of the time, you'll use all the different areas of the VRML interface, so you will need to import all three packages. Start the class by declaring its name and what classes it uses:

   ```
   import vrml.*;
   import vrml.field.*;
   import vrml.node.*;
   class replace_script extends Script {}
   ```

2. Next, create the `initialize()` method and use the `getField()` method from the Script class definition to get the variables belonging to the VRML Script node into Java. To do this, simply pass the method a text string with the name of the field you want. Because `getField()` returns a `Field`, you need

to cast it to be the correct field type so you can call the right methods. For example, use the following to get the strings corresponding to the external file:

```
class myscript extends Script {
    private MFString externalFile;
    void initialize(void)
    {
        externalFile = (MFString)getField("externalFile");
    }
}
```

By convention, all the script internal variables are declared private. You could make them public, but there's no point because nothing accesses them from outside. These internal variables can be named whatever you want, but they usually have the same name as the corresponding VRML field.

TIP: The `getField()` method is used only for retrieving the `field` type values from the script. To get the eventOut type values, use the `getEventOut()` method in the same way, remembering to cast the returned value. In JavaScript you could just assign a value to that eventOut reference to generate the event. You can do the same in Java, once you have retrieved the eventOut reference.

3. This leaves the eventIns. Now the Java model varies radically from the JavaScript one. In JavaScript, each eventIn in Script's VRML declaration requires a corresponding method. Java uses a different approach that has a single method taking a list of the current events to be processed; then you call the appropriate internal methods to deal with the information. If you have done any programming with the AWT package, then you should be fairly used to this approach. In the next section, you'll take a look at Java event handling.

CAUTION: In early drafts of the Java API, it was designed so that you wrote direct eventIn methods, just like the JavaScript way of doing things. Beta 1 and 2 versions of Sony's CyberPassage version 2.0 implemented this early form, and several early books on VRML 2.0 outlined this previous version of the Java API. This version is no longer current, however.

The change was made so that browsers could be written purely in Java. With the old draft versions, this wasn't possible.

 **TASK**

Dealing with Events

The previous section mentioned that the event-handling mechanism for Java scripts uses a single function as the interface point. To deal with events in a script, you need to take a few steps to get there:

1. Declare the `initialize()` method, and set the internal values using the `getField()` method. (This is the same as Step 2 in the previous task section.)

2. Create a series of private methods that you want to call for processing individual events.

3. Create one of the event-handling functions and use it to call the internal methods created in Step 1.

Events are passed to the script's event handler as an Event object type:

```
class Event {
    public String getName();
    public ConstField getValue();
    public double getTimeStamp();
}
```

As with all Java programming, if you want these methods to be called from outside, you must declare them public. An event coming into the script is like an external class calling methods from your class. In the Java API, event processing is done by one of two methods. The `processEvents()` method is used when there's more than one event generated at a particular timestamp, but the `processEvent()` method is called when there's only one event to be taken care of at that time.

The `processEvents()` method takes an array of event objects that you then analyze and pass to the various methods. This is no different from the way the AWT event-handling system works. A typical segment of code is demonstrated in Listing 21.1.

To see what a complete Java script source file looks like, declare just the `isOver` method for the moment so you can see the difference between the Java and JavaScript ways of handling the incoming events.

Timestamps are the same here as in JavaScript. The time the event was generated and the time it was received by the eventIn method could very well be different.

Listing 21.1. Converted version of one of the eventIn handlers from JavaScript to Java.

```
import vrml.*;
import vrml.field.*;
import vrml.node.*;

class replace_script extends Script
{
    // now we get all the class variables
    private SFBool pointerOver;

    //initialization
```

```
public void initialize(void)
{
    pointerOver = (SFBool)getField("pointerOver");
}

// now the eventIn declarations - only do the isClicked event for now
private void isOver(ConstSFBool value)
{
    if(value.getValue() == false)
        pointerOver.setValue(false);
    else
        pointerOver.setValue(true);
}

// now the event handling function
public void processEvents(int count, Event events[])
{
    int    i;
    for(i=0; i < count; I++)
    {
        if (events[i].getName().equals("isOver"))
            isOver(events[i].getValue());
        // collection of other else if statements here
    }
}
```

You could streamline this code by writing the method this way:

pointOver.setValues
(value.getValue());

However, the point is to show that Java uses proper boolean types, unlike JavaScript, which uses integers.

The second event handler method is processEvent(); since it deals with just a single event, the argument is only a single Event object. Therefore, the only difference between this method and the processEvents() method is that you don't need the for loop. The big if...else ladder of string comparisons remains, though.

When should you use the different event-handling functions? Take the following piece of VRML code as an example (this comes straight from the VRML specification):

```
Transform {
    children [
        DEF TS TouchSensor {}
        Shape { geometry Cone {} }
    ]
}
DEF SC Script {
    url     "Example.class"
    eventIn SFBool isActive
    eventIn SFTime touchTime
}
ROUTE TS.isActive  TO SC.isActive
ROUTE TS.touchTime TO SC.touchTime
```

Whenever the TouchSensor is touched, it generates two simultaneous events, so the script receives two. In this case, you need the processEvents() method that deals with a number of simultaneous events. If you were interested only in the isActive event, then you could use just the processEvent() method.

If you're not sure whether the script will receive more than one simultaneous event, then you can declare both methods. To save duplicating large amounts of code, you can put all the code to call the internal methods in the processEvent() method and just put a for loop that calls processEvent() with each individual event object in processEvents(). If this has confused you, then have a look at the following code fragment:

```
void public processEvent(Event e)
{
    if(e.getValue().equals("someEvent"))
        // call internal method
  else if ......
}
void public processEvents(int count, Event events[])
{
    int    i;
    for (i=0; i < count; i++)
        processEvent(events[i]);
}
```

Notice that a bit more work needs to be done to get an initial Java class file running. One advantage is that you declare only the fields you need to use. In Listing 21.1 you just wanted to use the pointerOver field from the VRML definition, so you left the rest out. The Java code is compiled independently of VRML source code, allowing you to take a staged approach to developing the code, adding variables and event handlers only when they're needed.

Outline of the VRML Java API

The Browser API defined in the previous chapter is also applicable to Java, but naturally there are Java methods for accessing the browser functionality. These methods can be accessed through the Browser class, so the syntax is almost the same as that in the previous chapter. The only thing that differs is what the various VRML types are in Java.

VRML types relate back to standard Java in the following manner (MF versions are just arrays of the SF type):

Table 21.1. Relationship of VRML types to Java types.

VRML Type	Java Type
SFString	String
SFFloat	float
SFInt32	int
MSString	String[]
MFNode	Node[]

Look again at the example of loading a world on demand and the `newNodesReady()` method that it called in Listing 21.2. You'll create the strings by using the Java `String` type.

Listing 21.2. Using the Browser class under Java.

```
public void newNodesReady(ConstMFNode node_list)
{
    String shape = "Shape { appearance Appearance {} }";
    String material = "Material { emissiveColor .2 .2 .2 }";
    String box = "Box { size 0.5 0.5 0.5 }";
    String sensor = "TouchSensor {}";
    Node shape_node;
    Node sensor_node;

    // create some nodes
    shape_node = Browser.createVrmlFromString(shape);
    sensor_node = Browser.createVrmlFromString(sensor);

    // assign some properties
    shape_node.postEventIn("material",
              (Field)Browser.createVrmlFromString(material));
    shape_node.postEventIn("geometry",
              (Field)Browser.createVrmlFromString(box));

    // update the internal field with the newly created
    // list of nodes
    newWorld.setValue(node_list.getValue());

    // now add the nodes to the scene
    secondObject.getValue().postEventIn("add_children",
                                        (Field)shape_node);
    secondObject.getValue().postEventIn("add_children",
                                        (Field)sensor_node);

    // finally add routes between the newly formed
    // touchsensor and the inputs to this script
    Browser.addRoute(sensor_node, "isActive",
                     this, "isClicked_new");
    Browser.addRoute(sensor_node, "isOver",
                     this, "isOver_new");
}
```

Java has a completely different structure. First, there's no way to directly assign values to the nodes' fields, as there was in JavaScript. If the node contains ordinary field types, then you must set them in the text string before you actually create the node; otherwise, you won't have access to it again. To write values to the fields that are eventIns or exposedFields, you must post an event to that field. You may remember from the last chapter that exposedFields can act just like eventIns and eventOuts combined. In the case of Java scripts, this is exactly how you must treat them.

Notice how much more object-oriented Java is than the JavaScript scripting; you can be sure Java is passing the correct types to the different nodes. There's more work involved to get the script up and running, but once you do, you can explore many other goodies.

The Beginning and the End

When you first add a behavior to a world, you might need to initialize some internal values. VRML allows the normal method of using the constructor method to perform any initialization that needs to be done internally.

The problem is that at the time the constructor is called, you probably won't have all the external access to the world enabled; even the values of the fields may not be valid yet because the world is still loading. To overcome this, the `initialize()` method was created. This function is, by default, empty, but can be overridden. The `initialize()` method is guaranteed to be called just after the entire world is created but before any external events are generated. It's called only once, and when it is, you know that you can read valid values for each of the script fields (using the `getField()` method) and can send events to other parts of the scene graph. This means everything in your world should function normally.

In the next section, you'll look at creating multithreaded scripts. When a node is about to be removed, you should clean up any extras that have been left lying around. The `shutdown()` method is a predefined method for all Script nodes that's called just before your script is removed. In this method, you place any cleanup code you need, such as killing threads you might have created.

Why Use Java?

JavaScript is fairly limited in what it can do. Besides some basic math and fetching files with http calls, you can't do much else. Basically, you can use it to write quick code to fulfill short-term needs. When you want to do something fairly complex with your world, then you need to switch to Java.

A good place to use Java is when you want to feed live data to the world. Java scripts can make use of any of the standard Java classes, which means the networking and threads classes are available. One typical use would be an external server sending data to your scene, which you then represent as 3D objects. The next section will outline how to do this.

So where do you use Java and where do you use JavaScript? It depends on what you want to do. Unfortunately, at this stage of the game, you're limited more by the browser than anything else. In time, you can expect to see browsers that support both

Java and JavaScript, as well as other languages. For the moment, just put on rose-colored glasses and assume an ideal world exists.

JavaScript is very handy for doing short little tasks when the compile-test cycle is too much effort. A good example is the toggle type of switch created in the previous chapter. Creating and compiling code for a three-line script isn't worth the trouble.

When you need greater flexibility and speed, then you should be using Java. The precompiled code combined with JIT compilers should make the code execution much faster, particularly in large complex worlds with many behaviors running continuously.

Using Other Java Classes

Developing a full networked and threaded example is beyond the scope of this book, but I can give you some outlines on how to go about it. A typical example is the stock market ticker that does a real-time display in 3D of your favorite stocks. At a stock market site, a server process would broadcast the information to whoever requests it. At the client end (your VRML world), you need to establish a link to receive the information.

The problem is that you want to keep the time spent in the script to an absolute minimum; also, the timing of when the script will be called is completely out of your control. The script may not be called at the same time that data is ready to be read from the network. What do you do? Well, since I have just been talking about threads, that should trigger something. Of course—you set up an independent thread containing all the networking code and then just report back to the world when there's more information to update.

When you first enter the world, the tracking should start. To do this, you take advantage of the creation method and start up the thread there. The thread code then starts up and installs any code it needs to monitor the network connection to the server. Such tasks as establishing the initial connection would all be handled in this separate task, so that the script can return to the browser as quickly as possible.

Having a separate thread that listens for new data is fine, but this thread needs to get information back to the VRML world. There are two ways to do that; in each method, you'll pass an instance of the Script node to the thread. First, you could just create another method that isn't an eventIn method, then call that method. Second, you could post events to that script just as any other node or script would. Using non-eventIn methods is questionable at the moment because there are no rules as to whether it's permitted. The safe bet is to post events back to the script so that they get dispatched and looked after in the same manner as all the other events.

Future Enhancements

Java scripting issues are not as complete as the JavaScript interface; for instance, there are no classes to represent the individual node types that exist in VRML. During the writing of the VRML 2.0 specification, there wasn't enough time to define these classes, so they were left out.

Many things, because of incompleteness, were left out of the specification, but will be left to the revised version 2.1 of the specification. There was a whole section on an external API that allowed outside programs to talk directly with the browser, and also the VRML world itself, that was left out. The external API was left out completely; it was not just the Java version.

Workshop Wrap-up

This is a limited look at what can be done with Java. Because Java is a full programming language, the scope for experimentation is wide, and the possibilities are endless. Keep in mind that you should be careful to not put too much code into the scripts. Every millisecond spent in the script is less time spent actually drawing the world onscreen. Make good use of threads where needed, and keep the scripts small.

One tool that hasn't been covered is the Liquid Reality toolkit from DimensionX. It has a complete set of classes that mimic the VRML nodes. It doesn't create a link for the scripts to interface with a particular browser; instead, you basically create your own browser by defining the nodes and their relationships, which are then drawn to the screen within the Java code itself. How Liquid Reality works, though, is more of a programming issue rather than a VRML topic, so it wasn't covered in depth in this book.

Next Steps

So what's left to do?

- ❏ In Chapter 22, "Adding Interactivity: The Future of VRML," you'll do a bit of crystal-ball gazing to see what's just around the corner for VRML. This chapter examines some of the higher level issues, like what you can and can't do with VRML and multi-user topics.

- ❏ In Chapter 23, "Real-Life Examples: A 3D Gallery: An Advanced VRML World," you finish developing the VRML gallery you started in Chapter 17. This chapter combines everything you've learned and adds a few extras for that touch of class.

Q&A

Q: What if I don't want to write my own Java behaviors but just view worlds that have behaviors? What do I need to have?

A: You still need to use Sony's CyberPassage to view them. No doubt there will probably be a few more browsers to add to the list as more companies release their offerings. You don't need to set the CLASSPATH variable, however, to use the Java behaviors.

Q: After compiling my code, it runs fine when I load it from the local drive. However, when I run it from the Web server, it doesn't work at all.

A: There may be two answers to your problem. First, the Web server might not be configured to handle the .class files. If so, then get your Web server administrator to add the following MIME type:

```
application/octet-stream.class
```

Second, CyberPassage has the same security rules as Sun's HotJava browser. It's possible you don't have the correct permissions set up to allow your browser to download the Java binaries from the Web server.

TWENTY-TWO

Adding Interactivity: The Future of VRML

—by Justin Couch

In this chapter, you

- ❏ Look at what's happening in the future with the VRML standard
- ❏ Learn what VRML's limits are and how to get around them
- ❏ See how to create your own avatar
- ❏ Combine VRML with HTML frames

Tasks in this chapter:

- ❏ Visiting Utopia with OnLive's Traveler
- ❏ Creating Your Own Avatar
- ❏ Using VRML with Frames

When the development of VRML first began, deliberate decisions were taken to design the language a step at a time. Version 1.0 was purely for static scenes. Version 2.0, which Part IV examined in detail, added behaviors that could be programmed. The future certainly has other surprises in store.

This chapter looks at some of VRML's possibilities, as well as some interesting current developments. This chapter includes the following topics:

- ❏ Where to next? A look at what's happening in the near future with the VRML standard. To get 2.0 out the door, a number of areas were left out because they were incomplete.
- ❏ It's always good to know what your limits are. VRML has its limits as well, and you'll learn what they are and the best means to get around them.
- ❏ So where is everybody else in cyberspace? A look at the various multiuser variants currently going around in VRML.
- ❏ Multiuser worlds will be taking off shortly, so you'll need a virtual body— you have to look like something. I outline some basic rules for creating your own character, called an *avatar*.

❏ Although the multiuser stuff is interesting, you really need to know how to mix VRML with other technologies on the Internet, such as frames. You'll learn about combining VRML with HTML frames, as well as how to create a very cool Web site.

Where to Next: The Future of the VRML Standard

As time for the release of VRML 2.0 grew closer and closer, the VRML development community realized that many of the hoped-for parts were not going to be finished in time. Instead of pushing back the release dates, the specification writers dropped a number of areas they felt were not yet complete. Among these was the VRML binary file format and the method of talking to a VRML world from another application.

Despite what has been said over the past years, virtual reality is still in its infancy. True VR requires the heavy use of 3D graphics and some serious hardware. Until the release of the Pentium CPU, there was never enough horsepower on the home PC to participate in a VR world—at least, not with any degree of speed. With the release of Microsoft's Direct3D standard, however, there has been a new interest in 3D graphics on the desktop. Now almost every major video card manufacturer has video cards offering 3D acceleration in the pipeline. The combination of the two has led to a rush of 3D applications on the desktop, with VRML leading the way.

Even VRML lacks some of the basic qualities required of a virtual reality system. Although it's possible to create a lot of the functionality for multiuser systems within VRML 2.0, there are no built-in capabilities within the language itself. Even some of that capability was left out in the effort to get VRML 2.0 ready by its release date.

VRML 2.1

Remember that shortly after the VRML 1.0 specification was released, a 1.1 update was underway. The 1.1 update was never released because the VRML development community decided to jump straight to 2.0. Version 2.1 is unlikely to be canceled because there is simply so much to digest with the 2.0 version.

Some of the unfinished portions of the 2.0 specification are slated for an update of the standard in version 2.1. This next version should be finished some time before the beginning of 1997. Don't worry; the plan is to not change the file format you have learned in this book and not to make incompatibilities between the two versions. You could say that 2.1 is more a maintenance release of VRML, with a few extra features thrown in.

Probably the first goal for 2.1 is to get the binary format sorted out, which will provide a customized format for distributing large VRML worlds across the Internet. Until now, users have had to rely on gzip, a compression program that compresses the text file before sending it to the end user. A binary format will provide an even better solution because extra space won't need to be wasted on text strings to define the world. Instead of, say, eight bytes to contain a node description, you will use only one.

The binary format is expected to be based on Apple's 3DMF format, which is the basis of many of its current offerings. 3DMF is more a method of producing these files than the actual format itself. Apple already has a QuickTime Movie and VR products based on it. This will be a welcome edition to VRML. If you learn by looking at other people's code, don't despair—you will have the ability to convert between text and binary formats. This was one of the implied requirements of the binary file format.

Next on the to-do list of 2.1 is the external API definition. This API will enable you to control the world from an outside application. As shown later in this chapter, it's possible to get the VRML world to control the HTML page in a limited way, but there's absolutely no way of doing the opposite. The external API contains all the functionality of the internal scripting browser interface and adds a little more. So if you have a Java or JavaScript program, you will be able to control what happens in your VRML world from a Web page or even a complete standalone program.

There are a few other issues related to 2.1. One of these is exactly which language will be supported in the Script nodes. When this issue was first raised, it resulted in a language war on the development mailing list. At the moment, there's no one required language that all browsers must support. To be completely cross-platform means you will need to write your behaviors in both Java and JavaScript.

VRML 3.0

My crystal ball (shown in Figure 22.1) is last season's model, so I hope it still works. Anyway, I'll give it a shot…

Figure 22.1.

Looking into the future of VRML, the wizard is unable to see a clear picture.

Based on the discussion undercurrents happening on the VRML development list (www-vrml), it seems there are several areas to be addressed in the next major version of VRML.

Multiuser Capability

This is a tricky topic—everybody has a favorite protocol he or she wants to use. However, with VRML 2.0, world writers have the ability to experiment freely and easily with protocol. It's likely that by the time VRML 3.0 is being discussed, a consensus on how to achieve this will be in place. This may not be an exact definition of a protocol, but maybe an agreement from the browser writers can be made that VRML 3.0 worlds will be inherently multiuser capable.

Seamless Worlds

There are already several proposals concerning the creation of seamless worlds in VRML 2.0. At the moment, VRML worlds are static in size. At some point, you reach the boundary and need to click on an object to go to the next part of the world. The current methods of providing seamless worlds are based on extending VRML 2.0 with Java so that this can be done. Where this could lead nobody knows. One possibility is that it ends up creating the equivalent of William Gibson's matrix on the Internet— a global 3D world accessible by everyone.

Heads-Up Displays

If you really want to know what's driving the development behind VRML, there are two books I suggest you read. On the www-vrml mail list, it seems everyone has read William Gibson's *Neuromancer* trilogy and Neal Stephenson's *Snow Crash*. When topics are being discussed, references to characters and events from these books always pop up. It's interesting to see how many of the things these authors wrote about are starting to come true. The ability to have some global network where everyone can get into a common virtual world is all but here.

Another interesting topic that will probably be addressed is the issue of heads-up displays (HUD) within the VR world. If you want to display text related to some particular part of the world, then you need to run a separate HTML window. VRML enables you to add head-mounted displays and data gloves so that you can have an immersive VR environment. When you are in an immersive environment, you lose the ability to use the flat screen, text-type pages you get on a screen. HUD capabilities have come up a number of times in the discussions of www-vrml, and it's likely some form of them will be in VRML 3.0.

The Limits of VRML

By now, you should have a pretty good idea of what VRML can and cannot do. Many of these restrictions depend on your own abilities and requirements. It wouldn't take much for the average programmer to code some solutions, but you probably aren't experienced enough in handling the complexities of TCP/IP communications to whip up your own multiuser scripts in a couple of days. After all, this book shows you how to enhance an existing site with VRML rather than show you the insides of VRML. How to write scripts in VRML can fill a book by itself.

VRML is still, by definition, a single-user world. Unless you go out of your way to include multiuser capabilities, you will be enjoying your own solitude in your virtual environment. To add multiuser capabilities, you will either have to write your own system for both the VRML end and the server to handle it or use somebody else's code and server. Later in this chapter, some of the systems that VRML browser companies have written using their own extensions are examined. In VRML 1.0, this meant you had to use that company's browser to access the world. In VRML 2.0, you just include the VRML extension mechanisms examined in the next chapter, so you no longer need to rely on one browser.

To a certain extent, seamless worlds can be created by placing proximity sensors around the edge of the world, then loading in the neighboring section when the user gets near the edge. This is a lot more complex than you might first imagine. It's a research topic all by itself. A number of companies and individuals (including myself) are actively trying to solve this problem in a useful way. This probably isn't a problem you will try to tackle yourself.

One problem not yet solved is interactions between objects already in the scene. Chapter 16, "Adding a Dash of Reality," looked at the Collision node. This node provides collision detection between the user and objects, but it doesn't cover what happens when your animated robot walks through a wall. Currently, the robot can walk straight through, but you aren't able to do so. The problem lies in the amount of CPU power it takes to compute the collisions. With the speed of current home computers, everything would be way too slow.

VRML also lacks the ability to type text into the world directly. Although you should be able to type text directly in the future, at the moment you must use the multiframed approach presented later in this chapter. You can't directly affect the world contents (at least not with VRML 2.0—though you will with the external API and VRML 2.1). The text documents need to present information in a way that the VRML world cannot. Jeff Sonstein's VRMLYahoo! front-end experiment combines the VRML part to provide the search capabilities with the HTML document to show the search results. The combination works effectively and probably means that direct input abilities to the VRML worlds will be a while in coming.

Making Friends in Cyberspace in 3D Chat Worlds

The popular press always seems to refer to the whole Internet/WWW thing as *cyberspace*. If you are a Gibson fan, you probably cringe every time you read about references to the whole Internet thing being cyberspace. However, there are companies out there trying to make cyberspace happen. Many of these companies use their own proprietary format for describing the worlds, so this chapter looks only at the ones that use VRML as the basic system.

CAUTION: OnLive and Worlds Chat work only on MS Windows 95 or 3.1. If you're using NT, you will have some problems with the system crashing. OnLive won't even install if it finds you have the incorrect hardware and software set up.

TASK Visiting Utopia with OnLive's Traveler

OnLive has a unique 3D chat environment where you can use your sound card with speakers and a microphone to talk and hear conversations, rather than typing messages as you do in other chat environments. OnLive can be found on the Web at `http://www.onlive.com/`.

OnLive's main product is called Traveler. It's the front-end that enables you to travel to other worlds and chat with online visitors. The main meeting world is called Utopia, but new worlds are showing up all the time, including some movie-related theme-based worlds.

So, ever wanted to go to Utopia? You need the right program to visit, and OnLive's Traveler works great (unless you're on Windows NT, as noted previously).

1. The first thing you need is the Traveler program. Start by visiting OnLive's Web site at `www.onlive.com` and move to its beta forum to download the Traveler program.

NOTE: You need to fill out a form to download the program. The program, currently in beta form, is still free.

2. Install the program by running the downloaded file to decompress its contents, then running the setup program.

NOTE: When running the setup program, Traveler becomes the default VRML browser for your browser. To change this, go to Options I General Preferences in the Netscape browser.

3. Once Traveler is installed, click on its icon to launch the program. The first dialog box you see is the Choose an Avatar selector. This is where you select your avatar. The avatar is seen by all other visitors within the world. Here you give your avatar a name, if you like the current model. (If you don't like the current model, you can create a new one.)

4. You can create your own avatar by clicking the Create New button. After clicking the Create New button, click the Avatar Models tab to select an avatar from the library of choices, as shown in Figure 22.2. You also can change the color of your avatar with the Color tab. When you're done modifying your model, click the OK button.

Figure 22.2.

Selecting an avatar using OnLive's Traveler.

Be sure to fill in the Profile tab, which gives information about yourself to the other visitors. It can be helpful to have this information when you start talking to others online.

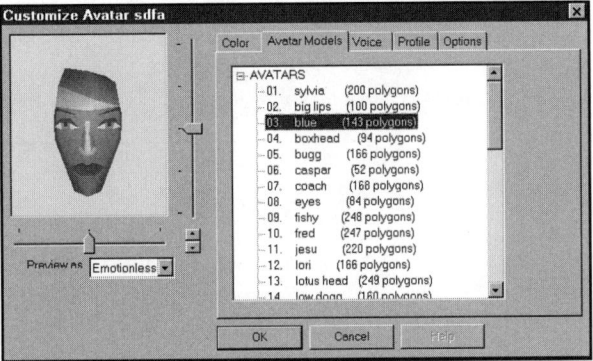

5. To visit the OnLive community, click the Go OnLive button. The Traveler window is displayed with several menu options. Traveler zips you to Utopia by showing you a series of boxes onscreen.

6. One of the first things you need to do is to set your microphone level. Use the Options command and select the Microphone tab. At the top of the dialog box is the Microphone Training Wizard button. Click this button to automatically set up your microphone. When you're ready to move on, click on one on the virtual worlds under the Portals menu option to move to another location.

7. To speak to people, hold down your space bar while talking. Be sure to be polite and let others speak in turn. Proper etiquette is a must in these worlds.

8. The buttons along the top of the window help you locate other people in this world and in the other communities. Figure 22.3 shows an image of Utopia.

Figure 22.3.

Using OnLive's Traveler program to visit the Utopia 3D chat world.

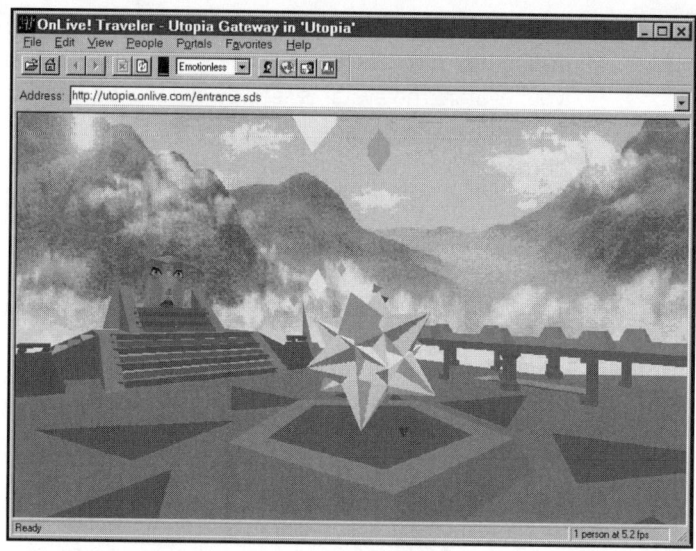

CyberPassage

The examples in this book have used version 2 of CyberPassage, so you should already be familiar with its interface. With the move to VRML 2.0, Sony dropped the support for their proprietary format. At the time this chapter was written, you needed to have two copies of CyberPassage: Version 1 for Sony's chat and version 2 for testing examples. The move to the VRML 2.0–based worlds should be complete by October 1996, and you will probably need only one browser—version 2.

CyberPassage takes a different view of the world from most of the other browsers. You may choose from only two Avatars. When you're wandering around in the world, it becomes difficult to spot who you're talking to because everybody looks the same.

Participating in Sony's worlds is similar to the Onlive method:

1. First, choose your avatar by going to the Avatar menu and selecting the View Avatar option. You need to be online to do this.

2. Type in the URL in the Open dialog box.

3. To see the conversation, select View I Chat. You can type in your speech in the bottom of the chat window.

BlackSun's CyberGate

This is probably the most popular of all the multiuser VRML browsers, and the one I spend too much time in. The browser is based on the principles outlined in the book *Snow Crash*. You can define personal and business cards for yourself, introducing what you do for a living, as well as your interests, hobbies, and so on, which can then be exchanged with other participants. (See Figure 22.4.) It also enables you to completely control how much information you want to reveal to others.

Figure 22.4.

A snapshot of PointWorld, the entry world for BlackSun users.

CyberGate is a bit different from the other browsers because all the areas for chatting and information are contained in one window.

1. All communications are text-based in the chat windows at the bottom of the screen. There are three separate classifications for the chats: public, groups, and private (known as 1:1). This enables full control of how many people you want to hear your mutterings.

2. The right side of the window contains the controls for the world. A tabbed section on the bottom provides access to almost all of the common functions. Here you can find out about others in the world, other popular worlds, group chat sessions, and your collection of cards from other people.

3. The Avatar window is the one you're likely to use the most. At the top is the list of this world's current participants. By clicking on the character name, you can get a slightly more detailed look. They may have a real-life name, interests, and a defined URL, which will show up in the corresponding windows.

   Below this list is a collection of buttons. After selecting a person, you can engage in a one-on-one chat by clicking the Chat button. If somebody asks you for a chat, then click the Accept button, shown on the lower-left side of the window. One of the best features is the ability to ignore obnoxious characters. Once you click the Ignore button, you never hear from them again for that session. Sadly, most of the other browsers do not have this feature.

Card exchanges can be done in a similar manner; select the person and then click the Exchange button. If you already have a card for that person, you can look at it by clicking the Show Card button.

4. The Worlds tab gives you a window that displays the list of the 10 most popular worlds at the moment. You can select one of them, then travel straight to it by clicking the Open World button.

5. If you want to have a group conversation, use the Group tab to get a list of the currently active groups. Select one of the groups, and the Description and Group Members fields are filled with the corresponding details. If you want to join a group, then select the one you want and click the Join button. To leave, click the Quit button in the left-hand chat window.

6. The last commonly used window is the Cards tab, which lists the current card collection. There are three card types—public, business, and personal. The public card is the one displayed when you select a person in the Avatar window discussed in Step 2.

Like most of the other browsers, you can use either a pre-built avatar or construct your own. Many people just go with the default avatars, but some regular users eventually create their own. You see some quite interesting ones out there. (Some of the interesting ones that I've seen recently include the U.S.S. Enterprise 1701-D, a toilet, a camera, and a pod of dolphins.) BlackSun avatars are any legal VRML 1.0 file, so whatever you create you can use—but it does have to follow the normal rules outlined later in this chapter.

> If at any stage you feel that things aren't correct, you can click the Refresh button that appears in several of the tabbed windows. Clicking this button makes the browser update the currently selected window.

Worlds Inc.

> You can find me in PointWorld and other BlackSun-enabled worlds almost every day, under the name Mithrandir. My avatar changes regularly, but if you see an old man with a walking stick, it's probably me.

Our final browser comes from Worlds Inc. The Worlds Chat environment was one of the first. At their Web site (http://www.worlds.net/), you'll find a demo of Worlds Chat, but a Gold version is also available that offers a lot more features. The demo version is a chopped down version of the commercial version, but you can still go online and chat with others.

Using the demo, your selection of pre-built avatars is limited to 15 and you can't assign your own name or custom avatar. The interface is nice to use, but the limitations of a 28.8K modem soon start showing in a busy world. The avatars are different as well—they are made of a series of images that change depending on the viewpoint. Figure 22.5 shows the avatar gallery, where you choose your persona.

Figure 22.5.
The entry of the space station of Worlds Chat.

Once you have an avatar, you can proceed to Worlds Chat by clicking on the Go To Worlds Chat. You appear in the Lobby along with several other somewhat lost-looking avatars. Your chat box shows the conversations. By clicking on the colored spheres in the lower-right corner (see Figure 22.6), you can port to different worlds.

Figure 22.6.
The Worlds Chat environment.

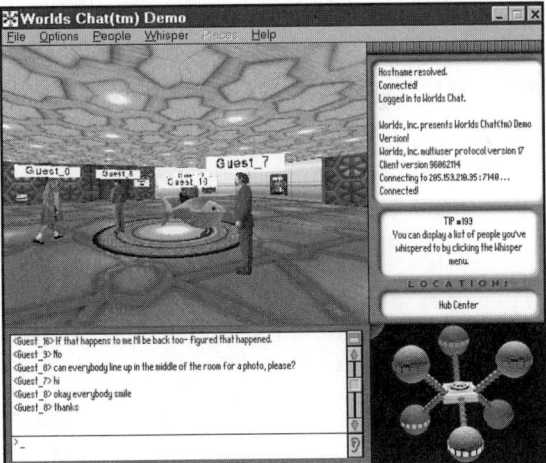

TASK Creating Your Own Avatar

One of the fun ways to roam about cyberspace is as an avatar you've created yourself. The problem is that what you create depends on which browser you're intending to use. At the middle of 1996, all the multiuser browsers were still VRML 1.0, which meant that what you used was completely dependent on the browser. Some used just a collection of pictures from different angles (like the creatures in DOOM), and others took any VRML 1.0 file you created. With the arrival of 2.0-based browsers, it's expected that all browsers will start using a VRML file for the body.

Many browsers offer a collection of basic avatars to choose from, as discussed in the preceding sections. Some worlds, like OnLive, let you make simple modifications like changing the avatar's dimensions or colors. It's even more interesting when the worlds support custom-built avatars.

When you create an avatar, there are a few rules of thumb to follow:

You can build avatars just like any other VRML world, with a text editor, but it's easier to use an avatar-building program. There are a couple of companies in the process of developing avatar-building programs. One such program, made by Hash Inc., should be out by September 1996.

1. Most of the worlds are made in human-size proportions, so your avatar should be no taller than about 2 units and a unit or so wide.

2. Don't make it too complex. A complex avatar doesn't slow your world down, but does slow things down for everyone else (making them inclined to leave).

3. BE CREATIVE. Remember, many people see you for the avatar you really are. A distinctive one leads to people instantly recognizing you whenever you enter—even when you're traveling through different worlds.

4. Currently, most avatars are built using standard VRML modeling tools, which usually include lights by default. If you're creating an avatar this way, then make sure there are no lights at all in the avatar file.

TASK Using VRML with Frames

One of the more interesting uses of VRML is to combine VRML with other Web technologies. When the specification was being written, the writers realized that VRML won't always be deployed the way you think it will. The parameters field in the Anchor node was the result of this realization. Besides using just the URL of the link, you may also want to communicate other values.

No doubt one of the most common ways of using VRML will be to use multiframe documents, with VRML in one frame and HTML in the others.

Remember the texture-mapped columns from Chapter 15, "Sprucing Up Models with Textures and Materials"? This example puts those plain VRML primitives representing the VRML logo in the middle of the room. Each one of them is linked to a different thing:

1. Begin with four frames. The left side one is the largest and contains the VRML world in the top and the HTML document in the bottom. The right side contains an index at the top and just a little logo at the bottom. This is aimed at frames-capable browsers, so an alternative non-frames version isn't provided.

   The frames declaration to produce a mixed VRML/HTML page is given in Listing 22.1.

Listing 22.1. The basic frames layout of the page.

```
<HTML>
<HEAD>
<TITLE>An example HTML and VRML World</TITLE>
</HEAD>
<!--
    An example of combining VRML and HTML together to provide
    interesting content for your world.
-->
<FRAMESET COLS="*, 120">
    <FRAMESET ROWS="75%, 25%">
        <FRAME SRC="column_world.wrl" NAME="vrmlFrame">
        <FRAME SRC="blank.html" NAME="docFrame">
    </FRAMESET>
    <FRAMESET ROWS="*, 120">
        <FRAME SRC="index_file.html" NAME="indexFrame">
        <FRAME SRC="vrml2.jpg">
    </FRAMESET>
</FRAMESET>
</HTML>
```

The early beta versions of CosmoPlayer didn't have the ability to use the named anchors for the cameras. When you clicked on the link, nothing happened. Check the latest version to see whether it now supports this ability. (This support is required in the specification.)

2. Once you have the basic frame layout, you can fill it in with other details, like what to put in each of the frames. The index frame is used like a tour guide to the world, showing points of interest. Named anchor tags, introduced in Chapter 16, are used to select the viewpoints from this frame.

3. The bottom frame is used as a place to put the documents from which you've been linked in the VRML worlds. A number of objects in the world itself contain links. You should be able to find the VRML logo in the center of the plaza. Each of the primitives points to a different HTML document. Appropriately, these are linked to the VRML Architecture Group's site for the latest version of the VRML specification, the CosmoPlayer site, and finally to a short document created by the authors.

4. Creating a mixed technology page is very simple. Just follow the normal steps for an HTML page, and substitute the VRML world where you want. You should be able to use the parameters field of the Anchor node to feed input to a window running JavaScript. To tell the browser that you want to put something in another frame, you put the string target=<frame name> into the parameter field.

You should recognize almost all the rest of the scene contents from previous chapters of this book. Texture-mapped columns, a little animated pig controlled by clicking on the control panel near the entrance, and a few trees make it environmentally friendly.

This is a good example of how combining different Web technologies can add more functionality to your Web page. The preceding example is shown in Figure 22.7.

Figure 22.7.
Combining frames and VRML can add another dimension to your VRML worlds.

Playing Multiplayer 3D Games on the Internet

Where do you go from here? With the ability to put in programmable behaviors, one of the most obvious uses for VRML is in front-ends for pre-existing games. There has been a DOOM WAD–to–VRML file converter around for some time, and without a doubt there will be a Quake front-end.

A DOOM-to-VRML 2.0 convertor is available from the Silicon Graphics VRML site (`http://vrml.sgi.com/`). The creatures aren't yet available, but all the doors and secret passageways are fully operational, just like the real thing. No doubt, people will be working on the gaming engine, so you'll be able to actually play DOOM in a VRML environment.

VRML is designed to create platform-independent content, so it will never run as fast or as smoothly as a custom-built game. VRML games are more likely to be of the not-so-high performance types, like mysteries and adventure games. However, some time in the not-too-distant future, there will be Internet games based on VRML worlds. Like all new technologies, this one is waiting to be explored.

A good preview of what's possible can be found at Keith and Margo's Murder Mystery, found at `www.murdermystery.com`. This mystery is composed of several VRML rooms that you explore to find clues. By solving the mystery, you qualify to win trips and prizes. This site, shown in Figure 22.8, is a good example of how VRML and frames can work well together.

Figure 22.8.

A scene from Keith and Margo's Murder Mystery VRML site.

Although VRML is and will be behind the gaming scene for a while, the gaming world isn't waiting around. The entire gaming industry is moving toward multiplayer games across the Internet.

The way to get around the bandwidth problems is for each player to have a copy of the game stored locally on their machine. That way, only the game updates, such as the positions of other players, need to be transmitted. Several hosting sites have begun to appear that enable you to play commercial games over the Web. One such site is the Total Entertainment Network, or TEN for short. At TEN you can play Duke Nukem 3D and Terminal Velocity, and they aren't stopping there.

Another good example is Internet Monopoly by Virgin games, and Looking Glass Software is planning to make multiplayer Internet games a regular feature on all their future games.

Workshop Wrap-up

You have almost reached the end. The tour of VRML has nearly ended, and you should be confident enough now to start making your own worlds. In the last VRML chapter, the finishing touches are added to your world, creating the full multimedia VR experience. In the following chapter, the world developed in Chapter 17, "Real-Life Examples: The VRML Art Gallery: A VRML World by Hand," has everything you learned in this part of the book put into practice. Hold on—it's one heck of a ride!

Q&A

Q: Will we ever see Gibson's matrix happening in the future? Is the Internet the start of it?

A: Tricky question. Certainly VRML has the makings to be the foundation of the matrix, but there other competing technologies out there. At the moment, VRML has the backing of just about every major computer company except Microsoft, which has decided to do its own thing. Whether Microsoft can steal the march from VRML remains to be seen.

Before users can go all out with immersive VR systems, a lot of work needs to be done. Remember that there are no defined multiuser protocols, and the current head-mounted displays are still cumbersome for extended periods of time. Besides, they aren't a common item you pick up at your local computer discount store. Bandwidth on the Internet is the other major problem. Cable modems and other solutions will be the start of developing the required high-capacity links.

Q: Can I incorporate other technologies, like Shockwave Director and RealAudio, into my worlds?

A: Currently, there's no real way to integrate Shockwave in a VRML world, but some sites use Shockwave as a front-end for a VRML world (the two technologies exist as separate elements on the HTML page).

Q: Where can I find out more about creating my own VRML avatar?

A: There are several sources on the Web, but take a look at Gerry Paquette's Avatar guide at `http://www.magmacom.com/~gerryp/howtoav.html`. This guide takes you through the process of building your own avatar by using Pioneer. Gerry is well known for his avatars in the CyberGate community and in several worlds he has built, one of which features a pool with sharks and a bartender you can order drinks from.

RealAudio is a real mystery. The definition of the sound system is examined in the next chapter, but for the moment, RealAudio inclusion will probably happen fairly quickly.

TWENTY-THREE

A 3D Gallery: An Advanced VRML World

—by Justin Couch

In Chapter 17, you created a VRML art gallery. It wasn't bad but it was still very, ummmm, uneventful. You could walk around, browse some pictures, go to a few other pages, but that was it. You could have created the site with any modeling package you saw in Chapter 13, "Exploring VRML Browsers and Development Tools," and exported it as a VRML 1.0 file.

Over the past few chapters you have been learning how to use the more advanced features of VRML 2.0—now you get to put them in practice.

- ❏ First, you'll rearrange the main file so that it quickly loads the basic world outline, then loads in the rest of the world as it goes along.
- ❏ Next, you'll add some behaviors. Animation will give you some of the tricks that can be used to create a great world.
- ❏ Once you've seen the basic world, then you'll enhance it a little by bringing in the example of the HTML frames-based document you experimented with in previous chapters.
- ❏ To finish the world, you need to add some noise. Until recently, cyberspace has been a pretty quiet place, but with VRML 2.0, you can place sound in the environment.

In this chapter, you

- ❏ Learn how to load your world efficiently
- ❏ Add behaviors to your world
- ❏ Enhance your world with an HTML frames-based document
- ❏ Add sound to the environment

Tasks in this chapter:

- ❏ Rearranging the Furniture
- ❏ Using Behaviors to Get Your Message Across
- ❏ Creating Complex Behaviors
- ❏ Adding One Last Touch: Sound

Rearranging the Furniture

If you open the VRML file from Chapter 17, "Real-Life Examples: The VRML Art Gallery: A VRML World by Hand," you'll notice that it's a rather large file, about 500 lines long. When you start to create large worlds, the file sizes can get unwieldy to work with. Another drawback to large worlds is that users must download the whole world before they can even start wandering around. Since you learned how to inline other files in Chapter 18, "Tricks to Optimize Your VRML Worlds for the Web," you'll apply that technique to the art gallery.

How should you divide up the world? Some general rules of thumb should be used:

1. All the global information, like WorldInfo, NavigationInfo, Backgrounds, and the Viewpoints, should be placed in the main file. The main file should also include the basic structure of the world—how all the little pieces fit together.

2. If you use a large collection of nodes that are used across several scenes or that fall into a single object that's reused often in a scene, then these nodes should be split into separate files.

3. Use one file for each separate entity. Each object should exist in its own file rather than all the objects being gathered in one external file.

Following those rules, the world can be split into the following groups:

1. The main world, consisting of the five islands, the connecting wooden planks, the pictures on each island, and the trees

2. The staircase with all its texturing as a single object

3. The marble archways; a problem because each arch has its own label, but you'll work around that by putting the labels for each arch in the main world

4. Some animated objects (to be developed later), each in a separate file

Once you have each of these parts, you can inline them back into the main file. Besides the islands and the picture definitions, you just have a series of Inline and Transform nodes to worry about.

Using Behaviors to Get Your Message Across

Some things you *must* do when creating a world. In this example, Cindy Reed has lent me her pig from her online VRML texture tutorials (`http://www.ywd.com/cindy/texture.html`), which I then converted to VRML 2.0. Having pigs in cyberspace? Well, I just had to make them fly. The first animation, then, isn't particularly useful, but it *is* fun and will also introduce a few important concepts about combining multiple scripts and interpolators to get complex behavior.

At the center of the middle island will be a collection of controls for the pigs' movement—one control to start and stop the pigs and two other controls to select their flying behavior. The pigs will have two different flying formations.

When the pigs stop flying, they need to rest somewhere; even in cyberspace, you need to let them rest. Having the pigs follow a circular flying path means they would continually crash through the resting point, so you need to add lead-in and lead-out paths. Here's where the fun begins. You may remember, from the section on events in Chapter 18, the idea of connecting the output of one node to many inputs of another node. You also used interpolators to control movement, starting and stopping it by controlling the enabled field. You'll use those methods now—and go one step farther.

Creating Complex Behaviors

A complex path for an object doesn't necessarily mean you need a complex script to control the path. There are three parts to the flying-pig problem: the pig taking off, the track during normal flying, and the track leading back to the take-off point. For each part of these paths, you can create a separate interpolator, then control which one is active by using the script to enable and disable the paths. The basic interactions of the scene's parts are shown in Figure 23.1.

Figure 23.1.

How the script controls the behavior of the pigs flying.

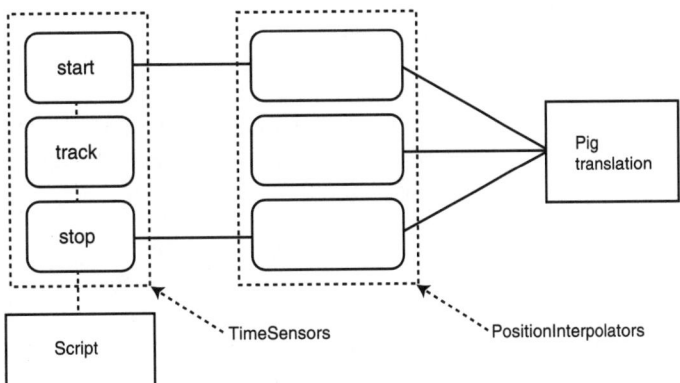

Now putting in the three parts of the pigs' journey will be fairly easy—just define the three paths you want them to take. However, getting things to match up and being nice in response to user input are important factors. For example, you should ignore a command to start a new flight if the pigs are still trying to land from the previous one.

1. Begin with the basics of trying to get two paths to match. The easiest way to do this is to take some predefined point on the path and make the pigs always join and leave from that point. If you look closely at the TimeSensor node, it supplies a fraction value, but it doesn't guarantee what values you will get out of this event, except for 0 and 1. The only time you're guaranteed to get values is at these two extremes.

2. Making the flight paths is now much easier. Simply create the interpolators so that the finish point of the starting interpolator and endpoint of the stop interpolator flights match with the stop/start points of the main flying behavior. Making these points match up requires the script to monitor the fraction value and check for a value of 1.

When you start creating complex behaviors, you need to define exactly what's going to happen where in the flight. For example, the logic for controlling the flight path is as follows: When the user first clicks the Go button, the animation begins with the start flight path. When the pig gets to the end of the start flight path, the script checks to see whether the Stop button has been clicked by looking at the field that checks for this value. If it has, then the pig begins the stop flight path. If it hasn't, then the pig continues on its normal flight path. At the end of each cycle (`cycleTime` event generated), the script again checks to see whether the Stop button has been clicked. If not, then the pig continues to orbit; if it has, then the stop flight path is executed. Any further commands are ignored until after the pig has landed.

That's it—now you can turn this logic into a script.

Starting the Flight

First, you need to insert the code for the toggle action switch developed in Chapter 19, "Using Built-in Animation Techniques," into the new script. The button will be a simple colored square and serve as both the start and stop for the animation. However, you can't just stop the pig dead in the middle of space.

As a result of clicking the switch, an event is sent to the script, which sets everything in action. In previous animation examples, the behavior was looped so that starting and stopping the animation was no problem. This time, however, the behavior lasts for just a set amount of time. To do this, set the loop field to FALSE for the TimeSensor node. Making an animation happen, then, becomes a matter of setting the startTime field. After setting the start time, the pig takes off on the first part of its journey, which is defined in startInterpolator. The start time is taken from the timestamp given in the parameters to the `isActive` event.

Listing 23.1. The outline of the code for the reaction to an `isActive` event (a mouse click on the switch).

```
function isActive(val, ts) {
    if(pointer_over == 1) {
        if(val == 0) {
            if(isRunning == 0) {
                isRunning == 1;
                isStarting == 1;
                startTime_changed = ts;
            }
            else
                isStopping == 1;
        }
    }
}
```

Transition to Normal Flying

To make the transition smooth, you need to know when the first part of the flight is finished. The easiest way to do this is keep track of the `isActive` eventOut field of the TimeSensor. When the TimeSensor has reached the end of its time, it will send the `isActive` eventOut a FALSE value. However, this same field is set to TRUE when it first gets activated from the code in Listing 23.1.

Within the function, you must check to see whether the event changes to FALSE. If so, then all you need to do is change a few internal condition variables and set the start time for the next TimeSensor. This time, you want the behavior to continue forever, so the loop field is set to TRUE. In Chapter 19, you learned that if the startTime was greater than the stopTime, the action would loop forever. Perfect! All you do is set the start time to be the same value as the timestamp, and all the flight paths merge together nicely.

Listing 23.2. The function called in response to the first TimeSensor's `isActive` field changing value.

```
function set_Started(val, ts)
{
    if(val == 0)
    {
        isStarting = 0;
        isTracking = 1;
        trackTime_changed = ts;
        track_changed = 1;
    }
}
```

Maintaining Flight

Maintaining the flight is the easy part. Because you've set the loop field to TRUE, then the pigs will fly around happily on the path forever. The problem is you need to be able to tell the pigs when to stop. There's no way to just break a loop and substitute your own behavior. What you want to do is check the flying behavior at a known point and then run the last part of the flight.

Like the start of the flight, you'll always be joining in the same place. You can do the same thing to end the flight, and the best place is at either the start or end of the loop. The TimeSensor node has one particularly nice feature: The cycleTime field sends out an event each time a new cycle starts, so you know not only the time, but also the object's position (the fraction value would be 0.0, making that the start of the interpolator position). When the event is received, check to see whether the flag telling you to stop has been set. If it has, just disable the TimeSensor input for the interpolator dealing with the current section of the flight and fill in the start time of the TimeSensor responsible for the last part, where the pigs fly back to the landing position.

Listing 23.3. The response to the cycleTime eventIn of the trackTime TimeSensor.

```
function trackCycleTime(ts)
{
    if(isStopping == 1)
    {
        isTracking = 0;
        track_changed = 0;
        stopTime_changed = ts;
    }
}
```

Safe Landing

The final section of the flight is the landing. At this point, the pigs are on their way, using the path given in the final interpolator. Unlike the other parts of the flight, there's no need to stop the flight; you just need to clean up a few internal variable values and re-enable the switch. The final part of the flight is triggered by looking at the isActive field of the final TimeSensor.

Listing 23.4. The final cleanup code for when the landing stops.

```
function set_Stopping(val)
{
    if(val == 0)
    {
        isRunning = 0;
        isStopping = 0;
    }
}
```

Now you have pigs that will take off, circle in flight, and land at your instruction. Try it out and see what happens!

Adding More Behavior: Follow Your Nose

When you tested out the flying pigs, what did you notice? If you saw nothing other than pigs flying around in a circle, run it again and take a close look at the pigs. Notice they're always pointing in the same direction, which isn't good. Not only can these pigs fly, but they can also fly backward and sideways—they're very talented pigs! However, you should change this behavior so that the pigs' noses are always pointing forward.

This is a fairly simple task. By now, you should be one step ahead of me, looking up the spec for an interpolator that works for rotation fields. You need to use the OrientationInterpolator, which takes a series of key/value pairs and works out return values from there. There's already a Transform node above the Pig node, so you can pass the SFRotation values straight into the rotation field of the Transform node. For consistency, you need to drive the new interpolator from the same TimeSensor as the tracking value.

You don't need special values for OrientationInterpolator; all you really need are three values for the two extreme points of the path and the part that smoothly links between repeats. If you remember back to the first couple of animation examples in Chapter 19, the OrientationInterpolator works in the same way as the sphere moving backwards and forwards—except it's dealing with a rotation rather than a position. There's not much need to do more than this. The OrientationInterpolator then looks like this:

```
DEF pigorientation OrientationInterpolator {
    keys [ 0, 0.5, 1 ]
    values [
        0 1 0 0,
        0 1 0 3.142,
        0 1 0 0
    ]
}
ROUTE tracktimer.fraction TO pigorientaion.set_fraction
ROUTE pigorientation.value_changed TO pigcontrol.rotation
```

Pigcontrol is the Transform node containing the inlined pig, allowing you to control the pig's position and orientation by setting the translation and rotation fields, respectively.

Creating a Familiar, Yet Exciting, World

You've seen how easy it is to create a basic world, but you've also seen the extra work needed to add behaviors. World behaviors, however, generally aren't that complex; a simple animation of an object in response to user input is fairly common. Whether behaviors are complex or simple, however, learning the basic interactions between the interpolators, sensors, and scripts is essential.

Combining HTML 3.0 and VRML 2.0

In the previous chapter, I introduced the use of multiframed documents that combine VRML and HTML. Now you're going to combine them again so that you have a Web site that uses the best of both technologies. (See Figure 23.2.)

In the Chapter 17 workshop, each picture was linked to an HTML document that explained how the picture was created and supplied other details. For this workshop, you'll use the same frame setup. The upper-right frame will contain a list of viewpoints to visit in this site. The lower frame will be the target for HTML files referred to in the VRML world. The only change you need to make is adding a Back button on each of these target pages so that the user can get back to the Intro page, if necessary.

Figure 23.2.
The final gallery with the flying pigs and the HTML frames.

TASK   Adding One Last Touch: Sound

I have resisted temptation until now, but it's time to make this world really interesting by adding some sound. The virtual gallery is very quiet at the moment, so it needs something to liven it up a bit. First, I'll add some background noise, and then I have convinced my co-author to put a microphone in his hand and speak to you about the work.

The Sound Node

Adding sound to a scene is relatively easy; it requires two nodes that work together because VRML splits multimedia capabilities into two parts. For both video and sound, one node handles the individual file format and another controls how that format (either sound or movie) appears in the world. For video, the MovieTexture and Appearance node are combined; sound uses the combination of the Sound and AudioClip nodes. Here's what the Sound node looks like:

```
Sound {
    exposedField SFVec3f  direction    0 0 1
    exposedField SFFloat  intensity    1
    exposedField SFVec3f  location     0 0 0
    exposedField SFFloat  maxBack      10
    exposedField SFFloat  maxFront     10
    exposedField SFFloat  minBack      1
    exposedField SFFloat  minFront     1
    exposedField SFFloat  priority     0
    exposedField SFNode   source       NULL
    field        SFBool   spatialize   TRUE
}
```

The Sound node is used to place sound in a scene. Basically, it controls how to put sound in by setting the direction and intensity of the noise. To put in the background music (this is an art gallery, after all), make it an ambient source of music. *Ambient sound* is created by setting the spatialize field to FALSE and the minimum values (minFront and minBack) to cover the area you want the sound to be heard in.

In complex worlds, there might be too many sounds for the user's computer to handle. The priority field lets you organize which sounds should be heard in preference to others. A value of 0 is the lowest priority and 1 is the highest.

If you wanted to create a "speaker effect" with directional sound, then use the direction field. Sound is oriented around this direction. By combining the direction field with the min/max fields, you can create directional sound. The minFront and minBack fields control the minimum distance that you can hear the sound at full volume, both in front of the location and behind it. The front is the side that the direction field points to. The maxFront and maxBack fields control the outer limits of the sound's audibility. To add to the effect of ambient sound, if you set minBack equal to minFront and maxBack equal to maxFront, you get sound with no direction at all, which gives you the full ambient effect.

Putting in Sound Sources

Notice how the Sound node has no ability to reference the sound file. That ability is left to another node that's placed in the source field. Chapter 15, "Sprucing Up Models with Textures and Materials," mentioned using MPEG sound in the scene. Here is where it gets used. To use the audio capabilities of MPEG1-Systems, place the MovieTexture node in the source field. Normally, you use the DEF keyword for the node in the appearance field and then insert the USE keyword in the source field. That way, you're guaranteed to get proper synchronization of sound and video.

The other option for adding sound to a world is to use the AudioClip node, which looks like this:

```
AudioClip {
    exposedField   SFString  description   ""
    exposedField   SFBool    loop          FALSE
    exposedField   SFFloat   pitch         1.0
    exposedField   SFTime    startTime     0
    exposedField   SFTime    stopTime      0
    exposedField   MFString  url           []
    eventOut       SFTime    duration
    eventOut       SFBool    isActive
}
```

You can play either MIDI or WAV files with the sound nodes because support for their file formats is required by the specification. As usual, you place the filename(s) in the url field, and the loop and description fields follow the normal rules for VRML that you have seen in other nodes. The startTime and stopTime fields are used for controlling when the sound plays. If you hook these time fields up to a TouchSensor node and add some scripts, you can make the sound play almost like a CD player. There are some limitations, like not being able to start at the middle of a sound file, but even that may be possible with a clever use of TimeSensors, scripts, and other nodes, such as Switch.

One method around this problem of starting halfway through a sample is the equivalent of the Fast Forward button. The pitch field controls how quickly the source should be played in relation to the original recording. If you set the pitch field to 2, then the sound plays twice as fast. For the more musically inclined, that means the sound is played up an octave, as well.

Therefore, you can create a fast forward option by connecting a sensor to a script that modifies the pitch field in response to user input.

The specification does allow other sources of sound. Sony's CyberPassage will handle standard MOD files as well, which is great if you want to put fully digitized, sampled music in your world. MOD files are usually large, so they might not be appropriate for Internet use.

Using Sound Nodes

I suppose I need to make up for the flying pigs example, so the background music will be a bit more traditional. Since this is an art gallery, I'll choose Mozart's "Eine Kleine Nachtmusik." Being such a popular piece of music, you can find literally hundreds of versions on the Internet.

The background music is added by including the code from Listing 23.5.

Listing 23.5. Code to put background music in the scene.

```
Sound {
    minFront 100
    minBack  100
    maxFront 150
    maxBack  150
    spatialize FALSE
    source AudioClip {
```

```
            description "Eine Kleine NachtMusik"
            loop TRUE
            startTime 1
            url "mozart.midi"
        }
    }
}
```

The other way of using sound in this demo world is to have it respond to user input. Again, you'll use the same basic TouchSensor and Script node combination to trigger the sound. Background music requires continuously playing the sound file without user intervention, but for a talking demo you need to just play it once. Therefore, the loop field is left at the default value of FALSE, and most of the other values are left at their default, too.

Starting the sound file requires that the startTime be set. It also means that the stopTime is set, too, because this isn't a repetitive sound source. Remember from Chapter 19, in the explanation of the input parameters for events, that the second field is the timestamp of when the event occurred. The AudioClip node contains an eventOut that gives the value of its sound file's duration. By combining these two, you can set the startTime (the event's timestamp) and the stopTime (timestamp + duration). The duration is an eventOut, which means that you need a corresponding eventIn for the script; it takes the value and stores it internally for later use.

The complete code to produce the Sound node is given in Listing 23.6. A small square acts as the switch to control the sound. The sound file could be anything, but in this case it's the voice of my co-author, explaining one of his images. By simply changing the file in the URL, you can put that sound in front of any picture in the scene.

Listing 23.6. Controlling a Sound node in response to user input.

```
Group {
    children [
        DEF soundsensor TouchSensor {}
        Shape {
            appearance Appearance {
                material Material { emissiveColor 0. 0.5 0.1 }
            }
            geometry Box { size 0.7 0.1 0.7 }
        }
    ]
}

Sound {
    source DEF audioout AudioClip {
        url "explain.wav"
    }
}

DEF soundscript Script {
    field SFBool   pointerOver FALSE
```

continued

Listing 23.6. continued

```
field SFTime    duration    0
eventIn SFBool isOver
eventIn SFBool isActive
eventIn SFTime set_duration
eventOut SFTime soundStopTime
eventOut SFTime soundStartTime
url "vrmlscript:
    function isOver(val) {
        pointerOver = val;
    }
    function isActive(val, ts)
    {
        if(pointer_over == 1)
        {
            if(val == 0) {
                soundStartTime = ts;
                soundStopTime = ts + duration;
            }
        }
    }
    function set_duration (val) {
        duration = val;
    }
    "
}

ROUTE audioout.duration TO soundscript.set_duration
ROUTE soundsensor.isOver TO soundscript.isOver
ROUTE soundsensor.isActive TO soundscript.isActive

ROUTE soundscript.soundStartTime TO audioout.startTime
ROUTE soundscript.soundStopTime TO audioout.stopTime
```

Defining Your Own Nodes

If you just read that last sentence in the previous section and despaired at having to cut and paste all this code every single time you want to put in a sound, don't worry. VRML gives you a mechanism for producing custom nodes within the specification; it's called PROTO. You can declare the code once at the top of the file with a specific name, and then use that name anywhere in the file, just as though it was an ordinary VRML node.

The syntax for using PROTO is a little different. First, you must tell the browser what fields and events it will handle; they're declared in square brackets. After that, declare how it works by using standard VRML syntax, which can include any legal combinations of nodes, scripts, and ROUTE commands.

Designing a PROTO

The type of the PROTO (for example, leaf, group, and so on) is defined by the type of the first node in the definition. This definition is then used by the browser to determine how the PROTO fits into the scene node structure.

Looking back at the previous section, controlling the music is definitely a candidate for being made into a PROTO. The basic implementation is the same; all you want to do is change the music file, which makes the interface to the PROTO easy. The design goes something along the following lines:

The sound can be any file you want, and it would be good to add the ability to change it on-the-fly. You can also change the geometry for the switch. Essentially, the PROTO should contain the behavior but let you do the customization on the visible parts.

Going through this and the code from Listing 23.6 shows that the fields need to be an exposedField MFString for the file URL and a field MFNode for the geometry. Now the Transform node also has add_children and remove_children events, so you need to replicate that.

From this description, you can work out that the PROTO definition needs to look like this:

```
PROTO NarrativeSound_X [
    field MFNode children []
    exposedField MFString url []
    eventIn MFNode add_children
    eventIn MFNode remove_children
]
{
    # the node definition in here
}
```

Connecting the External World to the Inside

The most important part of the PROTO declaration is that it can pass values straight from it to the internal nodes. To pass these values, you just declare the following:

```
<target fieldname> IS <source fieldname>
```

Naturally, they need to be of the same type for this to work. You can do this with anything, even the eventIn or eventOut. It works whether you're connecting to a script or just an ordinary node. Going back to Listing 23.6, you can see that you want to set the children of the Group node. To do this, you need the following declaration:

```
Group {
    children [
        IS children
        DEF soundsensor TouchSensor {}
    ]
    remove_children IS remove_children
    add_children IS remove_children
}
```

A script is basically the same, except you have the extra declarations of the access type and field type to place in front. To connect an `isOver` eventIn for the PROTO to a script, you would use this syntax:

```
EventIn SFBool isOverNow IS isOver
```

All that's left is putting everything together, which is shown in Listing 23.7.

Listing 23.7. The completed PROTO for the sound narrative.

```
#VRML V2.0 utf8
#
# A single-shot sound file player
#

PROTO [
    field MFNode    children         []
    exposedField MFString url         []
    eventIn MFNode add_children
    eventIn MFNode remove_children
]{
    Group {
        children [
            Group {
                add_children IS add_children
                remove_children IS remove_children
                children [
                    DEF soundsensor TouchSensor {}
                    IS children
                ]
            }

            Sound {
                source DEF audioout AudioClip {
                    url is url
                }
            }
        ]
    }

    DEF soundscript Script {
        field SFBool    pointerOver FALSE
        field SFTime    duration    0
        eventIn SFBool isOver
        eventIn SFBool isActive
        eventIn SFTime set_duration
        eventOut SFTime soundStopTime
        eventOut SFTime soundStartTime
        url "vrmlscript:
            function isOver(val) {
                pointerOver = val;
            }
            function isActive(val, ts)
            {
                if(pointer_over == 1)
                {
                    if(val == 0) {
```

```
                              soundStartTime = ts;
                              soundStopTime = ts + duration;
                          }
                      }
                  }
                  function set_duration (val) {
                      duration = val;
                  }
              "
          }

          ROUTE audioout.duration TO soundscript.set_duration
          ROUTE soundsensor.isOver TO soundscript.isOver
          ROUTE soundsensor.isActive TO soundscript.isActive

          ROUTE soundscript.soundStartTime TO audioout.startTime
          ROUTE soundscript.soundStopTime TO audioout.stopTime
      }
```

Once you have this PROTO declared at the top of your file, you can then use it like any other node. Since you have a Group as the first node, it means that this is a group node as well. To use this PROTO, you need to declare it at the top of the file. Within the file, you can use it like this:

```
Group {
    children [
        mynarrative {
            url "mozart.mid"
        }
    ]
}
```

Using PROTOs from Other Files

A major use for PROTOs is the ability to select them from other files, which requires using the EXTERNPROTO statement:

```
EXTERNPROTO protoname [
    #list of fields here
]
[ http://your.domain.here/filename.wrl ]
```

The last section is the list of URLs and URNs to this PROTO. They may also include the #anchor value, too. The name after the # is used to work out what the PROTO name is when you have a large collection of PROTOs sitting in one file.

TIP: You need to declare only the fields you will use. If you don't declare the extras, that's OK, but if there are extra ones or if none exist, then the browser will complain.

Workshop Wrap-up

That's it. Except for a few extras, you've learned enough VRML to keep you going for quite some time. VRML 2.0 has the potential to do things that haven't even been thought of yet. Indeed, some of the examples in this book will become staple nodes for use in your own worlds.

You should now have enough insight into VRML 2.0 to create your own compelling worlds. VRML 2.0 offers enough flexibility to be used for anything from desktop VR for corporate demonstrations and products right down to an individual's home page.

What's Missing?

There are a few sections of VRML that this book did not cover:

- ❏ 3D text with the Text node; this is a big, complex beast that allows you to place 3D text into your world.
- ❏ Geometry sensors; this class of sensors is similar to the TouchSensor but even more basic, allowing you to customize how to map user input to various geometric shapes.
- ❏ The switch node; this can selectively display one of several different children.
- ❏ Extrusion and ElevationGrid nodes; these two are fairly common. Extrusion acts like a cylinder, and ElevationGrid is a variant of IndexedFaceSet in terms of behavior.

These are complex features that require a thorough understanding of how VRML works and the use of scripting to get the most benefit from them.

Next Steps

The last part of this book deals with other 3D technologies on the horizon. The appendixes also cover some of the basic VRML information you can use as references while trying build your own creations.

- ❏ Appendix A, "3D Software Resource Guide," contains basic information on where to find resources on 3D graphics packages.
- ❏ A complete reference of the node definitions is included in Appendix B, "VRML 2.0 Node Specifications."
- ❏ Appendix C, "VRML Resource Guide," lists some cool worlds to visit that demonstrate interesting VRML concepts.
- ❏ Appendix D, "ActiveVRML Resources," lists Web resources for finding out more about Microsoft's ActiveVRML.

❏ A number of times I have used HTML pages as well as VRML, so head to Appendix E, "HTML Quick Reference," which lists HTML resources for you to visit.

Q&A

Q: I want to learn more about scripting and how to use it. Where else should I look for information?

A: If you need to do heavy programming, then books on Java and JavaScript are a must. Sams.net has a number of books on these topics, including *Tricks of the Java Programming Gurus*, which gives you an in-depth look at how to interface VRML and Java. Coincidentally, that chapter happens to be written by me.

Q: Where do I go from here?

A: Start writing your own VRML worlds. First, learn the basic worlds, and then head on to behaviors. There's always more than one way to approach a solution, particularly with the interaction between scripts and interpolators.

Q: What's likely to change in the future?

A: This book was written when Draft 3 of the VRML 2.0 specification was current. Between Draft 3 and the official release of verison 2.0, the only differences will be clarification and rewording of parts. You can sleep easily at night, knowing that what's in these pages won't go out of date too quickly.

Forthcoming revisions to the 2.0 standard will address parts of the specification that are still outstanding but don't affect the file format. The parts include things like the external API and binary file format, which means you can write your files now and still have them run on browsers in the future.

PART

VI

Appendixes

A
3D Software Resource Guide

—by Kelly Murdock

There are many, many software packages available with 3D features. They range from high-end systems that cost $10,000 or more to simple 3D packages that do extrusions for $49. This list isn't complete and is by no means exhaustive, but it gives you a sampling of what's out there.

Workstation-based, High-End 3D-Rendering, Modeling, and Animation Packages

Workstations were once the only machines that could create 3D images. As the lower-end machines grew more powerful, workstations kept pushing the limits of possibilities, at a cost: 3D packages for workstations can cost $10,000 or more, depending on the configuration.

Silicon Graphics' Wavefront/Alias

http://www.alias.com

These masters have been around for some time. With their products, including SGI's PowerAnimator ($9,995), currently in version 7.5, you'll find a lot of power. Silicon Graphics has recently introduced a WebAnimator package to create 3D graphics specifically for the Web. The package runs on high-end workstations and cost tens of thousands of dollars, but is also responsible for a majority of the special effects you see in movies.

ElectroGIG's GIG3DGO

http://www.electrogig.com/on/info/products/gig3d/gig3dgo.html

ElectroGIG is another company that specializes in advanced modeling and rendering solutions for workstation-class computers. Their main product, GIG3DGO, incorporates many of the latest developments in computer graphics, including iso-surface modeling and parametric raytracing.

Vertigo

http://www.vertigo3d.com/

Vertigo version 9.6 enables you to model with polygons or splines, which gives you great control and precision over your models. Vertigo also offers many animation advantages as well, such as the Mechanix feature, which lets you apply math to objects.

Side Effect's PRISMS

http://www.sidefx.com/prisms.html

PRISMS is based around a NURBS (*NURBS* stands for "non-uniform rational b-splines") modeler that gives you great control over your model. PRISMS also has motion capture, particles, metaballs, inverse kinematics, and image effects.

PC-based, High-End PC-Rendering, Modeling, and Animation Packages

In this category you'll find the powerhouse products of PC-based 3D graphics. These products are still expensive (in the range of several thousand dollars), but aren't nearly as pricey as workstation-based packages.

Microsoft's SoftImage

`http://www.microsoft.com/Softimage/`

Until recently, this package would have been confined to the preceding category, but under Microsoft's influence SoftImage has shown up on systems running Windows NT. These systems also are used to create movie effects. SoftImage doesn't look like a Windows program because the interface is identical to the SGI version, but it's still extremely powerful and costs several thousand dollars. Advanced features include its programmable Mental Ray renderer for precise control over scene elements.

Kinetix's 3D Studio Max

`http://www.ktx.com`

Autodesk broke off their multimedia division under the Kinetix banner. At around $4000, this package isn't cheap, but neither are the effects that it makes possible. 3D Studio Max is probably the most popular PC-based 3D package. 3D Studio is strengthened by its ability to include third-party add-in routines, called *IPAS*, that extend the product's functionality.

New Tek's Lightwave 3D

`http://www.newtek.com/3d/3danim.html`

A survivor of the Amiga system, it costs less than 3D Studio (around $1495), but is still very powerful and often used in television production. Lightwave versions are available for workstations also. Lightwave 3D just came out with version 5, which includes a whole slew of new and exciting features.

PC-based, Middle-End PC-Rendering, Modeling, and Animation Packages

These products are finally getting into the price range that 3D enthusiasts and hobbyists can afford. They range from a few hundred dollars to around $500. They are capable of creating some incredible images and animations. For most Web developers, these are the tools to consider for adding 3D to Web sites.

Caligari's trueSpace

`http://www.caligari.com/lvltwo/product/ts2.html`

Though currently in version 2, a lower cost special edition version is available. The trueSpace package sports an easy-to-use interface with many advanced features; it's one of the easiest to get you started.

Fractal Design Corporation's Ray Dream Studio

`http://www.raydream.com/`

Ray Dream is now part of Fractal Design Corporation. Ray Dream is an integrated studio with models and extensions as well as a powerful modeling package and animation capabilities. A Macintosh version is also available. Watch for the Ray Dream site moving over to Fractal's site in the near future. The current version under Fractal's name is 4.1.

Hash's Animation Master

`http://www.hash.com/`

This package uses patches (rather than polygons, as the other packages do) to represent models. Hash's main package, Animation Master, is in version 4, but an earlier version is now available for only $199, under the name Martin Hash's 3D Animation. It includes such advanced features as inverse kinematics.

Macromedia's Extreme 3D

`http://www.macromedia.com/software/extreme3d/index.html`

Extreme 3D is a fairly new, but powerful, package. This product replaces the Macromodel package with animation features. You can anticipate that Macromedia will introduce Shockwave for Extreme 3D in the future, making it easy to publish 3D artwork and animations on the Web.

Okino's NuGraf Rendering System

http://www.okino.com/nrs/nrs.htm

The NuGraf Rendering System has a strong array of conversion filters. It also has one of the fastest rendering engines available in this class. If you work with image libraries fairly often, you'll find the batch-conversion mode invaluable.

3D Eye's TriSpectives

http://www.3deye.com/

TriSpectives 1.0 and TriSpectives Professional 1.0 are both aimed at the CAD market. They ship with over 1,000 drag-and-drop models and are priced at around $300 and $500, respectively.

CrystalGraphics' Topas Professional

This is a DOS-based package with features that rival 3D Studio at a smaller price point. Topas is included in Topas Kaleidoscope, a suite of tools for 3D professionals that includes models, textures, and a Fractal Design Painter for $1995. CrystalGraphics doesn't have a Web site, but they can be reached at 800-979-3535.

Byte-by-Byte's Soft F/X

http://bytebybyte.com

Soft F/X, version 2.5, can run on various Windows platforms. Academic versions are also available. Byte by Byte also sells a Mac-based 3D package called Sculpt 3D, currently in version 4.1 for $500. Soft F/X cost $695, but competitive upgrade pricing is available.

Imagine's Impulse

http://www.coolfun.com/

Impulse is a DOS-based product that is another leftover from the Amiga world. Imagine is working on a Windows version, which will ship shortly. Check their Web site for pricing and upgrade options.

Visual Software's Visual Reality

http://www.micrografx.com/visualsoftware/e1.html

Now owned by Micrografix, this package supports a number of integrated packages, including Visual Model, Visual Font, Renderize Live, Visual Image, and a library of models.

PC-based, Low-End PC-Rendering, Modeling, and Animation Packages

At the low end are simple packages that usually cost under $100. They make some simple 3D effects available for people who want only an occasional 3D element.

Fractal Design Corporation's AddDepth

`http://www.raydream.com/all/html/shop/add.htm`

AddDepth is another product by Ray Dream that will now fly under the Fractal Design banner. It's great at extruding vector-based figures, whether text or symbols.

Visual Software's Simply 3D

`http://www.micrografx.com/visualsoftware/e2.html`

Simple 3D is another low-cost, extrusion-based 3D package. You can control lights and materials.

Asymetrix's 3DFX

`http://www.3dsite.com/cgi/software/asymetrix/3dfx.htm`

Marketed as drag-and-drop 3D, this product is very easy to use. Libraries of 3D models are included.

Macintosh-based PC-Rendering, Modeling, and Animation Packages

Many 3D graphics professionals prefer to work on Macintosh computers. Fortunately for them, there are several 3D packages to choose from.

Electric Image

`http://www.electricimg.com/`

A high-end tool for the Macintosh, Electric Image is often used to produce television effects and scenes. Although it's the most expensive Macintosh 3D package, its power rivals some of the workstation packages. It also sports the fastest rendering engine available.

Specular's Infini-D

http://www.specular.com/products/infini-d/infini-d.html

Specular is working to get version 3.5 out the door. This Macintosh-based package for the mid-range enthusiast is very versatile, and has an abundance of new features like SuperFlares, Animated Booleans, and Shadow Catchers.

Strata's Studio Pro

http://www.strata3d.com/Main.html

Studio Pro is another strong Macintosh product. Strata recently announced the release of version 2.0. This new version will have many new features, like Quicktime VR support, special effects, and a plug-in architecture.

Auto.des.sys' Form Z and RenderZone

http://www.formz.com/

Form Z is called the 3D form synthesizer. RenderZone adds advanced rendering capabilities to the product. Both versions are also available for Windows.

Yonowat's Amapi

http://www.yonowat.com/

Amapi is a model construction and assembly tool, capable of rapidly modeling complex shapes. The 2.11 version is available for Mac, Windows, UNIX workstations, and as a 3D Studio plug-in.

Special Function 3D Packages

Some packages focus on creating just one type of model or animation, and they can be invaluable for certain projects.

Fractal Design Corporation's Poser

http://www.fractal.com/poser/poser.html

Poser is used to create human models. It comes with several prebuilt models that can easily be moved around to just the right shape.

Virtual Reality Laboratories' VistaPro

http://www.callamer.com/vrli/vp.html

Currently in version 4, this Windows-based product creates terrain and scenery images. It also can use U.S. geographical data.

AnimaTek's World Builder

http://www.animatek.com/

At $1000, this isn't an inexpensive scenery generator, but the output is worth it. This package can handle trees, plants, shrubs, and fields of flowers.

Metatools' KPT Bryce

http://www.metatools.com/bryce/

Another strong landscape builder for the Mac, KPT Bryce is produced by the same group that made Kai's Power Tools. The current version is 2.0.

LightScape

http://www.lightscape.com/

This product specializes in radiosity-based models and architectural rendering of interior spaces.

B

VRML 2.0 Node Specifications

—by Justin Couch

This appendix contains a list of all VRML 2.0 nodes and their definitions. The nodes are grouped according to their function within the scene graph. Although Chapter 13, "Exploring VRML Browsers and Development Tools," discussed group nodes and leaf nodes, there are a few more types. The grouping here is the same as that used in the VRML 2.0 draft 3 specification.

It has been assumed that you already know how to use VRML and the syntax for piecing together a scene. This is merely a listing of each of the nodes, their fields, and the default value for each field.

Grouping Nodes

These nodes are primarily used to contain other nodes. Children nodes are always placed in the children field and are bounded by a box located at bboxCenter and of size bboxSize. Grouping nodes may contain any other nodes, including other grouping nodes, as children.

Anchor

```
Anchor {
  eventIn       MFNode   addChildren
  eventIn       MFNode   removeChildren
  exposedField MFNode   children       []
  exposedField SFString description    ""
  exposedField MFString parameter      []
  exposedField MFString url            []
  field        SFVec3f  bboxCenter     0 0 0
  field        SFVec3f  bboxSize       -1 -1 -1
}
```

Billboard

```
Billboard {
  eventIn       MFNode   addChildren
  eventIn       MFNode   removeChildren
  exposedField SFVec3f  axisOfRotation 0 1 0
  exposedField MFNode   children       []
  field        SFVec3f  bboxCenter     0 0 0
  field        SFVec3f  bboxSize       -1 -1 -1
}
```

Collision

```
Collision {
  eventIn       MFNode   addChildren
  eventIn       MFNode   removeChildren
  exposedField MFNode   children       []
  exposedField SFBool   collide        TRUE
  field        SFVec3f  bboxCenter     0 0 0
  field        SFVec3f  bboxSize       -1 -1 -1
  field        SFNode   proxy          NULL
  eventOut     SFTime   collideTime
}
```

Group

```
Group {
  eventIn       MFNode   addChildren
  eventIn       MFNode   removeChildren
  exposedField MFNode   children       []
  field        SFVec3f  bboxCenter     0 0 0
  field        SFVec3f  bboxSize       -1 -1 -1
}
```

Transform

```
Transform {
  eventIn      MFNode       addChildren
  eventIn      MFNode       removeChildren
  exposedField SFVec3f      center          0 0 0
  exposedField MFNode       children        []
  exposedField SFRotation   rotation        0 0 1  0
  exposedField SFVec3f      scale           1 1 1
  exposedField SFRotation   scaleOrientation 0 0 1  0
  exposedField SFVec3f      translation     0 0 0
  field        SFVec3f      bboxCenter      0 0 0
  field        SFVec3f      bboxSize        -1 -1 -1
}
```

Special Groups

Special groups are a subset of the grouping nodes that contain extra functionality. Each special group contains extra information in the scene graph that doesn't necessarily get displayed, even though the information exists in the file.

Inline

```
Inline {
  exposedField MFString url        []
  field        SFVec3f  bboxCenter 0 0 0
  field        SFVec3f  bboxSize   -1 -1 -1
}
```

LOD

```
LOD {
  exposedField MFNode   level      []
  field        SFVec3f  center     0 0 0
  field        MFFloat  range      []
}
```

Switch

```
Switch {
  exposedField MFNode   choice      []
  exposedField SFInt32  whichChoice -1
}
```

Common Nodes

Common nodes are common across the scene graph. They can be placed as children of other nodes or as standalones.

DirectionalLight

```
DirectionalLight {
  exposedField SFFloat ambientIntensity  0
  exposedField SFColor color             1 1 1
  exposedField SFVec3f direction         0 0 -1
  exposedField SFFloat intensity         1
  exposedField SFBool  on                TRUE
}
```

PositionLight

```
PointLight {
  exposedField SFFloat ambientIntensity  0
  exposedField SFVec3f attenuation       1 0 0
  exposedField SFColor color             1 1 1
  exposedField SFFloat intensity         1
  exposedField SFVec3f location          0 0 0
  exposedField SFBool  on                TRUE
  exposedField SFFloat radius            100
}
```

Shape

```
Shape {
  exposedField SFNode appearance NULL
  exposedField SFNode geometry   NULL
}
```

Sound

```
Sound {
  exposedField SFVec3f  direction    0 0 1
  exposedField SFFloat  intensity    1
  exposedField SFVec3f  location     0 0 0
  exposedField SFFloat  maxBack      10
  exposedField SFFloat  maxFront     10
  exposedField SFFloat  minBack      1
  exposedField SFFloat  minFront     1
  exposedField SFFloat  priority     0
  exposedField SFNode   source       NULL
  field        SFBool   spatialize   TRUE
}
```

AudioClip

```
AudioClip {
  exposedField  SFString  description        " "
  exposedField  SFBool    loop               FALSE
  exposedField  SFFloat   pitch              1.0
  exposedField  SFTime    startTime          0
  exposedField  SFTime    stopTime           0
  exposedField  MFString  url                []
  eventOut      SFTime    duration_changed
  eventOut      SFBool    isActive
}
```

Script

```
Script {
  exposedField MFString url            []
  field        SFBool    directOutput  FALSE
  field        SFBool    mustEvaluate  FALSE
  # And any number of:
  eventIn      eventTypeName eventName
  field        fieldTypeName fieldName initialValue
  eventOut     eventTypeName eventName
}
```

SpotLight

```
SpotLight {
  exposedField SFFloat ambientIntensity  0
  exposedField SFVec3f attenuation       1 0 0
  exposedField SFFloat beamWidth         1.570796
  exposedField SFColor color             1 1 1
  exposedField SFFloat cutOffAngle       0.785398
  exposedField SFVec3f direction         0 0 -1
  exposedField SFFloat intensity         1
  exposedField SFVec3f location          0 0 0
  exposedField SFBool  on                TRUE
  exposedField SFFloat radius            100
}
```

WorldInfo

```
WorldInfo {
  field MFString info  []
  field SFString title ""
}
```

Sensors

Sensors take external input and generate events to be passed to other nodes by routes. They have the ability to be enabled or disabled by setting the enabled field appropriately. Although they don't hold children nodes themselves, they use the children of their parent Grouping node as the geometry.

CylinderSensor

```
CylinderSensor {
  exposedField SFFloat    diskAngle  0.262
  exposedField SFBool     enabled    TRUE
  exposedField SFFloat    maxAngle   -1
  exposedField SFFloat    minAngle   0
  exposedField SFRotation offset     0 1 0 0
  exposedField SFBool     autoOffset TRUE
  eventOut     SFBool     isActive
  eventOut     SFRotation rotation_changed
  eventOut     SFVec3f    trackPoint_changed
}
```

PlaneSensor

```
PlaneSensor {
  exposedField SFBool   enabled              TRUE
  exposedField SFVec2f  maxPosition          -1 -1
  exposedField SFVec2f  minPosition          0 0
  exposedField SFVec3f  offset               0 0 0
  exposedField SFBool   autoOffset           TRUE
  eventOut     SFBool   isActive
  eventOut     SFVec3f  trackPoint_changed
  eventOut     SFVec3f  translation_changed
}
```

ProximitySensor

```
ProximitySensor {
  exposedField SFVec3f    center       0 0 0
  exposedField SFVec3f    size         0 0 0
  exposedField SFBool     enabled      TRUE
  eventOut     SFBool     isActive
  eventOut     SFVec3f    position_changed
  eventOut     SFRotation orientation_changed
  eventOut     SFTime     enterTime
  eventOut     SFTime     exitTime
}
```

SphereSensor

```
SphereSensor {
  exposedField SFBool     enabled          TRUE
  exposedField SFRotation offset           0 1 0 0
  exposedField SFBool     autoOffset       TRUE
  eventOut     SFBool     isActive
  eventOut     SFRotation rotation_changed
  eventOut     SFVec3f    trackPoint_changed
}
```

TimeSensor

```
TimeSensor {
  exposedField SFTime  cycleInterval 1
  exposedField SFBool  enabled       TRUE
  exposedField SFBool  loop          FALSE
  exposedField SFTime  startTime     0
  exposedField SFTime  stopTime      0
  eventOut     SFTime  cycleTime
  eventOut     SFFloat fraction_changed
  eventOut     SFBool  isActive
  eventOut     SFTime  time
}
```

TouchSensor

```
TouchSensor {
  exposedField SFBool  enabled TRUE
  eventOut     SFVec3f hitNormal_changed
```

```
eventOut       SFVec3f hitPoint_changed
eventOut       SFVec2f hitTexCoord_changed
eventOut       SFBool  isActive
eventOut       SFBool  isOver
eventOut       SFTime  touchTime
}
```

VisibilitySensor

```
VisibilitySensor {
  exposedField SFVec3f center    0 0 0
  exposedField SFBool  enabled   TRUE
  exposedField SFVec3f size      0 0 0
  eventOut     SFTime  enterTime
  eventOut     SFTime  exitTime
  eventOut     SFBool  isActive
}
```

Geometry

Pure geometry nodes can't be drawn on the screen by themselves. They must be used as the node in the geometry field of the Shape node. They contain no properties other than the basic geometrical characteristics.

Box

```
Box {
  field    SFVec3f size  2 2 2
}
```

Cone

```
Cone {
  field    SFFloat   bottomRadius 1
  field    SFFloat   height       2
  field    SFBool    side         TRUE
  field    SFBool    bottom       TRUE
}
```

ElevationGrid

```
ElevationGrid {
  eventIn      MFFloat   set_height
  exposedField SFNode    color          NULL
  exposedField SFNode    normal         NULL
  exposedField SFNode    texCoord       NULL
  field        MFFloat   height         []
  field        SFBool    ccw            TRUE
  field        SFBool    colorPerVertex TRUE
  field        SFFloat   creaseAngle    0
  field        SFBool    normalPerVertex TRUE
  field        SFBool    solid          TRUE
  field        SFInt32   xDimension     0
```

```
  field       SFFloat  xSpacing       0.0
  field       SFInt32  zDimension     0
  field       SFFloat  zSpacing       0.0
}
```

Extrusion

```
Extrusion {
  eventIn MFVec2f     set_crossSection
  eventIn MFRotation  set_orientation
  eventIn MFVec2f     set_scale
  eventIn MFVec3f     set_spine
  field   SFBool      beginCap         TRUE
  field   SFBool      ccw              TRUE
  field   SFBool      convex           TRUE
  field   SFFloat     creaseAngle      0
  field   MFVec2f     crossSection     [ 1 1, 1 -1, -1 -1, -1 1, 1 1 ]
  field   SFBool      endCap           TRUE
  field   MFRotation  orientation      0 0 1 0
  field   MFVec2f     scale            1 1
  field   SFBool      solid            TRUE
  field   MFVec3f     spine            [ 0 0 0, 0 1 0 ]
}
```

IndexedFaceSet

```
IndexedFaceSet {
  eventIn       MFInt32 set_colorIndex
  eventIn       MFInt32 set_coordIndex
  eventIn       MFInt32 set_normalIndex
  eventIn       MFInt32 set_texCoordIndex
  exposedField  SFNode  color            NULL
  exposedField  SFNode  coord            NULL
  exposedField  SFNode  normal           NULL
  exposedField  SFNode  texCoord         NULL
  field         SFBool  ccw              TRUE
  field         MFInt32 colorIndex       []
  field         SFBool  colorPerVertex   TRUE
  field         SFBool  convex           TRUE
  field         MFInt32 coordIndex       []
  field         SFFloat creaseAngle      0
  field         MFInt32 normalIndex      []
  field         SFBool  normalPerVertex  TRUE
  field         SFBool  solid            TRUE
  field         MFInt32 texCoordIndex    []
}
```

IndexedLineSet

```
IndexedLineSet {
  eventIn       MFInt32 set_colorIndex
  eventIn       MFInt32 set_coordIndex
  exposedField  SFNode  color            NULL
  exposedField  SFNode  coord            NULL
  field         MFInt32 colorIndex       []
  field         SFBool  colorPerVertex   TRUE
  field         MFInt32 coordIndex       []
}
```

PointSet

```
PointSet {
  exposedField  SFNode  color  NULL
  exposedField  SFNode  coord  NULL
}
```

Sphere

```
Sphere {
  field SFFloat radius  1
}
```

Text

```
Text {
  exposedField  MFString string    []
  exposedField  SFNode   fontStyle NULL
  exposedField  MFFloat  length    []
  exposedField  SFFloat  maxExtent 0.0
}
```

Geometric Properties

Geometric properties are property nodes for the different geometry nodes. These can be declared and have the DEF keyword placed in front of them once, then reused across a number of nodes, instantly. For example, you can declare one Coordinate node and use it in an IndexedFaceSet and PointSet node at the same time. The usual rules about the DEF and USE keywords apply.

Color

```
Color {
  exposedField MFColor color  []
}
```

Coordinate

```
Coordinate {
  exposedField MFVec3f point  []
}
```

Normal

```
Normal {
  exposedField MFVec3f vector  []
}
```

TextureCoordinate

```
TextureCoordinate {
  exposedField MFVec2f point  []
}
```

Appearance

This collection of nodes controls the visible appearance of the geometric surface. Although these nodes can't be used to alter geometric properties, they can enhance geometric surfaces when used wisely. The default color for the Appearance node is black.

Appearance

```
Appearance {
  exposedField SFNode material         NULL
  exposedField SFNode texture          NULL
  exposedField SFNode textureTransform  NULL
}
```

FontStyle

```
FontStyle {
  field SFString family       "SERIF"
  field SFBool   horizontal   TRUE
  field SFString justify      "BEGIN"
  field SFString language     ""
  field SFBool   leftToRight  TRUE
  field SFFloat  size         1.0
  field SFFloat  spacing      1.0
  field SFString style        ""
  field SFBool   topToBottom  TRUE
}
```

ImageTexture

At the time of this writing, the type of the justify string was under discussion. It may well become an MFString, with each string specifying a justification in each axis. Check the final release of the VRML 2.0 specification for the final result.

```
ImageTexture {
  exposedField MFString url       []
  field        SFBool   repeatS TRUE
  field        SFBool   repeatT TRUE
}
```

Material

```
Material {
  exposedField SFFloat ambientIntensity  0.2
  exposedField SFColor diffuseColor       0.8 0.8 0.8
  exposedField SFColor emissiveColor      0 0 0
  exposedField SFFloat shininess          0.2
  exposedField SFColor specularColor      0 0 0
  exposedField SFFloat transparency       0
}
```

MovieTexture

```
MovieTexture {
  exposedField SFBool    loop              FALSE
  exposedField SFFloat   speed             1
  exposedField SFTime    startTime         0
  exposedField SFTime    stopTime          0
  exposedField MFString  url               []
  field        SFBool    repeatS           TRUE
  field        SFBool    repeatT           TRUE
  eventOut     SFFloat   duration_changed
  eventOut     SFBool    isActive
}
```

PixelTexture

```
PixelTexture {
  exposedField SFImage  image     0 0 0
  field        SFBool   repeatS   TRUE
  field        SFBool   repeatT   TRUE
}
```

TextureTransform

```
TextureTransform {
  exposedField SFVec2f  center        0 0
  exposedField SFFloat  rotation      0
  exposedField SFVec2f  scale         1 1
  exposedField SFVec2f  translation   0 0
}
```

Interpolators

Given a set of keys and corresponding values, the input of a fractional value produces an output value that's the result of the linear interpolation between the appropriate pairs of values.

ColorInterpolator

```
ColorInterpolator {
  eventIn      SFFloat  set_fraction
  exposedField MFFloat  key             []
  exposedField MFColor  keyValue        []
  eventOut     SFColor  value_changed
}
```

CoordinateInterpolator

```
CoordinateInterpolator {
  eventIn      SFFloat  set_fraction
  exposedField MFFloat  key             []
  exposedField MFVec3f  keyValue        []
  eventOut     MFVec3f  value_changed
}
```

NormalInterpolator

```
NormalInterpolator {
  eventIn       SFFloat set_fraction
  exposedField MFFloat key            []
  exposedField MFVec3f keyValue       []
  eventOut      MFVec3f value_changed
}
```

OrientationInterpolator

```
OrientationInterpolator {
  eventIn       SFFloat    set_fraction
  exposedField MFFloat     key            []
  exposedField MFRotation  keyValue        []
  eventOut      SFRotation value_changed
}
```

PositionInterpolator

```
PositionInterpolator {
  eventIn       SFFloat set_fraction
  exposedField MFFloat key            []
  exposedField MFVec3f keyValue       []
  eventOut      SFVec3f value_changed
}
```

ScalarInterpolator

```
ScalarInterpolator {
  eventIn       SFFloat set_fraction
  exposedField MFFloat key            []
  exposedField MFFloat keyValue       []
  eventOut      SFFloat value_changed
}
```

Bindable Nodes

These nodes can be used only one at a time. The first one declared in the file is always the default. Any subsequent nodes can be made active by sending them a set_bind event. The current state can be found by reading the isBound eventOut field.

Background

```
Background {
  eventIn       SFBool    set_bind
  exposedField MFFloat    groundAngle    []
  exposedfield MFColor    groundColor    []
  exposedField MFString   backUrl        []
  exposedField MFString   bottomUrl      []
  exposedField MFString   frontUrl       []
  exposedField MFString   leftUrl        []
```

```
   exposedField MFString rightUrl     []
   exposedField MFString topUrl       []
   exposedField MFFloat  skyAngle     []
   exposedField MFColor  skyColor     [ 0 0 0 ]
   eventOut     SFBool   isBound
}
```

Fog

```
Fog {
   exposedField SFColor  color           1 1 1
   exposedField SFString fogType         "LINEAR"
   exposedField SFFloat  visibilityRange 1000
   eventIn      SFBool   set_bind
   eventOut     SFBool   isBound
}
```

NavigationInfo

```
NavigationInfo {
   eventIn      SFBool   set_bind
   exposedField MFFloat  avatarSize      [ 0.25, 1.6, 0.75 ]
   exposedField SFBool   headlight       TRUE
   exposedField SFFloat  speed           1.0
   exposedField MFString type            "WALK"
   exposedField SFFloat  visibilityLimit 0.0
   eventOut     SFBool   isBound
}
```

Viewpoint

```
Viewpoint {
   eventIn      SFBool     set_bind
   exposedField SFFloat    fieldOfView   0.785398
   exposedField SFBool     jump          TRUE
   exposedField SFRotation orientation   0 0 1 0
   exposedField SFVec3f    position      0 0 0
   field        SFString   description   ""
   eventOut     SFTime     bindTime_changed
   eventOut     SFBool     isBound
}
```

C

VRML Resource Guide

—by Justin Couch

Ah, so you want to look for additional VRML information. You even made it back here to the appendix section. There are a number of different topics for which you can find information: browsers, modeling tools, content, and online tutorials.

The lists presented here are by no means a definitive record of all the companies involved. Rather, these lists include the most popular and widely known companies and individuals.

General Sites

The following sites are of general interest to a VRML developer because they contain many links to all sorts of VRML resources. At these sites, you can find everything from browser software to philosophical discussion papers on the direction of VRML.

The VRML Repository

`http://www.sdsc.edu/vrml/`

Whenever you need to find information on VRML, the first place you should head is the VRML Repository. This site is run by the San Diego Supercomputing Center and was the first site to set itself up as the storage place of all things VRML. Among its large collection of pages you can find links to software, research, and companies in the VRML field.

The software ranges from free things, such as converters, to professional modeling packages. All the major companies listed in the later section of this appendix have links here. One of the more useful things is the links to freeware and shareware software for producing VRML files. The items vary from syntax checkers to browsers and modeling tools. A lot of the software in this category is multipurpose. For example, WCTV2POV (mentioned in Chapter 13, "Exploring VRML Browsers and Development Tools") doesn't export just VRML files, but a number of others, as well. Many of the modeling tools also are multipurpose.

Another interesting area fairly unique to this site includes links to research involving VRML. Papers exist for just about every area of the specification, covering current research on virtual environments as well as more general VR topics. A look through this page takes you right back to the very beginning of VRML, with papers on the design of various bits and pieces of the specification, proposals for new features, and much more.

Wired Magazine's VRML Site

`http://vrml.wired.com/`

One of the first companies to become interested in VRML was *Wired Magazine*. One of the staff members from the magazine was present at the first conference when VRML was born and offered space on the company's server to host a site. To this day, the company runs the mailing list server that has the 2000-odd people involved in the writing of the VRML specification. In contrast to the Repository, this site is full of information about current happenings in the VRML world, such as press releases, articles by famous people, and more general information.

Browser Companies

These companies produce the software for viewing a VRML world. Generally, you can't edit and browse worlds with one piece of software. However, a number of these companies offer a suite of tools for both building and browsing.

This section is divided into two parts. First, VRML 1.0 software is dealt with; then 2.0 companies are looked at.

VRML 1.0

Naturally, the first browser off the blocks is Netscape's Live3D. This comes as part of the standard beta versions of Navigator 3.0, giving everybody access to VRML worlds without requiring them to download yet another plug-in. For users of pre-3.0 versions of Netscape, the link to Live3D can be found under the Netscape home page.

Chapter 13 mentioned a few other browser companies, which are included in the following list.

VRScout	Chaco Communications	www.chaco.com
VRWeb	Univ. of Graz/NCSA	www.iicm.tu-graz.ac.at
Worldview	Intervista Software	www.intervista.com
CyberPassage v1.0	Sony	vsl.sony.co.jp
CyberGate	BlackSun Inc.	www.blacksun.com
Onlive	Onlive! Technologies	www.onlive.com
Voyager	Virtus Corp.	www.virtus.com

VRML 2.0

At the time of this writing, there are only two VRML 2.0 browsers available. Both of them are in the early beta-testing stage, so many of the nodes will either not work completely or just not be implemented.

The CD-ROM includes the latest beta versions at the time of publishing; however, you should check these sites for the latest versions:

CyberPassage V2.0	Sony	vsl.sony.co.jp
CosmoPlayer	Silicon Graphics	vrml.sgi.com/cosmplayer
Liquid Reality (Java VRML toolkit)	Dimension X	www.dimensionx.com
Pueblo	Chaco Communications	www.chaco.com

Other companies have browsers in the works. It would be a good idea to check the sites mentioned for 1.0 browsers to see the latest offerings.

Modeling Tools

Modeling tools can be subdivided into three types:

1. **Non-VRML**. Use external conversion programs to convert the exported files to VRML.

2. **Partial support**. Although not originally VRML, these now contain either exporters within the product or some ability to select VRML capabilities.

3. **Dedicated**. This software is designed to create VRML content. Some dedicated software also has the capability to export to other formats, but the main focus is VRML.

The first two categories of modeling tools are currently supported only by version 1.0. By the time you read this, there should be some proper 2.0 support in software.

Non-VRML

Just about anything supporting the DXF file format can be classified in this area. Programs like WCTV2POV can then be used to convert DXF to VRML 1.0 format. A few of the more popular packages used widely in the VRML community are listed here:

AutoCAD	AutoDesk Software	`www.autodesk.com`
3D Studio and 3D Studio MAX AutoCAD	AutoDesk Software	`www.autodesk.com`
trueSpace	Caligari	`www.caligari.com`

Partial Support

A number of plug-in exporters to popular products like 3D Studio and AutoCAD fall into this category:

Interchange	Syndesis	`www.threedee.com`
3D Builder	3D Construction Company	`www.elizabethton.ilinkgn.net/3d_construction/3dc.htm`
Walkthrough	Pro Virtus	`www.virtus.com`

Note: WCTV2POV converts many file formats to many others.

Dedicated VRML

These tools are dedicated to producing VRML content. At the time of this writing, they were capable of generating only 1.0 output, which would then need to be converted. At least some of these tools will have 2.0 capabilities for static scenes by the time you read this book.

Pioneer and Pioneer PRO	Caligari	`www.caligari.com`
V-Realm Builder	IDS Software	`www.ids-net.com`
Virtual HomeSpace Builder	Paragraph Intl.	`www.paragraph.com`
CyberPassage Conductor	Sony	`vs.sony.co.jp`
WebSpace Author	Silicon Graphics	`webspace.sgi.com`

Content

The following is a collection of interesting sites that showcase different uses of VRML. In addition, the VRML Repository listed earlier in this appendix contains a large list of VRML sites to visit.

Terra Vista Virtual Community

`www.terravista.org.`

This is a spin-off group from the VRML development mailing list that tries to apply the specification by stretching it as far as it will go. It contains no affiliations with any commercial company. All of Terra Vista's worlds are designed to be visited by any VRML-compliant browser.

People are free to come along and provide their own worlds, as long as they adhere to a few guidelines.

Graphman's VRML RollerSkater

`www.graphcomp.com/vrml`

This site uses CGI, HTML frames, and VRML together. The main page produces a rollerskater, but there are a number of different VRML pages and worlds to visit. They showcase various aspects of VRML not commonly used in day-to-day worlds.

Intellink CyberLife Worlds

`www.intellink.com/forum/`

These are a series of VRML worlds that have been created to take advantage of BlackSun's CyberHub Client multiuser extensions to Live3D. These worlds were used as part of the competition that launched CyberHub Client.

Many hidden objects are used in these worlds. For the casual observer, there is one set of things to view, but those who like to explore will find the world in a new light. These worlds are based purely on Live3D and CyberHub Client, so you need to have these loaded to enjoy the world properly.

Intel's Pentium World

`www.intel.com`

Here's an example of a high-end use of VRML for marketing purposes. It requires a fast Internet connection and computer—this world is definitely not for the 486 machine.

The world presents a fly-through of the Pentium chip and associated marketing information. It makes heavy use of texture mapping, but is a showcase for what can be done with VRML in marketing terms.

Len Bullard's Tale of the Talosians

`fly.hiwaay.net/~cbullard/talosf01.htm`

For something completely different, Len's Talosian world is a fantasy story about an alien race living on earth. It combines VRML, frames, and CGI to provide music on one page.

This world recently won first place in the V-Realm World Builder's contest. Most of the world was built using V-Realm Builder with a few hand tweaks, such as the Live3D Spin node extensions. The story is slowly developing, so keep visiting regularly.

Online Tutorials

Most of the tutorials presented here are for VRML 1.0. A few are slowly emerging to cover VRML 2.0, but everything has been slow because of the stability of the draft specifications. Now that VRML 2.0 has reached official status, expect some of these to be updated.

Cindy Reed's Texture Tutorial

`www.ywd.com/cindy/texture.html`

This is one of the best tutorials for working out the complexities of VRML texture mapping. It covers everything from applying simple texture maps to complex issues of applying them to IndexedFaceSets.

The pig you have seen floating around in a few of the book's examples was generously supplied by Cindy and is also used in this tutorial.

Pioneer Joel's VRML Tutorial

`vrml.asu.edu`

This is a complete overview of VRML 1.0 nodes and syntax. The tutorials are presented as a series of sample code and offer some explanation about why things happen the way they do.

Silicon Graphics VRML 2.0 Site

`vrml.sgi.com`

This location provides a series of demonstration examples about how to use the VRML 2.0 nodes and behaviors. This isn't a strict tutorial per se, but a series of examples you can download and examine at your leisure. Several are very large (more than 500K), and there are some very complex worlds here.

If you need some heavy-duty scripting examples, then look at the Robot example. If you try to run it, make sure you have lots of RAM and a fast CPU.

This site is also the site for CosmoPlayer and everything else Silicon Graphics produces for VRML. There are links to other VRML 2.0 tutorials at this site as well.

D ActiveVRML Resources

—by Kelly Murdock

ActiveVRML is Microsoft's answer to interactive 3D multimedia on the Web. It's a scripting language that enables you to create 3D worlds and 2D cel animations. ActiveVRML is embedded in your Web page as an ActiveX control and is available as part of the Microsoft ActiveX Development Kit.

The Microsoft ActiveX Development Kit

As part of Microsoft's effort to promote their ActiveX initiative, they made the ActiveX Development Kit available to developers in mid-1996. This kit was a valuable resource that included a lot of information on ActiveX controls, including a complete resource for ActiveVRML.

Included in the ActiveVRML resource section are samples, tutorials, complete documentation, and release notes. The entire resource is a series of HTML pages.

NOTE:
The ActiveVRML development team at Microsoft is currently developing a new release of ActiveVRML. The beta for this new release should be available in August of 1996.

The following pages are included in the ActiveVRML resource section of the ActiveX Development Kit:

- ❏ Setup Instructions
- ❏ Creating ActiveVRML Content
- ❏ ActiveVRML Samples
- ❏ ActiveVRML Homepage
- ❏ ActiveVRML Documentation
- ❏ ActiveVRML Release Notes

Reviewing these pages will give you an idea of what's possible with ActiveVRML.

Web Resources

There are several resources on the Web that can help you get a jump start into ActiveVRML. The most important site to check is at

`http://www.microsoft.com/workshop/prog/avr/`

This is the ActiveVRML site at Microsoft, where the latest news and developments in ActiveVRML are posted.

To understand the differences between VRML 2.0, the Moving Worlds specification, and ActiveVRML, jump over to the following page.

`http://reality.sgi.com/employees/gavin/vrml/ActiveVRMLResponse.html`

This page gives SGI's response to ActiveVRML. It also includes a comparison list between the two technologies.

There are several good tutorial pages about ActiveVRML found on the Web. One is found at the Folk Arts site:

`http://www.folkarts.com/activevrml/guide.html`

This site is the Dummy Guide to ActiveVRML. It offers a single example with some good background material.

Another good tutorial is maintained by Vijay Mukhi's Computer Institute hosted on NECA:

`http://www.neca.com/~vmis/avrml.htm`

This site has many examples in what is probably the best tutorial on ActiveVRML outside of Microsoft.

E HTML Quick Reference

—by Dick Oliver

This appendix is a reference to the HTML tags you can use in your documents. Unless otherwise noted, all of the tags listed here are supported by both Microsoft Explorer 3.0 and Netscape Navigator 3.0. Note that some other browsers don't support all the listed tags, and some of the tags listed as (MS) may also be supported in the final shipping version of Netscape 3.0.

The proposed HTML style sheet specification is also not covered here. Refer to the Netscape (http://home.netscape.com/) or Microsoft (http://www.microsoft.com/) Web sites for details about this and other late-breaking changes to the new HTML 3.2 standard.

HTML Tags

These tags are used to create a basic HTML page with text, headings, and lists. An (MS) beside the attribute indicates Microsoft.

Comments

`<! - ... ->`   Creates a comment. Can also be used to hide JavaScript from browsers that do not support it.

`<COMMENT>...</COMMENT>`   The new offical way of specifying comments.

Structure Tags

`<HTML>...</HTML>`   Encloses the entire HTML document.

`<HEAD>...</HEAD>`   Encloses the head of the HTML document.

`<BODY>...</BODY>`   Encloses the body (text and tags) of the HTML document.

Attributes:

`BACKGROUND="..."`	The name or URL of the image to tile on the page background.
`BGCOLOR="..."`	The color of the page background.
`TEXT="..."`	The color of the page's text.
`LINK="..."`	The color of unfollowed links.
`ALINK="..."`	The color of activated links.
`VLINK="..."`	The color of followed links.
`BGPROPERTIES="..."`(MS)	Properties of background image. Currently allows only the value FIXED, which prevents the background image from scrolling.
`TOPMARGIN="..."`(MS)	Top margin of the page, in pixels.
`BOTTOMMARGIN="..."`(MS)	Bottom margin of the page, in pixels.

\<BASE\> Indicates the full URL of the current document. This optional tag is used within \<HEAD\>.

Attribute:

HREF="..." The full URL of this document.

\<ISINDEX\> Indicates that this document is a gateway script that allows searches.

Attributes:

PROMPT="..." The prompt for the search field.
ACTION="..." Gateway program to which the search string should be passed.

\<LINK\> Indicates a link between this document and some other document. Generally used only by HTML-generating tools. \<LINK\> represents a link from this entire document to another, as opposed to \<A\>, which can create multiple links in the document. Not commonly used.

Attributes:

HREF="..." The URL of the document to call when the link is activated.
NAME="..." If the document is to be considered an anchor, the name of that anchor.
REL="..." The relationship between the linked-to document and the current document; for example, "TOC" or "Glossary".
REV="..." A reverse relationship between the current document and the linked-to document.
URN="..." A Uniform Resource Number (URN), a unique identifier different from the URL in HREF.
TITLE="..." The title of the linked-to document.
METHODS="..." The method with which the document is to be retrieved; for example, FTP, Gopher, and so on.

\<META\> Indicates meta-information about this document (information about the document itself); for example, keywords for search engines, special HTTP headers to be used for retrieving this document, expiration date, and so on. Meta-information is usually in a key/value pair form. Used in the document \<HEAD\>.

Attributes:

`HTTP-EQUIV="..."`	Creates a new HTTP header field with the same name as the attribute's value; for example, `HTTP-EQUIV="Expires"`. The value of that header is specified by the `CONTENT` attribute.
`NAME="..."`	If meta-data is usually in the form of key/value pairs, `NAME` indicates the key; for example, `Author` or `ID`.
`CONTENT="..."`	The content of the key/value pair (or of the HTTP header indicated by `HTTP-EQUIV`).

`<NEXTID>` Indicates the "next" document to this one (as might be defined by a tool to manage HTML documents in series). `<NEXTID>` is considered obsolete.

Headings and Title

`<H1>...</H1>`	A first-level heading.
`<H2>...</H2>`	A second-level heading.
`<H3>...</H3>`	A third-level heading.
`<H4>...</H4>`	A fourth-level heading.
`<H5>...</H5>`	A fifth-level heading.
`<H6>...</H6>`	A sixth-level heading.
`<TITLE>...</TITLE>`	Indicates the title of the document. Used within `<HEAD>`.

All heading tags accept the following attribute:

Attribute:

`ALIGN="..."`	Possible values are `CENTER`, `LEFT`, and `RIGHT`.

Paragraphs and Regions

`<P>...</P>`   A plain paragraph. The closing tag (`</P>`) is optional.

Attribute:

`ALIGN="..."`	Align text to `CENTER`, `LEFT`, or `RIGHT`.

`<DIV>...</DIV>`   A region of text to be formatted.

Attribute:

ALIGN="..."   Align text to CENTER, LEFT, or RIGHT.

Links

`<A>...</A>`   With the HREF attribute, creates a link to another document or anchor; with the NAME attribute, creates an anchor that can be linked to.

Attributes:

HREF="..."	The URL of the document to be called when the link is activated.
NAME="..."	The name of the anchor.
REL="..."	The relationship between the linked-to document and the current document; for example, "TOC" or "Glossary" (not commonly used).
REV="..."	A reverse relationship between the current document and the linked-to document (not commonly used).
URN="..."	A Uniform Resource Number (URN), a unique identifier different from the URL in HREF (not commonly used).
TITLE="..."	The title of the linked-to document (not commonly used).
METHODS="..."	The method with which the document is to be retrieved; for example, FTP, Gopher, and so on (not commonly used).
TARGET="..."	The name of a frame that the linked document should appear in.

Lists

`<OL>...</OL>`   An ordered (numbered) list.

Attributes:

TYPE="..."	The type of numerals to label the list. Possible values are A, a, I, i, 1.
START="..."	The value with which to start this list.

`<UL>...</UL>`	An unordered (bulleted) list.
Attribute:	

	`TYPE="..."`	The bullet dingbat to mark list items. Possible values are DISC, CIRCLE (or ROUND), and SQUARE.

`<MENU>...</MENU>`	A menu list of items.
`<DIR>...</DIR>`	A directory listing; items are generally smaller than 20 characters.
`<LI>`	A list item for use with `<OL>`, `<UL>`, `<MENU>`, or `<DIR>`.
Attributes:	

	`TYPE="..."`	The type of bullet or number to label this item with. Possible values are DISC, CIRCLE, (or ROUND) SQUARE, A, a, I, i, 1.
	`VALUE="..."`	The numeric value this list item should have (affects this item and all below it in `<OL>` lists).

`<DL>...</DL>`	A definition or glossary list.
Attribute:	

	COMPACT	The COMPACT attribute specifies a formatting that takes less whitespace to present.

`<DT>`	A definition term, as part of a definition list.
`<DD>`	The corresponding definition to a definition term, as part of a definition list.

Character Formatting

`<EM>...</EM>`	Emphasis (usually italic).
`<STRONG>...</STRONG>`	Stronger emphasis (usually bold).
`<CODE>...</CODE>`	Code sample (usually Courier).
`<KBD>...</KBD>`	Text to be typed (usually Courier).
`<VAR>...</VAR>`	A variable or placeholder for some other value.
`<SAMP>...</SAMP>`	Sample text (seldom used).
`<DFN>...</DFN>`	A definition of a term.
`<CITE>...</CITE>`	A citation.

`<B>...</B>`	Boldface text.
`<I>...</I>`	Italic text.
`<TT>...</TT>`	Typewriter (monospaced) font.
`<PRE>...</PRE>`	Preformatted text (exact line endings and spacing are preserved—usually rendered in a monospaced font).
`<BIG>...</BIG>`	Text is slightly larger than normal.
`<SMALL>...</SMALL>`	Text is slightly smaller than normal.
`<SUB>...</SUB>`	Subscript.
`<SUP>...</SUP>`	Superscript.
`<STRIKE>...</STRIKE>`	Puts a strikethrough line in text.

Other Elements

`<HR>`   A horizontal rule line.

Attributes:

`SIZE="..."`	The thickness of the rule, in pixels.
`WIDTH="..."`	The width of the rule, in pixels or as a percentage of the document width.
`ALIGN="..."`	How the rule line is aligned on the page. Possible values are LEFT, RIGHT, and CENTER.
`NOSHADE`	Causes the rule line to be drawn as a solid line instead of a transparent bevel.
`COLOR="..."` (MS)	Color of the horizontal rule.

`<BR>`   A line break.

Attribute:

`CLEAR="..."`	Causes the text to stop flowing around any images. Possible values are RIGHT, LEFT, ALL.

`<NOBR>...</NOBR>`	Causes the enclosed text not to wrap at the edge of the page.
`<WBR>`	Wraps the text at this point only if necessary.
`<BLOCKQUOTE>... </BLOCKQUOTE>`	Used for long quotes or citations.
`<ADDRESS>...</ADDRESS>`	Used for signatures or general information about a document's author.

`<CENTER>...</CENTER>`	Centers text or images.
`<BLINK>...</BLINK>`	Causes the enclosed text to blink irritatingly.
`<FONT>...</FONT>`	Changes the size of the font for the enclosed text.

Attributes:

`SIZE="..."`	The size of the font, from 1 to 7. Default is 3. Can also be specified as a value relative to the current size; for example, +2.
`COLOR="..."`	Changes the color of the text.
`FACE="..."` (MS)	Name of font to use if it can be found on the user's system. Multiple font names can be separated by commas, and the first font on the list that can be found is used.

`<BASEFONT>`   Sets the default size of the font for the current page.

Attribute:

`SIZE="..."`	The default size of the font, from 1 to 7. Default is 3.

Images, Sounds, and Embedded Media

`<IMG>` Inserts an inline image into the document.

Attributes:

`ISMAP`	This image is a clickable image map.
`SRC="..."`	The URL of the image.
`ALT="..."`	A text string that is displayed in browsers that cannot support images.
`ALIGN="..."`	Determines the alignment of the given image. If LEFT or RIGHT (N), the image is aligned to the left or right column, and all following text flows beside that image. All other values, such as TOP, MIDDLE, BOTTOM, or the Netscape-only TEXTTOP, ABSMIDDLE, BASELINE, and ABSBOTTOM, determine the vertical alignment of this image with other items in the same line.
`VSPACE="..."`	The space between the image and the text above or below it.

HSPACE="..."	The space between the image and the text to its left or right.
WIDTH="..."	The width, in pixels, of the image. If WIDTH is not the actual width, the image is scaled to fit.
HEIGHT="..."	The width, in pixels, of the image. If HEIGHT is not the actual height, the image is scaled to fit.
BORDER="..."	Draws a border of the specified value in pixels to be drawn around the image. In the case of images that are also links, BORDER changes the size of the default link border.
LOWSRC="..."	The path or URL of an image that will be loaded first, before the image specified in SRC. The value of LOWSRC is usually a smaller or lower resolution version of the actual image.
USEMAP="..."	The name of an image map specification for client-side image mapping. Used with <MAP> and <AREA>.
DYNSRC="..." (MS)	The address of a video clip or VRML world (dynamic source).
CONTROLS (MS)	Used with DYNSRC to display a set of playback controls for inline video.
LOOP="..." (MS)	The number of times a video clip will loop. (-1 or INFINITE means to loop indefinitely.)
START="..." (MS)	When a DYNSRC video clip should start playing. Valid options are FILEOPEN (play when page is displayed) or MOUSEOVER (play when mouse cursor passes over the video clip.

<BGSOUND> (MS)   Plays a sound file as soon as the page is displayed.

Attributes:

SRC="..."	The URL of the WAV, AU, or MIDI sound file to embed.
LOOP="..." (MS)	The number of times a video clip will loop. (-1 or INFINITE means to loop indefinitely.)

`<OBJECT>` (MS)	Inserts an image, video, Java applet, or ActiveX OLE control into a document.

NOTE: The full syntax for the `<OBJECT>` tag is not yet completely finalized. Check `http://www.w3.org/pub/WWW/TR/WD-object.html` and `http://www.microsoft.com/intdev/author/` for the latest attributes supported by the HTML 3.2 standard and implemented in Microsoft Internet Explorer.

`<EMBED>` (Netscape only)	Embeds a file to be read or displayed by a plug-in application.

NOTE: In addition to the following standard attributes, you can specify applet-specific attributes to be interpreted by the plug-in that displays the embedded object.

Attributes:

`SRC="..."`	The URL of the file to embed.
`WIDTH="..."`	The width of the embedded object in pixels.
`HEIGHT="..."`	The height of the embedded object in pixels.
`ALIGN="..."`	Determines the alignment of the media window. Values are the same as for the `<IMG>` tag.
`VSPACE="..."`	The space between the media and the text above or below it.
`HSPACE="..."`	The space between the media and the text to its left or right.
`BORDER="..."`	Draws a border of the specified size in pixels to be drawn around the media.
`<NOEMBED>...</NOEMBED>` (N)	Alternate text or images to be shown to users who do not have a plug-in installed.
`<OBJECT>` (MS)	Inserts an embedded program, control, or other object.
`<MAP>...</MAP>`	A client-side image map, referenced by `<IMG USEMAP="...">`. Includes one or more `<AREA>` tags.

<AREA>   Defines a clickable link within a client-side image map.

Attributes:

SHAPE="..."	The shape of the clickable area. Currently, only RECT is supported.
COORDS="..."	The left, top, right, and bottom coordinates of the clickable region within an image.
HREF="..."	The URL that should be loaded when the area is clicked.
NOHREF	Indicates that no action should be taken when this area of the image is clicked.

Forms

<FORM>...</FORM>   Indicates an input form.

Attributes:

ACTION="..."	The URL of the script to process this form input.
METHOD="..."	How the form input will be sent to the gateway on the server side. Possible values are GET and POST.
ENCTYPE="..."	Normally has the value application/x-www-form-urlencoded. For file uploads, use multi-part/form-data.
NAME="..."	A name by which JavaScript scripts can refer to the form.

<INPUT>   An input element for a form.

Attributes:

TYPE="..."	The type for this input widget. Possible values are CHECKBOX, HIDDEN, RADIO, RESET, SUBMIT, TEXT, SEND FILE, or IMAGE.
NAME="..."	The name of this item, as passed to the gateway script as part of a name/value pair.
VALUE="..."	For a text or hidden widget, the default value; for a checkbox or radio button, the value to be submitted with the form; for Reset or Submit buttons, the label for the button itself.
SRC="..."	The source file for an image.
CHECKED	For checkboxes and radio buttons, indicates that the widget is checked.

SIZE="..."	The size, in characters, of a text widget.
MAXLENGTH="..."	The maximum number of characters that can be entered into a text widget.
ALIGN="..."	For images in forms, determines how the text and image align (same as with the <IMG> tag).

<TEXTAREA>...</TEXTAREA>   Indicates a multiline text entry form element. Default text can be included.

Attributes:

NAME="..."	The name to be passed to the gateway script as part of the name/value pair.
ROWS="..."	The number of rows this text area displays.
COLS="..."	The number of columns (characters) this text area displays.
WRAP="..." (N)	Control text wrapping. Possible values are OFF, VIRTUAL, and PHYSICAL.

<SELECT>...</SELECT>   Creates a menu or scrolling list of possible items.

Attributes:

NAME="..."	The name that is passed to the gateway script as part of the name/value pair.
SIZE="..."	The number of elements to display. If SIZE is indicated, the selection becomes a scrolling list. If no SIZE is given, the selection is a pop-up menu.
MULTIPLE	Allows multiple selections from the list.

<OPTION>   Indicates a possible item within a <SELECT> element.

Attributes:

SELECTED	With this attribute included, the <OPTION> is selected by default in the list.
VALUE="..."	The value to submit if this <OPTION> is selected when the form is submitted.

Tables

<TABLE>...</TABLE>   Creates a table that can contain a caption (<CAPTION>) and any number of rows (<TR>).

Attributes:

BORDER="..."	Indicates whether the table should be drawn with or without a border. In Netscape, BORDER can also have a value indicating the width of the border.
CELLSPACING="..."	The amount of space between the cells in the table.
CELLPADDING="..."	The amount of space between the edges of the cell and its contents.
WIDTH="..."	The width of the table on the page, in either exact pixel values or as a percentage of page width.
ALIGN="..." (MS)	Alignment (works like IMG ALIGN). Values are LEFT or RIGHT.
BACKGROUND="..." (MS)	Background image to tile within all cells in the table that don't contain their own BACKGROUND or BGCOLOR attribute.
BGCOLOR="..." (MS)	Background color of all cells in the table that don't contain their own BACKGROUND or BGCOLOR attribute.
BORDERCOLOR="..." (MS)	Border color (used with BORDER="...").

`BORDERCOLORLIGHT="..."` (MS)	Color for light part of 3D-look borders (used with `BORDER="..."`).
`BORDERCOLORDARK="..."` (MS)	Color for dark part of 3D-look borders (used with `BORDER="..."`).
`VALIGN="..."` (MS)	Alignment of text within the table. Values are `TOP` and `BOTTOM`.
`FRAME="..."` (MS)	Controls which external borders appear around a table. Values are `void` (no frames), `above` (top border only), `below` (bottom border only), `hsides` (top and bottom), `lhs` (left-hand side), `rhs` (right-hand side), `vsides` (left and right sides), and `box` (all sides).
`RULES="..."` (MS)	Controls which internal borders appear in the table. Values are `none`, `basic` (rules between `THEAD`, `TBODY`, and `TFOOT` only), `rows` (horizontal borders only), `cols` (vertical borders only), and `all`.

<CAPTION>...</CAPTION>   The caption for the table.

Attribute:

`ALIGN="..."`	The position of the caption. Possible values are TOP and BOTTOM.

<TR>...</TR>   Defines a table row, containing headings and data (<TR> and <TH> tags).

Attributes:

`ALIGN="..."`	The horizontal alignment of the contents of the cells within this row. Possible values are LEFT, RIGHT, and CENTER.
`VALIGN="..."`	The vertical alignment of the contents of the cells within this row. Possible values are TOP, MIDDLE, BOTTOM, and BASELINE.
`BACKGROUND="..."`(MS)	Background image to tile within all cells in the row that don't contain their own BACKGROUND or BGCOLOR attributes.
`BGCOLOR="..."`	Background color of all cells in the row that don't contain their own BACKGROUND or BGCOLOR attributes.
`BORDERCOLOR="..."`(MS)	Border color (used with BORDER="...").
`BORDERCOLORLIGHT="..."`(MS)	Color for light part of 3D-look borders (used with BORDER="...").
`BORDERCOLORDARK="..."`(MS)	Color for dark part of 3D-look borders (used with BORDER="...").

\<TH\>...\</TH\>   Defines a table heading cell.

Attributes:

ALIGN="..."	The horizontal alignment of the contents of the cell. Possible values are LEFT, RIGHT, and CENTER.
VALIGN="..."	The vertical alignment of the contents the cell. Possible values are TOP, MIDDLE, BOTTOM, and BASELINE.
ROWSPAN="..."	The number of rows this cell will span.
COLSPAN="..."	The number of columns this cell will span.
NOWRAP	Does not automatically wrap the contents of this cell.
WIDTH="..."	The width of this column of cells, in exact pixel values or as a percentage of the table width.
BACKGROUND="..." (MS)	Background image to tile within the cell.
BGCOLOR="..." (MS)	Background color of the cell.
BORDERCOLOR="..." (MS)	Border color (used with BORDER="...").
BORDERCOLORLIGHT="..." (MS)	Color for light part of 3D-look borders (used with BORDER="...").
BORDERCOLORDARK="..." (MS)	Color for dark part of 3D-look borders (used with BORDER="...").

\<TD\>...\</TD\>   Defines a table data cell.

Attributes:

ALIGN="..."	The horizontal alignment of the contents of the cell. Possible values are LEFT, RIGHT, and CENTER.

`VALIGN="..."`	The vertical alignment of the contents of the cell. Possible values are TOP, MIDDLE, BOTTOM, and BASELINE.
`ROWSPAN="..."`	The number of rows this cell will span.
`COLSPAN="..."`	The number of columns this cell will span.
`NOWRAP`	Does not automatically wrap the contents of this cell.
`WIDTH="..."`	The width of this column of cells, in exact pixel values or as a percentage of the table width.
`BACKGROUND="..."` (MS)	Background image to tile within the cell.
`BGCOLOR="..."` (MS)	Background color of the cell.
`BORDERCOLOR="..."` (MS)	Border color (used with `BORDER="..."`).
`BORDERCOLORLIGHT="..."` (MS)	Color for light part of 3D-look borders (used with `BORDER="..."`).
`BORDERCOLORDARK="..."` (MS)	Color for dark part of 3D-look borders (used with `BORDER="..."`).
`<THEAD>` (MS)	Begins the header section of a table. The closing `</THEAD>` tag is optional.
`<TBODY>` (MS)	Begins the body section of a table. The closing `</TBODY>` tag is optional.
`<TFOOT>` (MS)	Begins the footer section of a table. The closing `</TFOOT>` tag is optional.
`<COL>...</COL>` (MS)	Sets width and alignment properties for one or more columns.

Attributes:

`WIDTH="..."` Width of column(s) in pixels or relative width followed by a * ("2*" columns will be twice as wide as "1*" columns, for example).

ALIGN="..." Text alignment within the column(s). Valid values are center, justify, left, and right.

SPAN="..." Number of columns that the properties specified in this <COL> tag apply to.

<COLGROUP>...</COLGROUP> Sets properties of a group of columns all at once (should enclose one or more <COL> tags).

Attributes:

ALIGN="..." Text alignment within the columns. Valid values are center, justify, left, and right.

VALIGN="..." Vertical alignment of text within the columns. Valid values are baseline, bottom, middle, and top.

Frames

<FRAMESET>...</FRAMESET> Divides the main window into a set of frames that can each display a separate document.

Attributes:

ROWS="..." Splits the window or frameset vertically into a number of rows specified by a number (such as 7), a percentage of the total window width (such as 25%), or as an asterisk (*) indicating that a frame should take up all the remaining space or divide the space evenly between frames (if multiple * frames are specified).

COLS="..." Works similar to ROWS, except that the window or frameset is split horizontally into columns.

<FRAME> Defines a single frame within a <FRAMESET>.

Attributes:

SRC="..." The URL of the document to be displayed in this frame.

NAME="..." A name to be used for targeting this frame with the TARGET attribute in <A HREF> links.

`<MARGINWIDTH>`	The amount of space to leave to the left and right side of a document within a frame, in pixels.
`<MARGINHEIGHT>`	The amount of space to leave above and below a document within a frame, in pixels.
`SCROLLING="..."`	Determines whether a frame has scroll bars. Possible values are YES, NO, and AUTO.
`NORESIZE`	Prevents the user from resizing this frame (and possibly adjacent frames) with the mouse.
`FRAMEBORDER="..."` (MS)	Specifies whether to display a border for a frame. Options are YES and NO.
`FRAMESPACING="..."` (MS)	Space between frames, in pixels.
`</NOFRAME>...</NOFRAMES>`	Provides an alternative document body in `<FRAMESET>` documents for browsers that do not support frames (usually encloses `<BODY>...</BODY>`).

Scripting and Applets

`<APPLET>`   Inserts a self-running Java applet.

NOTE: In addition to the following standard attributes, you can specify applet-specific attributes to be interpreted by the Java applet itself.

Attributes:

`CLASS="..."`	The name of the applet.
`SRC="..."`	The URL of the directory where the compiled applet can be found (should end in a slash / as in `"http://mysite/myapplets/"`). Do not include the actual applet name, which is specified with the CLASS attribute.
`ALIGN="..."`	Indicates how the applet should be aligned with any text that follows it. Current values are TOP, MIDDLE, and BOTTOM.
`WIDTH="..."`	The width of the applet output area in pixels.
`HEIGHT="..."`	The height of the applet output area in pixels.

`<SCRIPT>`   An interpreted script program.

Attributes:

`LANGUAGE="..."`	Currently only JAVASCRIPT is supported by Netscape. Both JAVASCRIPT and VBSCRIPT are supported by Microsoft.
`SRC="..."`	Specifies the URL of a file that includes the script program.

Marquees

`<MARQUEE>...</MARQUEE>` (MS)   Displays text in a scrolling marquee.

Attributes:

`WIDTH="..."`	The width of the embedded object in pixels or a percentage of window width.
`HEIGHT="..."`	The height of the embedded object in pixels or a percentage of window height.
`ALIGN="..."`	Determines the alignment of the text *outside* the marquee. Values are TOP, MIDDLE, and BOTTOM.
`BORDER="..."`	Draws a border of the specified size in pixels to be drawn around the media.
`BEHAVIOR="..."`	How the text inside the marquee should behave. Options are SCROLL (continuous scrolling), SLIDE (slide text in and stop), and ALTERNATE (bounce back and forth).

BGCOLOR="..."	Background color for the marquee.
DIRECTION="..."	Direction for text to scroll (LEFT or RIGHT).
VSPACE="..."	Space above and below the marquee, in pixels.
HSPACE="..."	Space on each side of the marquee, in pixels.
SCROLLAMOUNT="..."	Number of pixels to move each time text in the marquee is redrawn.
SCROLLDELAY="..."	Number of milliseconds between each redraw of marquee text.
LOOP="..." (MS)	The number of times marquee will loop. (-1 or INFINITE means to loop indefinitely.)

Character Entities

Table E.1 contains the possible numeric and character entities for the ISO-Latin-1 (ISO8859-1) character set. Where possible, the character is shown.

NOTE: Not all browsers can display all characters, and some browsers may even display characters different from those that appear in the table. Newer browsers seem to have a better track record for handling character entities, but be sure to test your HTML files extensively with multiple browsers if you intend to use these entities.

Table E.1. ISO-Latin-1 character set.

Character	Numeric Entity	Character Entity (if any)	Description
	&#00;–&#08;		Unused
	&#09;		Horizontal tab
	&#10;		Line feed
	&#11;–&#31;		Unused
	&#32;		Space
!	&#33;		Exclamation mark
"	&#34;	&quot;	Quotation mark
#	&#35;		Number sign
$	&#36;		Dollar sign
%	&#37;		Percent sign
&	&#38;	&amp;	Ampersand
'	&#39;		Apostrophe
(	&#40;		Left parenthesis
)	&#41;		Right parenthesis
*	&#42;		Asterisk
+	&#43;		Plus sign
,	&#44;		Comma
-	&#45;		Hyphen
.	&#46;		Period (fullstop)
/	&#47;		Solidus (slash)
0–9	0–9		Digits 0–9
:	&#58;		Colon
;	&#59;		Semi-colon
<	&#60;	&lt;	Less than
=	&#61;		Equals sign
>	&#62;	&gt;	Greater than
?	&#63;		Question mark
@	&#64;		Commercial at
A–Z	A–Z		Letters A–Z
[	&#91;		Left square bracket

Character	Numeric Entity	Character Entity (if any)	Description
\	&#92;		Reverse solidus (backslash)
]	&#93;		Right square bracket
^	&#94;		Caret
_	&#95;		Horizontal bar
`	&#96;		Grave accent
a–z	a–z		Letters a–z
{	&#123;		Left curly brace
|	&#124		Vertical bar
}	&#125;		Right curly brace
~	&#126;		Tilde
	&#127;–		Unused
¡	&#161;		Inverted exclamation
¢	&#162;		Cent sign
£	&#163;		Pound sterling
¤	&#164;		General currency sign
¥	&#165;		Yen sign
¦	&#166;		Broken vertical bar
§	&#167;		Section sign
¨	&#168;		Umlaut (dieresis)
©	&#169;		Copyright
ª	&#170;		Feminine ordinal
‹	&#171;		Left angle quote, guillemet left
¬	&#172;		Not sign
-	&#173;		Soft hyphen
®	&#174;		Registered trademark
¯	&#175;		Macron accent
°	&#176;		Degree sign

continued

Table E.1. continued

Character	Numeric Entity	Character Entity (if any)	Description
±	&#177;		Plus or minus
²	&#178;		Superscript two
³	&#179;		Superscript three
´	&#180;		Acute accent
µ	&#181;		Micro sign
¶	&#182;		Paragraph sign
·	&#183;		Middle dot
¸	&#184;		Cedilla
¹	&#185;		Superscript one
º	&#186;		Masculine ordinal
›	&#187;		Right angle quote, guillemet right
1/4	&#188;		Fraction one-fourth
1/2	&#189;		Fraction one-half
3/4	&#190;		Fraction three-fourths
¿	&#191;		Inverted question mark
À	&#192;	&Agrave;	Capital A, grave accent
Á	&#193;	&Aacute;	Capital A, acute accent
Â	&#194;	&Acirc;	Capital A, circumflex accent
Ã	&#195;	&Atilde;	Capital A, tilde
Ä	&#196;	&Auml;	Capital A, dieresis or umlaut mark
Å	&#197;	&Aring;	Capital A, ring
Æ	&#198;	&AElig;	Capital AE dipthong (ligature)
Ç	&#199;	&Ccedil;	Capital C, cedilla
È	&#200;	&Egrave;	Capital E, grave accent

Character	Numeric Entity	Character Entity (if any)	Description
É	&#201;	&Eacute;	Capital E, acute accent
Ê	&#202;	&Ecirc;	Capital E, circumflex accent
Ë	&#203;	&Euml;	Capital E, dieresis or umlaut mark
Ì	&#204;	&Igrave;	Capital I, grave accent
Í	&#205;	&Iacute;	Capital I, acute accent
Î	&#206;	&Icirc;	Capital I, circumflex accent
Ï	&#207;	&Iuml;	Capital I, dieresis or umlaut mark
Ð	&#208;	&ETH;	Capital Eth, Icelandic
Ñ	&#209;	&Ntilde;	Capital N, tilde
Ò	&#210;	&Ograve;	Capital O, grave accent
Ó	&#211;	&Oacute;	Capital O, acute accent
Ô	&#212;	&Ocirc;	Capital O, circumflex accent
Õ	&#213;	&Otilde;	Capital O, tilde
Ö	&#214;	&Ouml;	Capital O, dieresis or umlaut mark
×	&#215;		Multiply sign
Ø	&#216;	&Oslash;	Capital O, slash
Ù	&#217;	&Ugrave;	Capital U, grave accent
Ú	&#218;	&Uacute;	Capital U, acute accent

continued

Table E.1. continued

Character	Numeric Entity	Character Entity (if any)	Description
Û	&#219;	&Ucirc;	Capital U, circumflex accent
Ü	&#220;	&Uuml;	Capital U, dieresis or umlaut mark
Ý	&#221;	&Yacute;	Capital Y, acute accent
Þ	&#222;	&THORN;	Capital THORN, Icelandic
β	&#223;	&szlig;	Small sharp s, German (sz ligature)
à	&#224;	&agrave;	Small a, grave accent
á	&#225;	&aacute;	Small a, acute accent
â	&#226;	&acirc;	Small a, circumflex accent
ã	&#227;	&atilde;	Small a, tilde
ä	&#228;	&aauml;	Small a, dieresis or umlaut mark
å	&#229;	&aring;	Small a, ring
æ	&#230;	&aelig;	Small ae dipthong (ligature)
ç	&#231;	&ccedil;	Small c, cedilla
è	&#232;	&egrave;	Small e, grave accent
é	&#233;	&eacute;	Small e, acute accent
ê	&#234;	&ecirc;	Small e, circumflex accent
ë	&#235;	&euml;	Small e, dieresis or umlaut mark
ì	&#236;	&igrave;	Small i, grave accent
í	&#237;	&iacute;	Small i, acute accent

Character	Numeric Entity	Character Entity (if any)	Description
î	&#238;	&icirc;	Small i, circumflex accent
ï	&#239;	&iuml;	Small i, dieresis or umlaut mark
ð	&#240;	&eth;	Small eth, Icelandic
ñ	&#241;	&ntilde;	Small n, tilde
ò	&#242;	&ograve;	Small o, grave accent
ó	&#243;	&oacute;	Small o, acute accent
ô	&#244;	&ocirc;	Small o, circumflex accent
õ	&#245;	&otilde;	Small o, tilde
ö	&#246;	&ouml;	Small o, dieresis or umlaut mark
÷	&#247;		Division sign
ø	&#248;	&oslash;	Small o, slash
ù	&#249;	&ugrave;	Small u, grave accent
ú	&#250;	&uacute;	Small u, acute accent
û	&#251;	&ucirc;	Small u, circumflex accent
ü	&#252;	&uuml;	Small u, dieresis or umlaut mark
´y	&#253;	&yacute;	Small y, acute accent
þ	&#254;	&thorn;	Small thorn, Icelandic
ÿ	&#255;	&yuml;	Small y, dieresis or umlaut mark

APPENDIX

F

What's on the CD-ROM?

On the *Laura Lemay's Web Workshop: 3D Graphics and VRML 2.0* CD-ROM, you will find all the sample files that have been presented in this book, along with a wealth of other Windows and Macintosh applications and utilities.

NOTE: Everything on the CD-ROM is detailed in the Web pages on the CD-ROM itself. Open the index.htm document with your Web browser to begin exploring.

Windows Software

Models

- ❏ Viewpoint models
- ❏ Platinum Pictures models from 3D Café site
- ❏ Harry Chang's models
- ❏ Acuris models
- ❏ 3 Name 3D's CyberProp Models

Commercial Demos

- ❏ Caligari trueSpace2—30-day trial version
- ❏ Byte by Byte SoftF/X 2.5 demo
- ❏ Okino's NuGraf Rendering System and PolyTrans conversion program
- ❏ Yonowat's Amapi demo 2.11 for Windows 95
- ❏ EOS System's PhotoModeler LX
- ❏ Fractal Design Painter 4
- ❏ Richardson Systems' Model3DD demo and Model3DD Environment
- ❏ Radiance Software's Ez3D
- ❏ Adobe Photoshop 3.0.5
- ❏ VistaPro
- ❏ Bores Pro, LenZFX, and SandBlaster demos from Digimation

Photoshop Plug-ins

- ❏ Metatools' Kai's Power Tools 3 demo
- ❏ Alien Skin Software's The Black Box demo
- ❏ Andromeda Software's series 2 filters demo

3D Shareware Tools

- ❏ Landscape Maker 2.1
- ❏ WCTV2POV convertor version 2.7
- ❏ Silicon Software's Lace 3D, Partica, and Silly Space
- ❏ bCAD

- ❏ Yilsoft's KnowExec 2.0
- ❏ Breeze Designer 2.0
- ❏ Paint Shop Pro 3.12

VRML Tools

- ❏ Vream Inc's WIRL Lite
- ❏ Caligari's Pioneer 2.0

3D Chat Environments

- ❏ BlackSun's CyberGate
- ❏ World's Inc. Worlds Chat

Netscape Plug-ins

- ❏ Emblaze
- ❏ Sizzler

Other

- ❏ VRML 2.0 specification
- ❏ W3e HTML Editor version 4.2.1
- ❏ CSE 3310 HTML Validator for Windows 95/NT v1.00
- ❏ ThumbsPlus v3c-s 32-bit image viewer and browser
- ❏ WinZip for Windows NT/95
- ❏ WinZip Self-Extractor utility

Macintosh Software

Models

- ❏ Viewpoint models
- ❏ Platinum Pictures models from 3D Café site
- ❏ Harry Chang's models
- ❏ Acuris models
- ❏ 3 Name 3D's CyberProp models

Commercial Demos

- ❏ Adobe Photoshop 3.0.5
- ❏ Byte by Byte Sculpt 3D 4.1 demo
- ❏ Yonowat's Amapi demo 2.11 for Mac
- ❏ Fractal Design Painter 4

- ❏ Specular Infini-D 3.2
- ❏ Metatools' KPT Bryce demo
- ❏ Strata Demos
- ❏ Vistapro Mac
- ❏ Form Z Render Zone from auto.des.sys

Photoshop Filters

- ❏ Metatools' Kai's Power Tools 3 demo
- ❏ Andromeda Series 2 Filters
- ❏ Black Box 2.ob Cutout Filters

Netscape Plug-ins

- ❏ Totally Hip Software's Sizzler
- ❏ Emblaze from Geo Interactive Media Group

Other

- ❏ Adobe Acrobat reader

About Shareware

Shareware is not free. Please read all documentation associated with a third-party product (usually includes files named readme.txt or license.txt) and follow all guidelines.

INDEX

Laura Lemay's Web Workshop: Netscape Navigator Gold 3

— *Laura Lemay & Ned Snell*

Netscape Gold and JavaScript are two powerful tools for creating and designing effective Web pages. This book covers design elements and explains how to use the Netscape Gold WYSIWYG editor. The CD-ROM contains editors and code from the book, making the reader's learning experience a quick and effective one.

Teaches how to program within Navigator Gold's rich Netscape development environment

Explores elementary design principles for effective Web page creation and covers Web publishing

CD-ROM includes editors and all the source code from the book.

$39.99 USA/$53.99 CDN
ISBN: 1-57521-128-9
Internet-General

User Level: Casual — Accomplished
400 pages

Laura Lemay's Web Workshop: Graphics and Web Page Design

— *Laura Lemay & James Rudnick*

With the number of Web pages increasing daily, only the well-designed will grab the attention of those browsing the Web. This book illustrates, in classic Laura Lemay style, how to design attractive Web pages that will be visited over and over again.

Teaches beginning and advanced design principles

Covers the Internet

CD-ROM contains HTML editors, graphics software, and royalty-free graphics and sound files.

$55.00 USA/$77.95 CDN
ISBN: 1-57521-125-4
Internet-Online/Communications

User Level: Accomplished
500 pages

Laura Lemay's Web Workshop: Creating Commercial Web Pages

— *Laura Lemay & Daniel Bishop*

This book shows how to create commercial-grade Web pages using HTML, CGI, and Java. In the classic clear style of Laura Lemay, it explains not only how to create the page, but also how to apply proven design principles to make the Web page a marketing tool.

Teaches you how to use HTML, CGI, and Java

Illustrates corporate uses for Web technology—catalogues, cutomer service, and product ordering

CD-ROM includes the book's templates, HTML editors, graphics software, CGI forms, and more.

$39.99 USA/$56.95 CDN
ISBN: 1-57521-126-2
Internet-Business

User Level: Accomplished
400 pages

Laura Lemay's Web Workshop: Microsoft FrontPage

— Laura Lemay & Denise Tyler

This is a clear hands-on guide to maintaining Web pages with Microsoft's FrontPage. Written in the clear, conversational style of Laura Lemay, it's packed with interesting, colorful examples that demonstrate specific tasks.

Teaches how to maintain Web pages with FrontPage

CD-ROM includes all the templates, backgrounds, and materials you need.

$39.99 USA/$56.95 CDN
ISBN: 1-57521-149-1
Internet-Web Publishing

User Level: Casual — Accomplished
400 pages

Laura Lemay's Web Workshop: JavaScript

— Laura Lemay

Readers will explore different aspects of Web publishing—CGI scripting and interactivity, graphics design, or Netscape Gold—in more depth than they do in the *Teach Yourself* books.

Provides a clear, hands-on guide to creating sophisticated Web pages

Covers CGI

CD-ROM includes the complete book in HTML format, publishing tools, templates, graphics, backgrounds, and more.

$39.99 USA/$56.95 CDN
ISBN: 1-57521-141-6
Communications/Online-Internet

User Level: Casual — Accomplished
400 pages

Teach Yourself Web Publishing with HTML 3.2 in 14 Days, Professional Reference Edition

— Laura Lemay

This is the updated edition of Lemay's previous bestseller, *Teach Yourself Web Publishing with HTML in 14 Days, Premier Edition*. Readers will find advanced topics and updates to Web page creation, including adding audio, video, and animation.

Explores using CGI scripts, tables, HTML 3.2, Netscape and Internet Explorer extensions, Java applets and JavaScript, and VRML

Covers HTML 3.0

CD-ROM included!

$59.99 USA/$81.95 CDN
ISBN: 1-57521-096-7
Internet-Web Publishing

User Level: New — Casual — Accomplished
1,104 pages

Teach Yourself Web Publishing with HTML in 14 Days, Premier Edition

— *Laura Lemay*

This book teaches everything you need to know about publishing on the Web. Besides in-depth coverage of HTML, it also gives you hands-on practice designing and writing HTML documents.

Readers will learn how to upload their page to a server and how to advertise

Covers HTML 3.0

CD-ROM is Mac- and PC-compatible; includes applications for creating Web pages with graphics and templates.

$39.99 USA/$53.99 CDN　　　*User Level: New — Accomplished*
ISBN: 1-57521-014-2　　　　　*840 pages*
Internet-Web Publishing

Teach Yourself Java in 21 Days

— *Laura Lemay, et al*

The first, best, and most detailed guide to developing applications with the hot new Java language from Sun Microsystems.

Gives you detailed coverage of the hottest new technology on the World Wide Web

Explains browsing Java applications with Netscape and other popular Web browsers

CD-ROM includes the Java Developer's Kit.

$39.99 USA/$53.99 CDN　　　*User Level: Casual — Accomplished — Expert*
ISBN: 1-57521-030-4　　　　　*500 pages*
Internet-Programming

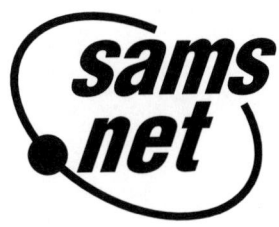

Add to Your Sams.net Library Today
with the Best Books for Internet Technologies

ISBN	Quantity	Description of Item	Unit Cost	Total Cost
1-57521-128-9		Laura Lemay's Web Workshop: Netscape Navigator Gold 3 (Book/CD-ROM)	$39.99	
1-57521-125-4		Laura Lemay's Web Workshop: Graphics and Web Page Design (Book/CD-ROM)	$55.00	
1-57521-126-2		Laura Lemay's Web Workshop: Creating Commercial Web Pages (Book/CD-ROM)	$39.99	
1-57521-149-1		Laura Lemay's Web Workshop: Microsoft FrontPage (Book/CD-ROM)	$39.99	
1-57521-141-6		Laura Lemay's Web Workshop: JavaScript (Book/CD-ROM)	$39.99	
1-57521-096-7		Teach Yourself Web Publishing with HTML 3.2 in 14 Days, Professional Reference Edition (Book/CD-ROM)	$59.99	
1-57521-014-2		Teach Yourself Web Publishing with HTML in 14 Days, Premier Edition (Book/CD-ROM)	$39.99	
1-57521-030-4		Teach Yourself Java in 21 Days (Book/CD-ROM)	$39.99	
		Shipping and Handling: See information below.		
		TOTAL		

Shipping and Handling: $4.00 for the first book, and $1.75 for each additional book. If you need to have it NOW, we can ship product to you in 24 hours for an additional charge of approximately $18.00, and you will receive your item overnight or in two days. Overseas shipping and handling adds $2.00. Prices subject to change. Call between 9:00 a.m. and 5:00 p.m. EST for availability and pricing information on latest editions.

201 W. 103rd Street, Indianapolis, Indiana 46290

1-800-428-5331 — Orders   1-800-835-3202 — FAX   1-800-858-7674 — Customer Service

Book ISBN 1-57521-143-2

CD-ROM

Installing
the CD-ROM

The companion CD-ROM contains all the source code and project files developed by the authors, plus an assortment of evaluation versions of third-party products. The Windows installation program installs the LLWW—3D Graphics and VRML 2 group to your Program Manager and places several icons in it that you can launch. To install, please follow these steps:

Windows 95 Installation Instructions

1. Insert the CD-ROM into your CD-ROM drive.
2. From the Windows 95 desktop, double-click on the My Computer icon.
3. Double-click on the icon representing your CD-ROM drive.
4. Double-click on the icon titled setup.exe to run the CD-ROM installation program.

Windows NT Installation Instructions

1. Insert the CD-ROM into your CD-ROM drive.
2. From File Manager or Program Manager, choose Run from the File menu.
3. Type `<drive>\setup` and press Enter; `<drive>` corresponds to the drive letter of your CD-ROM. For example, if your CD-ROM is drive D:, type `D:\SETUP` and press Enter.
4. Follow the onscreen instructions in the Guide to the CD-ROM program.

Macintosh Installation Instructions

1. Insert the CD-ROM into your CD-ROM drive.
2. When an icon for the CD appears on your desktop, open the disc by double-clicking on its icon.
3. Double-click on the file titled index.htm.